EARLY CHRISTIANITY IN CONTEXT

Editor
John M.G. Barclay

Editorial Board
Loveday Alexander, Troels Engberg-Pedersen,
Bart Ehrman, Joel Marcus, John Riches

ACTS IN ITS ANCIENT LITERARY CONTEXT

A Classicist Looks at the Acts of the Apostles

LOVEDAY C.A. ALEXANDER

t&t clark

Copyright © Loveday Alexander, 2005

Published by T&T Clark International
A Continuum imprint
The Tower Building, 11 York Road, London SE1 7NX
15 East 26th Street, Suite 1703, New York, NY 10010

www.tandtclark.com

British Library Cataloguing-in-Publication Data
A catalogue record for this book is available from the British Library

ISBN 0567082091 (hardback)

Typeset by Free Range Book Design & Production Ltd
Printed on acid-free paper in Great Britain by MPG Books Ltd, Cornwall

CONTENTS

List of Illustrations

Chapter 4

CHAPTER 5

ABBREVIATIONS

AB	Anchor Bible
ABD	David Noel Freedman (ed.), *The Anchor Bible Dictionary* (New York: Doubleday, 1992)
AJT	*American Journal of Theology*
ANRW	Hildegard Temporini and Wolfgang Haase (eds.), *Aufstieg und Niedergang der römischen Welt: Geschichte und Kultur Roms im Spiegel der neueren Forschung* (Berlin: W. de Gruyter, 1972–)
BETL	Bibliotheca ephemeridum theologicarum lovaniensium
BHT	Beiträge zur historischen Theologie
CBQ	*Catholic Biblical Quarterly*
CRINT	Compendia rerum iudaicarum ad Novum Testamentum
FGH	F. Jacoby, *Die Fragmente der griechischen Historiker* (Leiden: Brill, 1950–58)
GGA	*Göttingische gelehrte Anzeigen* (Göttingen, Akademie der Wissenschaften)
HNT	Handbuch zum Neuen Testament
HTR	*Harvard Theological Review*
Int	*Interpretation*
JBL	*Journal of Biblical Literature*
JJS	*Journal of Jewish Studies*
JRH	*Journal of Religious History*
JRS	*Journal of Roman Studies*
JSNT	*Journal for the Study of the New Testament*
JSNTSup	*Journal for the Study of the New Testament*, Supplement Series
JSOTSup	*Journal for the Study of the Old Testament*, Supplement Series
JTS	*Journal of Theological Studies*
Kühn	C.G. Kühn (ed.), *Galeni Opera Omnia* (20 vols; Leipzig, Car Cnobloch, 1821–33)
NovT	*Novum Testamentum*
NovTSup	*Novum Testamentum*, Supplements
NTS	*New Testament Studies*
OCD[2]	*The Oxford Classical Dictionary* (eds. N.G.L. Hammond and H.H. Scullard; Oxford: Clarendon Press, 1970).
PEQ	*Palestine Exploration Quarterly*

RE	*Real-encyclopädie der classischen Altertumswissenschaft* (Stuttgart: Metzler, 1893–1980)
RGG	*Religion in Geschichte und Gegenwart*
SBL	Society of Biblical Literature
SBLDS	SBL Dissertation Series
SBLMS	SBL Monograph Series
SBLSBS	SBL Sources for Biblical Study
SBLSP	SBL Seminar Papers
SNTSMS	Society for New Testament Studies Monograph Series
ST	*Studia theologica*
STK	*Svensk teologisk kvartalskrift*
TLZ	*Theologische Literaturzeitung*
TQ	*Theologische Quartalschrift*
WUNT	Wissenschaftliche Untersuchungen zum Neuen Testament
ZNW	*Zeitschrift für die neutestamentliche Wissenschaft*

FOREWORD

This volume charts the development of a number of trajectories opened up by my original doctoral project on *The Preface to Luke's Gospel*. It includes a series of exploratory readings of Acts alongside other ancient literary genres (biographies, novels, epic, apologetic), together with a reader-oriented approach to the unity of Luke-Acts. The final piece signals a return to the linguistic issue and the question of *Fachprosa*. Most of this material has been published separately, and I am grateful to the publishers for permission to reprint. In most cases, I have elected to reprint the papers substantially as they originally appeared, if only for ease of reference. This will inevitably mean some repetition: but it also means that footnote numeration should normally be the same as in the original, though we have added or adjusted cross-references to other articles reprinted in this book. Existing bibliographical references have been updated where relevant, but I have not attempted to provide a complete new bibliography for the older papers. The essays can be read separately as autonomous studies presented to a variety of academic audiences between 1993 and 2004; but they also form a coherent sequence as part of a larger endeavour which has been occupying my attention for the last ten years, whose roots go back to my original doctoral project, and which will eventually bear fruit (God willing) in a monograph on *Acts and the Ancient Reader* and a commentary on Acts for the *Black's NT Commentary* series (Continuum, forthcoming).

My thanks are due to: John Barclay and Joel Marcus, who accepted the original idea for a collection for the T&T Clark series 'Studies in the NT and its World'; to Rebecca Mulhearn and Becca Vaughan-Williams of Continuum; and to Audrey Mann, without whose help I would never have been able to get this collection together. Plus – of course – to all the colleagues and friends with whom I have discussed these ideas over the years, and especially to fellow-members of the SBL Luke-Acts Group and the Acts seminars of the SNTS and BNTS. I am particularly grateful to all those editors and programme chairs who have invited me over the years to present papers on Acts and to participate in the stimulating and challenging conversations on the genre of Acts that have engaged much of our scholarly attention over the past two decades.

Particular thanks are due to the following publishers for permission to reprint: – Brill Academic Publishers; Cambridge University Press; The Continuum International Publishing Group; Eerdmans Publishing Company; Labor et Fides; Oxford University Press; Paternoster Press; Peeters Publishers. Full details of the original publication are given at the beginning of each article.

Chapter 1

ON A ROMAN BOOKSTALL:
READING ACTS IN ITS ANCIENT LITERARY CONTEXT

There was once an editor of an organ of opinion catering for the literary wants of a western mining-camp who, sitting in his office one day, noticed a bullet crash through the glass of the window and flatten itself against the wall beside his head. Upon which a relieved and happy smile played over his face. 'There,' he exclaimed. 'Didn't I say so? I knew that Personal Column would be a success.'[1]

It is in something of the spirit of P.G. Wodehouse's editor that I have observed with interest a number of recent commentators taking issue with the central argument of my 1993 monograph on *The Preface to Luke's Gospel*.[2] It is always heartening to find that people take your work seriously enough to disagree with it, and that alone might have been sufficient encouragement to revisit that work, and to take the opportunity to assess how the argument has moved on since 1993. But this collection also owes its existence to a more positive kind of encouragement. In the summer of 2002, I was invited by Todd Penner and Caroline Vander Stichele to contribute a paper to the second of two sessions on 'Recent Approaches to Acts' at the International meeting of the SBL in Berlin, as part of a wider project on 'Methodology and the Future of Biblical Studies'.[3] There I was able to explain how my thinking has developed since the publication of *The Preface*, and was encouraged by the group's response to collect and publish some of my wider explorations in the ongoing enterprise of learning to read Luke's work as one book among many on the Greco-Roman bookstall.

Ever since I began the study of classical Latin (at 12) and Greek (at 13), I have been fascinated by the interface between the New Testament and the rich and

1. P.G. Wodehouse, *Bill the Conqueror* (London: Methuen, 1924), p. 92.
2. Loveday Alexander, *The Preface to Luke's Gospel: Literary Convention and Social Context in Luke 1.1–4 and Acts 1.1* (SNTSMS, 78; Cambridge; Cambridge University Press, 1993). The volume has now been reissued by Cambridge University Press in paperback. For a summary of critique and reviews, see especially David E. Aune, 'Luke 1:1–4: Historical or Scientific Prooimion?', in A. Christopherson, *et al.* (ed.), *Paul, Luke, and the Graeco-Roman World: Essays in Honour of Alexander J.M. Wedderburn* (JSNTSup, 217; Sheffield: Sheffield Academic Press, 2003), pp. 138–48.
3. These papers are now published in Todd Penner and Caroline Vander Stichele (eds.), *Contextualizing Acts: Lukan Narrative and Greco-Roman Discourse* (SBL Symposium series 20; Atlanta; SBL, 2003). See also Todd Penner's invaluable essay on recent Acts scholarship in 'Madness in the Method? The Acts of the Apostles in Current Study', in *Currents in Biblical Research* 2.2 (2004), pp. 223–93.

varied world of classical literature. As Dorothy L. Sayers complained many years ago, these are two parallel worlds which tend to be studied in isolation from each other.[4] Studying the literature of the Greco-Roman world, especially the multi-cultural world of the eastern Mediterranean in the second century CE, has always opened up for me the tantalizing possibility of hearing how the familiar texts of the New Testament sounded when they were fresh-minted, when the message of the Christian *euangelion* was not only *good* but *news* – something new, something that hadn't been heard before. But the new has to communicate itself in the linguistic conventions and literary forms that already exist – and those literary forms will themselves become part of the struggle to communicate, to find ways to express the inexpressible. In any given culture, language and convention create pressures and constraints on what can be said and on how it is perceived. The medium moulds the message just as the message forces the medium to expand and develop.

So when, as a classical graduate in the autumn of 1970, I moved from the Faculty of Literae Humaniores at Oxford to read for a DPhil in the Faculty of Theology, my aim was to place the New Testament writings firmly within their Greco-Roman context. The gospels seemed the obvious place to begin, and my original project was ambitious, not to say reckless, in its scope: 'The evangelists as historians in the light of contemporary historiography'.[5] It was, as I have explained to generations of research students ever since, a research topic crying out for focusing and redefinition (*all* the gospels? the *whole* of contemporary historiography?). Somewhere around the middle of that first year, I turned my attention to Luke's preface. Scholarly consensus at the time held that Luke's opening verses demonstrated conclusively that at least one of the evangelists intended his work to be read as 'history' in the great classical tradition. It was an assumption that I had initially shared, and hoped to use as a plank in a much bigger argument: Luke's preface seemed to be one of the more secure connections in the larger project of comparing the gospels with the work of the classical historians. Here at least we seemed to have a New Testament author who was consciously placing his work within the great literary tradition of his day, who was aware of the literary formalities of Greek historiography and was able to deploy them to good effect in his preface. But a more detailed examination of Cadbury's classic analysis of the preface[6] convinced me that there were serious flaws in this virtually universal assumption, and prompted a radical redefinition of the thesis. The bigger picture would have to wait.

---

4.   Cf. Chapter 7, p. 165.

5.   I must here pay tribute to my *Doktorvater* the Reverend Professor Dennis Nineham, then Warden of Keble, who provided invaluable support and guidance throughout my student years and beyond.

6.   Henry J. Cadbury, 'Commentary on the Preface of Luke', in Foakes Jackson and Kirsopp Lake (eds.), *The Beginnings of Christianity* (London: Macmillan, 1922), II, Appendix C, pp. 489–510.

The Preface to Luke's Gospel

In a paper published in 1986 as a digest and summary of the ensuing research project, I set out clearly the structure of the problem, which has both negative and positive components.[7] On the negative side, I detailed briefly the problematic aspects in Cadbury's analysis which had originally led me to question the prevailing assumption that the literary conventions used by Luke in his prefaces point to the genre 'Greek historiography'.[8] I then went on to develop the positive stage of the argument. If the literary conventions displayed in Luke's preface do not belong to the genre of Greek historiography, where do they belong? We need to spread our net wider, to map a greater range of Greek prose prefaces, if we are to arrive at a satisfactory analysis of the literary signals emitted by Luke's preface. An exhaustive survey of Greek prose prefaces from the fourth century BCE to the second century CE[9] brought me to the (quite unexpected) conclusion that the preface-type closest to Luke's is that found in a range of technical handbooks in subjects as diverse as engineering, rhetoric, and medicine – what the Germans call *Fachprosa* and I had labelled (somewhat misleadingly) the 'scientific tradition'.[10]

In the final part of the study, I set out two lines of further investigation opened up by this conclusion. The first follows a *socio-linguistic* trajectory linking the linguistic work of Albert Wifstrand and Lars Rydbeck with more recent studies on the social status of the first Christians, especially in the work of Abraham Malherbe and Wayne Meeks. Luke's preface has always carried a lot of socio-cultural freight. Many commentators have argued that Luke's choice of preface-conventions shows some kind of conscious intent to align his work with the 'High literature' of his day, to break out of the 'darkness of the conventicle' and articulate the gospel story in terms that would make sense within the public discourse of the Empire.[11] But if Luke's choice of preface-conventions aligns his work with *Fachprosa* rather than with Greek historiography, the social location of his work might look rather different:

---

7.   Loveday Alexander, 'Luke's Preface in the Pattern of Greek Preface-Writing', *NovT* 28.1 (1986), pp. 48–74.

8.   Alexander, 'The Pattern of Greek Preface-Writing', pp. 49–51. The differences between Luke's prefaces and those of the historians are set out in more detail in *The Preface*, ch. 3, and in Chapter 2 below.

9.   What I actually did was to move systematically along the shelves of the Lower Reading Room in the Bodleian Library (*in aeternum floreat!*) looking at the beginning of every Greek prose text written between the fourth century BCE and the second century CE.

10.   Alexander, 'The Pattern of Greek Preface-Writing', pp. 57–60. In retrospect, the choice of the word 'scientific' was misleading: it focused attention too much on content and too little on function and mode of delivery. 'Technical literature' is perhaps preferable (as long as it is understood that this includes for example a *techne* or handbook in a literary subject like rhetoric or epistolography): but English has no real equivalent to the German *Fachprosa*.

11.   Cf. Alexander, 'The Pattern of Greek Preface-Writing', p. 48 and Chapter 2, pp. 21–22 below.

If we can firmly say that Luke's work 'belongs' to this category of 'scientific literature' or 'technical prose', then we have an immediate link in to a large and neglected area of 'middlebrow' literature of the first century CE. The importance of this *Fachprosa* for New Testament linguistics has already been underlined by the work of Albert Wifstrand and more especially by his pupil Lars Rydbeck, whose study *Fachprosa, vermeintliche Volkssprache und Neues Testament* appeared in 1967.[12] Rydbeck shows that the New Testament writers use a language identical neither with the vernacular *Koine* of the papyri (probably as near as we can get to the spoken *Koine* of the streets and market-places of the Eastern Empire), nor with the classicizing prose of the *literati*. It is a 'Zwischenprosa', literate but not literary,[13] a written language designed primarily for conveying factual information; and it is chiefly preserved in the technical treatises of the scientific writers. As Abraham Malherbe has noted,[14] 'almost half of Rydbeck's references (in the NT) are to Luke and Acts'.[15]

These social implications are discussed more fully in *The Preface*, ch. 8, and I revisit them in Chapter 10 below.

The second trajectory follows up the more immediate – and in many ways more challenging – literary question: if my reading of the preface-conventions is correct, what does this tell us about the generic affinities of Luke's project as a whole? In what ways does it make *literary* sense to regard Luke as 'a writer within the scientific tradition'?[16] Here my 1986 article sets out two options. The first, given that the content of Luke's two volumes is mainly biographical narrative (i.e. stories about a teacher and his followers), would be to investigate further the role of such biographical material in the scientific tradition as a whole:

The problem of biographical content may be tackled in one of two ways. The first is to look at the uses of biography within the school traditions. Here most of the evidence comes from the philosophical schools. C.H. Talbert has made a number of important suggestions on this subject.[17] He sees Luke-Acts as falling into a pattern found in Diogenes Laertius, viz. *Life* of the founder of a school plus *Succession* or record of the transmission of authentic doctrine via the master's disciples… Evidence for biographical interest in the founders of other schools is less forthcoming… [Many of the] great

---

12.   Lars Rydbeck, *Fachprosa, vermeintliche Volkssprache und Neues Testament* (Acta Universitatis Upsaliensis: Studia Graeca Upsaliensia, 5; Uppsala: Berlingska Boktryckeriet, Lund, 1967). Rydbeck does not discuss the preface itself, and he insists (p. 16) that his study is concerned with 'linguistic-grammatical facts' and not with a 'technical prose style as such'. My analysis of the Lukan preface (which was completed in all essentials without knowledge of Rydbeck's work) therefore provides a separate and independent link with this body of literature.

13.   Cf. F.C. Grant, 'not illiterate, but certainly nonliterary': *The Gospels: Their Origin and Growth* (New York: Harper, 1957), p. 28.

14.   A.J. Malherbe, *Social Aspects of Early Christianity* (Louisiana: Louisiana State University Press, 1977), p. 41, n. 28.

15.   Cf. Alexander, 'The Pattern of Greek Preface-Writing', pp. 60–61.

16.   Alexander, 'The Pattern of Greek Preface-Writing', pp. 66–67.

17.   C.H. Talbert, *Literary Patterns, Theological Themes and the Genre of Luke-Acts* (SBL Monographs, 20; Missoula, MT: Scholars Press, 1974), ch. 8; *idem, What is a Gospel?* (Philadelphia: Fortress Press, 1977); *idem*, 'Biographies of Philosophers and Rulers as Instruments of Religious Propaganda in Mediterranean Antiquity', *ANRW* 2.16.2 (1978), pp. 1619–651.

figures of Greek science were remembered rather through biographical anecdote than through biography as such—as for example in the story about Archimedes told by Plutarch, *Marcellus* 14f. Here there is not the same ideological interest in the lifestyle of a founder as there is in the philosophical schools, but there were other reasons for preserving biographical details – bibliographical, chronographical, exemplary – as may be seen, for example, in the scattered notices (never part of a full 'biography') which make up the sum of our biographical information on the mathematician Hippocrates of Chios.[18] There is then some evidence that biographical information played a definite role in the traditions of the schools, chiefly but not exclusively the philosophical schools. Whether there is sufficient evidence at the right date to provide a possible model for Luke-Acts, and whether this kind of biographical activity (which is for the most part ancillary to a pre-existent and independent body of oral or written teaching) provides a proper parallel to the role of Gospel traditions in the life of the early Church, must remain matters for more detailed investigation.[19]

I return to that more detailed investigation (at least in regard to Acts) in Chapter 3 below.

There is however an alternative strategy, which is to stop looking at the preface as an indicator of genre and look at it in terms of function. This would open up the possibility of looking at Luke's work (indeed the gospel tradition as a whole) in the light of the school traditions of antiquity:

> The alternative and, I believe, preferable approach to the problem of the biographical character of Luke's Gospel is to look to the scientific tradition in the first instance for parallels not in content but in function. The texts I have studied differ widely as to content, and insofar as form is determined by content there is no uniformity once we leave the prefaces behind. What they do have in common is (in large degree) a similarity of function. They derive more or less directly from a school context: they are 'school texts', that is, not elementary, watered-down textbooks in the modern sense, but the written deposit of the *technē*, the distillation of the teaching of a school or a craft tradition as it was passed down from one generation to another.[20] Forms of presentation vary, some traditions preserving a style closer to that of the oral lecture, others reduced to different degrees of written systematisation;[21] but the variety of content is simply a reflection of the variety of teaching traditions embodied in the texts.[22]

I remain convinced that the Hellenistic schools have enormous potential as a social matrix for understanding early Christianity, and I have begun to explore

---

18.   RE 8.2 s.v. 'Hippokrates' no. 14 (1780–1801).

19.   Alexander, 'The Pattern of Greek Preface-Writing', pp. 68–69.

20.   This is, of course, a generalization of a complex situation. For fuller discussion see Alexander, *The Preface*, esp. pp. 204–10, and Loveday Alexander, 'The Living Voice: Scepticism towards the Written Word in Early Christian and in Greco-Roman Texts', in D.J.A. Clines, S.E. Fowl and S.E. Porter (eds.), *The Bible in Three Dimensions* (Sheffield: Sheffield Academic Press, 1990), pp. 221–47.

21.   Oral: e.g. Aristoxenus of Tarentum, *El. Harm.*, 3.59.6; P. Steinmetz, 'Die Physik des Theophrastus', *Palingenesia I* (1964), pp. 14ff. Systematic: see M. Fuhrmann, *Das systematische Lehrbuch: ein Beitrag zur Geschichte der Wissenschaften in der Antike* (Göttingen: Vandenhoeck & Ruprecht, 1960).

22.   Alexander, 'The Pattern of Greek Preface-Writing', p. 69.

this field in a series of papers which I hope soon to publish in a separate volume.[23]

Beyond the Preface

My initial work on the Lukan preface set out two primary research trajectories: the question of Luke's social location, and the question of the literary classification of his work. It is the second, the literary question – and specifically the question of the literary genre of Acts – that occupies most of the papers in this collection. Chapter 2, 'The Preface to Acts and the Historians', was written in response to an invitation from Ben Witherington III to contribute to his *History, Literature and Society in the Book of Acts*.[24] Here I take the opportunity to develop a fuller study of the preface to Acts than I had space for in *The Preface* (cf. *The Preface*, pp. 142–46). This paper sets out in detail the evidence for the use of dedication (second-person address) and recapitulatory prefaces in Greek histories and apologetic texts, and confirms my earlier conclusion that neither practice fits the normal generic expectations of historiography for Greek readers. Where these features do appear in Greek historiography, it is on the margins of the genre, where it comes closest to the conventions of technical prose. The article then examines the case for regarding Acts as a historical monograph[25] or as 'apologetic historiography',[26] and concludes that within the Greek historical tradition overall, the best parallels to Acts in terms of preface-convention lie in the latter area, that is precisely where historiography is least rhetorical and closest to its roots in the Ionian *historia*-tradition.

Back in 1986, I had already suggested that the most obvious way to fit Luke's work into the literary matrix of the school tradition was to treat it as an example of the biography of a great teacher; and this is the subject of Chapter 3, 'Acts and Ancient Intellectual Biography'. This was an invited contribution

23.   Alexander, 'The Living Voice', pp. 221–47; 'Schools, Hellenistic', in *ABD* V, pp. 1005–11; 'Paul and the Hellenistic Schools: the Evidence of Galen': in Troels Engberg-Pedersen (ed.), *Paul in his Hellenistic Context* (Philadelphia: Augsburg Fortress/Edinburgh: T&T Clark, 1994), pp. 60–83; 'IPSE DIXIT: Citation of Authority in Paul and in the Jewish and Hellenistic Schools', in Troels Engberg-Pedersen (ed.), *Paul beyond the Judaism-Hellenism Divide* (Louisville: Westminster John Knox, 2001), pp. 103–27. These papers are to be published in Loveday Alexander and Philip Alexander (eds.), *The School of Moses and the School of Christ* (forthcoming).

24.   Loveday Alexander, 'The Preface to Acts and the Historians', in Ben Witherington III (ed.), *History, Literature and Society in the Book of Acts* (Cambridge: Cambridge University Press, 1996), pp. 73–103.

25.   Cf. Chapter 2, pp. 37–40. On Acts as monograph, see further E. Plümacher, 'Die Apostelgeschichte als historische Monographie', in J. Kremer (ed.), *Les Actes des Apôtres: Traditions, rédaction, théologie* (BETL, 48; Leuven: Leuven University Press – Gembloux, 1978); repr. in E. Plümacher, *Geschichte und Geschichten: Aufsätze zur Apostelgeschichte und zu den Johannesakten* (ed. J. Schröter, R. Brucker; Tübingen: Mohr Siebeck, 2004), pp. 1–14; idem, 'Cicero und Lukas: Bemerkungen zu Stil und Zweck der historischen Monographie', *ibid.*, pp. 15–32.

26.   Cf. Chapter 2, p. 40. On Acts as apologetic, see further Chapter 8 in this volume.

to the first volume of Bruce Winter's monumental series on *The Book of Acts in its First-Century Setting* (1993). Richard Burridge's *What Are the Gospels?* had just appeared in 1992, and was beginning to reawaken interest in ancient biography as a genre for the Gospels.[27] But my study has a narrower focus on intellectual biography, that is writing that celebrates the lives of people who were famous for their intellectual achievements: poets and philosophers, doctors and mathematicians. Its starting point is Charles Talbert's brilliant hypothesis linking Luke's two-volume composition (Gospel + Acts) with the pattern of biographical writing found in Diogenes Laertius' *Lives of the Philosophers* (Life of Founder + Lives of Disciples).[28] This general pattern of 'succession literature' is widespread in the Hellenistic school tradition, and it demonstrates that biographical narrative, and the assurance of the stability of tradition, has an important role to play within the ongoing life of the schools.[29] The problem here is not function but form: Luke's free-flowing narrative has a very different literary texture from the thematic structures and analytical narrative mode of Diogenes Laertius (who though later than Luke-Acts is our best surviving exemplar of this tradition). Nevertheless, the biographical paradigms developed in this tradition (especially the unwritten 'Life' of Socrates) provide suggestive parallels with Luke's presentation of Paul in Acts and suggest a means by which Luke's readers could fit Paul's story – and by implication their own – into 'a story they already knew' (Chapter 3, pp. 62–68).

If the narrative texture of Acts is hard to parallel in biography, maybe we should cast the generic net more widely. Following up on the success of Richard Pervo's *Profit with Delight*, and in the context of a burgeoning interest in Greek fiction,[30] I set out at the same time to explore some of the more novelistic aspects of Luke's composition. Chapter 4, '"In Journeyings Often": Voyaging in the Acts of the Apostles and in Greek Romance' originally appeared in *Luke's Literary Achievement*, a product of many years' fruitful research collaboration with the Faculty of Theology in Lausanne and the Department of

---

27.   Richard A. Burridge, *What are the Gospels?* (SNTSMS, 70; Cambridge: Cambridge University Press, 1992). The second edition (Grand Rapids: Eerdmans, 2004) contains extended coverage of the biography debate since 1992 in ch. 11, 'Reactions and developments' (pp. 252–307).

28.   Cf. n. 17 above.

29.   Cf. now also Charles Talbert and Perry Stepp, 'Succession in Luke-Acts and in the Lukan Milieu', in Charles Talbert (ed.), *Reading Luke-Acts in its Mediterranean Milieu* (NovTSup, 107; Leiden: Brill, 2003), pp. 19–55; Perry L. Stepp, *Leadership Succession in the World of the Pauline Circle* (Sheffield: Sheffield Phoenix Press, 2005).

30.   Richard I. Pervo, *Profit with Delight: The Literary Genre of the Acts of the Apostles* (Philadelphia: Fortress Press, 1987). The 'Ancient Fiction and Early Christian and Jewish Narrative' section at the SBL provided (and continues to provide) a stimulating and companionable context for these explorations, which prompted further forays into the realm of Greek fiction: cf. my 'St. Paul and the Greek Novel', in Ron Hock (ed.), *Ancient Fiction and Early Christian Narrative* (SBL Symposium Series; Atlanta: Scholars Press,1998), pp. 235–256; and 'The Passions in the Novels of Chariton and Xenophon', in John T. Fitzgerald (ed.), *Passions and Progress in Greco-Roman Thought* (London: Routledge, forthcoming).

Religions and Theology in Manchester.[31] The voyage motif seems an obvious starting-point for a comparative reading of Acts and the Greek novels, since it is integral to both. Examining the journey-structures of Chariton and Xenophon of Ephesus reveals both intriguing parallels to Acts and significant differences. The mental maps of both novels are centred on the Mediterranean and reflect the geographical perspective of the old Ionian world-map. Luke's mental map shifts from the Jerusalem-centred perspective of the early chapters to a Mediterranean-centred map much closer to those of the novelists. This is matched by a shift in the mode of travel, as Luke's Paul (rather against the grain of the Paul of the Epistles) becomes a sea-voyager, effortlessly at home in the cultural territory claimed by the novelists as quintessentially 'Greek'. It is, I suggest, an act of narrative aggression as potentially disturbing to the Greek reader as the Egyptian invasion of the landscapes of Hellenism depicted in the Isis temple at Pompeii.

Chapter 5, 'Narrative Maps', continues this parallel exploration of the cultural worlds of Acts and Greek romance.[32] Originally written for a *Festschrift* for John Rogerson, this paper explores some of the ways in which the topographical nomenclature of a narrative can be used to reconstruct its 'implied map' (Chapter 5, pp. 98–100). Here the underlying point of comparison is found in the fact that the journeys of St Paul, as narrated by Paul himself in the Epistles and by Luke in Acts, take place in the same geographical theatre as the journeys of the heroes and heroines of contemporary Greek romance. Yet there is astonishingly little overlap in the toponymy of the four narratives: out of a total of 141 place-names, only four are found in all four narratives and only 13 in any three (Chapter 5, p. 110). Analysing these patterns creates a means of understanding the political and rhetorical filters which colour each narrative's landscape, and which in turn both reflect and create the differing cultural landscapes of the authors and their readers. Paul and (to a slightly lesser degree) Luke share a commitment to the realistic political landscape of the present which is notably missing in the novelists. Yet Luke's fascination with sea-voyaging, which makes its impact as much in the use of redundant names as in the descriptive detail he lavishes on Paul's voyages, allows him to link his story with the parallel epic of romance without losing its rootedness in the contemporary Roman world.[33]

---

31. '"In Journeyings Often": Voyaging in the Acts of the Apostles and in Greek Romance': in C.M. Tuckett (ed.), *Luke's Literary Achievement: Collected Essays* (JSNTSup, 116; Sheffield: Sheffield Academic Press, 1995), pp. 17–49.

32. Loveday Alexander, 'Narrative Maps: Reflections on the Toponymy of Acts', in M. Daniel Carroll R., D.J.A. Clines, P.R. Davies (eds.), *The Bible in Human Society: Essays in Honour of John Rogerson,* (JSOTSup, 200; Sheffield: Sheffield Academic Press, 1995), pp. 17–57.

33. Since the original publication of this study, the geographical horizons of Luke's work have been explored more fully by James M. Scott, in his *Geography in Early Judaism and Christianity: The Book of Jubilees* (SNTSMS, 113; Cambridge: Cambridge University Press, 2002), esp. pp. 44–96.

Chapter 6, 'Fact, Fiction, and the Genre of Acts', takes up the wider question of the construction of factuality in Greek literature. This is a fuller version of the paper originally presented in abbreviated form as a Short Main Paper at the SNTS meeting in Birmingham in 1997, and published in NTS the following year.[34] Behind the quest for the genre of Acts there often lies an unexpressed assumption that once we know its genre, we shall know whether to classify Luke's work as 'fact' or 'fiction'. But in fact it is clear that this equation is much too simple: the fact/fiction divide does not follow generic boundaries. The paper proposes an approach that focuses on the reader's expectations rather than on the author's intentions. What were the literary clues that disposed an ancient reader to classify a narrative as 'fact' or fiction'? Why did ancient historians come to acquire a reputation for mendacity? What were the danger signals that alerted ancient readers that they were approaching the domain of fantasy? Read this way, it becomes clear that Acts does not fit comfortably into either the 'fiction' or the 'non-fiction' shelves of the ancient reader's library.

Chapter 7, 'New Testament Narrative and Ancient Epic', deals with a different kind of literature, which seems at first sight to stretch the boundaries of comparative reading to breaking-point. This paper was originally presented in the 'Ancient Fiction and Early Christian Narrative' section at the SBL Annual Meeting in Toronto in 2002, and published in two sections, part in the Festschrift for Daniel Marguerat (2003), part as a review of Marianne Bonz's *The Past As Legacy* in TLZ.[35] Bonz's study, like the work of Dennis Ronald Macdonald,[36] performs an invaluable function in alerting us to the importance of the classical epics in the cultural script of antiquity. At the surface levels of discourse and narrative management, Acts is not an epic, and no ancient reader would suppose that it was. Luke's mythology, his language, his values, and his narrative structures all owe more to the Greek Bible than to Greek and Roman epic. Nevertheless, Luke's narrative contains subtle linguistic and symbolic clues which create hyperlinks with the narrative world of epic, most notably in the final voyage to Rome.

So far I have been focusing on narrative aspects of Luke's work, reading Acts alongside other narrative representations of personage, of place, and of adventure in Greco-Roman culture. In Chapter 8, 'The Acts of the Apostles as an

34. Loveday Alexander, 'Fact, Fiction, and the Genre of Acts', *NTS* 44.3 (July 1998), pp. 380–99.

35. Loveday Alexander, 'New Testament Narrative and Ancient Epic', in Emmanuelle Steffek and Yvan Bourquin (eds.), *Raconter, interpreter, annoncer: Parcours de Nouveau Testament. Mélanges offerts à Daniel Marguera pour son 60ᵉ anniversaire* (Le Monde de la Bible, 47; Genève: Labor et Fides, 2003), pp. 239–49. Also my Review of Marianne Palmer Bonz, *The Past As Legacy*, in TLZ 129 (2004), pp. 381–83.

36. Dennis R. MacDonald has explored parallels between New Testament narrative and Greek epic in a number of publications: see esp. *The Homeric Epics and the Gospel of Mark* (New Haven: Yale University Press, 2000); 'The Shipwrecks of Odysseus and Paul', *NTS* 45 (1999), pp. 88–107; 'Paul's Farewell to the Ephesian Elders and Hector's Farewell to Andromache: A Strategic Imitation of Homer's Iliad', in Penner and Vander Stichele (eds.), *Contextualizing Acts*, pp. 189–203.

Apologetic Text', the attention shifts to the rhetorical texture of Luke's work. Presented originally to an Oxford seminar on 'Apologetic in the Ancient World', this paper was also aired in research seminars at Yale and St Andrews, and published in 1999.[37] The lack of consensus over the scope and direction of Luke's apologetic in Acts arises partly, I suggest, out of a failure to attend to the surface structure of the text. 'Apologetic' is not an ancient genre-category in itself, but *apologia* – a word Luke is fond of – is a perfectly recognizable sub-genre of forensic rhetoric, a speech for the defence addressed to a definable audience on a particular occasion. Acts is not itself a speech in this sense, but Luke has structured his narrative in a way that heightens the importance of apologetic speech. The book contains a large number of dramatic scenarios which create opportunities for placing rhetorical speech on the lips of the characters, and many of these speeches – particularly in the final chapters – are explicitly described as *apologia*. These scenarios between them encompass all the varied audiences that have been posited for the book as a whole (Jewish, Christian, Greek, and Roman), but careful analysis reveals that the overwhelming majority of apologetic speech in Acts is addressed to a Jewish audience.

Chapter 9, 'Reading Luke-Acts from Back to Front' was presented originally at a Leuven colloquium organized by Jos Verheyden in 1998 on 'The Unity of Luke-Acts' and published in the colloquium volume of the same name.[38] It deals with the question, in what sense does the puzzling ending of Acts supply a closure to the whole two-volume work? Gérard Genette and others have argued that the beginning and ending of a book function as a framing device which serves to assist the reader's entry into and exit from the narrative world (Chapter 9, pp. 208–11). Approaching the ending in this way highlights a number of structural links and cross-references between the end of Acts and the beginning of the Gospel, all of which serve to reinforce both the prospective and the retrospective narrative unity of the whole work. But if the ending of Acts also functions as a bridge between the narrative world and the world of the readers, it seems likely that the book's final scenario in Rome, with Paul making his last *apologia* before the assembled leaders of the Jewish community (Acts 28.17–28) comes closer to the world of the readers than the opening scenes of the Gospel. Luke's short preface (Lk. 1.1–4) has a distancing effect, separating the world of the writer and his inscribed reader, Theophilus, from the tradition passed down by the eyewitnesses. His longer narrative prologue (Lk. 1.5–4.30) carefully creates an entrée into a narrative world where angels and heavenly voices are always on hand to explain the inner significance of the 'events fulfilled among us'. But the voyage which carries Paul to Rome also functions as a bridge back to the much more ambivalent world of the readers, 'a world where even the words of apostles are the subject of doubt and debate' (Chapter 9, pp. 227–29).

---

37.   Loveday Alexander, 'The Acts of the Apostles as an Apologetic Text', in Mark Edwards, Martin Goodman, Christopher Rowland (eds.), *Apologetics in the Roman Empire* (Oxford: Oxford University Press, 1999), pp. 15–44.

38.   Loveday Alexander, 'Reading Luke-Acts from Back to Front', in Jos Verheyden (ed.), *The Unity of Luke-Acts* (BETL; Leuven: Peeters, 1999), pp. 419–46.

It is fitting to close this collection with a paper which honours two of the finest and most acute exponents of the importance of placing New Testament texts on the bookshelves of the Greco-Roman world. Chapter 10, '*Septuaginta, Fachprosa, Imitatio*', was originally published in a *Festschrift* for Eckhard Plümacher[39] and arose out of an invitation from Lars Rydbeck and Stan Porter to provide a critical retrospective of the work of Albert Wifstrand for the 'Graeco-Roman World of the New Testament' seminar at the SNTS meeting in Durham in 2002. The paper takes us back to the question of *Fachprosa* and the sociolinguistic register of Luke's writings, and neatly brings together two of the dominant underlying themes that have emerged in this collection: Luke's relation to the literature of the classical world, and his relation to the Greek Bible. Considered against the whole spectrum of Greek linguistic usage, Luke's Greek is not the atticizing Greek of the second-century elite but 'an educated written language untouched by classicism', a form of 'standard Hellenistic prose' which also appears in the writers of *Fachprosa* (Chapter 10, pp. 235). This was the default Greek prose maintained by bureaucrats and technical writers for non-literary composition, a style which was still acceptable for historians at the end of the Hellenistic era but falls well short of the classicising standards of the prestige code of the first and second centuries CE. Luke's Greek is not 'classicizing' in this sense, but it does betray the influence of a different kind of classic, the Greek Bible, whose distinctive style pervades his narrative at every level (Chapter 10, pp. 242–43). It was Eckhard Plümacher who first (so far as I am aware) made the illuminating observation that Luke's 'biblicizing' Greek can itself be seen as a form of classicism, an example of the pervasive *imitatio*-culture of the Greco-Roman world;[40] but it is a form of classicism that would be meaningless outside the Jewish communities of the Diaspora. Within the Jewish communities, this Septuagintal language functioned as a prestige code, used for formal literary and liturgical composition; to non-Jews, it was simply another form of non-Attic ('barbaric') Greek. Even at the linguistic level, then, we can see that Luke's work seems to be located at the intersection of two distinct cultural codes.

39.   Loveday Alexander, 'Septuaginta, Fachprosa, Imitatio: Albert Wifstrand and the Language of Luke-Acts', in Cilliers Breytenbach and Jens Schröter (ed.), *Die Apostelgeschichte und die hellenistische Geschichtsschreibung: Festschrift für Eckhard Plümacher zu seinem 65. Geburtstag* (AGAJU, 57; Leiden: Brill, 2004), pp. 1–26.

40.   Eckhard Plümacher, *Lukas als hellenistischer Schriftsteller: Studien zur Apostelgeschichte* (Göttingen: Vandenhoeck & Ruprecht, 1972). On *imitatio*, cf. Loveday Alexander, 'Intertextualité et la question des lecteurs', in D. Marguerat and A. Curtis (eds), *Intertextualités: La Bible en échos* (Geneva: Labor et Fides, 2000), pp. 201–14; see also now Dennis R. MacDonald (ed.), *Mimesis and Intertextuality in Antiquity and Christianity* (Claremont Studies in Antiquity and Christianity; Harrisburg: Trinity Press International, 2001).

The Preface and the Critics

How has the argument fared since the publication of *The Preface* in 1993? Criticism of my thesis has tended to cluster around two poles: the negative argument that Luke's preface does not provide a good fit for the genre 'Greek historiography'; and the positive argument proposing 'the scientific tradition' (or 'technical prose') as an alternative. This introductory chapter gives me an opportunity not only to respond to some of the points raised by critics, but also to revisit the original question in the light of the wider explorations in Greek literature charted in this volume.

The first point to be made here is that we need to distinguish carefully between *literary* questions about genre and *historical* questions about reliability. For many Lukan scholars (notably in the Anglo-Saxon world), fitting Luke's preface into the genre of Greek historiography seems somehow to guarantee the historical reliability of Luke's work. Somehow, the implication seems to be, we can rest assured of the reliability of Luke's account of Christian origins if we can only demonstrate that Acts belongs to the genre of historiography – which in this context is normally taken to mean historiography as understood by the Greeks and Romans. Hence, casting doubt on the historiographical nature of the preface is equivalent to impugning Luke's reliability as a historian. This issue seems to lie behind a lot of the ire and contention that still (somewhat to my surprise) surrounds my argument that the preface does not support the generic classification of Luke's work as Greco-Roman historiography. Todd Penner's recent surveys of Acts scholarship show convincingly how much energy critical scholars have invested in finding some kind of historical kernel in and under Luke's story.[41] What is striking in Penner's analysis is the way he shows that this is true not only (as we might expect) for conservative scholars but unexpectedly – and perhaps even more – for those who refuse to take Luke's story at face value and yet have claimed to find a historical substratum in the Acts narrative by reading against the grain.[42]

So it is important to make it clear from the outset that my argument in *The Preface* was not about historicity but about a particular way of writing history and its peculiar etiquette of discourse. I was not making any claims as to the truth-value of Luke's narrative (which must be contested on other grounds). Nor was I claiming that Luke did not intend his work to be read as 'history,' if by that we mean a reliable account of events in the recent past. In fact (paradoxically enough), casting Luke as a sober, pragmatic, writer of 'scientific prose' might give us a much more secure handle on his reliability.[43] It is certainly

---

41. Todd Penner 'Madness in the Method', pp. 235–41; Penner and Vander Stichele (eds.), *Contextualizing Acts*, p. 11; Todd Penner, *In Praise of Christian Origins: Stephen and the Hellenists in Lukan Apologetic Historiography* (*Emory Studies in Early Christianity* 10; New York: T&T Clark International, 2004), ch. 1, pp. 1–60.

42. Penner, *In Praise of Christian Origins*, pp. 38–39.

43. On this see further Loveday Alexander, 'Formal Elements and Genre: Which Greco-Roman Prologues Most Closely Parallel the Lukan Prologues?' in David P. Moessner (ed.), *Jesus and the Heritage of Israel* (Harrisburg: Trinity Press International, 1999), pp. 9–26.

evident (as I have made clear all along) that the preface shows a strong interest both in 'reliability'[44] and in the preservation of authentic tradition.[45] What is interesting is that the pragmatic realism of Luke's preface is not accompanied by the normal markers of critical distance that Greek historical discourse uses to position itself within the territory of 'fact'. The narrative of Acts contains much that ancient readers would almost certainly have classed as fiction – which makes it all the more disconcerting that Luke apparently expects it to be taken at face value.[46]

Others, more circumspect, have rightly seen that the claim to be writing within the Hellenistic tradition of historiography is not an automatic guarantee of historical accuracy and might even militate against it (cf. Chapter 6 below).[47] But there is still somehow a perceived need to defend the generic link with Greek historiography, perhaps because of the huge vistas it opens up for structural and thematic comparisons with the classical and Hellenistic historians.[48] The potential value of this kind of comparison was observed as long ago as Cadbury's *Making of Luke-Acts* and Dibelius' essays on Luke the historian;[49] but it has been affirmed with renewed vigour – and with very fruitful results – in the last decade in the work of scholars associated with the SBL Luke-Acts group (David Balch, David Moessner, Greg Sterling, Charles Talbert) and more recently in the work of Todd Penner and Clare Rothschild.[50] If the preface does not fit the genre

---

44.   Cf. *asphaleia* Lk. 1.4, which should not be translated 'truth' as in many English versions.

45.   So, correctly, S. Byrskog in *Story as History—History as Story: The Gospel; Tradition in the Context of Ancient Israel* (WUNT, 123; Tübingen: Mohr-Siebeck, 2000), pp. 48–49: though he misses the force of my argument, which was much more focused on the vocabulary of Luke's preface than on the historians' use of eyewitness testimony. On the *autopsia*-convention and its potential for subversion, see further Chapter 6 in this volume; and on tradition, Alexander, 'The Living Voice'.

46.   Chapter 6, pp. 157–63.

47.   Cf. now Penner, *In Praise of Christian Origins*, ch. 3, e.g. p. 111: 'It is very difficult, if not impossible, to move beyond the framework, order, characterization, and style of the narrative to a concrete bedrock of assured reliable and verifiable data. The very understanding and practice of writing history in Luke's day would seem to bear this out.'

48.   Penner's *In Praise of Christian Origins* is committed to the view that Luke 'consciously aligns his work with the tradition of Greek historiography' (p. 220; cf. p. 59 'for the purposes of this study'), and this factor seems to underlie his critique of my work on the preface (p. 133, n.73). However, in *Contextualizing Acts* (pp. 14–16) he defends a much more holistic and open-ended approach to genre.

49.   H.J. Cadbury, *The Making of Luke-Acts* (New York: Macmillan, 1927). Cf. also C.K. Barrett, *Luke the Historian in Recent Study* (London: Epworth Press, 1961); M. Dibelius, *Studies in the Acts of the Apostles* (ed. H. Greeven; trans. M. Ling and P. Schubert; London: SCM Press, 1956), ET of *Aufsätze zur Apostelgeschichte* (Göttingen: Vandenhoeck & Ruprecht, 1951); now reprinted in a new format in M. Dibelius, *The Book of Acts: Form, Style, Theology* (ed. K.C. Hanson; Minneapolis: Fortress Press, 2004). The work of Eckhard Plümacher has been particularly influential in German-speaking scholarship: cf. the important series of essays now collected in Plümacher, *Geschichte und Geschichten*.

50.   Cf. Penner, *In Praise of Christian Origins*, esp. ch. 3; Clare Rothschild, *Luke-Acts and the Rhetoric of History* (WUNT, 2.175; Tübingen: Mohr Siebeck, 2004).

of Greek historiography, is all this excellent work ruled out of court? Clearly it is immensely illuminating to compare Luke's work with that of the Greek historians. Do not these parallels show Luke's work has more in common with Greek (and Roman) historiography than with any other ancient genre?

There are a number of points to be made in response to this. The first is that my original argument was about the preface and the preface alone. If we want to argue that the rest of Luke's work fits the generic expectations of Greek historiography, we are free to do so.[51] But (let us be clear), the preface must still be factored into the equation. We still have to take into account the negative fact that the conventions Luke uses in his preface, the most significant single place for ancient authors to make preliminary indications to their readers about genre and topic, are counter-indicative of Greek historiography. Of course, Luke might have just got his preface-etiquette wrong, or decided to do something different: but we have only to look at Josephus to see a Jewish contemporary who is painfully aware of the conventional code governing the composition of a historical preface. In other words, I would argue, a Greek reader would need strong generic indications within the narrative to outweigh the negative expectations induced by the preface. At the very least, we should be looking for Luke's generic models not among the great classical historians (Thucydides and Herodotus are probably the most difficult to square with the preface) but among the more marginal historians, closer to Luke in time, who do occasionally use preface-conventions closer to those found in *Fachprosa* – the antiquarians (Dionysius of Halicarnassus, Diodorus' opening books), the ethnic historians (Manetho, Josephus).[52] This is the line I would pursue if I wanted to follow Sterling's suggestion that Luke should be located in the area of 'apologetic historiography' or Hubert Cancik's interesting proposal that Acts represents an example of institutional historiography.[53]

Secondly, it is also important to remember that the Greek historians did not have a monopoly on history-writing in the ancient world: there are other ways of writing history in Greek, with different generic expectations. It is simply confusing the issue to say that Luke follows the conventions of Greek historiography but is *also* influenced by the historiography of the Greek Bible and the Hellenistic Jewish historians, as if biblical historiography were simply a subset

---

51.   As does Greg Sterling, *Historiography and Self-Definition: Josephos, Luke-Acts and Apologetic Historiography* (NovTSup, 64; Leiden: Brill, 1992), p. 341: 'Since I have placed Luke-Acts into the category of historiography on larger grounds, I will compare the statement with others in Hellenistic historiography'.

52.   But note, even so, that Josephus does not actually contravene the generic expectations of historiography by inserting a dedication into the opening the preface of the Antiquities. Epaphroditus is mentioned at *Ant.* 1.8, but only in the third person; the formal address does not appear until the epilogue of the *Life* (*Vita* 430), which originally appeared as an appendix to the *Antiquities*.

53.   Hubert Cancik, 'The History of Culture, Religion and Institutions in Ancient Historiography: Philological Observations Concerning Luke's History', *JBL* 116.4 (1997), pp. 673–95. See further Chapter 2 in this volume.

of Greek historiography.[54] Like all imperialistic cultures, the Greeks were always keen to fit other people's history and literature into their own – but it does not follow that we have to accept this colonialist perspective.[55] The fact is that biblical historiography belongs to an autonomous near eastern tradition of historiography which is in some respects parallel to the Greek (and may even have influenced it), but in others emphasizes aspects downplayed or ignored in the parallel tradition. A full study of Luke's historiographical praxis would have to take account of such structural features as the biographical aspects of ancient near eastern historiography, which appear in the court tales of Herodotus but were rigorously excluded from Thucydides' more democratic conception; the role of direct speech in the two traditions; the role of religion and the miraculous; or the strongly exegetical dynamic of Lukan rhetoric, which is much more obviously at home in the Jewish tradition than in the Greek.[56] To appreciate these cultural distinctives is not to hark back to some pseudo-essentialist opposition between 'Judaism' and 'Hellenism',[57] nor to seek some kind of refuge from the 'challenge' of locating Luke in the Greco-Roman world (which is after all what this volume is all about).[58] It is, rather, to recognize that the process of locating Luke's work on the map of Greco-Roman culture is not just a matter of identifying broad cultural patterns (important though that is), but also of differentiating the particular social or sectarian threads that make up the broader pattern. If we want to hear Luke's distinctive socio-cultural voice within the interlocking worlds of ancient Mediterranean discourse, we have to identify not only what game he is playing, but which team he plays for.[59]

54.   Thus a footnote in Penner, *In Praise of Christian Origins* (p. 146, n. 114) concedes that biblical historiography is 'worth considering' as a genre for Luke-Acts – but does not allow us to ponder what that might do for the label 'Greek historiography' and what might be the relationship between the two. Similarly Joel Green, *The Gospel of Luke* (NICNT; Grand Rapids: Eerdmans, 1997), moves smoothly from the statement that in describing his work as a 'narrative', Luke 'identifies his project as a long narrative account of many events, for which the chief prototypes were the early histories of Herodotus and Thucydides' to the recognition that 'many of Luke's predecessors in Israelite and Jewish historiography did not reflect on their aims and procedures within the writing itself' (p. 5), which seems to assume that 'Israelite and Jewish historiography' is part of the same literary tradition as Herodotus and Thucydides.

55.   On 'apologetic historiography' see further Chapter 2 and Chapter 8 in this volume. Rather than describing it as a separate genre (for which there is no ancient warrant), I would prefer to regard the texts Sterling includes in this category as one of the points where the Greek and the Jewish traditions intersects with those of its 'barbarian' neighbours – and I see no reason why we should accept the Greek view of what is happening at that point of intersection.

56.   Cf. Chapter 6 below; further, Loveday Alexander, 'Marathon or Jericho? Reading Acts in Dialogue with Biblical and Greek Historiography', in David J.A. Clines and Stephen D. Mooore (eds.), *Auguries: The Jubilee Volume of the Sheffield Department of Biblical Studies*, (JSOTSup, 269; Sheffield; Sheffield Academic Press, 1998), pp. 92–125. I pursue the comparison with Greek and Jewish historiography in more detail in *Acts and the Ancient Reader* (forthcoming).

57.   Cf. Engberg-Pedersen (ed.), *Paul beyond the Judaism-Hellenism Divide.*

58.   As Penner seems to imply, *Contextualizing Acts*, pp. 12–13.

59.   Loveday Alexander, 'IPSE DIXIT', pp. 103–27.

But there is a more fundamental point at issue here. I would not wish at this stage to invoke Sandmel's spectre of 'parallelomania';[60] but I think it is fair to ask whether the parallels that emerge from comparative readings of Acts alongside various types of Greek historiography are necessarily indications of genre. Too often there is a kind of illegitimate totality transfer (to borrow James Barr's phrase) which encourages the leap from *topos* or motif to genre. This tendency is evident in much of the recent discussion on the genre of Luke-Acts (cf., e.g., Chapter 7 below). Todd Penner argues persuasively that we need to construct 'a more pervasive literary and cultural environment...for interpreting Acts', looking for 'broad patterns of cultural communicative strategies surfacing in a wide array of literature in the ancient Mediterranean world', and seeking to uncover 'a base structure of communication and persuasion, which could and did take on differing manifestations of form and expression depending on individual factors relating to social, political, and ideological contexts situated in divergent locales and time periods'.[61] This, I believe, expresses precisely what I have been seeking to do in this long-term project of reading Acts in its ancient literary context. But – as Penner himself shows – what we are talking about here is a range of philosophical or rhetorical *topoi* and patterns of persuasive discourse, drawing on a deep-rooted training in the manipulation of narrative which pervades the whole culture of Greek education. These patterns are not confined to the genre of historiography, and it is misleading to identify them as indicators of genre. In a cultural context where (as Christopher Pelling notes), 'authors and audiences were peculiarly sensitive to genre',[62] the solution is not to conclude that genre did not matter (clearly it did, at least in certain contexts), but to find a more sophisticated vocabulary for analysing literary parallels, one that can distinguish genre-specific features from other cultural *topoi*, and one that takes as much account of the formal points of differentiation between genres as of their similarities.

This leads me to wonder, finally, whether the positive trajectory of my original project was correctly formulated. Having identified that the preface does not fit the genre of Greek historiography, it was natural to ask the question: what genre does it belong to? But was this the right question? Do 'scientific prefaces' function as genre markers at all? Several critics identified this as the main problem with the argument of *The Preface*: 'The work itself is obviously not a scientific or technical treatise', as David E. Aune puts it.[63] The apparent anomaly had not escaped me. The affinity of Luke's preface with prefaces found in *Fachprosa* was a conclusion that was forced on me by the evidence; and as long

---

60.   S. Sandmel, 'Parallelomania', JBL 81 (1962), pp. 1–13.

61.   Penner, *In Praise of Christian Origins*, pp. 218–19.

62.   C.B.R. Pelling, *Literary Texts and the Greek Historian* (London: Routledge, 1999), p. 2.

63.   Aune, 'Historical or Scientific Prooimion?' p. 143. Cf. Greg Sterling, *Historiography and Self-definition* p. 340, n. 140: 'The Achilles heel of A's proposal is that the preface must relate to the text in a meaningful way – even if it is detachable'. Joel Green makes a similar point (*Luke*, p. 4): 'Formal, grammatical features cannot mask the significant discontinuity one recognises when moving from the substance of the scientific tradition to the narrative of the third Gospel'.

ago as 1986, I had identified the problem and suggested some possible lines of investigation this apparently paradoxical conclusion might open up:

> How can Luke's two-volume narrative, based on traditional material rather than on 'eyewitness' research or the systematic sifting of new evidence, be compared with the treatises of Vitruvius or Hermogenes? What possible congruity can there be between Hero's *Mechanics* or Galen's *Anatomical Procedures* and Luke's story of the sayings and doings of a Galilean holy man and his followers? This is the nub of the problem with which the alignment of Luke's preface leaves us.[64]

One strategy is to question the whole idea that the preface is an indicator of genre. Suppose instead we accept Greg Sterling's proposal, that 'there was a common stock of terms used for prose prefaces in the Hellenistic world which transcended the boundaries of a single genre'?[65] That would accommodate the stray parallels quoted in other texts which apparently do not belong to the 'scientific tradition',[66] and leave us free to determine the genre of Luke's work on other grounds (which is effectively what Sterling does).[67] It would encourage us to look for other kinds of significance in the preface: for parallels in social function, or for a common mode of discourse calling on the detached, rational voice of Greek academic discourse.[68] It also encourages us to move beyond the preface and explore the generic characteristics of Acts as a whole (which is what this book is all about).

But my own feeling now is that if my original formulation was too narrow, Aune and Sterling formulate the problem too broadly. The preface-conventions Luke employs (like dedication) cluster in a variety of places in Greek literature: in technical treatises (*Fachprosa*); in antiquarian historiography; in marginal authors working on the edges of the Greek cultural tradition (including Jewish writers); in some forms of biography;[69] and occasionally among the literary essays of a Plutarch or a Lucian. But this is not simply a random pattern of distribution.

---

64. Alexander, 'The pattern of Greek Preface-Writing', p. 67.

65. Sterling, *Apologetic Historiography*, pp. 340–41; cf. Aune, 'Historical or Scientific Prooimion?' p. 144: 'A. should have argued that the use of prefaces reveals nothing about genre or provenance of texts…'

66. Aune, 'Historical or Scientific Prooimion?', pp. 145–47 cites parallels in the preface to Plutarch, *Septem Sapientium Convivium* (though this is clearly not a historical preface either).

67. Cf. n. 50 above.

68. Both of these possibilities are explored in *The Preface* (which devotes two chapters to the functions of prefaces in *Fachprosa*); cf. also Alexander, 'Formal Elements and Genre', p. 12: 'It would be going too far to claim that the stylistic register of the opening verse of Acts is sufficient to locate the text within a particular genre. "Greek academic prose" is not a genre but a wide field of discourse.'

69. Dedicatory passages appear in Diogenes Laertius, *Lives of Eminent Philosophers* 3.47, 10.29: and in some of Plutarch's *Lives* (*Theseus, Dion, Demosthenes*). Diogenes Laertius (whose work falls outside the chronological limits of my original study) falls well within the category of school literature (cf. Chapter 3 below). Plutarch's prefaces exhibit the kind of rhetorically-sophisticated variation we would expect of this writer, and apart from dedication, have little in common with the *Fachprosa* prefaces.

It is equally clear (and equally important) that there are places where these conventions are *not* used – and that these tend to be the literary genres which had a more clearly-defined set of formal generic expectations (like history, or epic). So I would now be inclined to re-formulate my conclusion thus: Luke's preface draws on a set of default preface-conventions used across a range of prose compositions which fall outside the more formally-defined prose genres of rhetoric and historiography. In a sense, then, the preface itself can be read as a mark of literary marginality. This literary marginality should not be equated too easily with social marginality: Plutarch, for instance, is clearly not a marginal figure in terms of Greco-Roman elite culture.[70] But in many cases where this pattern of conventional language appears, it does coincide with a marginal social position (manifested, for example, in the seeking of patronage), and thus reflects a sense of the appropriate social etiquette for the occasion.[71]

And this brings us back full circle to the question of *Fachprosa*. As we see in Chapter 10, sociolinguistics provides valuable conceptual tools for analysing the twin classicistic phenomena of 'Atticism' and 'Biblicism' as prestige or 'High' forms of standard Hellenistic prose. This latter was the default language of everyday written communication in the eastern Mediterranean, used widely in *Fachprosa* and also in a range of other compositions where (for a variety of reasons) the embellishments of Atticism were not considered necessary or even appropriate. Luke's language is not Atticistic: essentially it belongs within the upper reaches of this standard educated *Koine*, except where he introduces his own form of classicizing embellishment by giving his language a more biblical flavour (Chapter 10, pp. 242–46). This mirrors exactly the pattern we find with Luke's use of literary convention. The 'scientific' conventions Luke uses in his preface are just what we would expect from a writer whose default language belongs to the same register as *Fachprosa*. In this sense, the preface has clear affinities with prefaces produced by other Jewish-Greek writers when they seek to present their work to a wider audience, not because it reproduces a 'biblical' style (in fact there is no precedent in the Hebrew Bible for such a preface), but because these Jewish writers deployed the same formal conventions (and for more or less the same reasons) as the technical writers of *Fachprosa*.[72] But equally, it positions Luke's work quite clearly outside the more narrowly-defined literary genres where the canons of a progressively classicizing taste demanded ever closer fidelity to classical norms – historiography above all.

David Aune is thus quite correct when he concedes that most extant histories 'are written by authors with a social status to which Luke could never have aspired and in an elevated style he could never have emulated'.[73] But he is

---

70.   But for the cultural anxieties latent in the Second Sophistic, see Simon Swain, *Hellenism and Empire: Language, Classicism, and Power in the Greek World, AD 50–250* (Oxford: Clarendon Press, 1996).

71.   Cf. Alexander, *The Preface*, ch. 9. On the complex relation between register and social dialect, see now further Chapter 10 below.

72.   See Alexander, *The Preface*, ch. 7.

73.   Aune, 'Historical or Scientific Prooimion?', p. 142.

entirely missing the point when he posits that there must have been 'literally hundreds of histories written in *Zwischenprosa* that the educated would have considered mediocre and that have been lost'.[74] Adopting a high classicizing style was an integral part of the generic expectations associated with historiography: the writing of history demanded a certain grandeur, both in language and in scale. That is why history was naturally associated with the prestige code: to write a history in '*Zwischenprosa*' (standard Hellenistic prose) was effectively to rule oneself out of consideration as a serious historian – as Lucian's satire shows all too clearly. Once we admit that Luke does not match these exacting standards, in other words, we are effectively conceding that he is not attempting to write history within the very limited parameters imposed by the standards of educated taste – unlike Josephus, whose awareness of the standards of incipient classicism is painfully obvious. Luke may well be (in fact I believe he is) attempting to write a different kind of history – but that would take us further than we are able to go in this introductory essay.

Epilogue: Where Next?

There is inevitably an element of the centrifugal about a collection of studies like this. Each paper follows its own agenda, an agenda driven partly by the logic of the particular project for which it was originally conceived. In fact, I have deliberately taken advantage of these projects and invitations to open up a variety of new dimensions in my own study of Acts, and this has been one of the most enjoyable aspects of the whole process. Nevertheless, all of them are concerned to forward in one way or another my own original project of reading Luke's work in its ancient literary context: and it is appropriate at this point to reflect in a more concerted way on the underlying themes that emerge from the collection when viewed as a whole.

My original work on the preface approached the subject from a traditional author-centred approach, focusing on the question of authorial intention. But there is another way to set about this kind of literary comparison, and that is to approach it from the perspective of the readers (or hearers)[75] of Acts rather than of the author: that is, to look at where the text is going rather than where it is coming from. Even if we stay within the parameters of a broadly historical approach to the text, the reader-oriented perspective has several advantages. It encourages us to move away from scholarship's lengthy preoccupation with sources and influences (which tends to be pursued in a knock-out fashion, as if the demonstration of one kind of influence is sufficient to eliminate the possibility of others). A reader-oriented approach is less determinate, more open-ended: the text has (presumably) only one author, but it can have an infinite number of readers. And all of those readers will bring to the text their own

---

74.　Aune. 'Historical or Scientific Prooimion?' p. 142; cf. p. 148, 'hundred of lost mediocre histories'.

75.　Here and throughout, the concept 'readers' should be deemed to include 'hearers'.

reading experience: so that while we may legitimately doubt whether the *author* of Acts had read Vergil's epic or the Greek novels, there is no reason why we should not ask what happens if we approach the text from the perspective of a *reader* familiar with romance – or even with the *Aeneid*.

This reader-oriented perspective provides a unifying thread for many of the papers in this volume. Richard Burridge's work on biography picks up the concept of genre as a kind of contract negotiated between authors and readers.[76] Genre, on this view, becomes not so much a set of rules as a set of cultural expectations, which authors may subvert or transform but which they must somehow engage with if the process of communication is to get off the ground. This approach allows us to move inwards to the text, focusing initially on the generic expectations of competent contemporary readers. It encourages us to look forwards to where the text is going rather than backwards to where it came from, to think of our text as an act of communication, rather than simply analysing it as the end-product of a process of composition. And, by opening up the possibility of multiple readings, it suggests a strategy for accommodating the many fruitful readings of Acts that have emerged from the past two decades of comparative reading. Luke may not have intended his work to be located within the tradition of the great classical historians, but it is always instructive to approach it from the standpoint of readers whose expectations are formed by that tradition.

These comparative readings can be seen, then, as part of an open-ended process of learning to read Acts alongside a multiplicity of ancient readers, with a variety of reading competencies formed within distinct cultural locations.[77] It is evident that this comparative process has enormous potential for illuminating Luke's work. Reading Acts alongside the literature of the Greco-Roman world opens up a rich repertoire of narrative strategies and symbolic codes available to writers and readers in that world. But comparison is as much about difference as it is about similarity, and the two run through this exercise in comparative reading like contrapuntal themes. Many of these papers have brought to light a tension between deep functional parallels and differences in surface texture, a lack of 'fit' that operates at the formal levels of discourse across a whole range of Greek literary genres. And it is vital to be attentive to these discourse features, the differences as well as the similarities, if we are to understand how Acts functions as a piece of early Christian communication within the larger world of Greco-Roman discourse.

---

76.   Burridge, *What Are the Gospels?*, ch. 2.
77.   I hope to pursue this further in a companion volume to this series of essays entitled *Acts and the Ancient Reader*.

Chapter 2

THE PREFACE TO ACTS AND THE HISTORIANS[*]

The beginning of a text has a special place in the orientation process which forms an inevitable part of any reader's approach to a new book. In the ancient world, where a book had neither dust-jacket nor publisher's blurb, the opening of a book, whether or not it constituted a formal preface, was particularly important. It was frequently used to identify the subject of the text which followed, sometimes the author or a particular readership. It could also be used, less directly, to identify the genre of the text: in a literary world which operated with a relatively formal code (formal, that is, by twentieth-century standards), the conventions employed at the beginning of the text could alert the reader as to what kind of text to expect.[1]

The commentators on Acts have long been aware of the potential literary significance of its opening words. Cadbury, writing in 1922, stated clearly what was to become a datum of Lukan scholarship: '[Luke's] prefaces and dedications at once suggest classification with the contemporary Hellenistic historians.'[2] The influential commentaries of Conzelmann and Haenchen contain classic restatements of this position:

> Acts, as the second book of a large historical work, begins in accordance with literary forms with a renewed dedication (to Theophilus) and a backward glance to the first book . . . This opening verse shows that firstly: Christianity is adopting the literary forms. It is therefore on the point of leaving the milieu of ordinary folk and entering the world of literature, the cultural world of antiquity. Thus its aloofness from the 'world' in which it grew up, expecting the end of this aeon, is diminishing . . . (Haenchen)
>
> Since the opening includes at least the suggestion of a proem, Luke is making literary

[*]   Originally published as 'The Preface to Acts and the Historians', in Ben Witherington III (ed.), *History, Literature and Society* (Cambridge, 1999), pp. 73–103, used here with the kind permission of Cambridge University Press.
    1.   D. Earl, 'Prologue-form in Ancient Historiography', *ANRW* 1.2, pp. 842–56; L.C.A. Alexander, *The Preface to Luke's Gospel* (SNTSMS 79; Cambridge: Cambridge University Press, 1993), pp. 2, 4, 5, passim.
    2.   *The Beginnings of Christianity*, ed. F.J. Foakes Jackson and Kirsopp Lake (London: Macmillan, 1922), II, p. 15.

claims and introducing his book as a monograph. The dedication is also in accord with literary custom. (Conzelmann)[3]

Comments like these imply what Cadbury had explicitly stated: that the preface of Acts functions as a genre-indicator. The informed reader, beginning at the beginning of the book, is led immediately to place it in the category 'history' (Cadbury, Haenchen) or 'monograph' (Conzelmann). Whether the rest of the book lives up to these expectations is another matter; in any genre-contract, the reader may well be disappointed to find that the author is unable to fulfill her or his side of the contract.[4] For many scholars, the expectations aroused by the preface of Acts are fully satisfied in the text itself.[5] Others confess almost immediate frustration. Haenchen, oddly, blames the problems on the readers:

> The elegant exordium of the third gospel has left many scholars with the impression that Luke would have been capable of writing the history of the dawn of Christianity in the style of a Xenophon, if not a Thucydides. However, he lacked at least two requisites for such an undertaking: an adequate historical foundation – and the right readers.[6]

Others would be more inclined to locate the problem with the standards of historiography prevailing in Luke's day:[7] which is to say that although our expectations in reading Acts may be disappointed (if, that is, we expected a dispassionate, objective history of the early church), nevertheless the first-century reader, accustomed to rather different standards of historical writing, would find the outcome of the composition perfectly in line with the expectations set up by the preface. Either way the preface (which is all that concerns us in this chapter) is widely accepted as defining the rules of the particular game Luke is playing.

3.   E. Haenchen, *The Acts of the Apostles* (*The Acts of the Apostles* (Oxford: Blackwell, 1971), pp. 136–37; ET (rev.) of *Die Apostelgeschichte* (Mayer Kommentar, Göttingen, 1961), pp. 136–37; H. Conzelmann, *Acts of the Apostles* (Hermeneia; Philadelphia: Fortress Press, 1987, trans. from 2nd German edn. of 1972), p. 3. It is clear from the context that Conzelmann has in mind primarily the historical monograph.

4.   See R.A. Burridge, *What Are the Gospels?* (SNTSMS 70; Cambridge: Cambridge University Press, 1992), ch. 2, esp. pp. 35–36. For genre as 'a system of expectations', cf. p. 35, drawing on E.D. Hirsch, Jr, *Validity in Interpretation* (New Haven, CT: Yale University Press, 1967), pp. 83, 73; for genre as contract, *ibid.*, drawing on H. Dubrow, *Genre* (The Critical Idiom Series, 42; London: Methuen, 1982), p. 31.

5.   The position is classically stated by Sir W.M. Ramsay, *St. Paul the Traveller and the Roman Citizen* (London: Hodder & Stoughton, 1895), p. 34: 'I will venture to add one to the number of the critics, by stating in the following chapters reasons for placing the author of Acts among the historians of the first rank'. It has been defended many times in this century, notably in the work of F.F. Bruce; for a thorough recent treatment, see C. Hemer, *The Book of Acts in the Setting of Hellenistic History* (WUNT, 49; Winona Lake, IN: Eisenbrauns, 1990).

6.   Haenchen, *Acts*, p. 103.

7.   E.g. W.L. Knox, *The Acts of the Apostles* (Cambridge: Cambridge University Press, 1948), p. 4; C.K. Barrett, *Luke the Historian in Recent Study* (London: Epworth, 1961), pp. 9–12; E. Plümacher, *Lukas als hellenisticher Schriftsteller* (Göttingen: Vandenhoeck & Ruprecht, 1972); W.C. van Unnik, 'Luke's Second Book and the Rules of Hellenistic Historiography', pp. 37–60 of J. Kremer (ed.), *Les Actes des Apôtres: Traditions, rédaction, théologie* (BETL, 48; Leuven: Leuven University Press – Gembloux, 1978), esp. pp. 42–43.

Our question in this chapter is simply to ask how far this consensus assessment is justified. If the preface acts as a genre-indicator, have its signals been read aright? Have they been read in the way that an informed first-century reader would read them? This is not an invitation to psychologize, but an invitation to become readers ourselves: that is, to immerse ourselves in a wide range of contemporary literature in order to facilitate an informed judgment on the range of possible options for reading the preface. The code of etiquette governing genre and other aspects of literary convention should not be seen as setting up normative prescriptions for what authors might and might not do: rather, by focusing on what the informed first-century reader could reasonably expect, the literary code encourages us as twentieth-century readers to build up an awareness of what was regarded in the ancient world as normal or customary in a particular genre.[8]

I. *One Volume or Two?*

The recapitulatory nature of the opening sentences immediately raises the question of the relationship between Acts and the 'former treatise': more particularly for our purposes, the question how far the preface to the Gospel should also be treated as the preface to Acts. If Acts is 'Volume II' of a two-volume composition, does this mean that the preface to 'Volume I' (the Gospel) serves equally as a preface to Acts, rather like the preface to a multi-volume series in modern academic publishing? Or is the connection to be interpreted in a rather looser fashion?[9]

There is, of course, no serious dispute that the 'former treatise' of Acts 1.1 is the Gospel of Luke: quite apart from the similarities of style, the identity of the dedicatee suggests that at once, as does the fact that Luke's is the only one of the canonical gospels which fits the description in Acts 1.1. But the closeness of the relationship and its literary consequences have been variously assessed in recent scholarship. Standard estimates of the literary significance of Luke's prefaces, like those of Cadbury and Haenchen cited above, tend to treat both prefaces together; the assumption is that any genre-indications implied by the Gospel preface may be taken as assumed in the second volume. More recent scholarship, however, has begun to question the widely accepted assumption of

---

8.   Burridge, *Gospels*, p. 35. The literary 'code' might usefully be compared with the dress codes governing certain groups (e.g. schoolchildren) or activities (e.g. sport). Parents of schoolchildren know all too well that the peer group's unwritten conventions about 'what is being worn' can be much harder to defy than the school's more prescriptive rules. Similar unwritten codes govern what is (and perhaps even more what is not) worn when playing, e.g., at a golf tournament.

9.   I.H. Marshall, 'Acts and the "Former Treatise"' (in B.W. Winter and A.D. Clarke [eds.], *The Book of Acts in its First Century Setting*. I. *The Book of Acts in its Ancient Literary Setting* [Grand Rapids: Eerdmans, 1993], pp. 163–82) provides a helpful discussion of the options.

the unity of the two-volume work known to scholarship as 'Luke-Acts'.[10] This wider debate is of interest to us here only insofar as it concerns the preface.

There are in fact two distinct questions to be borne in mind: to ask 'Does the Gospel preface look forward to Acts?' is not the same as asking 'Does the preface of Acts look back to the Gospel?' From the starting-point of Lk. 1.1–4, it is a question that concerns the author rather than the reader. These verses contain no explicit indication that a second volume is in prospect: it is only with hindsight, after reaching the beginning of Acts, that the reader is encouraged to explore the connection. From the author's point of view, on the other hand, it is a real question to what extent Luke had Acts in mind when he wrote the preface to the Gospel. When he describes his work in terms of 'the tradition handed down to us by the eyewitnesses and ministers of the word' (Lk. 1.2), for example, does this also describe the content of Acts? When he implies that Theophilus has already received 'instruction' in the material he is about to read (Lk. 1.4), is this also true of Acts?[11] And what of the genre question? I have argued elsewhere that the conventions employed in the Gospel preface do not accord with the common classification of Luke's work with Greco-Roman historiography: the scope and scale are wrong, dedication is not normally found in historical writings, the customary topics for historical prefaces do not appear, and both the style and the motifs of the Lukan preface are better paralleled elsewhere, in the broad area of Greek literature (too broad to be called a 'genre') which I have called 'the scientific tradition'.[12] I do not intend to repeat the evidence for these statements here except insofar as they relate to Acts: but we do need to ask how far the genre-indicators implicit in the first preface (whatever they may be) are relevant to the second.

For the reader of Acts, however, the question has a rather different complexion. If at the beginning of the Gospel it is an open question how much the second volume is in view, at the beginning of Acts there is no such comfortable uncertainty. The text explicitly directs the attention of the reader to the earlier volume in its opening words: it presents itself as a continuation of the story begun there, and makes the closing scene of the first volume the

---

10.   Most recently in M.C. Parsons and R.I. Pervo, *Rethinking the Unity of Luke and Acts* (Minneapolis: Fortress Press, 1993); see also E. Plümacher, 'Die Apostelgeschichte als historische Monografie', in Kremer (ed.), *Les Actes des Apôtres*, pp. 457–66. Plümacher is followed by D.W. Palmer, 'Acts and the Ancient Historical Monograph', in Winter and Clarke (eds.), *The Book of Acts*, pp. 1–29.

11.   Alexander, *The Preface*, pp. 24, 14f, 206f. In fact it has been argued that some of the statements in Lk. 1.1–4 apply more to Acts than to the Gospel (see, e.g., Cadbury's argument discussed in Alexander, *The Preface*, pp. 128–30; Marshall, 'Former Treatise', pp. 172–74) – though these readings raise problems of their own given the lack of explicit direction to the second volume in Lk. 1.1–4. Conversely, even if it is accepted that Luke-Acts is a two-volume work, it is natural that the first volume should be more immediately in mind (both to author and to readers) at the point at which the preface appears. Thus few would wish to argue that the 'many' of Lk. 1.1 applies also to the Acts narrative; and it is possible to refer Luke's statements on 'tradition' primarily to the Gospel without necessarily calling into question the unity of the work.

12.   Alexander, *The Preface*, passim: for a definition of the 'scientific tradition', see pp. 21–22.

opening scene of the second.[13] The reader of Acts thus has little choice about taking account of the existence of the Gospel. What is not clear is exactly what implications this has for our reading.

At the most obvious (and practical) level, it serves as a warning that the narrative on which we are about to embark is not self-contained. Names and allusions will not necessarily be explained: Jesus, Holy Spirit, John, the apostles are introduced without further explanation: passion, resurrection, kingdom are briefly mentioned in the first few verses as if the reader knows exactly what they are. Moreover by using the first person (ἐποιησάμην), the author of Acts points the reader back to one specific gospel, the one that he wrote: he does not here allude (as he does in Lk. 1.1) to other versions of the story which could supply the same essential background information. How far those narrative presuppositions may be extended backwards (for example through allusions to events much earlier in the Gospel narrative) or forwards (will this kind of prior knowledge also be presupposed at later points in the Acts narrative?) cannot be determined from the preface alone, and the inquiry would take us too far outside our immediate brief. All that can be stated with certainty is that as a narrative, Acts presents itself quite clearly as a 'second volume', that is, as a continuation of a story already half-way through. 'New readers begin here.'

This does not, of course, settle the question of the unity of Luke-Acts by itself: Luke could well have conceived the Gospel as a single-volume work and then have added Acts as an afterthought. All that the preface tells us on its own is that the Gospel was already written when Luke wrote the opening verses of Acts, and that he wanted his readers to know that. If, however, the recapitulation with which Acts begins is a recognizable literary convention known from other texts in the Greco-Roman literary world, it is reasonable to ask what light those other texts might shed on the question of unity. Where such a recapitulation occurs, is it normally the case that the second (or subsequent) work is 'Volume II' (or III, or IV) in a multi-volume composition? And can the readers also take it for granted that the text they are about to encounter is the same kind of text as its predecessor?

Examination of a range of recapitulations in other ancient texts confirms that Greek literature contains numerous examples of multi-volume works linked by a recapitulatory sentence at the beginning of successive volumes: see, for example, the three volumes of the commentary of Apollonius of Citium on the *Hippocratic De Articulis*, or the five volumes of Artemidorus Daldianus' *Oneirocritica*.[14] But it is also true, as I have argued elsewhere, that 'the connection between two successive works of a corpus linked by recapitulations is not always as tight as we might expect'.[15] The writings of Theophrastus, for example, are linked by recapit-

---

13.   Whatever the literary relations between the two versions of the ascension story (on which see the commentaries), this is how the story is presented in the text as we have it. See Plümacher, 'Monografie', p. 460: Plümacher argues that the repetition of the ascension story in the first chapter of Acts underlines Luke's concern 'to present his two λόγοι as rounded narrative segments relatively independent of each other' ('seine beiden λόγοι als von einander relativ unabhängige, abgerundete und in sich einheitliche Geschehenablaufe darzustellen').

14.   Alexander, *The Preface*, pp. 143–46.

15.   Alexander, *The Preface*, p. 146.

ulatory sentences describing the contents of previous works, even where the units so linked are not treated (by editors or scribes) as parts of a single composition. Thus the *De Causis Plantarum* presupposes the *Historia Plantarum* (both themselves multi-volume works) and refers back to it in the opening sentence; similarly *De Ventis* Book 1 states at the outset that part of the topic has been treated 'previously' (πρότερον). Here Theophrastus reflects the characteristic Aristotelian concern for logical order and completeness in the arrangement of the whole scientific-philosophical enterprise, but with a relatively new interest in the corpus as a body of written texts.[16] Archimedes exhibits the same interest in the letters which accompanied his mathematical treatises across the Mediterranean.[17]

A similar concern may be seen in later large-scale scholarly enterprises. Philo shows it throughout the corpus (though more in the *Exposition* than in the *Allegory of the Laws*), where many texts begin with a transitional sentence summarizing the contents of the previous book (cf. the openings of *Plant.*, *Ebr.*, *Sobr.*, *Conf. Ling.*, *Quis Rerum*, *Somn.* 1, *Dec.*, *Spec. Leg.* 1, *Virt.*). There is no obvious formal distinction between these 'corpus' transitions and those between 'Book 1' and 'Book 2' of a multi-volume work: compare *De Vita Mosis* 2.1, ἡ μὲν προτέρα σύνταξίς ἐστι περὶ γενέσεως τῆς Μωυσέως καὶ τροφῆς with *Quis Rerum* I, ἐν μὲν τῇ πρὸ ταύτης συντάξει τὰ περὶ μισθῶν ὡς ἐνῆν ἐπ᾽ ἀκριβείας διεξήλθομεν. A similar phenomenon may be observed in Galen, where a one-volume work, or Book 1 of a multi-volume work, may easily begin with a reference to a previous work.[18] Josephus seems to have structured his own oeuvre with the same large-scale conception of the relation of the parts to the whole, or at least of subsequent compositions to what has gone before: thus the *Antiquities* makes a clear allusion (though not in a formulaic recapitulation sentence) to the *Jewish War*, and the *Apion* (in more formulaic fashion) in turn to the *Antiquities*.[19] Josephus is a particularly valuable instance of this habit in that it is clear that there was a considerable time lapse between the completion of the *War* and the publication of the *Antiquities*.[20]

16.   Cf. *De Signis Tempestatum*, 1.1. Texts in F. Wimmer (ed.), *Theophrasti Opera Omnia* (Frankfurt on Main: Minerva, repr. 1964; [Paris: Didot, 1866]).

17.   See *De Sphaera et Cylindro*, Book 1, *De Conoidibus et Sphaeroidibus*, and *De Mechanicis Propositionibus*, all of which refer to a previous work, although none of them is a 'second volume'.

18.   *De temp.*, Book 1, Kühn I.509; *De Anatomicis Administrationibus* Book 1, Kühn II.215; *De Sanitate Tuenda*, Book 1, Kühn VI.1; *De Causis Morborum*, Kühn VII.1; *De Sympt. Diff.*, Kühn VII.42; *De Tremore*, Kühn VII.584; *De Dignosc. Puls.*, Book 1, Kühn VIII.766, where the four books of *De Diff. Puls.* are treated as the first part of a larger project; *De Comp. Med. Sec. Locos*, Book 1, Kühn XII.378.

19.   As Darryl Palmer correctly observes, 'Monograph', (cited in n. 10), p. 25: cf. *Ant.* 1.4, *Apion* 1.1.

20.   *Ant.* 1.7 speaks of 'hesitation and delay' in beginning the *Antiquities*; the date of completion (20.267) suggests around 18 years from the publication of the *War* (Thackeray, Loeb Classical Library *Josephus*, IV, p. x). We might also compare Artemidorus Daldianus, *Oneirocritica* (R.A. Pack [ed.], *Artemidorus Daldianus. Onirocriticon Libri V* [Leipzig: Teubner, 1963]), where Book 3 in the 5-volume sequence is presented as an afterthought: (3, pref.; 4, pref., p. 237). The fourth book seems to have followed after a further interval: it addresses a new dedicatee after the death of the first, and takes up criticisms of the earlier books (4, pref., pp. 237f.).

Comparison with the conventional code governing the use of recapitulations thus establishes clearly that two works linked as Acts is to Luke's Gospel need not necessarily have been conceived from the start as a single work. The comparison cannot, however, of itself establish that they were not so conceived: the preface to Acts leaves both possibilities open. The genre question, however, is not so clear. Palmer argues that two works by the same author linked by a recapitulation need not necessarily be of the same genre, and therefore that the genre of Acts may be different from that of the Gospel.[21] Certainly there is good reason for assigning distinct genre-categories to Josephus' three major works: the *War* and the *Antiquities* belong, if not to two different genres, at least to two different subgenres of historical writing, and the *Contra Apionem*, as its name suggests, is structured as an apologetic argument rather than a narrative. However, in these cases the changed subject matter and genre of the new work are indicated clearly in the preface.[22] Acts, by contrast, contains no prospective summary to match the retrospective allusion to the previous volume in verse 1, which seems to make it less likely that a major change of genre is in view. In the case of Philo, the assignment of genre-categories within the corpus is much more problematic. Although it is tempting to regard the 'lives' of the patriarchs as belonging to a different genre from the treaties on the pentateuchal Law which follow, the same underlying exegetical structure underlies the whole series. In the *De Vita Mosis*, on the other hand, where there is a more obvious attempt to address a Greek audience with a self-contained text in a distinct genre, the preface makes the change abundantly clear: no previous knowledge of the corpus is assumed, and formal preface-conventions of a type hardly seen elsewhere appear.[23]

As far as the preface is concerned, then, we cannot rule out either option: Acts may be read either as 'Volume II' of a unified composition, or as an independent monograph which simply reminds the reader that its narrative is a sequel to the earlier work. In what follows, I have tried to allow equally for both possibilities. I shall not assume that the implications of the Gospel preface also hold good for Acts, but shall treat the preface to Acts on its own merits.

---

21.   Palmer, 'Monograph', p. 25.

22.   'While Polybius and the tradition of political and military historiography served as the primary model for the *War*, it was the antiquarian history represented by Dionysius of Halicarnassus which supplied the model for Josephus' next work': H. Attridge, 'Josephus and his Works', in Michael E. Stone (ed.), *Jewish Writings of the Second Temple Period*, (CRINT, 2; Assen: Van Gorcum; and Philadelphia: Fortress Press, 1984), pp. 185–232, (217). Cf. Gregory E. Sterling, *Historiography and Self-definition: Josephos, Luke-Acts and Apologetic Historiography* (NovTSup, 44; Leiden: Brill, 1992), pp. 240–45. The genre of the *Antiquities* (as well as its subject) is indicated clearly at 1.5 (τὴν παρ' ἡμῖν ἀρχαιολογίαν). The apologetic mode of the *Contra Apionem* is indicated in the preface equally clearly, though less directly, by a cluster of forensic terms: βλασφημίας, τεκμήριον, λοιδορούντων, ἐλέγχαι, ψευδολογίαν, μάρτυσι, κτλ.

23.   On the audience of the *De Vita Mosis*, see esp. E.R. Goodenough, 'Philo's Exposition of the Law and his De Vita Mosis', *HTR* 26 (1933), pp. 109–25; E.R. Goodenough, *An Introduction to Philo Judaeus* (Oxford: Basil Blackwell, 2nd edn, 1962), pp. 33–35; S. Sandmel, *Philo of Alexandria: An Introduction* (Oxford and New York: Oxford University Press, 1979), p. 47.

II. *Defining the Preface*

Our first task must be to define what we mean by the preface of Acts. Commentators differ markedly in their divisions of the text at this point: the first section is estimated variously from three verses to fourteen. But for our purposes in this chapter there is no real need to define the end of the preface, for the simple reason that in formal terms (that is, in terms of the formal Greek literary conventions which concern us here) the preface to Acts has no ending.

The point may be illustrated by comparison with the preface to 2 Maccabees (2 Macc. 2.19–32), a passage which clearly follows Hellenistic literary convention and which is distinctly demarcated from the beginning of the narrative with the formula (v. 32), 'it would be foolish to lengthen the preface by cutting short the history itself'.[24] Even where no such formula is used, syntax and style usually make it clear where the preface ends and the narrative or discourse proper begins: this is the case, for example, with the preface to Ben Sira and with Luke's own preface to the Third Gospel.[25] The preface to Acts, by contrast, has a curiously open-ended feel to it, not only because of the hanging μέν left without an answering δέ,[26] but also because the authorial first sentence merges uneasily into impersonal narrative, into indirect speech, and then into direct speech, with the transitions marked only by a series of unimpressive conjunctions and relative pronouns. Since the end of the preface is so ill-defined, our primary concern here will be with the beginning, where the use of Greek convention is clear. We shall consider the awkward transition from preface to narrative, and its implications for Luke's use of literary convention, at a later point.[27]

For our immediate purposes, then, the preface of Acts consists of an opening sentence in which the author speaks in the first person singular, addresses an individual (Theophilus) using the vocative, and alludes briefly to the subject matter of his own previous treatise. This brief summary of the previous work then becomes the opening scene of the narrative, which unfolds subsequently without any further return of the second-person address or of the authorial first person singular.[28] The preface thus employs at least three recognizable Greek literary conventions: the authorial first person (as distinct from the impersonal narrator); the dedication to a named second person; and the recapitulation or summary of the contents of the previous book in a series. The manner in which

24.   On this preface see Alexander, *The Preface*, pp. 148–51.

25.   See Alexander, *The Preface*, pp. 151–154 on Ben Sira; pp. 103–104 on other endings.

26.   See the commentaries and D.W. Palmer, 'The Literary Background of Acts 1.1–14', *NTS* 33 (1987), pp. 427–38.

27.   In common with most current scholarship, I shall treat the text as it stands on the assumption that any irregularities are Luke's own, and not the result of redaction or textual corruption.

28.   Wehnert rightly dissociates the 'we' of the we-passages from the authorial 'I' of the prefaces: J. Wehnert, *Die Wir-Passagen der Apostelgeschichle: Ein lukanisches Stilmittel aus jüdischer Tradition* (Göttinger Theologischer Arbeiten, 40; Göttingen: Vandenhoeck and Ruprecht, 1989), pp. 136–39.

the recapitulation merges directly into the narrative is also a formal feature (if only in a negative sense) for which we may fairly seek parallels, although it is possible that in this case we are dealing with authorial idiosyncrasy rather than with literary convention.

III. *The Preface to Acts and Greek Historiography*

We return now to the question with which we began. Do the conventions used in the preface suggest to the informed reader, in Cadbury's words, an immediate classification with contemporary Hellenistic historiography? Do they arouse literary expectations which, even if they are not fulfilled in the text of Acts, yet exhibit a degree of literary pretension unique in the NT? And how far does the subject matter of Acts and its predecessor, as presented to the reader in the preface of Acts, accord with contemporary expectations as to the proper subject matter for historical writing?

a. *Authorial First Person*
The use of the authorial first person in prefaces is common in Greek literature, and can readily be paralleled in historical writing. It appears occasionally in Thucydides (1.3.1, 9, 1.22.1, 5.26.4–6), and much more freely in Polybius (for example 6.2.1–7, 9.1.1–2.7, 9.1.1a–5) and Diodorus (for example, 1.3.1, 5, 1.4.1–53, 1.42.2, 2.1.2–3, 3.1.3). It should, of course, be observed that the phenomenon is too widespread to be accounted a genre-indicator on its own.[29]

It is worth observing, however, that historical writers were notably reluctant to break the mould of impersonal narration inherited from their epic predecessors. The opening words of Herodotus' preface introduce the author in the third person, and the same archaic convention is used by Thucydides (1.1.1, 5.26.1): it remains a recognizable stylistic marker for later historians eager to parade their Thucydidean aspirations.[30] Even where the post-classical convention of the recapitulation is used, the verbs employed may well be impersonal and passive: not 'I have written', but 'it was demonstrated' (as in the [editorial] internal prefaces in Xenophon's *Anabasis*, or in Diodorus 2.1 and 3.1–2). The same reluctance to use the first person is evident where the author is introduced as a character in his own narrative: Thucydides, and following him Xenophon and Josephus, describe their own actions in the third person, not the first – a point which should be remembered in relation to the so-called 'we-passages' of Acts.[31]

29. See Alexander, *The Preface*, pp. 18, 22, 45, 50, 70, 71 on the development of personal prefaces in Greek literature.
30. Alexander, *The Preface*, pp. 26–27.
31. Wehnert, *Wir-Passagen*, p. 143.

b. *Dedication*

The appearance of this literary convention at the beginning of Acts would not encourage the informed reader to think immediately of historiography. The habit of dedicating a treatise to a named individual was not at all common in historical writing:

> The apostrophe of the second person, whether in direct address (vocative) or in epistolary form, does not fit with the impersonal narrative style of history, and was generally avoided: in Herkommer's words (my translation), 'the dedication of historical works was not customary among the Greeks... Further, dedication does not belong by nature to Roman historical writing.[32]

In fact the first extant example of a dedicated historical work is Josephus' *Antiquities*, which was dedicated (as we learn from the end of the *Vita*) to Epaphroditus. Even here, however, the conventional code is not formally breached: the beginning of the Antiquities opens in orthodox fashion with a discussion of the author's predecessors in the field and of the magnitude of the subject matter.[33] Epaphroditus appears in the third person, apparently incidentally, at 1.8: the themes introduced here, of the author's reluctant yielding to persuasion and of the learned disposition of the dedicatee, are part of the characteristic courtesy of dedication,[34] but Josephus, sensitive as ever to the stylistic niceties, avoids using the second-person address until the very end of his work (*Vita* 430). Only in the *Contra Apionem* (1.1, 2.1), which is not a historical narrative, do we find dedication given literary expression in a second-person address at the beginning of the text: which seems to suggest that, whatever the underlying social matrix in terms of patronage or place-seeking, the literary code does not encourage the formality of a second-person address in a historical work.[35]

Evidence for earlier, now lost, histories which might have borne dedications is difficult to assess unless the opening of the work happens to have survived. Testimonies in later writers that a certain text was written 'for' a particular individual do not necessarily imply that a second-person address stood in the preface.[36] However, where possible dedications are attested, it is notable that they tend to cluster on the more 'antiquarian' side of Greek historiography (Apollodorus) and with authors who, like Josephus, stand in one way or another outside the mainstream of Greek culture (Berossus, Manetho). The evidence may be summarized as follows:

32.   Alexander, *The Preface*, pp. 27–29, with reference to E. Herkommer, 'Die Topoi in der Proomien der römischen Geschichtswerke', (Dissertation, Tübingen, 1968), p. 25.

33.   Alexander, *The Preface*, p. 31; Herkommer, 'Topoi', pp. 102–12, 164–74.

34.   Alexander, *The Preface*, p. 27 and n. 7, pp. 73–75.

35.   The relationship between patronage and dedication is more complex than is often assumed: see Alexander, *The Preface*, pp. 50–63 (esp. 62), 187–200 (esp. 194). Josephus also records that he presented copies of the *War* to Vespasian, and that Titus arranged for its publication (*Life* 363): yet neither is addressed in the preface. See Attridge, 'Josephus', pp. 192–93.

36.   As is clear from Josephus: see previous note. Cf. J. Ruppert, 'Quaestiones ad historiam dedicationis librorum pertinentes', (Dissertation, Leipzig, 1911), pp. 29–30.

1. The *Chronica* of Apollodorus. This, according to Pseudo-Scymnus, he 'composed for the kings in Pergamum' (τοῖς ἐν Περγάμῳ βασιλεῦσιν...συνετάξατ'); it was a didactic summary of world history in iambic verse, a sufficiently odd innovation for Pseudo-Scymnus (who uses the same metre for his geographical summary) to consider it worth a lengthy explanation. That this was a formal dedication at the head of the text is clear:

κεῖνος μὲν οὖν κεφάλαια συναθροίας χρόνων
εἰς βασιλέως ἀπέθετο φιλαδέλφου χάριν,
ἃ καὶ διὰ πάσης γέγονε τῆς οἰκουμένης,
ἀθάνατον ἀπονέμοντα δόξαν Αττάλῳ
τῆς πραγματείας ἐπιγραφὴν εἰληφότι.[37]

2. Berossus. Tatian preserves a testimony from Juba of Mauretania, one of the major excerptors of Berossus' work, to the effect that Berossus 'drew up the history of the Chaldeans in three books for Antiochus'. Neither Josephus nor Eusebius, our major sources for the text of Berossus, mentions the dedication, but there is nothing intrinsically improbable in Juba's testimony. The Antiochus in question was Antiochus 1 Soter, whose reign can be dated from 293/2 (or 280) to 261/0 BCE. Josephus quotes from Berossus' work (see, for example, C. Ap. 1.129–153), and may have been influenced by the literary conventions employed there.[38]

3. Manetho. No authentic dedication survives, but Syncellus preserves the information that Manetho's account of Egyptian history was addressed to Ptolemy II Philadelphus. Unfortunately at least one of the Syncellus texts connects the dedication with the Book of Sōthis, which is a digest of Manetho's work dating probably from the third century CE. The 'Letter of Manetho', although it may preserve some authentic information, is 'undoubtedly a forgery'.[39] Josephus quotes extensively from Manetho (see, for example, C. Ap. 1.73–105) without mentioning any dedication.

4. The *Libyan History* of Aristippus. According to Diogenes Laertius 2.83, Aristippus of Cyrene, one of the early Socratics, is credited, among other works, with 'three books of *historia* of matters concerning Libya, sent to Dionysius' (τρία μὲν ἱστορίας τῶν κατὰ Λιβύην ἀπεσταλμένα Διονυσίῳ). As so often with Diogenes Laertius, there are conflicting reports on the writings of

---

37.   For Apollodorus, see F. Jacoby, *Apollodors Chronik: eine Sammlung der Fragmente*, (Philogische Untersuchungen, 16; Berlin: Weidmann, 1902). The citations are from Pseudo-Scymnus, *Orbis Descriptio* 45–49 (C. Müller [ed.], *Geographi Graeci Minores* [Paris: Didot, 1855–1861], pp. 196–99).

38.   Berossus: texts and fragments in P. Schnabel, *Berossos und die Babylonisch-Hellenistische Literatur* (Leipzig and Berlin: Teubner, 1923), pp. 5–8. Discussion in Sterling, *Apologetic Historiography*, pp. 104–17.

39.   Waddell, Loeb Classical Library *Manetho*, p. xxviii; text of the letter in Appendix 1, pp. 208–10. On the Sōthis-book, see pp. xxviif. and 234–48; the Syncellus extracts appear on pp. 14, 208. See further Jacoby, *Die Fragmente der griechische Historiker* (Leiden: Brill, 1958), (*FGH*), IIIC609 (Syncellus = T11a, b); Sterling, *Apologetic Historiography*, pp. 117–35.

Aristippus: a second list attributed to Sotion and Panaetius (2.85) makes no mention of the 'history'. If it is authentic, the dedication would pre-date by several decades the earliest examples known to us in any literary tradition.[40] The *historia* in question clearly belongs to the geographical-ethnographical side of the Ionian tradition: the word could as well be translated 'inquiry' as 'history'.

5. Dionysius of Halicarnassus, *Ant. Rom.* 1.4.3. This refers to some of his predecessors who have 'dared to express such views [sc. critical of the origins of Rome] in the writings they have left, taking this method of honouring barbarian kings who detested Roman supremacy – princes to whom they were ever servilely devoted and with whom they were associated as flatterers – by presenting them with "histories" which were neither just nor true' (βασιλεῦσι βαρβάροις... οὔτε δίκαιας οὔτε ἀληθεῖς ἱστορίας χαριζόμενοι: Loeb trans.). Here again we are in the area of ethnography and 'archaeology', and again the practice of dedication is associated with the monarchies of the Hellenistic age (though Dionysius describes the recipients of these texts, whoever they were, as 'barbarians', i.e. non-Greeks). But again it must be stressed that, as we saw in the case of Josephus, the charge of 'writing to please' does not necessarily entail that a formal dedication stood at the head of the text. Dionysius himself is happy to admit (apparently without irony) that his own work is bias-free because he is making a 'grateful return' (χαριστηρίους ἀμοιβάς) to the city of Rome (1.6.5). Like Josephus, he is able to make a graceful gesture without marking any dedication with a formal address.

6. Phlegon of Tralles (*FGH* 257 *T*3) and Callinicus of Petra (*FGH* 281 *T*1). They date respectively from the second and the third century CE and are thus too late for our purpose of establishing literary custom in the first century.

c. *Recapitulation*
The brief (and by no means exhaustive) survey of recapitulations given above of itself raises the question of literary appropriateness. How far are the practical, academic concerns evidenced by this kind of transitional introduction compatible with the more rhetorical interests of Hellenistic historiography?[41] Theophrastus, Archimedes, Philo, and Galen could not be called by any stretch of the imagination historians: and it would be dangerous to take Josephus, an outsider always conscious of his literary shortcomings,[42] as typical of the whole Greek historiographical tradition.

In fact the construction of a preface in the form of a recapitulatory transition is the exception rather than the rule in Greek historiography. The fifth-century classics, Herodotus and Thucydides, did not divide their works into books, and thus had no need for secondary introductions to separate books. Thucydides

---

40.   Cf. Alexander, *Preface*, p. 53: perhaps (if genuine) the work should be ascribed to Aristippus' grandson? See further *RE* 2. 1 s.v. 'Aristippos' (8).

41.   Well summarized in Sterling, *Apologetic Historiography*, pp. 8–9.

42.   See *Ant.* 1.7; *Apion* 1.50.

does have a secondary preface at 5.26 which reestablishes his authorship of the second section of the History (Γέγραφε δὲ καὶ ταῦτα ὁ αὐτὸς Θουκυδίδης Ἀθηναῖος ἑξῆς, ὡς ἕκαστα ἐγένετο), but this is more concerned with bridging the interlude in the war (and counting its extent in years) than with summarizing the contents of the first part of the work. Conformably with his model Thucydides, Xenophon provides no internal prefaces to the *Hellenica*, and the recapitulations in the *Anabasis* are generally accepted as the work of a later redactor. Even when the practicalities of book production made the division of a longer text into volumes a familiar phenomenon, historical writers still preferred to do without recapitulations: in the words of Laqueur's classic 1911 study,[43]

> Josephus in the *Jewish War*, Arrian in his *Anabasis*, Tacitus in the *Annals* and the *Histories*, Herodian etc. dispense altogether with any stylistic demarcation of the individual book; we read from one book to the next without finding the slightest indication of the fact that we have got into a new book.

Narrative, it would seem, provides its own principles of internal organization: a clearly structured narrative with a firm chronological sequence can dispense with the external aids to logical ordering used in philosophical or scientific discourse.

The number of surviving recapitulatory prefaces (that is, books which begin with a recapitulation) in historical writing up to the second century CE is remarkably small given the size and scale of Greek historiography. Diodorus Siculus has four or five such prefaces in twenty books: eight further books have a recapitulation at the end of the preface, marking the transition to the narrative, but in these cases the preface itself is structured in a very different way (pp. 37–38 below).[44] Polybius has one at 2.1 and again at 4.1 (though the back reference is to Book 2, not Book 3). Book 5 has no introduction, and Book 3 begins effectively as if it were a new (and large-scale) preface to the whole composition. The prefaces to the remaining books are mostly lost, but the most

---

43. R. Laqueur, 'Ephoros I: Die Proomien', *Hermes* 46 (1911), pp. 161–206, 166f. (my trans.): 'Josephus im Jüdischen Kriege, Arrian in seiner Anabasis, Tacitus in (167) Annalen u. Historien, Herodian usw. verzichten überhaupt auf jede stilistische Herausarbeitung des Einzelbuches; wir lesen von einem Buche zum andern hinüber, ohne auch nur im geringsten die Tatsache angedeutet zu finden, dass wir in ein neues Buch geraten sind.'

44. Recapitulatory prefaces: 1.42.1, 2.1.1, 3.1.1, 11.1.1–2.1.41 is included as marking the transition to the second 'volume' of Book 1, though there are doubts as to the authenticity of the bulk of the recapitulation, which is written in the third person (unusually for Diodorus) and sits ill with the first-person prospective sentence at 42.2. Book 17, which is similarly split, has no such demarcation. Recapitulation at the end of the preface: 4.1.5–6, 12.2.2–3, 13.1.2–3, 14.2.3–4, 15.1.6, 18.1.6, 19.1.9–10, 20.2.3. To class all these together, as Sterling does (p. 331, n. 102) is therefore misleading: even here there is still a wide variety of styles, some being much more formulaic than others. What interests us here is the construction of a preface around a recapitulation and nothing else: Sacks, indeed, can say that 'books ii, iii and xi have only tables of contents', as opposed to the 'full prooemium' which appears in Diodorus' other books (K.S. Sacks, *Diodorus Siculus and the First Century* [Princeton: Princeton University Press, 1990], p. 9).

likely interpretation of his own words in 11.1 is that Polybius chose to preface each Olympiad (that is, every other book) with an integral *proekthesis* or 'introductory survey to a book or series of books'. These *proektheseis* should be distinguished from the recapitulations of the earlier books.[45] Dionysius of Halicarnassus has only one initial recapitulation in the ten books of the *Roman Antiquities*, at 2.1, and Josephus has four in the twenty books of the *Jewish Antiquities*, at 8.1, 13.1, 14.1, and 16. The last case is puzzling since there is no obvious reason why Josephus should have adopted this convention here and nowhere else: Laqueur suggests the influence of a lost source. But for Polybius, Dionysius, and Diodorus it is possible to see a practical reason for the employment of recapitulations in the early sections of the work, where an extended theoretical or 'archaeological' introduction could make it difficult for the reader to find his or her way around.[46] Once the narrative proper begins, this need disappears; and it is noticeable that neither Josephus nor Polybius seems to feel that a summary of the prospective book is necessary in narrative, even where the *anakephalaiosis* formula is used: Josephus *Ant.* 8.1 and 13.1 contain no forward summary, and *Ant.* 14.1 and 15.1, like Polybius 2.1, simply say, 'we shall now speak of the events that followed immediately'.

The use of a recapitulation at the beginning of a book cannot therefore be described as in any way *customary* or *usual* in Greek historiography, though there are examples to be found. From the perspective of the reader's expectations, it is also relevant to note that such beginnings are far more common elsewhere in Greek literature, notably in the vast and multiform body of texts associated with philosophical and scientific inquiry.[47] This fits with the reasonable presumption that these summary introductions serve practical rather than rhetorical ends (see n. 46 above): the influence of rhetoric on history writing produced a very different kind of preface, of which I shall say more below. It may also be relevant to note that the highest incidence of these prefaces is in the area of history which overlaps most with the broader *historia* of the Ionians and their successors. It has been argued on other grounds that this area of historiography operated with a conventional code distinct from that which governed contemporary historiography.[48] But for our immediate purposes the important point is that this feature alone is not sufficient to suggest an identification with Greek historiography to the informed reader beginning at Acts 1.1.

45.   F.W. Walbank, *A Historical Commentary on Polybius*, (Oxford: Clarendon Press, 1967), II, p. 266; Laqueur, '*Ephoros I*', p. 186.

46.   Laqueur, '*Ephoros I*', pp. 191–92: 'Ein praktissches Bedürfnis hat die ἀνακεφαλαιώσεις hervorgebracht und sie immer dann anwenden lassen, wenn die Verzahnung zum Verständnis der Composition eines Werkes notwendig war'.

47.   Alexander, *The Preface*, pp. 143–44.

48.   The *locus classicus* for the distinction between political history and 'archaeology' or 'antiquities' is A.D. Momigliano, 'The place of Herodotus in the History of Historiography', in *idem*, *Studies in Historiography* (London: Weidenfeld & Nicolson, 1969), pp. 127–42; see also 'Historiography on Written Tradition and Historiography on Oral Tradition' in the same volume. See also n. 22 above.

d. *Subject Matter*

Ancient authors often use the opening words of a preface (or of the text itself) to indicate their subject matter, either generically (as in Josephus *Ant.* 1.1, 'Those who attempt to write histories . . .'), or more specifically (as in Josephus *War* 1.1, 'Since the war of the Jews against the Romans. . .').[49] Where the opening sentence takes the form of a recapitulation describing the subject of the previous volume, we would naturally expect a prospective sentence to introduce the subject of the new book. With Acts the matter is complicated by the fact that we have only the summary of the previous volume: Luke plunges straight into his narrative at 1.3 without giving the reader any prior orientation as to its contents. Whether or not it can be paralleled (see next section), this purely retrospective *anakephalaiosis* does have the effect of limiting the reader's perception of what lies in prospect.

This means that even if Acts is to be read as a self-contained work, rather than a 'second volume' (see above), the brief description of the contents of the previous treatise provided in v. 1 is the only summary indication of genre the preface provides; and it is not one which would immediately register to the informed reader, 'This is a historical work'. The proper subject matter for history in the Greco-Roman tradition was *res gestae*, the actions (*praxeis*) of nations, or cities, or great men.[50] The teachings and doings of an individual (περὶ πάντων ὧν ἤρξατο ὁ Ἰησοῦς ποιεῖν τε καὶ διδάσκειν) are more properly the subject of a biographical work (and a philosophical one at that) than of a history.[51] And even allowing for the possibility of a change of genre between the two books, there is nothing in the succeeding verses to indicate that the second is any more of a history than the first. They provide merely a bewildering succession of unglossed religious terms clustering around the continued activity of the dead teacher described in the previous volume.

This is not to say that the preface does not contain clear pointers as to the subject of the book: simply that they are not the kinds of pointers used to

49. See Earl, 'Prologue-form'. See also P. Städter, *Arrian of Nicomedia* (Chapel Hill: University of North Carolina Press, 1980), p. 61: 'The subject is presented firmly, though indirectly: Alexander son of Philip. Each sentence [of the preface] discusses Alexander historians, and A.'s name appears five times in these few lines.' The habit was not confined to historians: see Alexander, *The Preface*, pp. 29, 42–46, 71–73. The fact that in both the cases cited Josephus is actually talking about his predecessors does not affect the fact that these words effectively inform the reader of the genre of the book: *The Preface*, pp. 107–108 and n. 7.

50. On the proper subjects for history, see Momigliano, 'Herodotus'; O. Geiger, *Cornelius Nepos and Ancient Political Biography* (Historia Einzelschriften, 47; Stuttgart: Steiner Verlag, 1985), pp. 21–29, 46–51, esp. p. 22: 'For the Ancients history was political history, its main characters and prime movers kings, statesmen and generals.' See also M. Hengel, *Acts and the History of Earliest Christianity* (London: SCM Press, 1979), pp. 13–14; van Unnik, 'Luke's Second Book', pp. 38–39. Most commentators believe that the title ΠΡΑΞΕΙΣ ΑΠΟΣΤΟΛΩΝ was attached to Acts at a later stage of the tradition: see Sterling, *Apologetic Historiography*, p. 314.

51. Classic in this field is A.D. Momigliano, *The Development of Greek Biography* (Cambridge, MA: Harvard University Press, 1993 [1971]). Burridge, *Gospels*, pp. 70–81 gives a good general introduction; on Acts as biography, see L.C.A. Alexander, 'Acts and Ancient Intellectual Biography', Chapter 3 below.

indicate 'history' on the Greco-Roman literary spectrum. For the informed reader (and Luke signals clearly in verse 1 that his implied reader is already acquainted with the Gospel) the opening verses of Acts place the narrative in sequence not only with the Gospel but with the larger narrative which forms its matrix, that is, the narrative of the Jewish scriptures. I shall return to this point in my conclusions.

e. *Transition*

Finally, what of the abrupt transition from recapitulation to narrative? Palmer argues that there are a number of parallels to this apparent irregularity, though the list is not in fact very long.[52] However, I know of no parallel which can match the oddity of Luke's opening sentence: even in the closest parallels, the distinction between authorial comment and narration is matched by a clear syntactical break. This irregularity may be due simply to lack of competence on Luke's part, or to lack of interest in maintaining the formal preface-style with which he begins.[53] But it must be recognized that it is an irregularity, and it must affect our assessment of the relationship between Acts and the Gospel. As I observed above, the Josephan parallels occur within a narrative which has sufficient momentum of itself to allow the author to dispense with a prospective summary. The whole force of such a preface depends on the continuity of the narrative: there is no question that it introduces a self-contained monograph, much less a new genre. Where Josephus does begin a major new work with a reference back to earlier compositions, the transition to the new subject is fully explained (see n. 22 above).

It is becoming increasingly clear that if we are to take seriously the signals emitted by the preface we must either admit that the beginning of Acts does not conform to the conventional etiquette of Greco-Roman historiography or look for a different type of historiography. In this context it is worth giving some attention to the suggestion made by a number of scholars that although the category 'Hellenistic historiography' is too broad to help the reader of Acts, there are useful parallels with more specialized types of historical composition. Two in particular will concern us here: the historical monograph, and the genre of 'apologetic historiography'.

---

52. Palmer, 'Monograph', pp. 22–23 cites Josephus, *Ant.* 8.1, together with the editorial additions to Xenophon, *Anabasis* (date unknown) and Herodian, who dates from the third century CE. Polybius 2.1.1–4, which he also cites, does have a prospective sentence, however brief: 'I will now attempt to give a summary view...of the events immediately following'; cf. the similar brief prospectus in Josephus *Ant.* 14, 15.1. And in all these cases the narrative transition is rounded off with the appropriate particle (δέ or νῦν) to match the opening sentence. Similarly in Galen, *De Meth. Med.* (Kühn X.594), the one case I have been able to find in scientific literature.

53. See Alexander, *The Preface*, p. 175 on the limitations of Luke's competence and/or interest in the *formalia* of the preface.

IV. *The Preface to Acts and the Historical Monograph*

Classification of Acts (or Luke-Acts) as a 'historical monograph' goes back to a suggestion of Conzelmann's which has been taken up in a number of more recent studies.[54] The definition of this subgenre is by no means clear (see especially Palmer's discussion of the wide range of options, both in ancient and in modern usage), and its usefulness for the reader of Acts is variously assessed. There are in effect two diametrically opposed approaches. One looks at multi-volume works which use internal prefaces to highlight the individuality of each volume, while the other focuses on smaller-scale works consisting of one or two volumes only. We begin with the former.

Conzelmann's note on Acts 1.1 (*Acts*, p. 4) includes an excursus on 'proems' which suggests that it is the very fact that Acts has a preface which marks it out as a 'monograph':

> Proems originally belonged to the epideictic genre... Their penetration into Hellenistic historiography is indicative that such literary products are thought of as monographs (Diodorus). Thus the presence of the Lukan proem argues against the thesis that Luke's Gospel and Acts originally formed a single work, separated only for 'technical and canonical' reasons.

The reference to Diodorus is elucidated by a footnote bibliography which includes the classic study by Laqueur to which I alluded earlier (n. 43 above). In this lengthy analysis of the Diodoran prefaces, Laqueur points out that there are two distinct types of preface in Diodorus' *Library of History*. The first, as we have seen, is the 'recapitulation' type found in the first three books. But from Book 4 onwards a completely different type of preface appears, described by Laqueur as 'a new form . . . unheard of in contemporary literature' (p. 195, my trans.). Instead of the transitional, purely informative summaries of the earlier books, we find in these new prefaces either a methodological discussion about historiography in general (for example, Book 15) or a moralizing introduction (Laqueur, p. 162) which approaches the theme of the book in an indirect fashion (for example, Book 14). These prefaces recall the varied opening gambits of epideictic oratory and may be traced back ultimately to Isocrates. But Diodorus found them, Laqueur plausibly argues, in the historical work of Ephorus of Cyme, who was a pupil of Isocrates and who, according to Diodorus himself, 'wrote thirty books attaching a *prooimion* to each one' (Diodorus 16.76.5: Laqueur, pp. 196–97). Margrit Kunz challenges Laqueur's assumption that

---

54.   Ward Gasque, 'A Fruitful Field: Recent Study of the Acts of the Apostles', *Interpretation* 42 (1988), p. 117–31 (129) suggests that while '[v]ery few contemporary scholars would say that Luke is a historian in the tradition of Thucydides or Polybius . . . [t]he consensus of opinion at present seems to be that Luke has written a historical monograph'. See especially Hengel, *Earliest Christianity*, pp. 14, 36f.; Plümacher, 'Monografie', pp. 457–66. Plümacher is followed by Palmer in 'Monograph', pp. 1–29, in which see p. 3, n. 9 for further references. Geiger, *Cornelius Nepos*, pp. 47–51 gives a useful summary of the evidence for historical monographs.

Ephorus was Diodorus' only source for the 'epideictic' preface-type,[55] but her detailed linguistic analysis confirms the distinction drawn by Laqueur between the rhetorically well-constructed 'epideictic' prefaces and the recapitulations. The monotonous construction and limited vocabulary of the latter point to Diodorus' own authorship (Kunz, 'Zur Beurteilung', pp. 67–68).[56]

Whether this innovation should be credited to Ephorus or to some other historian, the effect of adding an epideictic preface to every volume of a multi-volume work is that each book becomes a monograph, with its own rhetorically crafted *prooimion*, rather than a purely pragmatic division of a seamless historical narrative. But this is not the kind of preface we have in Acts: as we have seen, it is precisely the unrhetorical, recapitulatory prefaces of Diodorus' earlier books that Acts recalls. By alluding to the 'former treatise', in fact, Acts 1.1 actively resists categorization as a monograph (in this sense): whether or not the book was conceived as 'Volume II', its opening sentence directs the reader's attention to the relationship of the narrative to a larger whole. Similarly with the examples from Archimedes, Josephus, and Galen noted above, where a recapitulation is used to link separate works: the effect of the recapitulation is to place the current work in a sequence within the author's total *oeuvre*. In this sense, then, the preface to Acts would seem rather to militate against classification as a 'monograph'.

However, the concept of the historical monograph may have a wider relevance to Acts if it is conceived not in the 'Ephoran' sense but simply as a historical work of limited scope and/or scale.[57] Even as a two-volume work, Luke-Acts is much shorter than the major works of classical and Hellenistic historiography, and this disparity in scale is a serious obstacle to the identification of Luke-Acts as 'history'.[58] Hence a number of scholars have realized the importance of investigating the evidence for smaller-scale works dealing with a limited chronological period. Most of the evidence for these works is fragmentary, but the studies of Plümacher and Palmer (n. 10 above) focus on Sallust and Cicero as providing good examples of the kind of monograph which was being written (or in

55.   Margrit Kunz, 'Zur Beurteilung der Prooemien in Diodors historischer Bibliothek', (dissertation, Zurich, 1935), pp. 101–107. Sacks, *Diodorus* (also in 'The Lesser Proemia of Diodorus Siculus', *Hermes* 110 [1982], 434–43) goes further in the rehabilitation of Diodorus as author rather than compiler, but does not contest the distinction between the recapitulation and the *prooimion* proper: cf. n. 44 above and next note.

56.   See the *prooemium* to Book 13 (Kunz, 'Zur Beurteilung', pp. 87–88), where Diodorus professes to have no time for a real historical *prooimion*: 'If we were composing a history after the manner of the other historians, we should, I suppose, discourse upon certain topics at appropriate length in the introduction (ἐν τῷ προοιμίῳ) and by this means turn our discussion to the events which follow; surely, if we were picking out a brief period of history for our treatise [or: taking a little time out of our text], we should have the time to enjoy the fruit such introductions yield' (13.1.1, trans. C.H. Oldfather, LCL). What he does have time for (τοῦτο μόνον προειπόντας) (13.1.2) is a recapitulatory sentence summarizing the contents of the previous six books and of the present one (13.1.2–3): which seems to confirm that in Diodorus' eye the recapitulation does not constitute a *prooimion* proper.

57.   Palmer, 'Monograph', pp. 4–14; Plümacher, 'Monografie', pp. 464f.

58.   See Burridge, *Gospels*, pp. 117–19 on the generic significance of 'size and length'.

Cicero's case talked about) in Rome in the first century BCE. Despite the difficulty of defining a genre for which there is no single ancient term,[59] Palmer concludes (pp. 26–27) that Sallust's works 'conform to the theoretical requirements for a short monograph' (namely a single-volume work covering a limited historical period, with the focus on one theme and one person; its literary components include a prologue, narrative, speeches, despatches, and letters). Acts too is a single volume of moderate length, with a limited historical and geographical scope; it focuses on 'one leading figure at a time', and contains a prologue, narrative, speeches and letters (Palmer, pp. 28–29). There are a number of important issues here which are beyond the compass of this chapter: here we can concern ourselves only with the preface. The 'prologue' for Palmer is an important formal link between Acts and Sallust (of the Hellenistic Jewish texts which he classes as 'monographs', only 2 Maccabees has a comparable prologue: Palmer, p. 27). But the prefaces which Palmer uses elsewhere for comparison with the formal features of the Acts preface are not from monographs but from multi-volume works (Palmer, pp. 22–24) – inevitably, given the foregrounding of the recapitulation in Acts 1.1. Sallust's prefaces have none of the formal features we have identified in the preface to Acts except the use of the authorial first person, which is, of course, far too widespread to act as a genre-indicator on its own. Both books lead into their subject indirectly with a general discussion of historiographical methodology (*Jug.*) or of human ethics (*Cat.*) in a manner strongly reminiscent of the 'Ephoran' prefaces used by Diodorus – a fact noted by Quintilian, who ascribes it to the influence of epideictic oratory.[60] Whatever the rights and wrongs of this attribution,[61] we shall have to look further afield than Sallust to find parallels to the formal features of the Acts preface.

Arrian's *Anabasis of Alexander*, which has been described as 'the only perfect surviving example of a Greek historical monograph',[62] has no dedication and no recapitulations: Arrian favors a direct, workmanlike style, and displays a strong interest in the authenticity of his sources (*Anab.* 1, pref.), but apart from the use of the first person this preface has no formal parallels either with Sallust or with Acts 1.1 (or for that matter with Lk. 1.1–4).[63] A thorough search of the

59.   Palmer, 'Monograph', pp. 4–8.

60.   Quintilian 3.8.9, 'quos secutus [Isocrates and Gorgias] videlicet C. Sallustius in bello Iugurthino et Catilinae nihil ad historiam pertinentibus principiis ortus est'. See also Laqueur, '*Ephoros I*', p. 202.

61.   Earl, 'Prologue-form', pp. 846–49 contests Sallust's debt to epideictic and proposes instead that Sallust had been reading the newly rediscovered Aristotelian corpus: 'whether directly influenced by Aristotle's works or not, he began "Bellum Catilinae" and "Bellum Iugurthinum" as though they were not works of history but philosophical and ethical treatises' (p. 855).

62.   Geiger, *Cornelius Nepos*, p. 47. On the preface to the *Anabasis*, see Städter, *Arrian*, pp. 60–66.

63.   There is a dedication, interestingly (or at least a dedicatory epistle), in Arrian's *Discourses of Epictetus*, and the *Periplus* is structured as a letter to Trajan (Städter, *Arrian*, pp. 32–41); but neither of these is a historical monograph.

fragmentary remains might throw up some useful parallels (though, as I have observed elsewhere, it is precisely these relatively trivial *formalia* that tend to disappear in the process of epitomizing). But the problem seems to be that historical monographs still belong to the genre of history, and their prefaces display all the variety found in the larger genre: it does not seem possible to isolate a preface-style specifically associated with monographs, and the formal features found in the prefaces of Luke and Acts are no more at home here than they are in Greek historical writing generally.

V. *The Preface to Acts and 'Apologetic Historiography'*

The subgenre of the historical monograph, then, does not help us to locate the preface within a particular area of Greek historiography. A second, more recent approach may prove more promising. In an important monograph,[64] Gregory Sterling has posited a subgenre which he calls 'apologetic historiography' as the best location for Luke's work within the Greek historiographical tradition. Prime examples of the genre are Manetho and Berossus, along with the lost Hellenistic Jewish historians and Josephus. Whether this group of writings is sufficiently well defined to merit identification as a genre – and whether 'apologetic historiography' is the right name for it – are questions beyond the scope of this chapter.[65] What is significant for our purposes is that all the texts cited by Sterling would fall on the antiquarian-ethnographic side of Greek historiography, i.e. the side where we are most likely to find recapitulations marking the beginnings of books; and that this is also the area of historiography where dedication is best attested, especially among non-Greek writers (see above).

It would be too much to say that the preface of Acts offers positive support of Sterling's thesis: the formal features we have isolated are not sufficient of themselves to identify the genre of Acts as 'apologetic historiography'. Rather, Sterling's thesis, by focusing on this particular area of Greek historiography, evades the negative problems which we have identified in the preface.[66] If Acts belongs anywhere within the genre of historiography, this (broadly speaking) is the type of historiography which the conventions used in the preface would lead the informed reader to expect.

---

64.   Sterling, *Apologetic Historiography*.
65.   Palmer, 'Monograph', pp. 16f. raises the question 'whether the apologetic purpose is constitutive of this genre and limited to it'.
66.   Sterling accepts the standard view that the prefaces of Luke and Acts (which he treats as a unified work, *Apologetic Historiography*, pp. 331–39) reflect 'the primary and secondary prefaces so common in Hellenistic historiography' (p. 339; see also pp. 323–24, 330–46, 348, 367, 369), but does not give much attention to the *formalia* (especially dedication) which in my view act as counter-indicators.

VI. *Conclusions*

It seems clear, then, that in simple terms the answer to our initial question is 'No': the preface to Acts, taken on its own, does not set up expectations for the informed reader that the text which follows belongs to the genre 'Hellenistic Historiography'. It should be stressed that this preliminary conclusion concerns only the preface: there may be other good reasons within the body of the text which would encourage these same informed readers to revise their expectations, but these do not concern us in this chapter. All I have tried to do here is to establish the point, negatively speaking, that the opening conventions used in the Book of Acts are not sufficient to establish the genre of the work as 'history' within the frame of reference defined by Greek literary convention, whether because they are not sufficiently genre-specific or because they reflect literary customs not normally associated with historiography. Further than 'normally' it would be unwise to go: I have not been concerned here to discuss what is possible for the author, merely what the literary custom of the first century would lead the reader to expect.

This conclusion has both negative and positive implications for the genre of Acts. Negatively, it must be admitted that the formal features of the Acts preface, though they can be paralleled in Greek historiography, are not in any sense typical of that literature. On the positive side, these conventions (especially dedication and recapitulation) are more characteristic of other types of literature: where they occur in historiography, they cluster on the margins of the genre, where it is furthest from epic or rhetorical pretension and closest to the scholarly, scientific side of the Ionian *historia*-tradition: in fact, where historiography intersects with the broader, non-rhetorical tradition of philosophical and technical prose which I have called 'scientific literature (see n. 47 above).

This may be represented in the form of a simple diagram (see Figure 1). If we are to find a plausible location for Acts within the Greek historiographical tradition it should be where these circles intersect, i.e. on the more scholarly, less rhetorical side of history (archaeology, ethnography), and perhaps especially where the author and/or subject is non-Greek.[67]

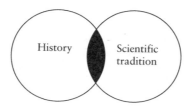

Figure 1

---

67. For the purposes of this chapter I have excluded from consideration (what a more extensive study would have to include) other prose narrative genres which overlap with history (and even with ethnography), such as travel writing and the novel. See on this whole area E. Gabba, 'True History and False History in Classical Antiquity', *JRS* 71 (1981), pp. 50–62.

One of the advantages of locating Luke's work in this area is that it allows us to place the text in a broader literary framework which is at least consistent with the indications of subject matter provided by the preface. It has long been recognized that the strongly 'biblical' language and subject matter of Acts place the book closer overall to biblical historiography than to the Greek tradition.[68] This suggests a possible literary matrix for the text among the lively and creative literary activities of the Greek-speaking Diaspora, which produced a significant number of biographical and historical monographs to set alongside the towering figure of Josephus.[69] None of the prefaces extant within this literature is close enough to that of Acts to suggest an immediate model, but there is sufficiently varied use of prefaces among Hellenistic Jewish writers to provide a literary context for Luke's. A more detailed study of the conventions used in these prefaces might well provide useful insight into the multifarious ways in which Jewish writers of Greek texts plug themselves into the dominant culture.[70]

And what, finally, of the Gospel preface? In this chapter I have deliberately focused on the preface to Acts alone: but it is pertinent in conclusion to bring the Gospel preface back into the picture. Nothing in this study of the preface to Acts has caused me to revise my view of the literary affinities of the Gospel preface. Both in different ways display a strictly limited range of literary conventions, and an equally limited interest in their development and use. In both cases, the literary etiquette displayed by Luke is fully at home in the broad tradition of technical prose, and much less so among the historians, who have a well-recognized repertoire of preface-topics which Luke does not use (and which I have not even touched on in this chapter).[71] There is no need, therefore, to argue for a different genre for the two works on the grounds of their prefaces (there may be other grounds, but they do not concern us here). Whether Luke and Acts are treated as separate works or as a two-volume set, their prefaces belong to the same literary code: and attentiveness to the nuances of this code, I would argue, can actually help us to resolve some long-standing questions about the genre of the two works.

68.   See on this E. Plümacher, *Lukas als hellenistischer Schriftsteller* (Gottingen: Vandenhoeck & Ruprecht, 1972); more recently Sterling, *Apologetic Historiography*, pp. 353–63; B.S. Rosner, 'Acts and Biblical History', in Winter and Clarke (eds.), *The Book of Acts*, pp. 65–82;

69.   The popularity of this subgenre among Hellenistic Jewish writers is clear from the surveys of Hengel (*Earliest Christianity*, p. 37), Geiger (*Cornelius Nepos*, p. 50, n. 49), and Palmer ('Monograph', pp. 18–21). Palmer notes that in fact the only single-volume historical monographs to survive before Acts, apart from Sallust's, are Jewish. Note also that these texts, like Acts, tend to fall at the overlap between history and biography (Geiger, *Cornelius Nepos*, pp. 50f; Palmer, 'Monograph', pp. 27f.) in a manner which conforms more with a long-established pattern of biblical historiography than with Greek: see on this Momigliano, *Development*, pp. 34–36.

70.   Alexander, *The Preface*, ch. 7. It should be stressed that 'Hellenistic Jewish literature' is not a genre so much as a literary matrix. Its writers intersect with the dominant Greco-Roman culture as individuals, not as a group, and there are many literary distinctions to be drawn between them. See esp. Sterling, *Apologetic Historiography*, ch. 5; H. Attridge, 'Historiography', in Stone (ed.), *Jewish Writings of the Second Temple Period*, ch. 4.

71.   Alexander, *The Preface*, ch. 3.

Chapter 3

'ACTS AND ANCIENT INTELLECTUAL BIOGRAPHY'[*]

Denn so ist es, Herr: dem Sokrates gaben sie ein Gift zu trinken, und unsern Herrn Christus schlugen sie an das Kreuz!

Theodor Storm, Der Schimmelreiter

I. *Introduction*

It is now almost 20 years since Charles Talbert put forward the brilliant proposal that the clue to the twofold structure of Luke-Acts was to be found in the compendium of philosophic biography which goes under the name of Diogenes Laertius' *Lives of the Philosophers*. Not that Diogenes Laertius could be in any direct sense Luke's literary model – the probable date of the compendium is the early-third century CE[1] – but he attests to a long tradition of writing up the lives of great teachers, and to an interest in the 'succession' by which a particular tradition was passed on and developed from the founding teacher to a series of disciples. Diogenes Laertius cites a variety of sources, the bulk of them dating from the Hellenistic period, i.e. 3–1 BCE:[2] and it is among these sources, Talbert postulates, that the model for Luke's two-volume work is to be found:[3]

---

[*]   Originally published as 'Acts and Ancient Intellectual Biography', in Bruce Winter and Andrew D. Clarke (eds.), *The Book of Acts in its First Century Setting*. I. *Ancient Literary Setting* (1993), pp. 31–63, reprinted here with the kind permission of the co-publishers Eerdmans Publishing Company and Paternoster Press.

1.   See the discussion in J. Mejer, *Diogenes Laertius and his Hellenistic Sources* (Hermes Einzelschriften, 40; Wiesbaden: Franz Steiner, 1978). Diogenes' citation of secondary sources like Favorinus makes a late second century date the earliest possible.

2.   On the hellenistic substance of Diogenes' work, cf. R.D. Hicks, *Diogenes Laertius* (Loeb Classical Library; 1925), p. xxxii: 'scarcely any allusion is made to the changes of the three centuries from 100 BC to AD 200'. For more recent discussion of Diogenes' sources, see Mejer, *Diogenes Laertius and his Hellenistic Sources* and B.A. Desbordes, 'Introduction à Diogène Laërce. Exposition de l'Altertumswissenschaft servant de préliminaires critiques à une lecture de l'oeuvre' (Doctoral Thesis; Utrecht: Onderwijs Media Institut, 1990), vols. I and II.

3.   Charles H. Talbert, *Literary Patterns, Theological Themes and the Genre of Luke-Acts* (SBLMS 20; Missoula, MT: Scholars Press, 1974); *idem, What is a Gospel?* (Philadelphia: Fortress Press, 1977); *idem*, 'Biographies of Philosophers and Rulers as Instruments of Religious Propaganda in Mediterranean Antiquity', *ANRW* 2.16.2 (1978), pp. 1619–1651; *idem*, 'Biography, Ancient', *ABD*, I, pp. 745–49.

> The similarities between the lives of the founders of philosophical schools presented by Laertius and Luke-Acts are remarkable. First of all, as to content...Luke-Acts, as well as Diogenes Laertius...has for its contents (a) the life of a founder of a religious community, (b) a list or narrative of the founder's successors and selected other disciples, and (c) a summary of the doctrine of the community. In the second place, in *form* Luke-Acts, like Diogenes Laertius' *Lives*, has the life of a founder as the first structural unit, followed by a second, namely, the narrative of successors and selected other disciples. . . There is furthermore a similarity of *purpose* between Luke-Acts and the Lives of philosophers following this pattern, whether they are collections or individual Lives. Both are concerned to say where the true tradition is to be found in the present... [T]he conclusion seems inescapable. Luke-Acts, just as Diogenes Laertius, derived the pattern for his work, (a) + (b), from the widespread use of it since pre-Christian times in portraying the lives of certain philosophers. If so, then Luke-Acts, to some extent, must be regarded as belonging to the genre of Greco-Roman biography, in particular, to that type of biography which dealt with the lives of philosophers and their successors. (*Literary Patterns*, 125–34).

Most of the recently-revived interest in ancient biography has been centred, naturally enough, on the Gospels,[4] and most readers would probably concur with Aune's bald statement that Luke 'does not belong to a type of ancient biography for it belongs with Acts, and Acts cannot be forced into a biographical mold'.[5] However, I believe that the reader of Acts has much to learn from the study of ancient biography; and Talbert's proposal makes a good starting-point in a number of ways.

First of all, the 'succession' structure deals precisely and neatly with Aune's problem of the structure of Luke's double work (and incidentally enables us to avoid the potentially ridiculous situation in which Matthew, Mark and John may be regarded as biographies but Luke may not). This does not entail trying to 'force Acts into a biographical mold', but it does mean taking seriously the extent to which the narrative of Acts is structured around a series of individual apostles, and in particular the extent to which one story-line, that of Paul, progressively dominates from his first, low-key introduction at 7.58. Paul is in fact the sole hero of the narrative from ch. 13 to ch. 28, that is for more than half the book, and Acts conveys far more information about Paul than about any other apostle.[6]

---

4.   The revival of interest in biography among students of the NT is exemplified by the reprint in 1970 of Clyde Weber Votaw's classic study, 'The Gospels and Contemporary Biographies in the Greco-Roman World', *American Journal of Theology* 19 (1915), pp. 45–73 and 217–49; (repr. Facet Books, Biblical Series 27; Philadelphia: Fortress Press, 1970). For more recent studies see: R.A. Burridge, *What Are the Gospels?* (SNTSMS 70; Cambridge: Cambridge University Press, 1992); K. Berger, 'Hellenistische Gattungen im Neuen Testament', *ANRW* 2.25.2 (1984), pp. 1034–1380, esp. pp. 1231–45.

5.   David E. Aune, *The New Testament in its Literary Environment* (Cambridge: James Clarke, 1988), p. 77. Cf. Burridge, *Gospels?*, pp. 243–47.

6.   Paul plays a major role in every episode from 13.4 to the end of Acts, except 18.24–28 (Apollos). The Jerusalem conference (15.1–29) is not a real exception: Paul is still the hero here, Peter a secondary character. Burridge points out, *Gospels?*, p. 246, that Paul is named in 14.5% of the sentences in Acts, a higher proportion than any other human character (Peter scores 6%). For comparison, analysis of an acknowledged biography like Tacitus' *Agricola* reveals that the hero figures as the subject of 18.1% of the verbs. A similar analysis of Paul in Acts would be well worth while.

Indeed this is one of the difficulties in classifying Acts as a 'history of the church' or even as 'The Acts of the Apostles': it is too lop-sided to sit comfortably with either title. Acts is not just a biography of Paul, but it contains a Pauline biography in the same way that the books of Samuel contain the Davidic 'succession narrative', or Genesis contains the story of Joseph – and this story-line can be studied in exactly the same way. But Talbert's hypothesis also alerts us to look at the way in which the Pauline story-line is embedded in the larger narrative, particularly at the way in which relationships with the other apostles are handled.

Secondly, Talbert's proposal encourages us to focus on a particular area of ancient biography. Ancient biography is a notoriously confusing field to understand, especially since it never attained the status of the genres recognized by classical rhetoric.[7] But there is a lot to be said for limiting our explorations to an area which may be loosely defined as 'intellectual biography', i.e. biography of individuals distinguished for their prowess in the intellectual field (philosophers, poets, dramatists, doctors) rather than in the political or military arena (kings, statesmen, generals). This gives us the initial advantage of limiting the field to Greek texts, since the bulk of political biography dates from the Roman period.[8] It also limits the field to the central core of undisputed biographical writing from the hellenistic age, which, as Gigon has pointed out, was largely confined to literary and philosophical heroes and hence to the sphere of private rather than public life.[9] This is clearly the sphere to which Paul belongs, and indeed the most obvious parallels are with the biographical material connected with philosophical teachers. However, philosophical biography is in many ways only a sub-group of intellectual biography, and although it is an important sub-group which may well prove to have unique features, it shares many formal features with the larger group.

Within this broader field, to restrict our lines of investigation to the philosophical 'succession-literature' highlighted by Talbert would be too narrow, especially since most examples of the genre are lost; and in fact Talbert himself

---

7.   Burridge, *Gospels?*, provides a helpful recent discussion with bibliography. Major general studies (where more specialist bibliography may be found) include F. Leo, *Die griechisch-römische Biographie nach ihrer Literarischen Form* (Leipzig: Teubner, 1901); D.R. Stuart, *Epochs of Greek and Roman Biography* (Berkeley: University of California Press, 1928); A. Momigliano, *The Development of Greek Biography*, now available in a new expanded edition (Cambridge, MA: Harvard University Press, 1993); originally published as *The Development of Greek Biography* and *Second Thoughts on Greek Biography*, both 1971; Albrecht Dihle, *Studien zur griechischen Biographie* (Göttingen: Vandenhoeck & Ruprecht, 1956); *idem*, *Die Entstehung der historischen Biographie* (Sitzungsberichte der Heidelberger Akademie der Wissenschaften, phil.-hist. Klasse 1986/3; Heidelberg: Carl Winter, 1987).

8.   It has even been suggested that political biography properly so called did not exist before Cornelius Nepos – though this is largely a matter of definition (J. Geiger, *Cornelius Nepos and Ancient Political Biography* [Historia Einzelschriften, 47; Wiesbaden/Stuttgart: Franz Steiner, 1985]).

9.   O. Gigon, 'Biographie. A. Griechische Biographie', *Lexikon der Alten Welt*, pp. 469–71. The major collection of literary biography is A. Westermann (ed.), *Biographi Graeci Minores* (Braunschweig: 1845; repr. Amsterdam: Hakkert, 1964).

points to a number of other aspects of philosophical biography which are potentially illuminating for the reader of Acts. In his major *ANRW* article he suggested a five-fold classification of biography according to social function:

> A. To provide the readers with a pattern to copy.
> B. To dispel a false image and provide a true one to follow.
> C. To discredit by exposé.
> D. To indicate where the true succession is to be found.
> E. To validate and/or provide a hermeneutical key to a teacher's doctrine.[10]

Besides Type D, the interest in the 'succession' of a great teacher's disciples which we have already mentioned, two of these indicate areas of interest in the ancient biographical tradition which are of particular significance for the reader of Acts.

(i) Type E: the 'hermeneutical key'. The description of biography as providing a 'hermeneutical key' to the teacher's doctrine underlines the fact that many intellectual biographies are ancillary to an independent and pre-existent body of writings. To put it more logically, much intellectual biography takes its starting point from the fact that its subject is independently known as an author; that is why he or she gets written about in the first place.[11] In this respect, as I have suggested on another occasion, Talbert's model works better for Acts than for the Gospel. Luke's account of Paul's missionary activities could well be seen as a biographical/hagiographical appendage to the corpus of genuine and deutero-Pauline epistles, put together as an accompaniment to this pre-existent body of Pauline teaching. Acts would in fact make a lot of sense as 'the product of a "Pauline school" which was also indulging in the typical "school" activities of collecting a corpus of letters and expanding it along lines deemed to express the master's thought in changing circumstances.[12]

(ii) Type A: the teacher as exemplum. The idea that the lifestyle (*bios*) of great teachers is as important in the education of their students as their sayings or writings is well attested in antiquity. Seneca provides a good example from the first century:

---

10.   Talbert, 'Biographies of Philosophers', pp. 1620–23. The usefulness of this typology has not been universally accepted. Talbert himself excludes a whole class of biography which he calls 'non-didactic' ('Biographies of Philosophers', p. 1620), and the attempt to provide a single grid of social functions to account for the whole range of biographies of 'philosophers and rulers' incurs the charge of over-simplification: cf. Dihle, *Studien zur griechischen Biographie*, p. 8. But we are only concerned here with the philosophical side of the grid, and in order to pursue the parallel with Acts we only need to establish that there were some ancient biographies with some of these functions.

11.   See especially Janet Fairweather, 'Fiction in the Biographies of Ancient Writers', *Ancient Society* 4 (1974), pp. 231–75; Mary Lefkowitz, *The Lives of the Greek Poets* (London: Duckworth, 1981).

12.   Loveday Alexander, *The Preface to Luke's Gospel* (SNTSMS, 78; Cambridge: Cambridge University Press, 1993), pp. 203–204.

Cleanthes would never have been the image of Zeno if he had merely heard him lecture; he lived with him, studied his private life, watched him to see if he lived in accordance with his own principle. Plato, Aristotle and a host of other philosophers all destined to take different paths, derived more from Socrates' character than from his words. It was not Epicurus' school but living under the same roof as Epicurus that turned Metrodorus, Hermarchus and Polyaenus into great men.[13]

Lucian's *Life of Demonax* provides a classic expression of this ideal in the form of biography:

> It is now fitting to tell of Demonax for two reasons – that he may be retained in memory by men of culture as far as I can bring it about, and that young men of good instincts who aspire to philosophy may not have to shape themselves by ancient precedents alone, but may be able to set themselves a pattern [κανών] from our modern world and to copy [ζηλοῦν] that man, the best of all philosophers whom I know about. (Lucian, *Demonax* 2, LCL).

Here the Life exists not to provide information ancillary to a pre-existent body of writings but to act as a 'template' for the readers to pattern their own lives on.[14] The importance of this function in ancient biography is widely recognized, especially among students of the biography of the later Empire, both pagan and Christian.[15] Reading Acts along these lines would encourage us to explore the ways in which Paul is presented as a pattern for imitation, a narrative extension of the process already visible in the epistolary corpus by which, in Conzelmann's words, 'with Paul's death not only his teaching but also the image of his work becomes the content of the tradition'.[16]

Talbert's hypothesis offers the further potential of anchoring the literary comparison to a specific social context, that of the hellenistic schools. In his 1974 study (cited in n. 3), he explicitly associates the collection and maintenance of the lives of philosophers and their disciples with the interests of the schools as communities:

> The most striking similarity...is that between the function of Luke-Acts and the individual lives of philosophers with an (a) + (b) pattern. Both are cult documents intended to be read and used within the community which produced them and in the interests of its ongoing life (*Literary Patterns*, p. 134).

The commitment of discipleship (whatever the formal setting) is presupposed even more strongly where the biography also has the function of setting forth

13. Seneca, *Ep.* 6.5, trans. Campbell (*Seneca: Letters from a Stoic* [Harmondsworth: Penguin Books, 1969], p. 40).

14. I am indebted to Susie Orbach, writing in 'The Guardian' on 27 March 1993, for this useful term.

15. Cf. e.g. P. Rousseau, *Ascetics, Authority and the Church in the Age of Jerome and Cassian* (Oxford: Oxford University Press, 1978), pp. 11–18, 68–74; Patricia Cox, *Biography in Late Antiquity* (Berkeley: University of California Press, 1983), *passim*.

16. Conzelmann, 'Luke's place in the development of early Christianity', in L. Keck and J.L. Martyn (eds.), *Studies in Luke-Acts* (London: SPCK, 1968), p. 307.

the sage as a pattern to imitate. The possibility of using the hellenistic schools (philosophical and other) to provide a social model for the early church is one which has aroused increasing interest over the years.[17] Especially in connection with the collection and publication of the Pauline letters,[18] it suggests a much needed concrete setting for a whole range of 'deutero-Pauline' literary activities (collecting and editing of genuine letters, production of pseudepigrapha, biographical narration), all of which can be paralleled among philosophers (Socrates, Plato, Epicurus), and in other technical traditions.[19] But only a detailed comparison can reveal how well the analogy works in practice.

The 'school' context also ties in with my own long-term investigation of the conventions employed in the Lukan preface, which led me to the conclusion that the web of expectations set up by the highly conventional language of the preface would lead the ancient reader to expect, not a work of historiography in the classic mould of Thucydides, Polybius or Josephus, but a technical treatise emanating (at whatever remove) from some kind of 'school' setting.[20] In fact Diogenes Laertius, though he did not figure in the original study because of his date, does contain a brief preface which parallels many of the features found in the technical prefaces which formed the subject of this study,[21] and thus falls broadly within the same literary category. Putting Acts in this context would also provide one possible solution to a literary problem raised by the Lukan preface. At the

17.　　Cf. Wayne Meeks, *The First Urban Christians* (London and New Haven: Yale University Press, 1983), pp. 75–84. A.D. Nock, *Conversion* (Oxford, 1933). E.A. Judge, 'The Early Christians as a Scholastic Community', *JRH* 1 (1960), pp. 4–15, 125–37. I have pursued this interest at greater length (and suggested other parallels) in 'The Living Voice: Scepticism towards the Written Word in Early Christian and in Greco-Roman Texts', in D.J.A. Clines, S.E. Fowl and S.E. Porter (eds.), *The Bible in Three Dimensions* (Sheffield: Sheffield Academic Press, 1990); *eadem*, 'Schools, Hellenistic', in *ABD*, V, pp. 1005–11; *eadem*, 'Paul and the Hellenistic Schools: the Evidence of Galen', in Troels Engberg-Pedersen (ed.), *Paul in his Hellenistic Context* (Philadelphia: Fortress Press, 1994).

18.　　H. Conzelmann, 'Paulus und die Weisheit', *NTS* 12 (1965), pp. 231–44 (esp. 233); 'Luke's Place in the Development of Early Christianity', in Keck and Martyn (eds.), *Studies*, pp. 298–316 (esp. 307–308). Cf. among more recent examples Mark Kiley, *Colossians as Pseudepigraphy* (Sheffield: JSOT, 1986), pp. 91ff.; but the term tends to be used with little if any attention to its precise social significance. Cf. Alexander, *The Preface*, p. 204 n. 29. Alan Culpepper's useful study *The Johannine School* (SBLDS, 26; Missoula: Scholars Press, 1975) was precipitated by a similar lack of precision in Johannine studies.

19.　　Wesley D. Smith, *Hippocrates: Pseudepigraphic Writings* (Studies in Ancient Medicine, 2; Leiden: Brill, 1990); Jody Rubin Pinault, *Hippocratic Lives and Legends* (Studies in Ancient Medicine, 4; Leiden: Brill, 1992). Pinault suggests (p. 33) that the composition of the Life of Hippocrates was closely linked with the publication of the Letters, which themselves constituted a kind of 'novella in letters' (Smith, *Hippocrates*, 20).

20.　　Alexander, *The Preface*, pp. 200–210.

21.　　The beginning of the work is lost, but the account of Plato's thought is introduced at 3.47 with a classic prefatorial passage addressed to Diogenes' unnamed (female) dedicatee. Note the following parallels (refs. to Alexander, *The Preface*): use of φιλο- compounds in dedication (p. 100); opening reference to dedicatee's disposition (p. 74); author's decision as main verb (p. 70); contents of book as object to main verb (pp. 71–73); modesty about presentation (p. 99); purpose clause as final element in long dedicatory sentence (pp. 74–75).

surface level, its most obvious message is that the author is promising to act as a faithful conduit for traditional material.[22] This is easy to understand for the Gospel, less so for Acts: recent scholarship has on the whole been reluctant to assign a large role to tradition in the composition of Acts (although the possibility has received new attention latterly in the work of Jervell and Lüdemann).[23] Looking at the role played by biographical traditions in the hellenistic schools could help us to a better understanding not only of the function of such traditions but also of their shaping: how they are structured and what is narrated. Finally, note that my use of the term 'hellenistic' should not be taken to imply a sharp distinction between 'Hellenism' and 'Judaism'. Many of the questions asked here about the role of biography in the hellenistic schools could also be asked of the rabbinic academies – and in fact I believe that a true appreciation of the social model of the 'school' as a tool for understanding early Christianity will only arise from a 'compare and contrast' exercise setting early Christian social structures alongside both hellenistic and rabbinic 'schools'. Only limitations of space prevent my pursuing the parallel here. (Cf. further Chapter 1 n. 23)

II. *Luke-Acts and Diogenes Laertius: A Narrative Comparison*

The parallel between Diogenes Laertius (DL) and Luke-Acts (LA), then, is one which for many reasons I would like to make work. The problem is that the closer we look at the comparison in literary terms, the more obvious it seems that DL is a 'bad fit', at any rate for Acts. The most obvious difficulty for the comparison is that Diogenes Laertius dates from the early third century CE and is therefore too late to act in any direct sense as a literary model for Luke-Acts. Talbert's comparison is not between Luke-Acts and Diogenes Laertius but between Luke-Acts and Diogenes' sources: 'Luke-Acts, just as Diogenes Laertius, derived the pattern for his work...from the widespread use of it since pre-Christian times in portraying the lives of certain philosophers'.[24] There is nothing wrong with this procedure in principle, since Diogenes quotes a large number of sources, most of them from the hellenistic period; but it has had the effect of diverting attention away from the text of Diogenes to a body of material which survives, if at all, only in the form of epitomes and quotations, for many of which Diogenes himself is our best witness. Scholars have recently begun to question the consensus view on Diogenes' sources: no-one doubts that they existed, but the difficulty of determining their precise form and extent has probably been underestimated.[25] For our purposes, this concern to get 'behind' Diogenes has

22.   Alexander, *The Preface*, pp. 201–202, 207.
23.   J. Jervell, 'The Problem of Traditions in Acts', *ST* 16 (1962), pp. 25–41, repr. as pp. 19–39 of *Luke and the People of God: A New Look at Luke-Acts* (Minneapolis: Augsburg, 1962); Gerd Lüdemann, *Early Christianity According to the Traditions in Acts* (London: SCM Press, 1989).
24.   Talbert, *Literary Patterns*, p. 134.
25.   See especially Mejer, *Diogenes Laertius and his Hellenistic Sources* and Desbordes, 'Introduction à Diogène Laërce'.

masked a number of obvious differences between the two texts at the level of the narrative. Only by giving full weight to the comparison at this surface level can we begin to appreciate the achievement of the author of Acts in shaping one of early Christianity's most important bodies of story.

1. *The Narrative Agenda*

The first question to ask is a simple one: what is narrated? What do Luke on the one hand, and DL on the other, think that their readers should be told? For simplicity's sake, I use here a list of the typical features of DL's lives cited by Ingemar Düring.[26] Düring stresses that not all items always appear: if the information was not available, DL did not include it. But the list is a useful indicator of the kinds of information that DL wanted to convey to his readers: and it cannot be solely dependent on the amount of material available to DL from his sources, for there are some cases, like Xenophon and Socrates, where we know that DL had far more information available about the character from literary sources than is given here.

1. Origin, pedigree (*genos*)
2. Relation to a philosophic school; scholarchate, διαδοχή
2. Education
4. Character, often illustrated by anecdotes and apophthegms
5. Important events of life
6. Anecdotic account of his death, usually followed by an epigram
7. ἀκμή (i.e. period when the philosopher 'flourished') and related chronological data
8. Works (list of book-titles)
9. Doctrines
10. Particular documents, wills, letters
11. Homonyms (other people of the same name)

A tabular summary will show how this works out in practice (using Düring's example of the Aristotle biography in Diogenes): see Table I. It will readily be observed that the order of topics is not preserved even in this example ('Character', and even 'events of life' actually come after 'death' in this case), but it is widely agreed that the order varies widely in Diogenes. What is important, and is generally agreed, is that the list represents fairly the narrative range of Diogenes' Lives; a cursory read confirms the constant recurrence of most of these items, even though not all of them occur in any one Life, and even though there might be better ways of classifying the material.

It is clear that Diogenes had very little information on many of his minor philosophers, and that (not surprisingly) the fullest Lives are those of the founders of schools. It is also clear that some information was available for certain schools only: e.g. the wills figure mostly in the Lives of the major Peripatetics. 'Education' does not figure in the Life of Aristotle, and is hard to distinguish in general from item (2): but many of the Lives contain a short note on the occupation of the philosopher before he or she entered the philosophic life, and some at least of these

26. I. Düring, *Aristotle in the Ancient Biographical Tradition* (*Studia Graeca et Latina Gothoburgensia*, 5: Göteborg: Elanders, 1957), pp. 77–78.

traditions may have the function of pointing up a contrast with the philosophic life.[27] The list of Works figures in almost every Life, but the major section on Doctrines tends to be attached to the founders of major schools.

Table I: Narrative Topics in Diogenes Laertius

	ARISTOTLE (DL bk. 5)	PAUL (Acts)
1. Genos (origin, pedigree)	5.1	22.2f, 28; 21.37, 39f.; 23.6, 34
2. School (scholarchate, διαδοχή)	5.2	ch. 9?
3. Education		22.3; 23.6; 26.4f.
4. Character (anecdotes and apophthegms)	5.17–21	
5. Events of life	5.3–11	chs. 13–19
6. Death (epigram)	5.6	chs. 20–28
7. Chronology (ἀκμή)	5.6, 9–10	11.28; 12.18
8. Works	5.21–27	
9. Doctrines	5.28–34	speeches?
10. Documents (wills, letters)	5.7–8; 5.11–16	speeches? 20.18–35
11. Homonyms	5.35	

Note: Each chapter in DL represents around 12 lines of Greek.

Even at a quick glance, it is evident that there are similarities and differences here. On the one hand, under '*Genos*' DL includes information about city of origin, parentage (if known) and family connections; like Acts (and unlike Luke's Gospel) he rarely shows any interest in birth stories, miraculous or otherwise. On the other hand Acts never makes any explicit remarks about Paul's character, and the anecdotal material which is used to illustrate character in DL (and there is a lot of this) is not easy to parallel in the Pauline tradition. Paul's story is much less anecdotal than that of Jesus, as a comparison between Luke's Gospel and Acts makes clear. The other major gap is 'Works': notoriously, Luke never mentions Paul's letters, and scholarship has often worked on the assumption that he did not know them. If he did not, then another possible parallel is removed: for the easiest way to parallel the 'Doctrines' section in DL is to think of Acts as a biographical introduction to the Epistles, which would then represent the 'Doctrines' of the apostle. But if Luke did know the Epistles, then (on the

27. O. Gigon, 'Antike Erzählungen über die Berufung zur Philosophie', *Museum Helveticum* 3 (1946), pp. 1–21 (esp. 2–3).

Diogenes model) we would expect him to mention them. The Pauline speeches in Acts might in theory be thought of as an equivalent: but that brings us up against another difficulty, which deserves a separate section.

2. *Narrative mode*

If it is not easy to argue for a good match between Acts and Diogenes at the level of agenda – i.e. in terms of topics covered – it becomes downright difficult when we turn our attention to the mode of the narrative, i.e. not just to what is told (informational content) but to how it is told. This means paying attention to a number of concrete factors which affect the structure of the narrative in significant ways.

1. *Genos*. This is always the first item of information in Diogenes, conveyed directly by the narrator in the opening words. The subject of the Life is normally the grammatical subject of the first sentence. In Acts the meagre information we are given about Paul's origins (and it does not include the names of his parents, as is normal in Diogenes) is conveyed indirectly, at a late stage in the story, and comes from the lips of Paul himself. It is often observed that Luke tells us that Paul was a Roman citizen: in fact Luke the narrator does not 'tell' us this, but allows his character Paul to tell us instead.

2. *School affiliations*. This is normally conveyed along with the opening information about name and parentage in Diogenes, and clearly forms one of the major organizing principles of the collection. More information may be given in the second paragraph. In the case of Paul, there is no difficulty with Talbert's suggestion that this idea of maintaining the correct 'succession' of the 'living voice' can be paralleled in Paul's struggles with the Jerusalem apostles and that the same kind of concern lies behind Paul's concept of his own apostleship (cf. esp. Galatians 1–2). The problem is with the expression of the idea in Luke's narrative. Where Diogenes is direct and unambiguous, Luke is indirect and ambivalent. On the one hand Paul's commission from the resurrected Jesus (the basis for Paul's own Christian affiliation in Galatians 1) is narrated fully no less than three times, once in the narrator's words (ch. 9) and twice in Paul's. As Ronald Witherup has pointed out recently, this certainly indicates that the episode is important for Luke's narrative.[28] On the other hand, though, Luke (notoriously) differs from Paul in making it appear that Paul had some contact with the Jerusalem apostles soon after his conversion (9.27), which some have seen as an attempt to imply dependence on Jerusalem (this thought underlies Talbert's view of Acts as 'succession narrative'). But in fact Luke carefully refrains from saying that Paul received any teaching from the apostles at this or at any point: if he does want to convey some kind of 'succession', he does it in an indirect and allusive fashion very different from that of Diogenes.[29]

---

28.   Ronald D. Witherup, 'Cornelius over and over and over again: "Functional Redundancy" in the Acts of the Apostles', *JSNT* 49 (1993), pp. 45–66.

29.   Talbert is aware of this difficulty: cf. 'Biography, Ancient', *ABD* I, p. 749: LA 'shares with certain biographies a concern to say where the true tradition is in the present, even if his sense of the radical difference between apostolic and post apostolic times caused him to eschew use of the typical succession vocabulary'.

3. *Education.* Again, this information in Acts is conveyed indirectly by the character Paul, not directly by the narrator. But, as we have seen, this item does not figure large in Diogenes' agenda: as in Acts, there is little or no trace of the theme of 'childhood brilliance' associated with more romantic biography. What we find in Acts, as in the Epistles, is rather a contrast, not between Paul the Pharisee and Paul the Christian but between the persecutor and the follower of Jesus.[30] A number of philosophical biographies similarly stress the dramatic nature of the first encounter with philosophy (which may well be structured as a 'conversion') and the previous unsuitability of the subject to the philosophic life.[31]

4. *Character.* We have already mentioned the obvious formal difference (one of the major difficulties in the way of reading any biblical narrative in terms of Greco-Roman biography) that Diogenes describes the ethos of his characters directly, and then cites a number of anecdotes to prove the point, whereas Luke conveys it indirectly through the story itself. It is of course an important question in itself to what extent the biblical writers share the modern novelist's preoccupation with 'character', but all that concerns us immediately is the formal difference.

5. *Events of Life.* In fact this item on the agenda is hard to distinguish from (4), and it might be better to say simply that Diogenes tends to fill a section of his Lives with disconnected anecdotes, some illustrative of character and some filling out of the life story of the hero. In many cases, this information was clearly very meagre: but it is worth noting that it seems to have formed a relatively unimportant part of the agenda even when more information could easily have been put in: Xenophon, for example, gets only a very short narrative section here, despite the fact that his own writings provided plenty of information for the biographer (DL 2.48–59). Paul's life, by contrast, is given full and detailed narrative treatment in Acts. The difference is visible at every level. Where Diogenes uses the curtly-formulated anecdote as the raw material for his narrative, Luke uses fully-narrated episodes, packed with irrelevant detail of the sort the *chria*-form was designed to eliminate. Like the Gospel writers, but to a much greater degree, Luke provides a connected narrative in Acts with full travel details to cement the link between one episode and another. This is 'thick' narrative if anything is: the contrast could hardly be greater with Diogenes' brief summary statements.[32]

6. *Death.* Diogenes appears to have had an interest in death scenes, which may be traced back to the hellenistic biographical tradition. But his accounts (often multiple) of the deaths of his philosophers are formulated in the same curt and

---

30.   Acts 7.58–8.1, 9.1–2; Gal. 1.13–14, Phil. 3.6, 1 Cor. 15.9–10.
31.   Cf. Gigon, 'Antike Erzählungen'; Nock, *Conversion*, ch. 11. The most dramatic 'conversion' story in DL is that of Polemo, 4.16.
32.   The Aristotelian anecdotes in DL 5.17–21 take up about 3 lines of Greek each. The total allotted to 'events of life' in 5.3–11 (a generous estimate including non-narrative excurses) is 99 lines. By contrast, Acts 14 (3 episodes plus a travel summary) takes 63 lines, and this is just one chapter out of 17 devoted to Paul in Acts.

factual fashion as the rest of his narrative, and treated with a disarming mixture of irony and *Schadenfreude*. Socrates' death is narrated with the reverence we would expect of the prototypical martyr of the philosophic tradition, but other philosophers die from a variety of undignified causes: gout, a broken finger, and falling over a chamber pot are in turn drily narrated and celebrated with the little epigrams composed (as he proudly tells us) by Diogenes himself.[33] Luke, by contrast, notoriously does not narrate the death of his hero at all, so strictly speaking this item should not appear under Acts. On the other hand, as Robert Maddox points out, the trial and impending death of Paul dominate the last few chapters of the book to a remarkable degree. The trial and journey to Rome occupy slightly more narrative space than the mission, and account for 'some 23.5% of the text of Acts and 12% of the whole of Luke-Acts' (a proportion comparable with the narrative time devoted to the passion of Jesus in the Gospel). If we take the Pauline narrative alone and include ch. 20, the point at which it is clearly established that Paul is to die (20.25), Paul's 'death' takes up more than half the time devoted to his story.[34] This is an important structural point to which we shall return.

7. *Chronology*. As one would expect in such a compendious collection, chronology, relative and absolute, is important to Diogenes and usually gets a direct statement to itself.[35] It is much less important to Luke: the Gospel begins with a proper comparative dating (3.1–2), but Acts contains no parallel to this. External dating criteria, like the death of Herod or the expulsion of the Jews by Claudius, are mentioned as part of the narrative, not allotted separate statements of their own. Relative chronology is notoriously vague in Acts.

8. *Works* and 9. *Doctrines*. Both these have already been mentioned: again, even if we admit the speeches or the letters as an equivalent to these items in the Diogenes *Lives*, there is no formal parallel to the method of their introduction. Direct speech in Diogenes is limited to the apophthegms (one-liners) or to the hymns, poems and letters which are sometimes quoted. Doctrine is summarized by Diogenes in his own voice, not expressed in direct speech placed on the lips of the philosophers themselves. And the listing of titles of books is an important part of the agenda.[36]

10. *Documents*. The wills quoted by Diogenes occur chiefly, as already stated, in the Peripatetic Lives; other documents, like letters, are occasionally included

33.　　DL 5.68. (Lycon); 7.28 (Zeno); 4.14–15 (Xenocrates). On the death theme and Diogenes' epigrams cf. Mejer, *Diogenes Laertius and his Hellenistic Sources*, pp. 46–50.

34.　　Robert Maddox, *The Purpose of Luke-Acts* (Göttingen: Vandenhoeck & Ruprecht, 1982), pp. 66–67.

35.　　DL frequently cites the *Chronica* of Apollodorus: e.g. 5.9. Cf. Mejer, *Diogenes Laertius and his Hellenistic Sources*, p. 34

36.　　Some lives consist of little more than a list of titles, e.g. Simon the Shoemaker (2.122), Cebes (2.125), although not all philosophers were known as authors, e.g. Hipparchia (6.96–98). The list can run to several pages, e.g. Theophrastus (5.42–50).

(e.g. Epicurus).[37] It is tempting to read Paul's farewell speech in Acts 20.18–35 as some kind of 'Testament', but this does not make it a formal parallel to the Testament of Aristotle: the wills quoted by Diogenes are real ones, legal documents concerned with the disposition of property and family arrangements, not ideological constructs like those of the biblical tradition. Conversely, the documents quoted by Luke (such as the letter of Claudius Lysias in Acts 23.26–30) form part of the narrative.[38]

11. *Homonyms*. Acts offers no parallel to this rather odd feature of Diogenes' compendium. It clearly derives from one of the many hellenistic sources he quotes, and expresses well the concern for cataloguing which dominates so much of this literature.[39]

It may be seen from this analysis that even where there are parallels in content between Acts and the Lives of Diogenes Laertius, detailed examination at the level of narrative mode points up as many contrasts as similarities. Acts uses full narrative where Diogenes makes summary statements; Acts uses indirect narrative (information conveyed by the characters) and indirect characterization where Diogenes always gives the bare facts; episodes from the life of the hero are structured in a completely different way. Acts gives us 'thick' narrative where Diogenes gives us 'thin'. It may in fact be doubted whether Diogenes' story can be dignified with the name 'narrative' at all: it might be better to say that Luke tells his story in 'narrative mode' while Diogenes' is much closer to the 'analytical mode'.[40] Luke speaks throughout with the unified voice of a narrator. Diogenes' work, by contrast, contains a strong authorial presence which repeatedly draws attention to a plurality of narrators, some anonymous ('they

37.   Epicurus: will 10.16–21; letters 10.22, 35–83, 84–116. Cf. the exchange of letters and decree cited in 7.7–9, 10–12 (Zeno).

38.   So, rightly, H.J. Cadbury, *The Making of Luke-Acts* (New York: Macmillan, 1927), pp. 190–199.

39.   On Demetrius of Magnesia, whom DL cites as his source for the homonyms, cf. Mejer, *Diogenes Laertius and his Hellenistic Sources*, pp. 38–39.

40.   'Mode': I borrow the term from John Douglas Minyard, *Mode and Value in the De Rerum Natura* (Hermes Einzelschriften, 39; Wiesbaden: Franz Steiner, 1978), ch. 4. Of the narrative mode he says (pp. 90–91): 'Narrative works are concerned with the sequential ordering of topics, not with the hierarchies of logical relations (as in analytical works)… They spend their energies on the development of an appropriate rhythm and verbal design, associative connections, the recollection or intimation of earlier events by later ones, the qualities of feeling which can be incorporated in a recreation of an incident or particular description, and the stabilization of attitudes and perspectives through a variety of incidents. The narrator does not assert logically testable propositions, he does not argue a case, and the narrative voice is not pluralized so that the incidents are seen from different points of view. The order is sequential (whether progressive or paratactic), and the narrative voice is unitary. Unity in the whole is founded upon the stabilization in style, incident, perspective and narrative voice.' The 'analytical' mode, by contrast is described on pp. 89–90: 'Works in the analytical mode try to create an order based upon logical relationships in an effort to explain a process of reasoning or aspect of reality. They strive for logic in argument, the clear statement of testable propositions, and the systematic analysis of public proofs…'

say'), others named.[41] From the formal perspective, what is interesting is not the identification of these 'sources' but Diogenes' attitude to them. He repeatedly draws attention to their existence, sometimes quoting chapter and verse (correctly). This maintains a constant distance between the implied author and what he narrates and creates a sense of detachment which is increased on the not infrequent occasions where Diogenes points out a conflict in his sources.[42] Luke makes use of a similar authorial voice in his prefaces (Lk. 1.1–4, Acts 1.1), but that voice never intrudes itself into the narrative. Even the 'we-passages', I would argue, do not constitute a breach in the narrative framework of Acts: the narrator there simply (and oddly) becomes a temporary character in his own narrative, but there is no consciousness of a plurality of narrators, much less of conflicting narratives, such as there is in Diogenes.

III. *Behind Diogenes Laertius: Biography in the Hellenistic Schools*

It is clear from this comparison that, while Luke and Diogenes Laertius share a certain number of narrative concerns, they differ considerably in their manner of expression. One response to this is to stress the catholicity of the genre, as do both Talbert and Burridge in different ways;[43] but this is to lessen the usefulness of the genre-description as a distinctive, and has the effect of blurring precisely those details of presentation which constitute the individuality of one kind of story-telling over against another. If we are to use the category of intellectual biography in any way to assist our understanding and appreciation of the narrative of Acts, it is worth persisting with the comparison; but it is clear that we must move behind Diogenes himself to the hellenistic biographical tradition on which he drew.

The comparison between Luke and DL tacitly assumes this move, as we saw earlier; but it also assumes that the tradition which underlies Diogenes' work was different in significant ways from the collection as we have it now. This assumption is in tune with recent scholarship on Diogenes which has begun to stress his own contribution as an author, in contrast with an earlier scholarship which saw him simply as a compiler; the epigrams, the doxographical sections, and perhaps other elements of the overall structure of the work should probably be credited to Diogenes himself.[44] Moreover there is evidence from the papyri that some earlier biographical narration was less compressed than that of

---

41.   Cf. Desbordes, 'Introduction à Diogène Laërce', I, p. ii: 'le moi-narrateur ne peut renvoyer à aucun fait biographique réel'.

42.   Conflicting sources: e.g. 7.28 (Zeno's age at death); 5.2 (different reasons for name 'Peripatetic').

43.   Talbert, 'Biography, Ancient', *ABD* I, distinguishes the 'essential' from the 'accidental' in ancient biography; Burridge, *Gospels?* draws up an intentionally wide list of constitutive features.

44.   See especially the work of Mejer, *Diogenes Laertius and his Hellenistic Sources* and Desbordes, 'Introduction à Diogène Laërce', with further references there.

Diogenes.[45] But there is a limit to what can be discovered about the narrative mode of lost or fragmentary sources, since it is precisely the surface structure that tends to disappear in the process of epitomizing and excerpting;[46] and there does seem to be a constantly recurring pattern of biographical *topoi* very similar to that of Diogenes' Lives both among his sources and in other forms of intellectual biography.[47]

To conduct a thorough survey of narrative agenda and narrative mode in all the biographies which can be dated before the second century CE is outside the scope of this paper. But it is necessary for the comparison with Acts to understand something of the nature of the hellenistic tradition, and for these purposes the question of function is crucial. We began by selecting three possible functions for biography among those put forward by Talbert's hypothesis which could be useful for understanding Acts. Two at least of these, the 'succession' type and the 'exemplary' type, presuppose a stance of commitment to one particular school or teacher; and the hypothesis of a 'school' setting also depends on such a stance.[48] But it is precisely this sense of commitment which is absent from Diogenes Laertius at the level of narrative mode;[49] and indeed it is hard to see how a compendium which narrates the lives of philosophers from all the competing schools of Greek philosophy could serve the interests of any one school in this way. Diogenes himself is described by Ingemar Düring as 'an erudite amateur, isolated and without personal connections with the contemporary schools of learning'[50] – and as we have seen, this estimate is borne out by a detailed study of Diogenes' work. But the very act of compilation distances the biographer from commitment to any one teacher. To make the paradigm work, we have to assume that behind a collection like Diogenes' lie a number of single Lives (and successions), originating in the different schools.

45.   The biography of the Epicurean Philonides found at Herculaneum (P. Herc. 1044) is in a tantalisingly fragmentary state, but it looks to have contained real narrative, not just disconnected anecdotes: see Italo Gallo, *Frammenti Biografici da Papiri* (Rome: Ateno & Bizarri, 1980), II, pp. 55–95. The Ptolemaic 'Life and Apophthegms of Socrates' contained in P. Hibeh 182 includes a fuller form of the story told at DL 2.34; structurally, however, this is little more than a collection of anecdotes with some doxography (Gallo, *Frammenti Biografici da Papiri*, pp. 177–199).

46.   The publication in 1912 of a papyrus containing Satyrus' biography of Euripides (using a totally unexpected dialogue form) revealed how fragmentary our knowledge is and how dangerous it is to make assumptions on the basis of negative evidence: cf. Momigliano, *Development*, 115.

47.   Cf. Mejer, *Diogenes Laertius and his Hellenistic Sources*, pp. 92–93. Compare the *Life of Hippocrates* attributed (probably correctly) to Soranus (Pinault, *Hippocratic Lives*, pp. 7–8), which is different from the *Lives* of DL but not markedly so.

48.   Cf. Talbert, *Literary Patterns*, p. 134 ('cult document') and 'Biographies of Philosophers and Rulers', p. 1626, 'Do any Greco-Roman biographies arise out of, presuppose, or function in the interests of religious /worshipping communities?'

49.   As a colleague observed at a seminar conducted on DL, 'He doesn't appear to like any of these guys very much'.

50.   Düring, *Aristotle*, p. 469.

This is where our first problem lies, for most of the committed, individual Lives cited by Talbert are post-Christian in date (*Secundus*, Lucian's *Demonax*), some of them substantially so (Philostratus, *Porphyry*). For pre-Christian Lives we are reliant largely on citations and allusions in later authors, or on biographical remains (mostly fragmentary) in the papyri. Clearly there is a need for a thoroughgoing study of all the evidence here: but, it seems clear from the evidence we do have (and from Diogenes Laertius himself) that single, committed Lives of the type posited by Talbert would be the exception rather than the rule in the hellenistic biographical tradition.

The *Successions* of Sotion, one of Diogenes' most important predecessors, dating from the mid-second century BCE, traced 'the roster of teachers and pupils in a continuous series from the earliest times down to his own day': like Diogenes' work, this seems to have been an even-handed, disinterested study of all the philosophical schools.[51] Fraser argues that Sotion drew most of the substance for his work from 'a more elaborate work by Theophrastus': 'Such "successions" were already known in outline to Plato and Aristotle and were much elaborated by Theophrastus, from whom apparently Sotion extracted the biographical and discarded the purely philosophical elements'.[52] The writing up of 'successions' may thus be seen as part of the Peripatetic interest in drawing up a universal history of the intellectual life.[53] 'Successions' devoted to the work of a single school were 'apparently far less popular'; Mejer cites eight known examples, of which two are from Plutarch and two from Galen.[54]

Diogenes' other major predecessor, Hermippus of Smyrna, was contemporary with or slightly earlier than Sotion. His work was even wider in scope: 'Hermippus' *Lives* contained biographies of eminent men, arranged according to their field of activity: of the Seven Wise Men, of distinguished lawgivers, philosophers and others. The *Lives* thus supplemented the largely bibliographical information to be found in Callimachus' *Pinakes*'.[55] Hermippus (whose work is described by Fraser as 'unreliable and scandalous')[56] seems to owe less to the ideals of philosophical *imitatio* than to the bibliographical labours of Callimachus, engaged in cataloguing the Alexandrian library: it is a type of biography which has been aptly called 'pinacographic'. Again, this kind of biography seems to have been compilatory in origin: Satyrus' more elaborate *Lives of the Tragedians*, of which only the *Life of Euripides* survives, was also a compilation, and the tradition continues down to the *Lives of the Poets* and other so-called 'minor biographers'.[57] It is this fact that leads Mejer to the conclusion, 'It is in fact difficult

51.   P.M. Fraser, *Ptolemaic Alexandria* (Oxford: Clarendon Press, 1970), I, p. 453. On Sotion and the 'Succession' literature in general, see Mejer, *Diogenes Laertius and his Hellenistic Sources*, pp. 40–42, 62–74.

52.   Fraser, *Ptolemaic Alexandria*, p. 469.

53.   Cf. Momigliano, *Development*, p. 119 on the Peripatetic interest in historical research.

54.   Mejer, *Diogenes Laertius and his Hellenistic Sources*, pp. 74–75.

55.   Fraser, *Ptolemaic Alexandria*, I, p. 781. Cf. also Mejer, *Diogenes Laertius and his Hellenistic Sources*, pp. 32–34, 90–93.

56.   Fraser, *Ptolemaic Alexandria*, I, p. 453.

57.   Cf. works listed in n. 9 and n. 11 above.

to find any difference between biographies of philosophers and those of other types of personalities except perhaps that the former contained more apophthegms and anecdotes involving sayings. That there was little or no difference is also indicated by the fact that the more prolific authors of biographies were not philosophers. Thus, we have no reason to assume that the motivation for writing biographies of philosophers was any different from the general motive of Hellenistic biography, sc. the wish to, depict a famous personality's ἦθος and πράξεις'.[58] Even among the biographers who can more properly be assigned to the Peripatetic school, with its interest in the moral qualities associated with the philosophic life, much of the material of which we have evidence seems to be compilatory and comparative rather than individual.[59] The typical title is περί βίων, not βίος τοῦ δεῖνού: *On the Tyrants of Sicily, On the Socratics, On Poetry and Poets*: the whole is seen by Stuart as a subdivision of the hellenistic impulse to 'polymathy'.[60] Such material could be used in the polemics between the different schools, but its character was in many ways anything but philosophical:

> Hellenistic biography was far more elaborately erudite than any previous biographical composition. It was also far more curious about details, anecdotes, witticisms and eccentricities. In so far as it supported one philosophy against another and helped its readers to understand writers and artists, it can be said to have pursued professional aims... But...men did not write biographies because they were philosophically-minded or because they were engaged in some kind of intellectual or political controversy. The educated man of the Hellenistic world was curious about the lives of famous people.[61]

There is, then, little evidence to support the assumption that Diogenes Laertius put his collection together from a number of originally separate, single biographies originating in the different schools. What seems to lie behind Diogenes (as is in fact perfectly clear from his own allusions to his sources) are more compilations, showing all the variety of interests of hellenistic erudition. Some of the material must go back to the archives of the individual schools: letters and wills fall most obviously into this category. Some is drawn directly from known literary sources (Xenophon, Plato). Chronological notices go back to the bible of hellenistic chronology, Apollodorus' *Chronica*; the lists of 'Homonyms' which close every Life come, as Diogenes tells us himself, from a treatise on 'Men of the Same Name'. The gossipy notes about the bisexual love-lives of the philosophers may go back in some cases to a polemical source like Aristoxenus' hostile biography of Socrates,[62] but Diogenes himself ascribes them to a treatise 'On the Luxury of the Ancients' which must have made fruity reading. It is no wonder that, at a seminar which I conducted recently on Diogenes, one participant suggested that his work looks like 'a kind of coffee-table book, with just the information that the educated person needs to know': and this character must

58. Mejer, *Diogenes Laertius and his Hellenistic Sources*, p. 93. Cf. Momigliano, *Development*, p. 84.
59. Cf. especially Stuart, *Epochs of Greek and Roman Biography*, ch. 5.
60. Stuart, *Epochs of Greek and Roman Biography*, p. 129.
61. Momigliano, *Development*, pp. 119–120.
62. Stuart, *Epochs of Greek and Roman Biography*, pp. 132–54.

be seen in large part as an accurate reflection of the hellenistic biographical tradition on which he drew.

So the origins of the 'heroic' biography of the philosopher seem as elusive as those of the so-called 'aretalogy of the divine sage' which in many ways it resembles.[63] Behind the encyclopaedic compilations of the early Empire lie, for the most part, not individual Lives but more series and collections. Behind them, and feeding into this literary activity at every stage, seem to be the real hard currency of biography in the hellenistic schools: sequences and catalogues, floating anecdotes and sayings, a name attached to a teacher, a name or an anecdote attached to a doctrine or discovery, archival collections of letters or wills. The process may be illustrated briefly by looking at the meagre biographical information preserved by the tradition about Hippocrates of Chios, not the famous doctor but a mathematician of the fifth century BCE of whom virtually nothing is known and of whom no 'Life' was ever written.

Björnbo in the *RE* article which bears his name,[64] argues that the biographical tradition about this Hippocrates rests on three pieces of evidence:

a) a notice in Proclus, believed to go back to Eudemus, which places H. in a chronological sequence: 'After Pythagoras. . .came Anaxagoras and Oinopides, who was younger than Anaxagoras. . .and after them Hippocrates of Chios, who discovered the quadrature of the moon, and Theodorus...'

b) Aristotle, *Meteor.* 1.342b35ff.: 'Hippocrates of Chios and his disciples held views similar to this'.

c) Aristotle, *Eth. Eud.* 8.2.5 1247a17–20: <do men succeed because of wisdom? no:> 'for example, Hippocrates was skilled in geometry but was thought to be stupid and unwise in other matters, and it is said that on a voyage owing to foolishness he lost a great deal of money taken from him by the collectors of the two-per-cent duty at Byzantium'.

Here we have three isolated biographical details, linked (a) to chronological sequence, (b) to a particular scientific hypothesis, and (c) to an ethical point. The last belongs clearly to a well-known class of anecdotes on the foolishness of philosophers and mathematicians, of a type which Jaeger calls the 'absent-minded astronomer'.[65] The three illustrate neatly, albeit at a very early stage of the tradition, the three major loci for biographical interest in the hellenistic schools: sequencing and chronology; doxography/bibliography; and ethics. In the last, which clearly alludes to a fuller narrative whose details may have been already lost when Aristotle cited the example, we have a type of moral paradigm expressed in the form of a biographical anecdote. This particular topos seems to express popular sentiment of a mildly (though generally affectionately) anti-philosophical flavour, but there is a related group, going back to the fifth

---

63.   See on this especially Cox, *Biography in Late Antiquity*, pp. 30–44.

64.   *RE* 8.2 (1913), pp. 1781–1801, art. 'Hippokrates (14)'.

65.   Werner Jaeger, *Aristotle: Fundamentals of the History of his Development* (trans. R. Robinson; Oxford: Clarendon Press, 2nd edn, 1948) Appendix II, pp. 426–61, 'On the Origin and Cycle of the Philosophic Ideal of Life'.

century, which 'owe their coinage entirely to men of a different class, men who were themselves full of the ethos of what was later called the "theoretic life", and made themselves a sort of symbol for it in the striking utterances of the wise men of old'.[66] It is here that we come closest to the biography of the sage as a paradigm for the philosophic life, but this function inheres in the isolated anecdote: there is no biography as such. We are of course largely dependent on literary sources, some of which in the later period are biographical, for the preservation of most of these 'floating' anecdotes; but the evidence of the papyri, as well as the existence of unattached anecdotes like this, confirms that they also circulated independently.[67]

In terms of the 'development' of intellectual biography, then, what we seem to have is not the expected progression

Anecdote → Life → Collected Lives

but one which misses out the middle stage:

Anecdote → ... → collection

– but the collection may just as well be a series of anecdotes (*Chriae*) or a series on a topic as a collection of *bioi*. When and why this pattern changed to encourage the composition of individual Lives remains a mystery. It would be a mistake to take it as an inevitable development: the rabbinic school tradition, with an essentially similar repertoire of catalogues and anecdotes, never developed individual biography.[68] Whatever the explanation, it seems to be the fact that the crucial steps were taken in a number of adjacent areas at around the turn of the eras: Andronicus' *Life of Aristotle* (perhaps),[69] the Epicurean *Life of Philonides* (P. Here. 1044), Philo's *Vita Mosis*, the Gospels and Acts, and then the second-century examples like Secundus the Silent Philosopher and Lucian. Perhaps we should remember Ben Perry's famous warning about looking for the 'development' of the novel: 'The first romance was planned and written by an individual author, its inventor. He conceived it on a Tuesday afternoon in July'.[70]

IV. *The Genre of Acts*

It is time to return to Acts, and ask how this material may help us to read Luke's composition. On the face of it, intellectual biography in the hellenistic period fails to provide a clear literary model for Acts, at least if by that we mean a full biography committed to an individual school and describing the teacher's life in

66.   Jaeger, *Aristotle*, p. 428.
67.   Cf. Gallo, *Frammenti Biografici da Papiri*, II, pp. 221, 229–30, 317, 331–33, 345, 351, 363, 371, 385–86.
68.   P.S. Alexander, 'Rabbinic Biography and the Biography of Jesus: A Survey of the Evidence', in C.M. Tuckett (ed.), *Synoptic Studies* (JSNTSup, 7; Sheffield: JSOT Press, 1984), pp. 19–50.
69.   On Andronicus, see esp. Düring, *Aristotle*, pp. 413–67. D. argues that Andronicus' work was not in fact a biography of Aristotle but a kind of 'catalogue raisonné' in which biographical data were used to determine the chronology and authenticity of the texts discussed.
70.   B.E. Perry, *The Ancient Romances* (Sather Classical Lectures, 37; Berkeley: University of California Press, 1967), p. 175.

such a way as to provide a moral paradigm for imitation. Biographical texts of this kind, widespread as they are in the period of late antiquity, seem to have been far from typical of the hellenistic tradition. But if we broaden our definition of biography to include not only the fully-fledged biographical texts but also the underlying traditions and patterns of thought, it is not difficult to see many points of interest for Acts.

The hellenistic school tradition offers clear evidence of biographical interest clustering around three foci: chronology and succession; doxography and bibliography; and the paradigm of the sage. This interest is expressed in biographical anecdotes and notices which circulate independently and may be combined in a variety of different 'collections'. I would suggest that the existence of these varied foci of biographical concern is of considerable interest to students of Acts. In all the years of debate about the existence or non-existence of 'sources' or 'traditions' behind the narrative of Acts, few have paused to ask what kind of social context might provide a matrix for the production or preservation of such material. It seems to me that the hellenistic school tradition provides just such a social matrix whose value has yet to be exploited for Acts. Parallels worth exploring include: the preservation of isolated anecdotes about famous teachers; the interest (as Talbert rightly saw) in the arrangement of disparate teachers into a 'succession'; concern for chronology and sequence; and the tendency to extract biographical details from a writer's works (especially letters) in default of external biographical information. And this interest was not limited to the philosophical schools; the preservation of the prefatorial letters of Archimedes and Apollonius of Perge, the Hippocratic pseudepigrapha and the Lives which they apparently inspired, and the bibliographical 'autobiographies' of Galen suggest that similar interests, if less frenetically expressed, existed in mathematical and medical circles.[71] As we argued above, the very fact that all this 'historical' activity was going on in the schools has relevance for the genre of Acts, which does not fit easily into the patterns of political historiography.

In this final section I would like to explore one particular template from the repertoire of hellenistic philosophical biography which I think did exert some influence on the structuring of Luke's Pauline narrative, and that is the hugely – perhaps uniquely – influential paradigm of Socrates. Socrates, though he figures as one philosopher among others in Diogenes Laertius, is actually in a rather different position from most of the subjects of philosophical biography. Historians of the genre dispute whether or not the Socratic writings of Plato and Xenophon are to be classified as 'biography'.[72] What is important for our purposes, however, is that what lies behind the tradition, in this case, is not a series of disconnected anecdotes or doxographical notices, but a substantial body of written texts operating on a level of literary complexity which Diogenes Laertius lacks. Here, as nowhere else in the hellenistic biographical tradition, are

---

71.   For Hippocrates, cf. n. 19 above. Galen's two short treatises, *De libris propriis* and *De ordine librorum suorum* may be found in vol. II of the *Scripta Minora* in the Teubner edition (Kühn, vol. XIX).

72.   Momigliano, *Development*, p. 17.

detailed narrative and first-person discourse; even if we discount the bulk of the Platonic dialogues,[73] Xenophon's less ambitious *Memorabilia* describe Socratic encounters with far more detail than the curtly-formulated *chriae* of Diogenes Laertius. Moreover, we know that this was not a fossilized literary tradition. Socratic anecdotes (not derived from Plato or Xenophon) are almost as common as chriae relating to the Cynic Diogenes of Sinope; Diogenes Laertius knows some of them, and some are collected in P. Hibeh 182.[74] A vigorous letter-writing activity clustered around the fourth-century sage and his disciples, probably dating from the Augustan age.[75] Socrates is cited as a moral paradigm by first-century writers like Seneca, Dio Chrysostom and Epictetus. And, perhaps most significant for us, episodes from his life (and even more, his death) provided a template for describing the lives of others in a number of texts dating from the first century and the beginning of the second.[76]

1. *The divine call.* The story of Paul's 'call' occupies a prime position at the beginning of his biography in Acts (ch. 9), and its twofold repetition in chs. 22 and 26 keeps it at the forefront of the readers' attention.[77] Similarly, Socrates' mission begins with an oracle from Delphi (Plato, *Apol.* 20e–22a) which inspires his mission and which he regards in the light of a military commission: 'the God gave me a station, as I believed and understood, with orders to spend my life in philosophy and in examining myself and others' (Plato, *Apol.* 28e, LCL; cf. Epictetus 1.9). This oracle figures prominently in Diogenes Laertius' account, where it is described as 'universally known' (2.37, Yonge); it also provided a template for a number of other 'call' stories attached to the lives of philosophers.[78] Note that the primary literary expression of this call is in the first-person *Apology* in which Socrates, on trial for his life, defends his own obedience to the divine message: compare Paul's dual first-person account of his call in his own *apologia*, Acts 22 and 26.

2. *The mission.* Paul's divine call points directly to his mission, which forms the central section of his biography (Acts 13–19). For Socrates, too, the Chaerephon-oracle is the beginning of a lifelong commitment: 'therefore I am still even now going about and searching and investigating at the God's behest anyone, whether citizen or foreigner...and by reason of this occupation I have no leisure to attend to any of the affairs of the state worth mentioning, or of my own, but

---

73. As ancient scholars seem on the whole to have done: DL 2.45.

74. Cf. nn. 67 and 45 above.

75. A.J. Malherbe (ed.), *The Cynic Epistles* (SBLSBS, 12; Missoula; Scholars Press, 1977), p. 2.

76. The data are collected in Klaus Döring, *Exemplum Socratis: Studien zur Sokratesnachwirkung in der kynisch-stoischen Popularphilosophie der frühen Christentum* (Hermes Einzelschriften, 42; Wiesbaden: Franz Steiner, 1979). See also A. Ronconi, 'Exitus illustrium virorum', in T. Klauser (ed.), *Reallexikon für Antike und Christentum* (Stuttgart: Hiersemann, 1966), VI, cols. 1258–68.

77. Cf. n. 28 above.

78. Cf. Gigon, 'Antike Erzählungen'.

am in vast poverty on account of my service to the God' (Plato, *Apol.* 23b LCL; cf. DL 11.21–22). Dio Chrysostom models his own mission on Socrates' in the *De Fuga* (*Or.* 13). Like Socrates', Dio's mission begins with an inquiry to the oracle (422R, 243.1–12 Teubner); unlike Socrates', it involves travel 'until you come to the farthest part of the earth' (243.10–11), an Odyssean lifestyle only bearable under direct orders from God (243.12–17).[79] The detailed rationale of this mission is presented as 'some ancient discourse, said to be by a certain Socrates, which he never ceased proclaiming, shouting and raising his voice everywhere and before everybody, both in the palaestras and in the Lyceum and before the law courts and in the market-place, like a *deus ex machina*, as somebody said' (244.17–22).[80]

3. *The daimonion*. One of the charges against Socrates is that of 'introducing new gods (καινὰ δαιμόνια) which the city does not believe in' (Plato, *Apol.* 24b, DL 2.40). The charge arises out of Socrates' claim to receive divine guidance at every step from his own *daimonion* (Xenophon, *Mem.* 1.2–5; DL 2.32). The identity of this *daimonion* was receiving renewed attention at the end of the first century; Socrates was also acquiring an enhanced mantic reputation as a 'prophet'.[81] Paul too experienced direct divine guidance at perplexing moments (e.g. 16.6–10), and was accused (in Athens) of introducing new gods (ξενὰ διαμόνια: Acts 17.18). Luke's choice of words is interesting here. This is the only occasion in the New Testament where διαμόνια is used in a non-pejorative sense: by implication, the word refers to 'Jesus and the resurrection', and the charge is never denied.[82] Note also that in Diogenes Laertius the Areopagus is regularly the scene for the trial of a philosopher.[83]

4. *Tribulations*. The mission is described by Socrates as involving 'herculean' labours. The Hercules metaphor is expanded in the Cynic tradition, but others know of extensive catalogues of Socrates' 'labours': commentators have long suspected that this kind of list provided the model for Paul's own catalogue of his labours in 2 Corinthians 10–13.[84] Seneca, *Ep.* 104.27–28 provides a good example of such a catalogue:

> If, however, you desire a pattern (*exemplum*), take Socrates, a long-suffering old man, who was sea-tossed amid every hardship and yet was unconquered both by poverty

---

79.   DL 2.22 seems to presuppose a pattern of the philosophic life which does involve travel (ἀποδημία): Socrates did not travel, but most philosophers did.

80.   Cf. also Epictetus 3.1.19–20, 3.21.19, 1.12.3 (S. paired with Odysseus), 3.22.26.

81.   Plutarch, *De genio Socratis* (*Moralia*, 575b–598f.); Döring, *Exemplum Socratis*, pp. 11–12.

82.   Socratic allusions in Acts 17 are suggested tentatively by Hans Dieter Betz, *Der Apostel Paulus und die sokratische Tradition* (BHT, 45; Tübingen: Siebeck-Mohr, 1972), p. 38 and n. 182; more decisively Karl Olav Sandnes, 'Paul and Socrates: the Aim of Paul's Areopagus Speech', *JSNT* 50 (1993), pp. 13–26.

83.   Trials on the Areopagus: DL 2.101, 2.116, 7.169.

84.   Cf. Betz, *Der Apostel Paulus*, passim.

(which his troubles at home made more burdensome) and by toil (*laboribus*), including the drudgery of military service. (LCL).[85]

Socrates is not the only example cited, however. Like Lucian (*Demonax* 2), Seneca feels the need to present an *exemplum* nearer home, so he follows the catalogue of Socrates' troubles with a parallel list of Cato's who, 'just as much as Socrates, declared allegiance to liberty in the midst of slavery' (§§ 29–33). The fact that the actual circumstances of the two lives were quite different does not affect the parallel.

5. *Persecution*. For Socrates, obedience to the divine call is accompanied from the start by hostility and persecution from his fellow-citizens (Plato, *Apol.* 22e–23a); in fact much of the *Apology* is an expansion on this theme. Diogenes Laertius links the two directly:

> very often, while arguing and discussing points that arose, he was treated with great violence and beaten, and pulled about, and laughed at and ridiculed by the multitude. But he bore all this with great equanimity. So that once, when he had been kicked and buffeted about, and had borne it all patiently, and some one expressed his surprise, he said, 'Suppose an ass had kicked me, would you have had me bring an action against him?' (DL 2.21, tr. Yonge).

The link is made even more explicitly in Acts, where the apostle's call is to persecution as much as to mission (9.16; 22.18; 26.17) and the narrative devotes as much time to the former as to the latter.

6. *Trial*. The culmination of years of hostility, and the focal point of the Socrates tradition, is the trial which leads to his death: the accidents of literary history mean that a disproportionate amount of Socratic biography takes the form of *apologia*, i.e. his own defence speech spoken in the first person. For Paul, too, the series of trials which brings Acts to an end takes up an apparently disproportionate amount of narrative space (below), and involves a substantial amount of first-person *apologia*. Note here again Luke's choice of words: ἀπολογία and its cognate verb occur seven times in this context, more than anywhere else in the New Testament. Socrates was of course the philosophical martyr par excellence, the prototype of a long line of sages confronting tyrants: 'the first philosopher who was condemned to death and executed' (DL 2.20 tr. Yonge) but not the last. Epictetus is particularly fond of citing Socrates as a paradigm for courageous opposition to tyranny.[86] John Darr in a recent book draws attention to Luke's casting of Herod Agrippa in the 'tyrant' role in the Gospel

---

85.   Note that Gummere (LCL translator) implies a metaphorical shipwreck even for this most landlocked of sages: *iactare* is often cited in the context of a storm at sea, cf. C.T. Lewis and C. Short, *A Latin Dictionary* (Oxford: Clarendon Press, 1879), sv.

86.   Cf. 1.19.6 ('Who becomes a zealous follower of yours [ζηλωτής] as [men did] of Socrates?'), 1.29.16ff., 29; 2.2.8ff., 15ff.; 2.5.18–19; 2.13.24; 4.1.123 (parallel with Helvidius); 4.7.28.

accounts of the trial of Jesus: there are several contenders for this role in Acts, but there can be no doubt that the part of the philosophic hero falls pre-eminently to Paul.[87]

7. *Prison*. 'When we read Acts as a whole, rather than selectively, it is Paul the prisoner even more than Paul the missionary whom we are meant to remember.'[88] As the dramatic setting for two of Plato's most famous dialogues, prison inevitably figures just as large in the biography of Socrates.[89] Two linked motifs are relevant here. Socrates, like Paul, sings hymns in prison: this minor detail of Plato's account (*Phaedo* 60d) is mentioned by Diogenes Laertius (2.42) who cites the actual words of the hymn in question. In Epictetus' hands, however, the episode becomes not an opportunity for pedantry but a pattern of philosophic constancy:

> A platform and a prison is each a place, the one high (ὑψηλός), the other low (ταπεινός); but your moral purpose can be kept the same, if you wish to keep it the same, in either place. And then we shall be emulating (ζηλωταί) Socrates, when we are able to write paeans in prison. (2.6.27, cf. 4.4.23).

The theme may be a development of a longer passage in the *Phaedo*, where Socrates compares his deathbed discourses with the songs of the swans who 'when they feel that they are to die, sing most and best in their joy that they are to go to the God whose servants they are' (84e–85b). A Socratic reading of Acts suggests that we might see not only Paul's hymn-singing in Philippi (Acts 16) but also his Paul's determination to carry on 'preaching and teaching' in his Roman prison (Acts 28.23–30) in the same light.

8. *Death*. The Socratic paradigm was, above all, a paradigm for facing death: in Seneca's words (*Ep.* 104.22) Socrates 'will show you how to die if it be necessary'. Epictetus makes the point countless times: Socrates' conviction that his accusers 'may kill me, but they cannot harm me' is cited on several occasions in the *Discourses* and is the motto chosen to close the *Enchiridion* (53.4).[90] His death, moreover, was explicitly paralleled with those of contemporary martyrs among the Stoic opposition under Nero and Domitian: with Helvidius Priscus (Epict. 4.1.123), with Cato and other Roman heroes of an earlier age (Seneca *Ep.* 98.12, 104.27–33). Seneca himself seems to have consciously modelled his own death on that of Socrates, and it seems clear that Tacitus' written account of the episode has the Socratic paradigm in view, following the precedent of

---

87.   John A. Darr, *On Character Building: The Reader and the Rhetoric of Characterization in Luke-Acts* (Westminster: John Knox Press, 1992), ch. 6; cf. Ronconi, 'Exitus illustrium virorum' (RAC 6.1264) on the death of Herod in Acts 12.23. ·

88.   Maddox, *The Purpose of Luke-Acts*, p. 67; cf. Richard Pervo, *Profit with Delight* (Philadelphia: Fortress Press, 1987) on the prominence of prison scenes in Acts.

89.   Esp. Epictetus: e.g.1.1.23–24, 1.4.24, 1.12.23.

90.   Döring, *Exemplum Socratis*, p. 45 and following.

Thrasea Paetus, Junius Rusticus and other Stoic biographers who patterned their subjects' deaths on that of their most famous predecessor.[91]

What about Acts? As we have seen, the last nine chapters of Acts are structured around an event which is never narrated directly, Paul's impending death. In Maddox's words, 'Since we have on other grounds every reason to judge that Luke composes with a careful eye to the dramatic movement and balance of his work, we may regard this long, final section as intended by the author to carry an emphasis and to form at least in some degree the goal and climax of his composition'.[92] A Socratic reading of Acts may provide at least a partial explanation for this remarkable structure. Chapters 20 and 21 play a crucial role here: the renewed insistence on Paul's readiness to face 'imprisonment and afflictions' (20.22–24), repeated prophecies of disaster (20.23; 21.10–11)[93] and the tearful farewells (20.36–37; 21.5; 21.12–13) which do nothing to break Paul's resolve (21.13–14). Note the sudden appearance of 'wives and children' in 21.5, and the implied inclusion of the daughters of Philip among 'the people there' in 21.12: this is very much a 'women's scene' in Socratic tradition, based on the removal of the weeping Xanthippe in *Phaedo* 60a and Socrates' refusal to be swayed by the claims of wife and children (*Crito* 45cd). The fact that this is a 'we-section' increases the Socratic effect (the narrative of the *Phaedo* is also in the first person plural): the final scene (21.12–14) strongly recalls the weeping of Socrates' friends in *Phaedo* 65–67, and his words of acceptance to Crito: 'if this is the will of the gods, so let it be'.[94]

V. Conclusion

The Socratic paradigm which I have sketched here does not exist in this form in any known biography of Socrates. It is not a 'genre' or a 'literary model' so much as a narrative pattern familiar to a wide range of writers in the first century CE, and used by them in a wide variety of styles and literary *Gattungen*. In these texts and others like them we can see the life of Socrates being used as a template for describing crucial events in their own lives or in the lives of more immediate heroes, particularly by those writers concerned with chronicling the deaths of philosophers who had faced martyrdom under Nero and Domitian. In the words of a modern novelist, 'Most people like to fit themselves into a story they already know; it makes them feel a bigger part of life than they are'.[95] I would suggest that

91. Oswyn Murray, 'The "Quinquennium Neronis" and the Stoics', *Historia* 14 (1965), pp. 41–61; Miriam Griffin, *Seneca: A Philosopher in Politics* (Oxford: Clarendon Press, 1976), ch. 11; Ronconi, 'Exitus illustrium virorum'.

92. Maddox, *The Purpose of Luke-Acts*, p. 66.

93. Note Diogenes Laertius relates a tale of a magus coming to Athens from Syria and foretelling Socrates' violent death (2.45).

94. *Crito* 43d, cited by Epictetus, *Ench.* 53.3 and elsewhere, cf. Döring, *Exemplum Socratis*, p. 45.

95. Amanda Cross, *No Word from Winifred* (London: Virago, 1987), p. 30.

this Socratic paradigm was available to Luke's readers and offered them the possibility of fitting Paul's story – and by implication their own – into 'a story they already knew', one which could work alongside the paradigm of the prophet which Luke employs to such good effect in the Gospel and in the first half of Acts. In Storm's words, 'so *ist* es, Herr'; that's how it *is*, this story from the past tells us something about our own lives: 'dem Sokrates gaben sie ein Gift zu trinken, und unsern Herrn Christus schlugen sie an das Kreuz!'

Chapter 4

'IN JOURNEYINGS OFTEN':
VOYAGING IN THE ACTS OF THE APOSTLES AND IN GREEK ROMANCE*

Voyaging is integral to the plot of both Acts and Greek romance. In Acts, right through from the opening mission statement at 1.8, geographical movement is a central component in the narrative: travel is not an optional extra for Jesus' followers, and especially not for Paul. For the Greek novels,[1] too, it may justly be claimed that the voyage is not simply one adventurous element among others that may befall the hero and heroine: it is *the* adventure which undergirds the plot of ancient romance. In Reardon's words, 'In the novel, the obstacles that circumstance puts in the way of a happy union are those consequent upon extensive travel in the Eastern Mediterranean and its hinterland – from Sicily to Babylon, from the Bosporus to Ethiopia'.[2] The travel motif thus provides a good starting-point for a comparative analysis of Acts and the Greek novels: good, because it is a motif essential to the plot of both; but also manageable in that it makes it possible to select salient narrative features for analysis. We are beginning

---

*   Versions of this paper have been read at the Centre for East Roman Studies, University of Warwick; at the Manchester-Lausanne Colloquium; and at the International Meeting of the SBL, Leuven 1994. I am grateful to friends and colleagues in all these places for their many helpful comments. It was first published as '"In Journeyings Often": Voyaging in the Acts of the Apostles and in Greek Romance', in C.M. Tuckett (ed.), *Luke's Literary Achievement: Collected Essays* (JSNTSup, 116; Sheffield: Sheffield Academic Press, 1995), pp. 17–49, reprinted here with the kind permission of the Continuum International Publishing Group.

1.   There is a growing and vigorous scholarly literature on the Greek novel. For trans-lations and fundamental bibliography, see B.P. Reardon (ed.), *Collected Ancient Greek Novels* (Berkeley: University of California Press, 1989 [hereinafter: Reardon, *Novels*]). T. Hägg, *The Novel in Antiquity* (English edn [revised]; Oxford: Blackwell, 1983) provides a readable and insightful introduction to the genre; J.R. Morgan and R. Stoneman (eds.), *Greek Fiction: The Greek Novel in Context* (London: Routledge, 1994) is a wide-ranging and stimulating collection of essays. The most concerted and convincing comparison with Acts to date may be found in R.I. Pervo, *Profit with Delight: The Literary Genre of the Acts of the Apostles* (Philadelphia: Fortress Press, 1987).

2.   B.P. Reardon, 'The Greek Novel', *Phoenix* 23, 1966, pp. 291–309 [hereinafter: Reardon, 'Greek Novel']), pp. 292–93; cf. also *idem, The Form of Greek Romance* (Princeton: University Press, 1991 [hereinafter: Reardon, *Form*]) pp. 15–16, 25. The obvious exception is Longus' *Daphnis and Chloe,* but even this is described by Reardon as 'a journey in time' (*Form*, p. 33).

to make great strides in the understanding of the literary environment of the NT texts;[3] but if this form of literary analysis is to make any progress, I believe, it is time to move beyond the often vague and general observations of the pioneers and undertake serious and concerted comparative studies with an eye to the differences as much as to the similarities between texts.

In a single article only a limited amount of such study can be attempted, and the texts chosen will perforce be selective. Greek romance is a large and complex phenomenon; here I have chosen to focus on the earliest of the full novel-texts we possess, Chariton's story of *Chaereas and Callirhoe*[4] and the *Ephesiaca* of Xenophon of Ephesus.[5] These are not only the closest in date to Acts but also (by common consent) the least 'sophistic': which is not to say that they lack literary art, but that they are the closest of the novels to the popular roots of Greek romance. And even within the theme of 'voyaging' I cannot hope to do justice to all its possible ramifications. For this reason I have largely (though not entirely) avoided the 'shipwreck' theme, which has received its fair share of attention. Instead I have tried to isolate three areas for concerted comparison within the broader theme: the structure of the voyage in terms of plot; the mental maps which the narrative presupposes; and the significance of the sea as a mode of travel.

The Voyage as Plot

'This book will make a traveller of thee.'[6]

The use of a voyage, real or imaginary, to provide the essential structure for a narrative must be one of the oldest plot-devices in literature, and is certainly not unique to Greek romance. The journey is a simple means of providing momentum and maintaining interest. Movement in space carries the story-line forward in 'alternating marches and halts', and provides a thread on which a whole series of adventures can be hung: as Philip Städter has observed in a different context, 'It is one of the features of a journey narrative, whether

---

3.   Notably (for example) D.E. Aune, *The New Testament in its Literary Environment* (Cambridge: James Clarke, 1988); K. Berger, 'Hellenistische Gattungen im neuen Testament', *ANRW* 2.25.2 (1984), pp. 1034–1380.

4.   Chariton: see Reardon, *Novels*, pp. 17–124. Greek text with French translation in the Budé series: *Chariton: le Roman de Chairéas et Callirhoé* (ed. G. Molinié; Paris: 'Les Belles Lettres', 1979). Reardon (*Novels*, p. 17) dates the text 'around the middle of the first century A.D.', Molinié (p. 2) between the third quarter of the first century and the first quarter of the second. [Note: G.P. Goold's Loeb edition of Chariton's *Callirhoe* (LCL 481; Cambridge, MA: Harvard University Press, 1995) was not available when this paper was first published. Goold dates the novel to the late first century.]

5.   Xenophon: see Reardon, *Novels*, pp. 125–169. Greek text with French translation in the Budé series: *Xénophon d'Éphèse: Les Ephésiaques*, (ed. G. Dalmeyda; Paris: Les Belles Lettres, 1962). Xenophon is generally dated around the beginning of the second century CE.

6.   John Bunyan, *The Pilgrim's Progress* (from 'The Author's Apology for his Work').

periplus or land journey (such as those of Xenophon and Alexander), that it may be expanded at will at any point'.[7] The travelling itself may simply serve as a linking device which transports the characters from one scene to another, so that the exotic location (and the adventures which take place there) are more important in narrative terms than the route by which it is reached; or the travel may itself become the focus of attention.

The travel plot in Chariton is relatively simple. In the opening scene the lovers meet, marry and are divided: Chaereas' baseless jealousy of his pregnant wife causes him to give her a kick, which leads to her apparent death and (real) burial. Pirates break in to rob the tomb, find Callirhoe recovering consciousness, and abduct her as part of their booty. The rest of the narrative recounts the separate adventures of the parted lovers: when they meet again, we know we have reached the climax of the story and the expected 'happy ending'. But before this can happen, the pair have to travel from Sicily in the far west of the Greek world to Babylon beyond its eastern frontiers: Chaereas follows the trail of Callirhoe to Miletus, where he is himself captured and enslaved in nearby Caria; both are then taken by circumstances beyond their control to Babylon, where a sensational trial scene reveals them to each other but fails to resolve the complex situation that prevents their reunion; war with Egypt takes both to Syria and Phoenicia, where Chaereas' military prowess finally rewards him with the recapture of his wife on the island of Aradus. The final scene recounts their return to Syracuse to live 'happily ever after' (Figure 1).

Xenophon follows essentially the same plot-structure, but with more complicated travels. His hapless pair, Anthia and Habrocomes, are likewise married in the opening scene (in Ephesus), set out on a honeymoon voyage (by which means their parents unaccountably hope to escape the perils prophesied by an oracle), are captured by pirates, sold as slaves, and separated: the rest of the narrative recounts Habrocomes' search for Anthia in Syria and Cilicia, then in Egypt and Ethiopia, finally in Sicily and Italy, before the two are reunited in Rhodes and sail back to Ephesus to begin their married life (Figure 2).

In a sense, then, both plots follow the familiar *nostos* structure of the Odyssey, in which the voyage achieves its closure with a return to the point of departure. By comparison with the Odyssey, however, Chariton devotes far more attention to the voyage out than to the homeward journey, which takes up only a few lines of narrative. Xenophon's structure is a little more symmetrical, though his chaotic management of narrative time makes it hard to be dogmatic.[8] In both the primary motivation for the voyage is the separation of the hero and heroine, which means that both are also committed to following the simultaneous adventures of two protagonists, not one – a problem which Chariton solves with characteristic grace and economy, Xenophon rather more creakily: 'Xenophon can think of no very effective means of conducting the parallel actions, and ends

7.   P. Städter, *Arrian of Nicomedia* (Chapel Hill: University of North Carolina Press, 1980), pp. 76, 126

8.   Part or all of the text may be an epitome: see T. Hägg, 'Die *Ephesiaka* des Xenophon Ephesius: Original oder Epitome?', *Classica et Mediaevalia* 27 (1966), pp. 118–61.

up moving his characters more and more wildly around the Mediterranean, like demented chessmen'.[9] In Chariton's narrative, Chaereas and Callirhoe actually are never very far from one another: geographically, Chaereas succeeds in dogging his wife's footsteps fairly closely throughout, and the barriers to their reunion are as much social as geographical (a possibility exploited much more fully later in *Daphnis and Chloe*).[10] Xenophon's more complex plot is still worked out in terms of paired voyages (tripled at times where the robber chief Hippothous becomes a third major character): but the underlying shape of a single journey, with the movement following a fundamental loss + search + finding structure, is clearly visible in both.

The overall motivation of the voyaging is thus tied to the essential plot-motif of separation, and in the hands of a competent narrator like Chariton this aspect of the plot is generally managed in a plausible fashion. In Xenophon, the travels of the protagonists are noticeably less well-motivated: in other words it becomes more obvious with Xenophon that the voyage is a plot necessity which over-rides the novelist's 'literary conscience'.[11] Some journeys are completely unmotivated (like Habrocomes' trip to Italy), others simply puzzling (like the original honeymoon trip, which seems precisely the wrong response to an oracle predicting disaster at sea).[12] Sometimes it is simply not clear whether travel is undertaken for the sake of adventure, or whether adventures occur in order to provide an excuse for travel: Habrocomes' trial 'before the prefect of Egypt' seems to be little more than a device for getting the hero to Alexandria after he has inconveniently got himself shipwrecked at the wrong end of the Delta (3.12.6). Even in Chariton, where motivation is generally speaking more plausible, the referral of the trial to the Persian King (4.6–7) can be seen as a device for creating geographical movement to an exotic location; and travel is clearly seen as an adventure in its own right, as part of the *pathos* which the characters have to endure before they can be re-united. Thus Chariton's last book begins:[13]

> Now that Chaereas had made honourable amends to Love, in that he had wandered the world from west to east and gone through untold suffering, Aphrodite took pity on him; having harassed by land and sea the handsome couple she had originally brought together, she decided now to reunite them (8.1).

What happens if we try to read Acts against this background? The use of the voyage motif shows both similarities with and differences from its use in the

9.   Reardon, *Form*, p. 36. Cf. T. Hägg, *Narrative Technique in Ancient Greek Romances: Studies of Chariton, Xenophon Ephesius, and Achilles Tatius* (Skrifter Utgivna av Svenska Institutet i Athen, ser. 8, VIII; Uppsala: Almqvist & Wiksell, 1971), ch. 4.

10.   Reardon, *Form*, pp. 30–34.

11.   The phrase is Reardon's: 'Greek Novel', p. 297.

12.   Honeymoon: 1.6–7; Italy: 4.4 (cf. note *ad loc.*, Reardon, *Novels*, p. 157 and n. 2).

13.   In the New Testament, the idea of travel as *pathos* is perhaps best exemplified not in Acts but in Paul's own account of his travels in 2 Cor. 11.23–27. It is a salutary reminder that Acts is not the only, and not even the most romantic, New Testament narration of the travels of the apostle.

novels. The surface motivation for the journeyings of Acts is of course different: the underlying plot, with a series of voyages motivated by a divinely-inspired mission to preach the word, suggests a parallel rather with philosophical biography[14] than with the romance plot of the separation of lovers. But the journey-narrative, as we have observed, has its own structural logic irrespective of motivation: and the novels provide an unparalleled resource for understanding the management of this structure in popular narrative (roughly) contemporary with Acts – something which cannot be matched in philosophical biography.[15] It is worthwhile, therefore, to proceed with the comparison on a 'compare and contrast' basis without at this stage raising questions of sources or influence.

It is not difficult, as we have observed, to view the whole narrative of Acts as a voyage, that is as a description of the geographical expansion of the Gospel message outwards from Jerusalem 'to the end of the earth' (1.8): the words already imply a divine bird's-eye view of the world, and Luke's continued use of the Greek term *oikoumenē* reinforces the sense of a mission with a strong territorial imperative.[16] In Robert Maddox's words, 'the story of Jesus and of the church is a story full of purposeful movement'.[17] But structurally this voyage-plot differs in two important ways from the plot of romance. First, if the whole narrative is viewed as a voyage, there is no single traveller to act as focus. If we ask who (or what) travels in this narrative, we are left with many named and nameless individuals (8.4), working under the guidance of a divine spirit (chs. 13, 16): stirring stuff, but not easily paralleled with the plot of romance.[18] The hero of this relentless expansion is not any single individual, but 'the church' (8.1) or perhaps 'the Word'.[19] And secondly, the thrust of this expansive movement is centrifugal: Acts, seen as a whole, does not share the outward-and-return structure of the novels.

Luke's predilection for structuring his narrative in terms of journeying has already been demonstrated in the 'travel-narrative' of the Gospel. In Acts it is of course seen most clearly in the Paul narrative, and it is this which has most obviously attracted comparison with Greek romance. Here too we are struck at

---

14. Cf. L.C.A. Alexander, 'Acts and Ancient Intellectual Biography', in B.W. Winter and A.D. Clarke (eds.), *The Book of Acts in its First Century Setting. I. Ancient Literary Setting* (Grand Rapids: Eerdmans, 1993), pp. 31–63 (= Chapter 3 in this volume).

15. Alexander, 'Biography', pp. 43–48 on the lack of 'real' narration in Diogenes Laertius. The travel element is best paralleled in the life of Pythagoras, and reappears later in Philostratus' *Life of Apollonius of Tyana*: but it is not typical of the philosophical *bios*.

16. The word occurs more often in Luke-Acts than in the rest of the New Testament put together. Paul uses it only once (Rom. 10.18), in an Old Testament quotation.

17. R. Maddox, *The Purpose of Luke-Acts* (Göttingen: Vandenhoeck & Ruprecht, 1982), p. 11.

18. The parallelism between Peter and Paul does not extend to parallel travel-narratives: Peter has only two trips to Joppa, and disappears from the main narrative line after ch. 12, reappearing only briefly in ch. 15 as a secondary character in a scene in which Paul is still the protagonist.

19. Cf. Lk. 3.2 – the first actor in Luke's account of Jesus' ministry is 'the word of the Lord'.

first sight by the centrifugal thrust of the plot: in geographical terms (as in much else) Acts is much more open-ended than the classic *nostos*. Paul's final destination is not Jerusalem but Rome. But the narrative significance of this final move may be thrown into relief by the predominantly outward-and-return structure of the Pauline journeys up to the climactic arrest in Jerusalem. What we seem to have is a series of shorter trips out and back from the Antioch base enfolded (in a kind of multiple *inclusio*) in a broader journey which begins and ends in Jerusalem (7.58; 21.17) (Figure 3).

The narrative pull exerted by Jerusalem in Luke's story has often been observed,[20] and it is particularly strong in the closing stages of the travel narrative, where from 19.21 onwards Paul, like his master before him, has firmly 'set his face to go to Jerusalem'.[21] The importance of this structure for Luke is highlighted by a comparison with Paul's own account of his mission in Rom. 15.17–29, which has a much simpler outward momentum 'from Jerusalem as far round as Illyricum', capped by prospective visits to Rome and Spain. For Paul, the impending visit to Jerusalem (15.25) is a temporary detour which he had hoped to be able to avoid (1 Cor. 16.3–4). Luke's different emphasis may be no more than the inevitable result of hindsight.[22] But what is important for our purposes is that this return to Jerusalem gives the journey narrative in Acts a distinctive shape which is much closer to the shape of voyaging in the novels than in the Epistles. Moreover Luke notoriously (and puzzlingly) fails to pick up on the practical motivation for the last Jerusalem visit which is explicit in the Epistles: the 'collection' is never mentioned in Acts, and as a result Paul's conviction that he must return (and that he must 'see Rome' is left without motivation. As so often in the novels, it seems that the voyage is predetermined by the author (in this case, Luke implies, by the divine author) before the plot has had chance to provide sufficient motivation. Paul has already indicated that this journey is a 'necessity', and has received divine confirmation in a dream (23.11), long before he calls into play the legal mechanism which actually motivates the journey.[23]

It may be objected that Luke's Pauline narrative is much less neat than those of Chariton and Xenophon, each of which, for all their convolutions, may be viewed as a single voyage. On the traditional reckoning Acts narrates four Pauline journeys (three 'missionary journeys' plus the final trip to Rome), which contrasts not only with the novels but with the single geographical sweep of Rom. 15.19. The contrast may be more apparent than real, however. Clearly Acts

---

20.   Cf. commentaries and standard works on Pauline chronology: R. Jewett, *A Chronology of Paul's Life* (Philadelphia: Fortress Press, 1979); G. Lüdemann, *Paul, Apostle to the Gentiles: Studies in Chronology* (London: SCM Press, 1984).

21.   Lk. 9.51. Cf. Maddox, *The Purpose of Luke-Acts*, pp. 66–67, 76–80 for a cautious overview of the parallelism between Paul and Jesus in Luke-Acts.

22.   I would agree with Ed Sanders that it is unlikely Luke could have written a totally fictitious account of events which must have been public knowledge: E.P. Sanders, *Paul* (Past Masters series: Oxford: Oxford University Press, 1991), p. 15.

23.   I am grateful to Cheol-Won Yoon for the observation that the appeal to Caesar functions (in plot terms) as the motive force to get Paul to Rome.

gives detail where Paul summarizes, and it is the reconstruction of the geographical data which has led to the accepted schema of 'missionary journeys'. But in narrative terms (i.e. in terms of what the narrator signals in the text) the three-journey structure is much less obvious. There is only one formal commissioning by the church and only one 'sending out' by the Spirit (13.1–4), followed by a second divine intervention in the call to Macedonia (16.6–10), which is not a new voyage but a decision made *en route*. The first voyage is brought to a clear closure with the return to the place 'from which they had been committed to the grace of God for the work which they fulfilled' (14.26), but there is no corresponding closure between the 'second' and the 'third' journeys: within the space of a few verses, Paul is refusing speaking engagements in Ephesus, promising to return, sailing to Caesarea, going up and greeting 'the church',[24] visiting Antioch, and off again strengthening disciples in Phrygia and Galatia (18.20–23). A much more obvious narrative closure marks the end of Paul's whole missionary activity with the (multiply-signalled) return to Jerusalem, which dovetails with the equally clear signals of the impending journey to Rome. Note also that both the opening stages of the missionary journey (13.4) and its decisive change of direction (16.11) are marked by the fact that the party immediately puts to sea – for the Greek reader, a sure sign that real voyaging is under way. We shall return to this point below.

Mental Maps

'...from the map to learn up painted worlds'[25]

It is an index of the centrality of the voyage motif that the reading of both Acts and the novels seems to demand a map: as Tomas Hägg puts it,[26] 'A map of the Mediterranean region showing the routes of the hero and heroine of a novel inevitably brings to mind the school-bible's map of the travels of St. Paul'. But the juxtaposition immediately raises another question: what kind of geographical conceptions would have been shared by the authors and readers of these texts?[27] What kind of mental maps do the narratives presuppose? A 'mental map' in this sense is not simply a chart of the areas of a reader's knowledge or ignorance (a concept which itself assumes that the familiar modern map of the Mediterranean is 'the real map': it is of course itself a construct).

---

24.   Perhaps in Jerusalem, but the text does not say so. Cf. Lüdemann, *Chronology,* pp. 141–57.

25.   *E tabula pictos ediscere mundos* (Propertius 4.3.33–40).

26.   See the endpapers to Tomas Hägg, *The Ancient Novel.*

27.   I have not attempted to provide a full bibliography of the geographical perspectives of biblical and Graeco-Roman literature. For a fuller discussion of the former, see P.S. Alexander, 'Geography and the Bible, Early Jewish', *ABD* II, pp. 977–88 and now J.M. Scott, 'Luke's Geographical Horizon', in D.W.J. Gill and C. Gempf (eds.), *The Book of Acts in its First Century Setting.* II. *Graeco-Roman Setting,* (Grand Rapids: Eerdmans, 1994), pp. 483–544. Scott's paper (which I did not see until after the completion of my own) confirms a number of the points made here.

Human beings appear to have a fundamental need to project order onto the space in which they live and move: they process spatial data received through the senses, relating one element to another and abstracting a mental map or model which functions as a constant frame of reference for all their activities.[28]

In the words of cognitive geographers Gould and White,

Man [sic] exists in what the psychologist David Stea has called 'invisible landscapes', which shape quite strongly his mental images and his behaviour... We are slowly realizing that people's perception of places is one of the things we must consider as we try to understand the pattern of man's work on the face of the earth.[29]

A cognitive map in this sense does not have to be drawn out on paper, but it can be projected from the patterns of behaviour and language of an individual or group: conversely, pictured maps can be used to illuminate a group's worldview and frame of reference.

The mental map underlying Chariton's voyage narrative is highly schematic and mirrors rather precisely the old Ionian map which dominated the Greek world (and this is very definitely a Greek world, not a Greco-Roman one).[30] Like the Ionian map, Chariton's mental map is an oblong shape longer than it is wide – or it has breadth but no depth, if you prefer.[31] The action swings from one end of this oblong to the other and finally back again, and its dramatic centre is also the geographical centre, at Miletus, plumb on the Ionian meridian which ran down the western coast of Asia Minor from Lysimachia on the Propontis to Alexandria.[32] The sea is at the centre of this view of the world, and its major routes are sea-routes. Most of the action happens along a longitudinal axis drawn along the Mediterranean from Sicily in the West to the crossing of the Euphrates at Zeugma or Thapsacus – though as we shall see, Chariton's knowledge of the East beyond the Euphrates is distinctly woolly. This axis corresponds closely to Dicaearchus' *diaphragma*, which was, according to Agathemerus,

a straight line line drawn from the Pillars through Sardinia, Sicily, Peloponnessus, Ionia, Caria, Lycia, Pamphylia, Cilicia, and the Taurus, one after another, up to the Imaus mountains.[33]

28.   P.S. Alexander, 'Geography and the Bible, Early Jewish', p. 978.

29.   P. Gould and R. White, *Mental Maps* (Harmondsworth: Penguin, 1974), pp. 141, 45.

30.   On ancient maps in general see O.A.W. Dilke, *Greek and Roman Maps* (London: Thames & Hudson, 1985). On the Ionian map, see W.A. Heidel, *The Frame of the Ancient Greek Maps* (New York: Arno Press, 1976; repr. of original edn, New York: American Geographical Society, Research Series no. 20, 1937).

31.   Heidel, *Frame*, p.17.

32.   Heidel, *Frame*, pp. 124–25

33.   Heidel, *Frame*, pp. 111–12, citing Agathemerus 1.5 (ed. C. Müller, *Geographi Graeci Minores* [Paris: Didot, 1861], vol. II p. 472). Heidel continues: 'This line, we know, was adopted by Eratosthenes as the main longitudinal axis of his chart (Strabo 2.1.1). ... [I]t practically coincided with the equator of the Ionian map between the Pillars and Asia Minor. From thence the text of Herodotus based on the "Persian map" indicates a line, marking the boundary between the tract (*akte*) of Asia Minor and that of Syria, in the same direction as far as the Eastern limits of Persia.'

Although this line is roughly parallel with the Equator, it produces an elongation of the Mediterranean (and especially of the 'Ionian Sea' which figures so large in Chariton's narrative) which can clearly be seen in reconstructions of the world map of Eratosthenes (Figure 4). According to Strabo (Figure 5), Eratosthenes placed even Athens on the same parallel (*Geog.* 67–68 [2.1.1]):

> In the third book of his Geography Eratosthenes, in establishing the map of the inhabited world, divides it into two parts by a line drawn from west to east, parallel to the equatorial line... He draws the line from the Pillars through the Strait of Sicily and also through the southern capes both of the Peloponnesus and of Attica, and as far as Rhodes and the Gulf of Issus...and indeed our whole Mediterranean Sea itself extends, lengthwise, along this line as far as Cilicia...then the line is produced in an approximately straight course along the whole Taurus range as far as...India so that in like manner both the Taurus and the Sea from the Pillars up to the Taurus lie on the parallel of Athens.

If we trace Callirhoe's journey on one of these maps rather than on a modern projection, it becomes clear that the whole of her journey (including the stop 'opposite Athens') is along this same west-east axis, and she scarcely deviates from it on her return when she is incarcerated on Aradus. Chaereas is allowed a little more north-south movement, but not much: the initial search-party taking him toward North Africa is narrated in the briefest of summaries and does not really form part of the narrative at all; and the Egyptian king is well into Phoenicia before Chaereas catches up with him.

But what of the great set-piece journey to Babylon, which (as we all know) is well to the south of this line? We may know it, and Chariton's contemporary Arrian knows it, as his account of Alexander's expedition makes clear, but I am not sure that Chariton does. There is nothing in the text to indicate that Dionysius' party turn south (or 'down-river') after the crossing of the Euphrates, and I suspect that for Chariton, Babylon (which represents the Oriental world) is simply 'East of the River'.[34] This is why Mithridates and his party, travelling from Caria via Armenia, actually arrive in Babylon faster than Dionysius travelling through Cilicia – which is a little surprising on any cartographic projection. Chariton's knowledge of the route to Babylon is a classic example of what Gould and White call travelling through a 'tube of ignorance', illustrated by overheard conversations of the form:

'We went to Majorca for our holidays'

'Where is Majorca?'

'I don't know exactly, we flew'.[35]

Habitual motorway drivers experience a similar phenomenon, in which geographical space is understood not as territory on a two-dimensional map projection but as a series of points on a one-dimensional itinerary: as in the *Peutinger Tafel*, the spatial relations of points on different itineraries are distorted

---

34. Contrast Arrian's detailed knowledge of the topography of the river crossings and the approach to Babylon: cf. *Anab.* 3.7–8, 15–16.

35. Gould and White, *Mental Maps*, pp. 119–20.

because they are not important (Figure 6). The Euphrates crossings at Zeugma and Thapsacus are, as it happens, more or less due East of Syracuse and Miletus: therefore to all intents and purposes Babylon is 'in the East' (since you get to it by travelling East), and Callirhoe's trial takes place on the eastern limits of Chariton's Greek world (Figure 7).

Xenophon's narrative world is equally centred on the Mediterranean, though its proportions are slightly different from Chariton's: this mental map has depth as well as breadth. Again, the Ionian meridian forms its primary axis, with the action starting and finishing in Ephesus. The couple's disastrous honeymoon trip is heading due south down this meridian to Alexandria when it is rudely inter-rupted by pirates: the maritime location of the disaster is undefined (1.13.3), but its source is identified as Rhodes, where the pirates first catch sight of their prospective booty (1.13.1). Fittingly, the final resolution also takes place in Rhodes (5.10–15), which as the point of intersection between the prime meridian and Dicaearchus' longitudinal axis qualifies as the geographical centre of this particular mental map (cf. Figure 4). Before that point, however, the lovers have travelled East, South and then West in a hectic tangle of separate journeys. The Orient for Xenophon is represented by Syria, with Cilicia and Cappadocia as extensions of the eastern voyage, I think, rather than a separate northern expedition.[36] After failing to meet in the East, the lovers follow separate sea-ways south to Egypt and Ethiopia, followed doggedly on land by the bandit chief Hippothous who has fallen for Habrocomes. Both thus eventually reach Alexandria, the destination of their original voyage, but separately and in various harrowing circumstances. Habrocomes gives up at this point and heads off to the West: it is left to Anthia and Hippothous to explore Ethiopia, the tradi-tional southern extremity of the Ionian maps[37] (and an area fruitfully exploited by the later novelist Heliodorus). Anthia is threatened with an even longer voyage, as she leaves Egypt en route for India (4.3.1). On Xenophon's mental map, India is 'south' in the same sense as Chariton's Babylon is 'east': the important fact is that the route to India (at least one of the major trading routes) runs south through Egypt and Ethiopia before heading for the Indian Ocean at Coptos.[38] The final phase of this exercise in 'boxing the compass' is westward, when the three all find themselves (for different reasons) in Greater Greece (Sicily and southern Italy) before heading back to the centre for their reunion in Rhodes (Figure 8).

Xenophon's map, then, seems best explained in terms of travel-routes rather than of territorial overview. As with Chariton the patterns of movement are highly schematic: but Xenophon's pattern is triangular rather than linear. Some of these routes are better known than others. Xenophon knows of three routes

36.   North is represented by Hippothous' story of his own origins at Perinthus (3.2), but this is not part of the primary narrative.

37.   Strabo, *Geog.* 3 (1.1.6); Heidel, *Frame*, pp. 26–28.

38.   4.1.5. For the importance of this route, cf. L. Casson, *The Periplus Maris Erythraei*, (Princeton: University Press 1989), pp. 13–14.

from Cilicia to Egpyt (though details along the way are decidedly sketchy);[39] and it is interesting that he knows the trade-route to India via Coptos, which as he tells us himself attracts 'a great crowd of merchants passing through for Ethiopia and India'.[40] But the sea-route from Alexandria to Italy is described in the minimum of words (4.4.2; 5.1.1), and Habrocomes' final route home (Sicily-Crete-Cyprus-Rhodes) looks like a nonsense, except perhaps on the assumption that the list represents a well-known list of destinations for ships heading into the eastern Mediterranean from Sicily (cf. the return voyage of Chaereas and Callirhoe) in which the order of the ports of call has been muddled.

The predominance of the Ionian mental map and the centrality of the sea for the voyages of Greek romance throw into relief the rather different geographical perspectives of Acts. Luke's story really has two mental maps, one centred on Jerusalem and one on the Mediterranean, and the movement from the one to the other enables us to chart a profound cultural shift within early Christianity. The geographical importance of the list of nations in Acts 2.9–11 has long been recognized. Whether or not the table has affinities with 'astrological geography',[41] it is clear that it presupposes a vision of the world centred on Jerusalem, like the later mediaeval Christian maps and like the contemporary map presupposed by the book of Jubilees.[42] Richard Bauckham in a recent lecture argues rightly, I think, that the names in the table are best understood as representative of different directions viewed from Jerusalem (Figure 9): the East (Parthians, Medes, Elamites and residents of Mesopotamia), the centre (Judaea), the North (Cappadocia, Pontus, Asia, Phrygia and Pamphylia), the South-West (Egypt and Libya), the West (Rome and Crete) and the South (Arabia).[43] Rome stands for the West because that is the direction from which its representatives appear – and Crete is on their direct route. Luke resists the temptation to take his primary narrative into these unexplored regions, though the episode of the Ethiopian

39. Cf. Dalmeyda on 4.1.1–5 'Cet itinéraire d'Hippothous est d'une aimable fantaisie. Rohde dit avec raison que ce sont là proprement dit des μυρμήκων ἀτραποί. Xénophon se pique de géographie, mais sa science ne va pas très loin et il semble ici jouer avec des noms de localités égyptiennes' (Dalmeyda, *Xénophon*, p. 49 n. 2)

40. 4.1.5; Schedia (4.1.3, 5.2.7) must have been also well known to traders: Strabo, *Geog.* 800 (17.1.16) describes it as 'the station for paying duty on the goods brought down [sc. down-river] from above it and brought up from below it'.

41. S. Weinstock, 'The Geographical Catalogue in Acts II,9–11', *JRS* 38 (1948), pp. 43–46; J.A. Brinkman, 'The Literary Background of the "Catalogue of the Nations"', *CBQ* 25 (1963), pp. 418–27; B.M. Metzger, 'Ancient Astrological Geography and Acts 2.9–11', in W.W. Gasque and R.P. Martin (eds.), *Apostolic History and the Gospel: Biblical and Historical Essays presented to F.F. Bruce on his 60th Birthday*, (Exeter: Paternoster Press, 1970), pp. 123–33; Scott, 'Luke's Geographical Horizon', pp. 527–30.

42. P.S. Alexander, 'Geography and the Bible, Early Jewish', pp. 980–82; Scott, 'Luke's Geographical Horizon', pp. 524–44.

43. R. Bauckham, 'James at the Centre: A Jerusalem Perspective on New Testament History and Canon', (Inaugural Lecture, St Andrews, 1994). [Subsequently published as Richard Bauckham, 'James and the Jerusalem Church,' in Richard Bauckham (ed.), *The Book of Acts in its First Century Setting. IV. Palestinian Setting* (Carlisle/ Grand Rapids: Paternoster/Eerdmans, 1995), pp. 415–80, esp. pp. 417–27.]

eunuch allows the reader to feel that the narrative has touched the exotic at one remove (much as Chariton is able to bring a southern dimension into his tale through the secondary narrative of the Egyptian king). But the implied narratives of the other, unnamed travellers of Acts 2 serve to back up the claim that the preaching of the gospel is a world-wide event: the charge of 'turning the world upside down' (17.6, 24.5) is welcomed rather than refuted (26.6).

Viewing the world from this Jerusalem-centred perspective has some interesting side-effects. It means that the Aegean is masked from sight, an unexplored backwater into which the westward-bound traveller has no need to penetrate (an effect which is exaggerated in later Christian maps, where it has shrunk to the size of a creek) (Figure 10). This may be one reason for the puzzling omission from Luke's list of Macedonia and Achaia, the areas where Paul is to spend so much of his time. But the omission may also be precisely *because* Paul is to spend his time there: it allows Luke to present these areas as virgin territory unreached by the gospel (unlike Rome, which already has a church when Paul arrives), and to assign to Paul an exploratory role which reverses the presuppositions of the Greek geographers. To explore is to travel beyond the boundaries of the known world. For Greek romance with its Ionian worldview, this means pressing beyond the known world of the Aegean to the unknown East (Syria, Phoenicia, Babylon) or South (Egypt, Ethiopia) or West (Sicily, Italy). But to a worldview centred on Jerusalem, the Aegean may be equally unknown territory, and its penetration by the emissaries of the gospel is a geographical achievement worthy of celebration. Paul's ministry in Macedonia and Greece simply does not fit into the world-map of Acts 2: his crossing of the Bosporus marks a breaking out of the known world, a new step carefully signalled in the narrative by a series of false moves successively blocked by the Spirit (16.6–8). It is hardly surprising that the decisive move requires the explicit guidance of a dream (16.9–10).

The voyages of Acts 16 and onwards, then, have already extended the boundaries of the mental map of Acts 2. By the final phases of the narrative the perspective has shifted decisively to a Mediterranean-centred map whose co-ordinates reflect those of Chariton and Xenophon. Jerusalem is the place where Paul's story begins (for narrator and readers: it is only later that we learn of his birth in Tarsus) and the goal to which it has been reverting from 19.21 onwards. But Paul's final voyage takes him by carefully-charted stages in a new direction (also announced in 19.21) from which the narrative offers no return: Jerusalem is no longer the centre of a circle but the eastern edge of a westerly voyage which follows the sea-routes more familiar to the Greek reader than to the Bible.

The Significance of Sea-Travel

As some grave Tyrian trader, from the sea,
Descried at sunrise an emerging prow...
And knew the intruders on his ancient home[44]

----

44.   Matthew Arnold, *The Scholar-Gipsy*.

This shift in geographical perspective is reflected in an equally significant shift in the mode of travel. We noted above that decisive stages in Paul's missionary journey are marked not only by divine guidance but also by the fact that the journey becomes (however briefly) a sea-voyage. The commissioning of the Spirit in Acts 13.4 leads the party directly to the port of Seleucia, from where they sail (ἀπέπλευσαν) to Cyprus: the same verb marks their return to Antioch with the commission fulfilled (14.26). Similarly the crossing from Asia Minor to Macedonia in Acts 16.11 is described in terms which emphasize the nautical nature of the voyage (ἀναχθέντες, εὐθυδρομήσαμεν). Indications of sea-travel recur at intervals throughout the Aegean ministry, clustering particularly around the return to Jerusalem, and reaching a climax in the final voyage to Rome.[45] The narrative of ch. 27 is (as commentators have long observed)[46] richly embellished with nautical terms, and full of realistic detail which ensures that the reader cannot forget that Paul's last journey is a *plous*, a sea-voyage.

To appreciate the full force of the lexical choices made here by Luke, we have only to look at Paul's own vocabulary of travel. Paul never uses the verb πλέω or any of its cognates, but speaks of his extensive journeys in non-specific terms (ἔρχομαι, πορεύομαι): it would be hard to tell, from Romans 15, that any sea-travel at all was involved in the projected trip to the West. This may be because from Corinth, where Paul is writing, it is more natural to contemplate the short crossing to Italy via Brundisium,[47] or it may be that Paul simply did not like the sea (his attitude to it in 2 Corinthians 11 certainly suggests that).[48] But it is not the possible authorial motives that interest us here so much as the effects on the reader. Acts foregrounds an aspect of Paul's travels which Paul himself prefers to ignore, or at least (except in the notoriously rhetorical passage 2 Corinthians. 11) to downplay. Moreover Luke has carefully prepared the ground in such a way that Paul (and his party) are the only characters who travel by sea in the whole two-volume narrative: Galilee for Luke is a 'lake' (λίμνη), not the sea (θάλασσα or πέλαγος), so that, in Vernon Robbins' words, 'Only Paul and his associates face the challenge, adventure, and destiny of voyaging across the sea'.[49] It is well known that this proliferation of nautical terms is almost (but not quite) co-extensive with the 'we-passages'. But again, it is no part of my purpose here

45.   20.6, 13–16, 38; 21.1–3, 6–7; 27 *passim*.
46.   See on this passage E. Norden, *Agnostos Theos: Untersuchungen zur Formengeschichte religiöser Rede* (Stuttgart: Teubner 1956 [1913]), pp. 313–27; M. Dibelius, *Studies in the Acts of the Apostles*, (ed. H. Greeven; London: SCM Press, 1956), pp. 7–9, 204–206; V.K. Robbins, 'By Land and by Sea: The We-passages and Ancient Sea-Voyages', in C.H. Talbert (ed.), *Perspectives on Luke-Acts* (Edinburgh: T&T Clark, 1978), pp. 215–42. Cf. further n. 50.
47.   The mention of Illyricum in the same passage suggests that the land routes were in his mind.
48.   Paul uses θάλασσα only in Old Testament allusions apart from 2 Cor. 11.26, which speaks in lurid terms of 'danger by sea'. This passage also includes (v. 25) the dramatic ἐναυάγησα and ἐν τῷ βυθῷ, which echoes LXX Ps. 106 (I am indebted to Brian Dodd for this observation). Does Acts 20.3, 13 reflect a known apostolic distaste for sea travel?
49.   Robbins, 'By Land and by Sea', p. 216. The nearest any other character gets to the sea is Acts 10.6, where we are told that Peter is staying 'by the sea' at the point when he receives his horizon-extending dream.

to explore the many theories about the possible reasons for this odd phenomenon.[50] Rather than speculating about the author and/or his sources, I am interested to explore its effects on the readers, and especially on readers acquainted with Greek romance.

The theme of jouneying by sea is not of course unique to the novel in Greek literature. Its obvious and ever-present archetype is the *Odyssey*, which has its Roman counterpart in the *Aeneid*. For both these foundational narratives, the hero reaches his goal via a sea-voyage, in which islands are more familiar than the continental interior, and whole regions are known solely by their coastlands and ports. The popularity of this kind of voyage-narrative among the Greeks (as among the Irish and the Scandinavians) must reflect the importance of the sea, and especially of the coastal voyage, in the Greek perception of the world. For much of Greek history, sea-travel was quicker and more convenient than land-travel. Thus, for Xenophon's mercenaries, in a famous scene, a distant glimpse of the sea means release from a nightmare and the prospect of homecoming (*Anabasis* 4.7.20–27). Traveller's tales appeared in prose as well as in verse: the *periplous* and the *periegesis* provided a convenient and durable format for scientific exploration for merchant handbooks, as a basis for mapping, and (increasingly under the Empire) for a growing public of armchair travellers which enjoyed reading lengthy geographical descriptions in the form of a voyage around the coasts of the Mediterranean.[51]

This literary context is important to bear in mind when we consider the role of the sea in the novels of Chariton and Xenophon. For both, voyaging begins with embarkation, and ends with a triumphant landfall.[52] Nautical terminology defines the means of travel: these adventurers 'sail' from one theatre of action to another; 'finding a ship' is an important event.[53] The sea is a potential source of danger and disaster: crossing it is an adventure in itself, yet it unites the lovers

---

50.   See in addition to the literature cited in n. 46 S.M. Praeder, 'The Problem of First Person Narration in Acts' (*NovT* 29 (1987), pp. 193–218); J. Wehnert, *Die Wir-Passagen der Apostelgeschichte: Ein lukanisches Stilmittel aus jüdischer Tradition* (Göttingen: Vandenhoeck & Ruprecht 1989); Stanley E. Porter, 'Excursus: The "We" Passages', in D.W.J. Gill and C. Gempf (eds.), *The Book of Acts in its First Century Setting*. II. *Graeco-Roman Setting* (Grand Rapids: Eerdmans 1993), pp. 545–74.

51.   Dilke, *Greek and Roman Maps,* ch. 6 gives a useful survey of the genre. For the *periplous* format in exploration, cf. Hanno, Scylax, Arrian, Nearchus; for merchant handbooks, cf. the *Periplus Maris Erythraei* (above n. 38). For the (sometimes uneasy) relationship between these accounts and the mapmakers, cf. F.W. Walbank, 'The Geography of Polybius', *Classica et Mediaevalia* 9 (1948), pp. 155–82; C. van Paassen, *The Classical Tradition of Geography* (Groningen: J.B. Wolters, 1957); P. Pédech, *La méthode historique de Polybe* (Paris: Les Belles Lettres, 1964), ch. 12; and compare the extensive discussion in book two of Strabo's *Geography*. (e.g. 71 [2.1.11]: even the astronomer Hipparchus 'trusted the sailors'). For armchair travellers, cf. Aelius Aristides, *Or.* 14.226.4–8 (Dindorf I.366). For *Periegeseis* of the Mediterranean, cf. Pseudo-Scymnus, Dionysius Calliphontis (C. Müller, *Geographi Graeci Minores* [Paris: Didot, 1855], I, pp. 196–237, 238–39).

52.   Chariton: 1.10.8–11.1, 3.3.8, 4.17, 5.1–9, 8.6.1–12. Xenophon: 1.10.3–11.6, 5.15.1.

53.   E.g. Xenophon 3.10.4, 4.10.2.

as well as separating them.[54] And, as Chariton especially makes clear in a number of set-piece speeches, the Mediterranean is seen as 'the Greek sea', the area where his Greek characters feel at home and where they can effortlessly triumph over the massed forces of oriental despotism.[55] This feeling is made explicit on Callirhoe's inland journey to Babylon: the narrator tells us that

> Callirhoe was distressed to be taken far from the Greek sea; as long as she could see the harbors of Miletus, she had the impression that Syracuse was not far away; and Chaereas' tomb in Miletus was great comfort to her (4.7.8).

As 'an island woman' (νησιῶτις) she expresses poignantly her feelings on crossing the Euphrates, 'beyond which there is a vast stretch of unending land':

> Now it is not Ionia where you [Fortune] keep me exiled; the land you allotted to me up to now was admittedly a foreign country, but it was Greek, and there I could take comfort in the thought that I was living by the sea. Now you are hurling me from my familiar world – I am at the other end of the earth from my own country. This time it is Miletus you have taken from me; before, it was Syracuse. I am being taken beyond the Euphrates, shut up in the depths of barbarian land where the sea is far away – I, an island woman! What ship can I hope will come sailing after me from Sicily now? (5.1.5–6).

The sea, then, is an important mode of travel in the novels and provides the opportunity for many of their adventures. Despite its dangers it is seen as a natural route of communication, linking the Greek cities and islands across the Mediterranean seaboard. Inland are no cities (no Greek cities, that is) but the lands of the barbarians, peopled with bandits – and foreigners. Beyond the Euphrates, as we have seen, lie the 'unending lands' of 'the king's great empire' (5.1.3); but even Caria, in Chariton's historical imagination, is a citiless desert, the territory of a Persian satrap worked by chain-gangs (3.7.3; 4.2.1ff.). Chariton's Babylon is rather like Mozart's *Seraglio*, a stereotype of the oriental court, characterized by the scheming of eunuchs and the 'kow-towing' of courtiers;[56] this is a thorough-going case of 'Orientalism',[57] redeemed only by the humanity and irony of this author's characterization.[58] Xenophon is less concerned than Chariton with creating a 'historical' setting for his tale, but his view of the lands travelled by his characters is equally depressing. Phoenicia is 'a barbarian land' peopled by 'lustful pirates' (2.1.2), and Syria is little better: Anthia spends her time there with a country goatherd. Egypt, despite the endeavours of the 'prefect', is overrun with bandits; and Psammis, the Indian merchant-prince, is not only naturally lustful

---

54.　E.g. Chariton 3.5.9, 6.6, 10.8; 4.1.5–6, 7.8; and cf. 1.14.9, where Reardon accepts Hercher's conjecture πελάγει.

55.　Cf. e.g. 7.5.8, 6.1–2; 8.2.12.

56.　Reardon's apt equivalent for *proskunēsis* (p. 79 n. 79). The 'orientalism' of the Babylonian court is carefully conveyed through the use of stock characters (the satraps, the eunuch, the queen and her ladies) and behaviour (e.g. 5.9.1; 6.3.1–7.10) as well as by set-piece descriptions (5.4.5–6; 6.4).

57.　I owe the term to E. Said, *Orientalism* (London: Routledge & Kegan Paul, 1978).

58.　E.g. 5.3.1–10; 8.3.1–11.

(the collocation with ἄνθρωπος βάρβαρος suggests that the two facts are connected) but also 'superstitious like all barbarians' (δεισιδαίμονες δὲ φύσει βάρβαροι, 3.11.4).[59]

Against this background we may begin to appreciate the full effects of Luke's presentation of Paul as a sea-voyager. We have already noted that the Jerusalem-centred perspective of the first half of Acts entails a reversal of the usual Greek perspective on the world: for Luke's hero, Syria and Phoenicia are home ground, while the Aegean is unexplored territory. The reversal is highlighted by occasional touches of regional characterization. The only 'barbarians' in Acts are in the West, not in the East (28.2); and it is the Athenians, in the heartland of Greek culture, who are described as 'superstitious' (δεισιδαιμονεστέρους, 17.22).[60] For the Greek reader, this is 'turning the world upside down' (17.6) with a vengeance.

The cultural significance of the Athens episode has been well analysed by a number of commentators: here Paul is presented as a new Socrates, beating the philosophers at their own game.[61] Paul's sea-voyages, I would suggest, represent a parallel act of narrative aggression. Chariton claims the sea as Greek cultural territory (much as the British used to do), and it is a claim with which readers of the Greek classics could easily identify.[62] Moreover it is not a claim which many readers of the Bible would care to dispute: in the book of Jonah, which offers the only parallel narrative in the Hebrew Bible, the hero's sea-trip is a disastrous mistake; and in the New Testament the book of Revelation notoriously (and to the lasting regret of that very British poet Rudyard Kipling) looks forward to an eschatological future in which 'the sea was no more' (Rev. 21.1). Paul himself, as we have seen, describes his experiences of sea-travel in lurid terms scarcely bettered by the novelists (2 Corinthians 11), and carefully avoids drawing attention to the practicalities of his journeys. Like a presidential candidate on the campaign trail, the apostle travels from venue to venue without having to think about the means of travel at all, relying on his team to study the timetables and make the reservations. For the narrator of Acts, by contrast, sea travel is a matter of consuming interest. This narrator (note the association of 'we-narration' with the sea) is perfectly at home on the sea, able to find seagoing connections with ease, familiar with the names of winds and harbours, alert to the complexities of shipping traffic in the Aegean and the Mediterranean.[63] The sea is presented as a proper sphere of activity for the emissaries of the gospel.[64]

---

59.   The identical reaction of Polyidus to Anthia at 5.4.5–7 is not described as 'barbarian'. For a similar combination (φύσει ... τὸ βάρβαρον γυναιμανές), cf. Chariton 5.2.6.

60.   Chariton's picture of Athens is also slightly ironic: compare 1.11.6–7 with Acts 17.21.

61.   For full discussion and bibliography, cf. Alexander, 'Biography', pp. 31–63 (= Chapter 3 in this volume, pp. 43–67).

62.   For a full collection of texts, cf. A. Lesky, *Thalatta: der Weg der Griechen zum Meer* (New York: Arno Press, 1973).

63.   Acts 20.13–16; 21.1–3; 27.1–2, 4–8, 12–16; 28.11–13.

64.   For this concept, cf. V.K. Robbins, 'Luke-Acts: A Mixed Population Seeks a Home in the Roman Empire', in L.C.A. Alexander (ed.), *Images of Empire* (JSOTSup, 122; Sheffield: JSOT Press, 1991) pp. 202–221; but I would be inclined to see the relationship with Greek aspirations here as more aggressive, less 'symbiotic' than Robbins does.

The hero on his last voyage is calm in the face of the storm, better at forecasting wind and weather than helmsman and captain, able to dominate the panic-stricken crew in the shipwreck.[65] Jonah's situation is reversed: far from being the cause of the ship's peril, Paul is the reason for its salvation. It is because of his mission, and his destined arrival in Rome, that its 276 souls will be delivered 'all safe to land'.[66] Clearly, as many commentators have seen, there is a theological claim implicit in the shipwreck narrative of Acts 27. Paul's God dominates and controls the sea crossing for him just as Aphrodite and Isis do for the heroines of the novels:[67]

> Just before she went on board, Callirhoe made an obeisance to Aphrodite. 'I thank you, lady', she said, 'for what is happening now. You are reconciled to me now; grant that I see Syracuse too! A great stretch of sea separates me from there; an ocean is waiting for me that is frightening to cross; but I am not frightened if you are sailing with me' (8.4.10).

But a comparison with the geographical perspectives of the novels also makes it clear, I would suggest, that the narrator is implicitly laying claim to a cultural territory which many readers, both Greek and Judaeo-Christian, would perceive as inherently 'Greek'.[68]

Conclusions

It is time to try to draw some tentative conclusions. It seems clear from this preliminary exploration at least that the comparison between Acts and the novels is well worth pursuing: even the limited topic of voyaging has thrown up a variety of leads which could be pursued at greater depth than has been possible here. But the exercise must also take note of differences as well as similarities, and should ideally be pursued in full awareness of the broader cultural context: romance does not have a monopoly on voyage-narratives. I would like to finish by making some observations on this broader context.

Frederick Brenk has demonstrated in a recent article[69] how the wall-paintings of the temple of Isis at Pompeii suggest ways in which the Roman worshipper could be

65.   27.9–10, 21–26, 30–36.
66.   Cf. nn. 46, 50 above for bibliography on Paul's shipwreck.
67.   On the identification of Aphrodite with the sea, cf. Lesky, *Thalatta*, pp. 279–82. For the parallel role of Isis in the *Ephesiaca*, cf. Dalmeyda, *Xénophon*, pp. xvi–xvii, and esp. 5.13.2–4.
68.   The Romans also had an interest in claiming dominance of the sea (and the claim was asserted in imperial monuments found in Chariton's home town of Aphrodisias: C. Nicolet, *Space, Geography, and Politics in the Early Roman Empire* [Jerome Lectures, 19; Ann Arbor: University of Michigan Press, 1991 (ET of *L'inventaire du monde: Geographie et politique aux origines de l'Empire Romain* [Libraire Arthème Foyard, 1988])], pp. 45–47): but we cannot pursue this important topic here.
69.   F.E. Brenk, 'A Gleaming Ray: Blessed Afterlife in the Mysteries', *Illinois Classical Studies* 18 (1993), pp. 147–64 (157–64).

successively drawn deeper and deeper into the profundities of Egyptian religion and thus transformed... The painting, like the architecture, innocently Greco-Roman in appearance, becomes more dangerously religious as one 'zooms in' on a world continually more mysterious and Egyptian in imagery and theme.

The comfortable and familiar landscapes of 'romantic Hellenism' are seen on closer inspection to be dotted with Egyptian buildings and symbols, so that 'seemingly innocent and innocuous iconography, veiled in familiar garb, only gradually begins to reveal its deeper meaning'. At one level we may legitimately, I think, compare Luke's use of the narrative techniques of romance with the 'innocuous iconography' of these wall-paintings, a device to introduce the Greek or Roman reader to a new and 'exotic' religion by easy stages. But at the level of the narrative itself the position is reversed. Luke cannot dot the romantic landscape with 'Christian' buildings and symbols because such things do not exist: even the 'synagogues' which form the most prominent feature of his cities are community groups rather than architectural features rivalling the temples of the Greek gods. Instead, we have suggested, Luke structures his narrative in such a way that his hero is presented as 'invading' Greek cultural territory: first the 'hidden' ports of the Aegean, then the 'Greek sea' itself. It is as daring in its way as the paintings of the Iseum, and potentially – at least for the Greek reader – much more disturbing.

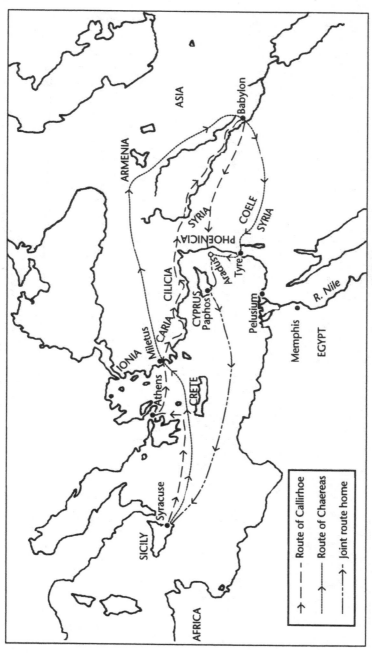

Figure 1. Chariton: The Travels of Chaereas and Callirhoe

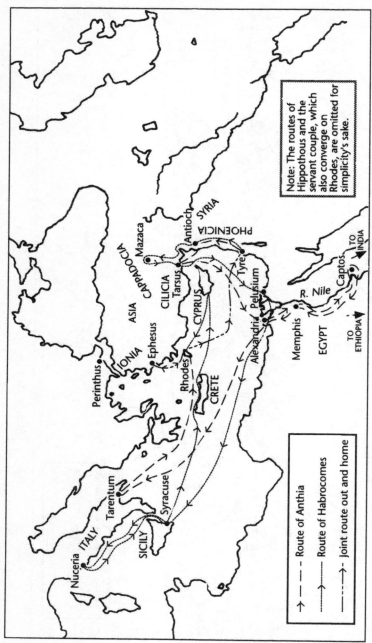

Figure 2. *Xenophon: The Travels of Anthia and Habrocomes.*

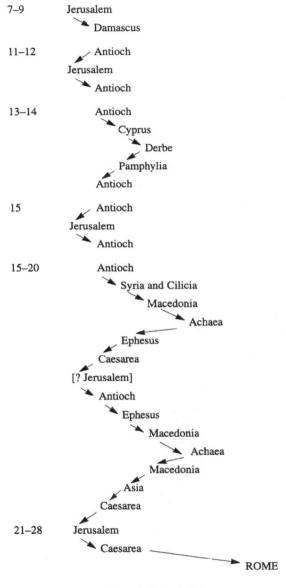

Figure 3. *Inclusio Diagram*

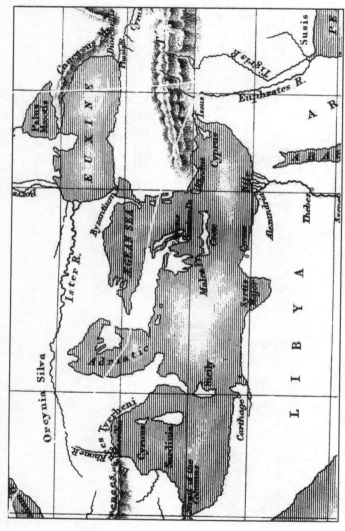

Figure 4. *Reconstruction of Eratosthenes' Map of the World (detail).*
From E.H. Bunbury. *A History of Ancient Geography*, I (London: John Murray, 2nd edn, 1883), after p. 660.

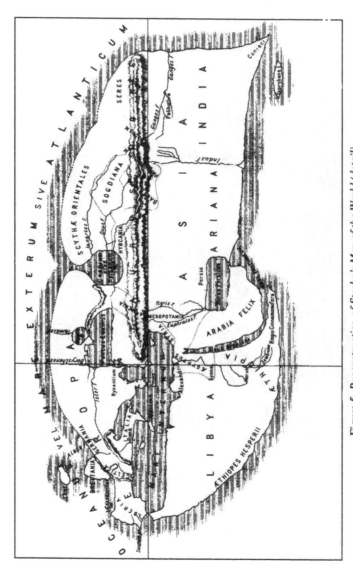

Figure 5. *Reconstruction of Strabo's Map of the World (detail).*
From H.F. Tozer, *A History of Ancient Geography*, (Cambridge: Cambridge University Press, 1897), facing p. 239.

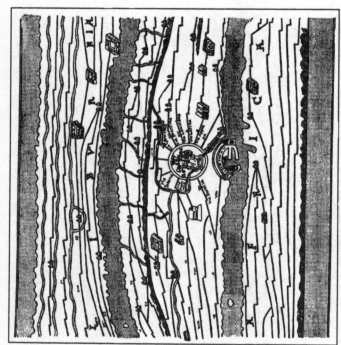

Figure 6. *Detail from the Peutinger Tafel (fourth cent. CE), Showing Roads Leading to Rome.* From M.B. Synge, *A Book of Discovery* (London: T.C. & E.C. Jack, n.d.), p. 62.

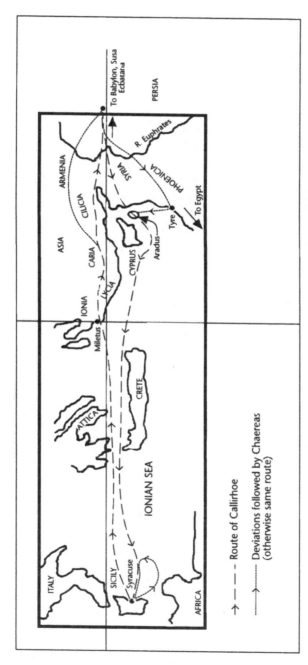

Figure 7. *Chariton: Schematic Route Maps for Main Characters Based on Eratosthenes' Projection.*

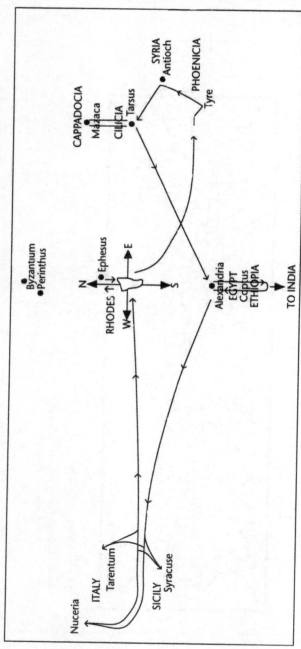

Figure 8. Xenophon: Schematic Route Maps for Main Characters Based on Eratosthenes' Projection.

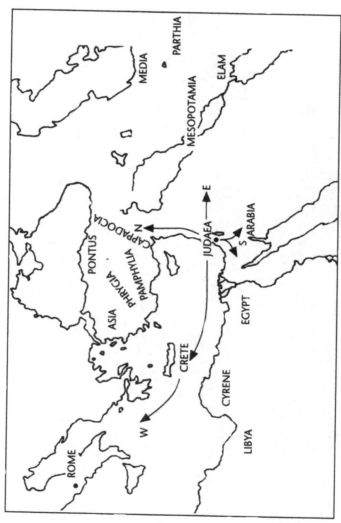

Figure 9. *A World View Centred on Jerusalem: The Regions of Acts 2.9-11.*

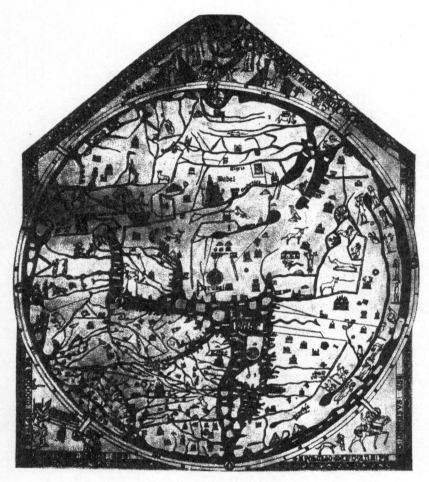

Figure 10. *The Hereford World Map,* drawn by Richard de Haldingham and
Lafford in 1280 CE.
Jerusalem lies at the centre of this Christian map, which is orientated with East
at the top. Note how Babylon, Jerusalem and Rome all appear on the same
(vertical) E-W parallel, and how the Aegean and Adriatic have shrunk in size.
From M.B. Synge, *A Book of Discovery* (London: T.C. & E.C. Jack, n.d.),
after p. 134.

Chapter 5

NARRATIVE MAPS:
REFLECTIONS ON THE TOPONOMY OF ACTS*

How many miles to Babylon?
Threescore miles and ten.
Can I get there by candlelight?
There and back again.
(Old nursery rhyme)

One of the pleasures of my association with John Rogerson has been a shared fascination with maps and a rooted conviction of their importance. It is only fitting, then, that this Festschrift should contain some reflection of this important aspect of John's scholarly activity. The *New Atlas of the Bible*, according to its editor's Preface, sets itself the task of 'seeking to elucidate the geographical conventions that were shared by the biblical writers and their first readers', and in this it 'reflects a current trend in biblical studies towards an appreciation of these narratives as stories in their own right'.[1] The Atlas thus fits well within the wider sensitivity to narrative structures which has been one of the most significant developments in biblical studies during John's time at Sheffield. But the elucidation of a narrative's geographical conventions, it may fairly be argued, does not sit easily within the familiar geographical categories: it shares neither the 'geographical' orientation of the *New Atlas* nor the 'historical' approach of the traditional Bible Atlas. Though linked with both of these, its natural home is within the province of 'Cognitive Geography', a relatively new branch of geographical study which reflects a suitably postmodern awareness that the mental maps which we carry around in our heads may be worth studying in their own right, not simply as approximations to a 'correct' or 'scientific' view of the world.

One way to approach the cognitive geography of an ancient narrative is to look at the shape of the world as presupposed in contemporary geographical

*   First published in M. Daniel Carroll R., D.J.A. Clines and P.R. Davies (eds.), *The Bible in Human Society: Essays in Honour of John Rogerson* (JSOTSup, 200; Sheffield: Sheffield Academic Press, 1995), pp. 17–57, reprinted here with the kind permission of the Continuum International Publishing Group.
        1.   J.W. Rogerson, *The New Atlas of the Bible* (Oxford: MacDonald, 1985), p. 12. Cf Mark Allan Powell, *What Is Narrative Criticism?* (Minneapolis: Fortress Press, 1990), pp. 70–72: 'the geographical setting of a narrative can play a significant role in its total effects'.

texts.[2] This approach has been used with some success to elucidate the Pentecost narrative of Acts 2,[3] and I have used it in another paper to explore the co-ordinates of the journey narratives in the latter part of Acts.[4] In this paper, however, I would like to explore some ways in which the toponymy of a narrative – that is, the selection and distribution of geographical names – may be used to reconstruct its 'implied map', that is the mental map which the text creates for the readers. The sheer familiarity of the Acts map may blunt our perception of its particularity: so the use of comparative maps from contemporary or near-contemporary texts is a useful tool to aid awareness here. Paul's own mental map provides one obvious control; and I shall also try to construct parallel mental maps using the narratives of the two earliest extant Greek novels, Chariton's *Chaereas and Callirhoe* and Xenophon of Ephesus' *Ephesiaca*. These two texts, which are both relatively close in time to Acts,[5] provide an excellent base for comparison because of the prominence of the voyage motif in texts which are not (on the face of it) primarily geographical.

Plotting names on a mental map is a useful way of charting knowledge of and interest in a particular region's geography. But the relationship between the two is not always a simple one. Studies of schoolchildren in Norway and Sweden have revealed the expected correlation between toponymical density and knowledge of the home area, so that the latter shows up as an 'information bump' in relation to the blanker areas further from home.[6] But artificial barriers,

2.   On ancient maps in general see O.A.W. Dilke, *Greek and Roman Maps* (London: Thames & Hudson, 1985). Theophrastus' will provided that 'the tablets (*pinakes*) containing maps of the world (*periodoi gēs*) should be set up in the lower portico' (Diogenes Laertius 5.51; Dilke, p. 31). More public was the map of Agrippa, commissioned and completed by Augustus for public display in Rome: Pliny, *Natural History* 3.16–17; Dilke, pp. 41–53; Claude Nicolet, *Space, Geography and Politics in the Early Roman Empire* (Jerome Lectures, 19; Ann Arbor: University of Michigan Press, 1991; ET of *L'inventaire du monde: Géographie et politique aux origines de l'Empire Romain* [Librairie Arthème Fayard, 1988]), ch. 5. The use of such a map 'for educational purposes' is well illustrated in the later empire by Eumenius: 'Let the schoolchildren see it in those porticoes and look every day at all lands and seas and every city, race or tribe that unconquerable emperors either assist by their sense of duty or conquer by their valour or control by inspiring fear' (XII *Panegyrici Latini* IX [IV]: cited from Dilke, p. 54).

3.   See most recently J.M. Scott, 'Luke's Geographical Horizon', in D.W.J. Gill and C. Gempf (eds.), *The Book of Acts in its Graeco-Roman Setting* (Grand Rapids: Eerdmans and Carlisle: Paternoster, 1994), pp. 483–544.

4.   L.C.A. Alexander, '"In Journeyings Often": Voyaging in the Acts of the Apostles and in Greek Romance', in C.M. Tuckett (ed.), *Luke's Literary Achievement* (JSNTSup, 116; Sheffield: Academic Press, 1995), pp. 17–39 (Chapter 4 in this volume, pp. 69–96).

5.   See B.P. Reardon, *Collected Ancient Greek Novels* (Berkeley: University of California Press, 1989), for translation and introduction. This translation is the one cited in the text unless otherwise stated. The most extensive comparative study of the novels and Acts is that of R.I. Pervo, *Profit with Delight: The Literary Genre of the Acts of the Apostles* (Philadelphia: Fortress Press, 1987). See also J.R. Morgan and R. Stoneman (eds.), *Greek Fiction: The Greek Novel in Context* (London: Routledge, 1994) for a stimulating collection of articles with more recent bibliography.

6.   P. Gould and R. White, *Mental Maps* (Boston: Allen & Unwin, 2nd edn, 1986), pp. 96–114.

like political frontiers, have the effect of distorting the correlation between information and geographical proximity, while conversely certain distant places also featured on the mental maps of even the youngest children, whether because they were popular holiday destinations or because they were prominent in news items at the time the survey was carried out. And religion, culture and history provide an extra dimension to the bare outlines of geographical information, which will be reflected in the selection and distribution of place-names on the mental map. Some years ago, there was a popular song based on the words of Psalm 137 which made it into the UK charts. I remember sitting (in Manchester) with an Iraqi friend, watching his small son singing along to the music. It was Ja'afar who remarked on the irony of the situation: if we were by the rivers of Babylon, he tried to explain to his son, we would be at home, not in exile. In the Judaeo-Christian tradition which underlies so much of Western European culture, Babylon has a significance almost entirely divorced from any knowledge of its present geography, much less of the emotions of its present inhabitants: it exists in a cultural space labelled 'exile' and can – if you are young enough – be reached before bed-time.[7]

Within the New Testament, it is the 'Journeys of St Paul' which most obviously and inevitably seem to require cartographic representation: any Bible Atlas worth its salt will have some sort of map to aid the reader of Acts and the Epistles. It is, however, surprisingly difficult to find any atlas which attempts to distinguish between the mental maps of the two bodies of literature: most present an amalgam of information from Acts and from Paul, with the emphasis overwhelmingly on the former. In addition, many maps include names which we, the readers, know from elsewhere: Sicily, for example, is not named anywhere in the New Testament, yet it frequently appears on maps of Paul's travels. This is not a matter of knowledge or ignorance: there is no reason to doubt that both Paul and Luke[8] knew the name of the island in which Syracuse is situated. It is rather a matter of paying attention to the precise contours of the geographical information an author chooses to highlight: and to do that, we need first to find a way to depict exactly the information given in the text. Only then can we proceed to evaluate its narrative significance.

Our primary concern in this exercise is with the use of geographical names within a given narrative, not with the identification of locations on a modern map. We shall concern ourselves only with the names which actually occur in the text, and the first step is to categorize them according to their function within the narrative. I have divided these geographical names into three categories: primary toponyms (places which occur within the main narrative); secondary toponyms (places which occur within implied or reported narrative); and decorative toponyms (places which supply local or historical colour in a more indirect fashion). Within the first two categories, we may further distinguish

---

7.   A British television documentary some years ago showed the arrival of a group of Russian Jews in Israel. They registered nothing on being told that their destination was 'Nazareth': as the commentator pointed out, this prominent feature of the Christian map of the Holy Land meant nothing to them.

between three classes of name: regional names, city names, and local names, such as names of streets or districts which serve to provide further definition in a locality already named. A narrative map should also be able to distinguish redundant place-names, that is, places that are not themselves locations for adventure but that give added topographical depth to a locality or a journey.

Paul

It is often forgotten that the primary narrative of Paul's journeys is the one he provides himself (if indirectly) in scattered 'travel notes' in the Epistles,[9] and these reveal that Paul sees his world almost entirely in regional terms. Given the extent of the apostle's travels, in fact, it is surprising how few place-names occur in the body of his letters. City names tend to occur most often in the epistle addresses (Rome, Corinth, Philippi, Thessalonica), occasionally in a direct address in the body of the letter (Phil. 4.15; Rom. 1.15). Otherwise Paul prefers to identify churches by regional names (Achaea, Asia, Judea, Macedonia, Galatia): in the last case, the regional name completely swamps the local names even in the letter address (Gal. 1.1; 3.1).[10] Similarly phrases referring to individual church members ('brothers', 'believers', 'firstfruits') tend to be tagged with regional names (Rom. 16.5; 1 Cor. 16.15; 2 Cor. 9.4, 11.9; 1 Thess. 1.7, 4.10), as do phrases referring to the spread of the gospel (1 Thess. 1.8; cf. 2 Cor. 11.10).[11] In fact (outside the letter addresses) there is only one place where the word *ekklesia* occurs in conjunction with a local name, and that is Rom. 16.1, where the recommendation of Phoebe presumably made it essential to distinguish the church in Cenchreae from the rest of the 'churches of Achaea'. Even more surprisingly, regional names also predominate in Paul's travel plans[12] and in his rare moments of autobiography.[13] It is also noticeable (as Edwin Judge has pointed out)[14] that Paul uses the Roman provincial names for the territories of his mission: Illyricum, Spania (not the Greek Iberia), Achaia. Pausanias tells us specifically that the Greeks disliked this last name because the Romans used it as a reminder of the humiliation of the Achaean League.[15] Paul's mental map is

8.   I use the name 'Luke' here and throughout as the conventional designation for the author of Acts.

9.   For the sake of brevity I have restricted the scope of this enquiry to the 'uncontested' epistles: Romans, 1–2 Corinthians, Galatians, Philippians, 1 Thessalonians, Philemon. A comparison of this group with the mental maps of the disputed Paulines might well prove profitable.

10.   Rom. 15.26, 1 Cor. 16.1, 19; 2 Cor. 8.1, 9.2; Gal. 1.22; 1 Thess. 2.14.

11.   Unbelievers are also classified by region: Rom. 15.13.

12.   Rom. 15.24, 28; 1 Cor. 1.16, 16.5; 2 Cor. 1.16, 2.13, 7.5.

13.   Rom. 15.19; 2 Cor. 1.8; Gal. 1.17, 21; Phil. 4.15.

14.   In a paper entitled, 'The Social Distinctiveness of the New Testament Churches', delivered at the British New Testament Conference (Halifax Hall, University of Sheffield) in September 1991.

15.   Pausanias 7.16.10: 'The Romans call him the governor, not of Greece (Ελλάς), but of Achaea, because the cause of the subjection of Greece was the Achaeans, at that time the head of the Greek nation'.

totally lacking in sentimentality: his mission is set very firmly in the contemporary political scene, and he has no qualms about a strategic approach which mirrors the Roman attitude to its conquered territories (see Map 1).[16]

Cities, by contrast, scarcely exist on the Pauline mental map except as locations for churches. Rome and Philippi are never mentioned outside the letter addresses; Corinth occurs once as a place to which Paul 'comes' in 2 Cor. 1.23, but there is a close link with the 'you' of the address. Thessalonica is mentioned once as a place (Phil. 4.16). The precise locations of the Galatian churches, as we have observed, are never named by Paul at all. The other cities named *as places* in the letters are Ephesus (1 Cor. 15.32; 16.8), Athens (1 Thess. 3.1), Damascus (2 Cor. 11.32; Gal. 1.17) and Troas (2 Cor. 2.12) – a pretty thin tally for one who prided himself on the extent of his travels (2 Cor. 11.26). The only city that receives more than a passing mention in Paul's letters is Jerusalem, which achieves a multi-dimensional status all the more striking because of its rarity. Jerusalem exists in geographical space, both as the place from which the mission began (Rom. 15.19) and as a place to which one travels (Rom. 15.25; 1 Cor. 16.3). It also exists in ecclesiastical space, a location for apostles (Gal. 1.17, 18; 2.1) and saints (Rom. 15.25, 26) – though not of an *ekklēsia* – and as the destination of Paul's 'service' in the collection (Rom. 15.31; 1 Cor. 16.3). But, uniquely in the Pauline topography, Jerusalem also reveals a theological dimension. In Gal. 4.25–26 Paul draws a distinction between 'the now Jerusalem' and 'the Jerusalem above', 'who is our mother' – a tacit recognition of the symbolic importance of this central Biblical location.

This passage, in fact, shows Paul fully aware of the multi-layered potential in cognitive mapping. Sinai and Jerusalem (which share the same meridian on the *Jubilees* map)[17] exist both in symbolic space and in the real world. Arabia, however, is not a location on the Biblical map: it belongs on the ruthlessly contemporary (Roman) map of Paul's own world, and in describing Sinai as 'a mountain in Arabia' Paul (I think) implicitly degrades it from the symbolic realm to the banal level of the contemporary traveller. Arabia is somewhere you can journey to: Paul himself has been there, as the reader of Galatians already knows (1.17). The effect is rather like saying (for the reader of the Robin Hood tales), 'We pulled off the motorway and had a picnic in Sherwood Forest', or perhaps (for the viewer of Westerns), 'We pulled up at a gas station in Tombstone Gulch' (see Map 2).

Chariton

Chariton's narrative, by contrast, is carefully located in the historical past. The novel was written in the first or second century CE, but its heroine is the daughter

---

16.　On Roman mapping see Nicolet, *Space, Geography and Politics*, esp. ch. 5.
17.　P.S. Alexander, 'Notes on the *Imago Mundi* in the Book of Jubilees', *JJS* 33 (1982), pp. 197–213.

of Hermocrates, a Sicilian general of the fourth century BCE who makes a brief appearance in the pages of Thucydides' *History of the Peloponnesian War.* Chariton's characters, therefore, move through a consciously archaic landscape from which all traces of the author's present have carefully been removed. Regional and city names are those of the classical past: Sicily, Attica, Ionia; Asia is used in the Ionian sense, not the Roman one (1.11; 3.6; 5.3, 5). But even within this 'historical' framework, Chariton is surprisingly grudging of place-names: he is solicitous (and largely successful) in avoiding anachronism,[18] but makes no attempt to reproduce the topographical richness of a Thucydides or a Xenophon. The result is a curiously empty scene, reminiscent of the painted landscapes of the villas of Pompeii (or of the paintings of Claude and Watteau) – largely pastoral, decorated with occasional monumental structures (tomb, temple), the viewpoint controlled by what is visible from the sea.[19] The point can be illustrated clearly by plotting Chariton's toponymy on to a series of maps: that is, by indicating on a simple outline map the place-names which actually occur in the text.

Primary Toponyms

The first category includes all locations for action involving the main characters in the primary narrative: since Chariton structures his narrative around the paired voyages of heroine and hero, this means all the places to which either of them goes in the main narrative. Despite the huge geographical extent of their journeys from Sicily to Babylon and back, topographical detail is surprisingly sparse. The dramatic action of the book is concentrated in three major locations, Syracuse, Miletus and Babylon, with the small and insignificant island of Aradus providing an unexpected setting for the dramatic reunion of the lovers (7.5).[20] With the action so focused on a small number of geographical areas, we might expect to find a disproportionate number of local place-names fleshing out their geographical characterization: but movement within the locality is described in generic terms (city, country estate, farm, desert, sea) rather than by the aggregation of local names. Athens has its Areopagus (1.11.7), and Dionysius' country house near Miletus is by 'the harbour called Docimus' (3.2.11); otherwise, the

---

18.   The route of Hyginus' journey (4.5.2) suggests that Chariton may have had Aphrodisias, his own home town, in mind as a locus for Mithridates' headquarters (Reardon, *Novels*, p. 71 n. 71); the mention of a port at Paphos (8.2.7) is another anachronism, possibly deliberate (Reardon, *Novels*, p. 113 n. 123).

19.   Visible from the sea: cf. 1.6.5; 1.11; 3.2.11–14; 3.4.18; 4.1.5. On the general importance of the sea in the narrative, see esp. 5.1 and further, Alexander, 'Voyaging', pp. 31–37 (Chapter 4 in this volume, pp. 80–85).

20.   Arrian's *Anabasis of Alexander*, which was probably written at around the same time as Chariton's novel, provides an instructive comparison. Arrian's acount of the expedition of Alexander shows clear affinities with the narratives of the great classical historians, and it is not difficult to see why he attracted comparison with Xenophon even in his own day. But a glance at the *Index to Proper Names* in the Loeb edition of Arrian shows a density of toponyms which Chariton cannot match: even within the area of the Aegean basin, which we can assume would be relatively well known to the readers of both texts, Arrian names a substantially greater number of places.

novel's key locations are characterized by their buildings and institutions rather than by place-names. Thus Syracuse is characterized by its democratic institutions (assembly, theatre, gymnasium), where typically 'Greek' activities take place (voting, decrees, embassies, the granting of citizenship: cf. esp. 8.6–8). Babylon is quintessentially 'oriental', with an emphasis on the importance of satraps' residences and royal palaces (5.2): the elaborately-described trial setting is dominated by the King's throne, indicative of the un-Greek centrality of an autocratic ruler even in the courts of justice (5.4). The Greek cities of the Aegean basin, though more 'Greek' (and therefore more 'free') than Babylon, are not accorded the full civic dignity of Syracuse: Miletus has temples, harbours and slave-markets, but no democratic assembly, and Priene, like Athens, is distinguished purely for its 'Greek' inquisitiveness (4.5.4; 1.11.6).

Chaereas' search for his wife involves him in some more extensive travelling on his own, but the search 'towards Libya' is described in summary fashion, and the location of his servitude under Mithridates is described simply as 'Caria'.[21] In Book 7 he does some successful campaigning in 'Syria and Phoenicia', but the only city named is Tyre,[22] and even after his liberation of the city, Chaereas refuses to participate in civic festivities (7.1–4). Details of the voyages between one location and another are equally meagre. Callirhoe views Athens from a distance (1.11), and the pair call in briefly to visit the temple of Aphrodite in Paphos on their way home (8.2.7). The 'Ionian Sea' which looms so large in the characters' thoughts is actually crossed in a very short amount of narrative time.[23] On land, too, redundant place-names (that is, names which create a sense of movement in a voyage narrative but do not form locations for significant action) are virtually non-existent in the primary narrative, and are used chiefly to emphasize the remoteness of Babylon. Callirhoe's route to Babylon takes her from Ionia via 'Syria and Cilicia' (in that order) to the Euphrates crossing, beyond which she sees only 'a vast stretch of unending land' labelled 'Bactra and Susa' (5.1.3–7); Chaereas' 'faster' route takes him from Caria via Armenia (5.2.1).[24] The return trip takes both parties back 'across the river' into Syria (7.2.1), rather mysteriously allowing the King to deposit his womenfolk in the island of Aradus en route (7.4.11–5.1). The names of Tyre and Sidon, Coele-Syria and Phoenicia are sufficient to establish a loose sense of location for the war with the Egyptians; the mysterious Chios (8.5.2) may be due to textual corruption.[25] Redundant place-names, in this most economical of narratives, are few and far between (see Map 3).

---

21.   Sicily, Italy, Libya and the Ionian Sea are covered in a matter of 3 lines: 3.3.8. Caria: 3.7.3; 4.7.4; 5.1.1.

22.   Sidon gets a brief mention at 7.4.11 as an object of concern to the Persian king, but does not play any part in the action.

23.   See below p. 116.

24.   Neither route inspires great confidence in Chariton's acquaintance with the geography of the Eastern provinces (cf. Alexander, 'Voyaging', pp. 26–28, [Chapter 4 in this volume, pp. 76–78]).

25.   Reardon, *Novels*, p. 117 n. 128. Karl Plepelits, *Chariton von Aphrodisias, Kallirhoe* (Stuttgart: Anton Hiersemann, 1976), p. 189 n. 190 suggests that the name may conceal a Phoenician one.

Secondary Toponyms

Unlike some of the later novelists, Chariton does not make much use of reported narrative or flashback. The Sicilian search-parties report back on their fruitless quest for Callirhoe in the briefest of terms (3.3): more dramatic significance is attached to the misfortunes of the pirate chief Theron, told in a (largely fictitious) first-person flashback, which adds the names Cephallenia and Crete to the novel's narrative map (3.4). The revolt of the Egyptian king allows the addition of a southern dimension: Memphis, Pelusium and the Nile make a brief appearance in the summary report of the uprising (6.8; 7.3), but do not significantly disrupt the East-West alignment of the main narrative.[26] More significant for the narrative is the opportunity afforded by this episode for adding a depth of local colour to the Babylonian setting through the invocation of the more distant Persian regions of Bactra and Ecbatana (6.8). The 'vast unending tract of land', evoked so feelingly when Callirhoe crosses the Euphrates, is here fleshed out with names which give the narrative map a semblance of geographical depth (see Map 4).

Decorative Toponyms

Finally, we should note how Chariton adds further depth to his topographical characterization through a scattering of names whose function in the narrative might be described as purely decorative. Place-names are used to label the fabrics and hangings of Babylon in a way that adds a richness of local colour to the elaborate picture of the fabulous East built up by the narrative. Like the careful descriptions of the throne-room or the king's hunting accoutrements, they serve to distance the Greek reader from the exotic world in which the novel's characters find themselves.[27] Chariton uses a similar technique to provide both local colour and historical depth to his heroes' Sicilian homeland through the use of topographical surnames. Acragas and Rhegium (1.2), Thurii and Messana (1.7) play no part in the narrative directly, but they serve to flesh out the topographically flat portayal of Sicily in the primary narrative, as does the (anachronistic) introduction of Sybaris into Theron's false account of Callirhoe's origins (1.12; 2.1): the names' associations add a further dimension to the irony of the tale.[28] These names also serve to remind the reader that Sicily and southern Italy were essentially Greek territory at the dramatic date of the story, thickly dotted with Greek colonies. The name 'Greek' itself, which is frequently invoked by the novel's heroes, indicates not the Greek mainland but the larger, more nebulous linguistic and cultural domain including Magna Graecia and the Ionian coast.[29] But perhaps the most interesting feature of Chariton's narrative map at this level of decorative toponymy is the cluster of names around the classical Greek heartlands of Attica and the Peloponnese. Lacedaimonians (Spartans), Corinthians and Peloponnesians

---

26.   Cf. Alexander, 'Voyaging', pp. 26–28 and Figure 7, (Chapter 4 in this volume, pp. 76–78, 93).

27.   Cf. 6.4.2 (Nisaean horse, Tyrian purple, Chinese quiver and bow); cf. 8.1.6

28.   Cf. Reardon's note (*Novels,* p. 35 n. 29).

29.   Cf. e.g. 7.2.3 'we are Greeks; we are of noble family in Syracuse'. Conversely, Athens is located not in 'Greece' but in 'Attica' (1.11.4).

figure prominently in Chaereas' band of champions against Tyre;[30] the battles of Salamis, Marathon, and Thermopylae are invoked to inspire both hero and heroine to courage against the barbarians.[31] These are not geographical locations for any action in the narrative, primary or secondary: rather they serve to provide a cultural location for the whole story within Chariton's chosen time-frame.[32] Their density creates an 'information bump' on the map which ensures the surprising prominence of a region in which none of the novel's action takes place, but which clearly plays a vital role in the cultural identity of its implied readers (see Map 4).[33]

Xenophon

In topography, as in so much else, Xenophon is markedly less sophisticated than Chariton: in Dalmeyda's words, 'in general, his great love-affair with geography is very poorly rewarded'.[34] Scene-painting is sketchy, with little topographical detail to enliven the empty, bandit-ridden landscapes. The chronological location is never clearly defined, but the effect is broadly that of a timeless 'hellenistic' setting. Hellenistic foundations like Antioch and Alexandria figure prominently in the 'New World' of Syria and Egypt alongside the older Greek settlements of Sicily and the Aegean, but Roman names are conspicuous by their absence. The regional geography of Asia Minor, as in Chariton, reflects the survival of the older Greek nomenclature (Lycia, Phrygia, Pamphylia), but it is too imprecise to allow any clear correlation with Roman toponymy. 'Asia' occurs once, at 1.1.3, to denote the region to which dramatic news from Ephesus is broadcast: but this usage is consistent both with the Roman period, in which Ephesus is the centre of the province of Asia, and with the older Ionian usage (reflected in Chariton) in which the Greek cities of the Ionian seaboard are seen as the frontage to a whole continent. The occasional title of a local magistrate can be used to provide a *terminus post quem* for the author, as in 2.13.3, where Perilaus is identified as 'eirenarch' of Cilicia, a post-Trajanic office: but Xenophon's phraseology here seems an unconscious betrayal of his own period, reflecting a naive lack of chronological sensitivity, rather than a conscious attempt to provide a temporal location for the narrative.[35]

30. 7.3.7; cf. also 8.2.12.

31. Salamis and Marathon are invoked by Callirhoe at 6.7.10, Thermopylae by Chaereas at 7.3.9. Cf. also Olympia and Eleusis, 5.4.4.

32. The comparison with Medea at 2.9.3, which introduces Scythia into the narrative map, is a further connection with the narrative world of Greek myth.

33. Cf. Alexander, 'Voyaging', pp. 34–35, (Chapter 4 in this volume, p. 83).

34. G. Dalmeyda, *Xénophon d'Ephèse: Les Ephésiaques* (Paris: Les Belles Lettres, 1962), p. xii: 'en général, son grand amour de la géographie est très mal payé de retour' (my translation).

35. Perilaus is described not as εἰρηνάρχης but as ὁ τῆς ἐν Κιλικίᾳ προεστώς. Hägg's assertion that 'the novel takes place in the same Near East, governed by the Romans, as the New Testament' (*The Novel in Antiquity*, [Oxford: Blackwell, 1983], p. 30) seems overstated: the 'prefect of Egypt' which appears in translations at the point cited (4.2.1) is simply an ἄρχων, a much more inclusive title, and the use of a cross (σταυρός) as a means of execution appears also in Chariton's carefully Rome-free narrative (though the method of attachment is different: 3.4.18). In both cases it may well be an unconscious reflection of the time-frame of the author – but that is very different from the chronological setting of the narrative.

Primary Toponyms

The distinction between primary and secondary toponyms is less obvious in Xenophon's work. The total number of geographical names in the two novels is almost identical, but in Xenophon most of them occur in the primary narrative as locations for adventures. Thus where Chariton concentrates his dramatic action into three major settings, Xenophon (in a shorter text)[36] spreads his in a more episodic fashion across a much wider range of locations. The story begins and ends in Ephesus, which is doubly anchored in Ionia and in Asia.[37] After their capture by pirates somewhere on the 'Egyptian sea' (1.12.3), the protagonists are taken first east (Phoenicia, Syria and Cilicia, with a detour to Cappadocia and Pontus), then south to Egypt and Ethiopia , then west to Italy and Sicily before making their way back to Rhodes for a tearful reunion. Within this framework, the sense of journeying is achieved for the most part in the simplest possible fashion, by naming destinations: Phoenicia, Cappadocia, Ethiopia, India, Italy.[38] In the novel's final scene, Anthia catalogues the various attempts on her virtue by geographical region: 'No one persuaded me to go astray: not Moeris in Syria, Perilaus in Cilicia, Psammis or Polyidus in Egypt, not Anchialus in Ethiopia, not my master in Tarentum' (5.14.2). The accumulation of these names allows the author to create a general sense of location in east, south or west without attempting any very precise topography. Regions are generally characterized by naming one major city: Tyre in Phoenicia (1.14.6); Antioch in Syria (2.9.1); Xanthus in Lycia (2.10.4); Tarsus in Cilicia (2.13.5), Mazacus in Cappadocia (3.1.1).[39] Travel between one location and another is generally accomplished in the minimum of narrative time, with little attention to travel detail, nautical or otherwise (see Map 5).[40]

There are however two areas which show up on Xenophon's mental map as clusters of 'redundant' place-names. The first of these, naturally enough, is around the author's home ground of Ephesus:

> It cannot be doubted, then, that Xenophon speaks to us here of 'things seen' and of a land which he knows well. He volunteers precise geographical information which his narrative does not require: he will tell us, for example, that Xanthos is not on the coast but 'inland' [2.10.4]; that the processional route which leads from the city to Artemision is seven stades [1.2.2]; that, by sea, it is no more than 80 stades from Ephesus to the sanctuary of Apollo at Colophon [1.6.1]. These details hold all the more interest for us in that our author does not always display the same exactitude: outside Asia Minor, with

---

36.   It is possible that the text as we have it may be (at least partly) epitomized: cf. Reardon, *Novels*, p. 126; T. Hägg, 'Die *Ephesiaka* des Xenophon Ephesius: original oder Epitome?' (*Classica et Mediaevalia* 27 [1966], pp. 118–61.

37.   1.1.1, 3. Asia seems to denote the continent, in the Ionian sense: cf. also 3.2.11.

38.   E.g. 1.13.2; 2.14.3; 3.1.1; 4.3.1; 4.3.3; 5.1.1.

39.   Sicily and Italy, unusually, muster four city names (Syracuse, Tarentum, Tauromenium, Nuceria), perhaps as the simplest means to allow for the separate destinations of the three protagonists.

40.   Cf. e.g. the brief voyages to the west at 5.1.1; 5.3.3; 5.5.4; 7; 5.6.1.

which he appears to be tolerably well acquainted, his itineraries can be strange and disconcerting.[41]

As so often, the depth of information available on the 'home' locality has a distorting effect on the mental map. Thus we are told that 'the temple of Apollo in Colophon is...ten miles' sail from Ephesus' (1.6.1), and the honeymoon voyage between Ephesus and Rhodes seems long in proportion to other narrative journeys because of the listing of intermediate stages on the route: Samos, Cos, Cnidus (1.11.1–6). A proliferation of nautical business increases the sense of journeying which is so prominent at this stage of the narrative, and so lacking elsewhere. Similarly the banishment of Leucon and Rhode to Xanthus in Lycia, 'a town some distance from the sea' (2.10.4) sounds like one of the longest journeys in the book; yet the distance covered is relatively small in comparison with the narrative map as a whole (see Map 5a).

The same technique of creating an itinerary by the use of redundant place-names is used in Egypt to enrich the sense of travel in an exotic location, but here Xenophon's local knowledge fails him. 'Egyptian' names are fired at the narrative in a scatter-gun effect which looks impressive but fails to make geographical sense (4.1.1–5): to quote Dalmeyda again, 'This itinerary of Hippothous is a kind of amiable fantasy'.[42] A comparison with Strabo shows by contrast the weakness of Xenophon's conception of this area: certain features of the standard merchant route to India appear, but on the whole Xenophon's picture of the Nile Delta is thin on detail and – quite simply – confused (see Map 5b).[43]

Secondary Toponyms

Secondary narrative in Xenophon is limited, but it does have the effect of increasing the text's geographical scope. Hippothous' lachrymose reminiscences provide a brief excursion to the northern end of the Aegean (Perinthus, Byzantium, Thrace; Lesbos, Phrygia Magna, Pamphylia: 3.2). The implied travels of Psammis, the Indian merchant prince, provide a southern dimension to the novel (Anthia is 'rescued' by the bandits en route to India, but gets no further than a cave in Ethiopia: 4.3). And several names from the Greek

---

41.   Dalmeyda, *Xénophon*, pp. xi–xii: 'Il n'est donc pas douteux que Xénophon nous parle ici de "choses vues" et d'un pays qu'il connaît bien. Il donne volontiers des précisions géographiques que son récit n'exigeait pas: il nous dira, par exemple, que Xanthos n'est pas sur le littoral, mais "dans les terres" [2.10.4], que le trajet de la procession qui va de la ville à l'Artémision est de sept stades [1.2.2]; que, par mer, il n'y a pas plus de quatre-vingts stades d'Éphèse au sanctuaire d'Apollon à Colophon [1.6.1]. Ces détails ont pout nous d'autant plus d'intérêt que notre auteur n'a pas toujours la même exactitude: hors de l'Asie-Mineure, dont il paraît avoir quelque connaissance, ses itinéraires sont, parfois, étranges et déconcertants.'

42.   Dalmeyda, *Xénophon*, p. 49, my translation: 'Cet itinéraire d'Hippothoos est d'une aimable fantaisie'; cf. Reardon, *Novels*, p. 155.

43.   Strabo mentions (going eastwards along the mouth of the Delta from Alexandria) Schedia (C800/17.1.16), Hermupolis, Mendes, Leontopolis (C802/17.1.19), and Pelusium (C803/17.1.21). For Memphis and the temple of Apis, cf. C807/17.1.31. There is another Hermopolis ('the Hermopolitic garrison, a kind of toll-station for goods brought down from the Thebais') above Memphis: C813/17.1.41. For Coptus, cf. C815/17.1.44–5.

heartland (Sparta, Argos, Corinth) are entered on the narrative map through the autobiography of Aegialeus (5.1.4–13), the poor fisherman whom Habrocomes encounters in Syracuse who turns out to be a 'Lacedaemonian Spartan' exiled for love – a thoroughly classical provenance for this model of faithfulness to love in adverse circumstances.

Decorative Toponyms
These are relatively few, given Xenophon's rather two-dimensional narrative style. Xenophon shares to the full Chariton's 'Greek' disdain for 'barbarians',[44] but he shows no interest in creating a cultural hinterland to the novel in the way that Chariton does through literary and historical allusion (above pp. 104–105). Only the opening description of the nuptial bedchamber (1.8.2) is rich enough to allow for decorative detail: 'Babylonian tapestry' and 'Nabatean ostriches'[45] seem to be used as an indicator of luxury (cf. 2.7.3). But there is a sense in which the whole Egyptian narrative is overshadowed by the implied travels of the merchants who made Egypt, as Strabo tells us, 'the greatest emporium of the *oikoumenē*'.[46] The constant stream of traffic up and down the Nile, from the commercial ports of Alexandria, past the duty-station at Schedia to Coptos and ultimately via the Red Sea ports to India,[47] is the motive force that brings Psammis to Alexandria and attracts Hippothous to Coptos as a likely spot for a bit of banditry (4.1.5) (see Map 6).

Acts
The toponymy of the Paul narrative in Acts need not be described here in detail: see the Appendix (pp. 120–22) for a summary. It is one of the most striking features of this narrative that the reader is suddenly swamped with geographical information, much of it presented with a prolixity of redundant detail (names underlined in the Appendix) which is surprising after the sparse and imprecise geography of the gospels.[48] This cartographic complexity has suggested to more than one reader a parallel with the more fantastic realms of Greek prose narrative. Tomas Hägg's classic study of *The Novel in Antiquity* notes in passing that 'a map of the Mediterranean region showing the routes of the hero and heroine of a novel inevitably brings to mind the school-bible's map of the travels of St Paul'.[49] Conzelmann makes a similar comparison with Xenophon of Ephesus: 'The addition of unimportant stopping-places along the way can be explained on literary grounds… [C]f. the extended description in Xen. Eph. 1.11–12.'[50] We are now in a position to pursue this comparison in more detail by setting the familiar

44.   Cf. Alexander, 'Voyaging', p. 35 (= Chapter 4, pp. 83–84).
45.   See Reardon's note *ad loc.*
46.   Strabo, *Geog.* C798 (17.1.13).
47.   Schedia: 4.1.3; cf. Strabo, *Geog.* C800 (17.1.16). Coptos: 4.1.4; cf. Strabo, *Geog.* C815 (17.1.45).
48.   M.A. Powell, *What Is Narrative Criticism?* (Minneapolis: Fortess Press, 1990), p. 71.
49.   Hägg, *The Novel in Antiquity*, endpapers.
50.   H. Conzelman, *Acts of the Apostles* (Hermeneia; Philadelphia: Fortress Press, 1987; trans. from 2nd German edn of 1972), p. xl and n. 88.

mental map of Acts alongside those of Paul, on the one hand, and the two novels on the other. In this final section I shall suggest some ways in which the insights of cognitive geography may be used to sharpen our perceptions of these narrative landscapes, and the similarities and differences between them.

1. *The Geographical Horizon*

For the purposes of this study, I have largely limited the comparison with Acts to the Pauline narratives, that is chs. 13–28. This clearly excludes a number of Palestinian names (Galilee, Samaria, Gaza, Joppa, Lydda, Sharon), as well as the Diaspora centres named in the Pentecost narrative at 2.9–11. All of these are significant for the contours of the total narrative map of Acts, especially as adding to the information density on its eastern side.[51] But the limitation provides a more straightforward comparison, in that from ch. 13 onwards Acts becomes more obviously a narrative of Mediterranean travel – a fact which is itself of some significance within the context of biblical geography, marking a decisive shift from the Jerusalem-centred perspective of the earlier part of Acts. Paul the traveller moves in an area bounded by Syria-Palestine in the east and Sicily-Italy in the west – which is very much the same geographical arena as the novels.

But this central Mediterranean arena, which represents the primary location for action in all four mental maps, should not be conceived as a closed system comprising the sum of these texts' geographical horizons. For all of them, the immediate horizon of the known and familiar is breached by the implied narratives of travellers from more distant regions – pilgrims or merchants, or destinations planned but never reached. These implied narratives form 'information corridors' like those observed in twentieth-century mental maps linking home territory to vacation destinations – though ideas of the actual location of these destinations may be hazy.[52] Paul's own mental map, interestingly enough, is the only one of the four to extend its horizons westward beyond Italy – the planned trip to Spain would have taken him into territory unexplored in the novels. Xenophon's map is breached at its southern extremity, with Anthia's threatened abduction to India via Ethiopia.[53] Chariton's map opens out towards the east, with a major scene set in Babylon ('Beyond the River') and further horizons implied through the use of eastern names – Bactra, Susa, and Ecbatana, with a glimpse of China in the distance. For Acts, it is the implied narratives of the pilgrims which most obviously open up the narrative map: Parthia, Media, Mesopotamia and Elam to the east (2.9), Arabia, Egypt and Ethiopia to the south (2.10–11; 8.27–39). Westwards, however, Luke's geographical horizon, like that of the novels, reaches no further than Sicily and Italy.

---

51.   Alexander, 'Voyaging', p. 30, (Chapter 4 in this volume, p. 80).

52.   On 'information corridors', see Gould and White, *Mental Maps*, p. 103. On 'location', cf. their comment that many travellers (especially by air) are content 'to be transported through a tube of ignorance' (Gould and White, *Mental Maps*, p. 83). Cf. further Alexander, 'Voyaging', pp. 27–28, (Chapter 4 in this volume, pp. 77–78).

53.   Alexander, 'Voyaging', pp. 28–29 with Figure 8, (Chapter 4 in this volume, pp. 78, 94).

2. *Invisible Landscapes and Spatial Biases*

It is the Mediterranean basin, then, that all four narratives have in common –
or, more accurately, its eastern half. But within that common geographical
framework there is room for enormous variation, both in the areas explored and
in the details of their toponymy. Out of a total of 141 names, the combined
mental map contains only four – an astonishingly low total – in common
between all four narratives (Corinth, Asia, Cilicia, Syria). If we extend this to
include names held in common by any three, we can add a further nine: Ephesus,
Antioch, Athens, Syracuse, Crete, Lycia, Cyprus, Phoenicia and Tyre. Thus the
common mental map of the Mediterranean area, taken from four broadly
comparable travel accounts written no more than a century apart, reveals a
surprisingly small degree of compatibility: 13 toponyms out of a total of 141.
The lack of overlap here cannot be accounted for by the relative paucity of names
in Paul. Paul's map contains only 21 names, but this includes two not shared by
any of the other narratives (Spain, Illyricum) and a further 11 [12] shared only
with Acts (Rome, Macedonia, Thessalonica, Philippi, Achaea, Cenchreae, Troas,
Galatia, Judaea, Jerusalem, Damascus, [Arabia]).[54] This means that over half of
the names on Paul's map (13 out of 21) do not correspond at all with the
toponymy of the novels, despite the fact that they are talking about travels within
the same geographical area. Acts has a greater degree of overlap, with a total
of 17 names in common with one or both novelists – but of these only six overlap
with both (Syracuse, Crete, Lycia, Cyprus, Phoenicia, Tyre).[55] And these common
lists are completely overshadowed by the long lists of toponyms unique to each
narrative: 23 in Xenophon, 28 in Chariton, and 38 in Acts.[56]

These statistics already underline the stark contrasts in the implied maps that
different narratives can construct for the same geographical location. This
implied map may well be much less extensive – and more schematic – than the
actual geographical knowledge of the actual author and readers. Narrative, like
cartography, involves selection from a bewilderingly large and inchoate mass of
data in order to construct a two-dimensional account on paper. Nevertheless,
the limitations of the implied map are an important feature of the total rhetorical
effect of the narrative, an effective part of the filter by which the narrator
controls the reader's perception of the narrative world. Where that world is –
or purports to be – also a report of the readers' real world, these limitations may
have a significant effect on readers' perceptions of the world outside the text.
They may also reflect, in a more obvious fashion, the perceptual filter which
governs the author's own view of the world:

> Human behaviour is affected only by that portion of the environment that is actually
> perceived. We cannot absorb and retain the virtually infinite amount of information that

54.   Arabia (Gal 1.17): cf. 'Arabs', Acts 2.11.
55.   Overlap with Xenophon only: Chios, Cos, Cnidos, Rhodes, Phrygia, Pamphylia,
Tarsus, Alexandria (plus Pontus if we include Acts 2). Overlap with Chariton only: Rhegium,
Miletus, Paphos.
56.   These figures do not include overlapping names from Acts 2 and 8: Cappadocia and
Ethiopia (Xenophon), Media and Libya (Chariton).

impinges upon us daily. Rather, we devise perceptual filters that screen out most information in a highly selective fashion… Our views of the world, and about people and
places in it, are formed from a highly filtered set of impressions, and our images are
strongly affected by the information we receive through our filters.[57]

Analysing the differences between the narrative maps in our study may give us
some clues as to the perceptual filters which have created them – and which they
create.

3. *The Political Landscape*

One of the filters most obviously at work here is political. The novelists select
their toponyms in such a way as to create a Rome-free landscape which must
(in the first or second century CE) be deliberate. Chariton does this by
constructing a dramatic chronology anchored at a point in the historical past;
Xenophon, less precise but equally resolute, by painting a timeless hellenistic
landscape. Acts, by contrast, shares Paul's commitment to the realistic political
landscape of the first century. There are 13 names unique to Paul and Acts: Spain,
Illyricum, Arabia, Rome, Macedonia, Thessalonica, Philippi, Achaea, Cenchreae,
Troas, Galatia, Judaea, Damascus, Jerusalem. Of these, the majority are Roman
or are used in a distinctively Roman fashion.[58] This is particularly evident in Sicily
and Italy, where both the novelists studiously avoid mentioning Rome and
focus on the old Greek colonies of Magna Graecia. Acts, by contrast, includes
not only Rome itself but also three local staging-posts with disinctively Latin
names (Puteoli, Appii Forum and Tres Tabernae)[59]. It is no part of my purpose
here to enter into the lengthy debate over the accuracy of Luke's political map
for the precise date of the events he records. The point is a more general one:
whether Acts was written in the first century or the second, its mental map
exhibits a realism about the Roman dimension of the Mediterranean
environment which is not mirrored in the romantic hellenism of the first- and
second-century novelists.

Where Acts differs from Paul, clearly, is in the addition of extra geographical
detail which gives the toponymy of Acts a depth and variety lacking in Paul's
much briefer travel notes. This makes Luke's map less starkly Roman than Paul's:
but it remains firmly rooted in the contemporary political world. Thus Acts
includes some of the older Greek regional names (Lycia, Pamphylia, Phrygia),
which persisted in use throughout the Roman period and which are also reflected
in the novels – though neither Xenophon nor Chariton shares Acts' knowledge
of the inland regions of Galatia and Lycaonia. 'Asia' appears to be used broadly
in the Roman sense to denote the province which included within its borders
Chariton's more archaic 'Ionia' and 'Caria'.[60] Luke shows no compunction in

---

57. Gould and White, *Mental Maps*, p. 28.
58. Cf. pp. 100–101, for Paul's use of Roman names.
59. Strabo, writing at the beginning of the first century, still uses the older Greek name
for Puteoli, Dicaearchia: cf. C793 (17.1.7).
60. P. Trebilco, 'Asia', in Gill and Gempf (eds.), *The Book of Acts in its Graeco-Roman
Setting*, pp. 291–362 (292, 300–302).

following Paul's usage of 'Achaea' (18.12, 27; 19.21), though he does once replace it with the less offensive 'Hellas' (20.2). But neither of the novelists refers to Greece in this way: they prefer in more classical fashion to talk of 'Attica', 'Lacedaimonia', and 'the Peloponnese' (much as the inhabitants of the political territory known to the world as 'Great Britain' tend to refer to their homeland as 'England', 'Wales', or 'Scotland').

4. *The Emotional Landscape*

Another filter which affects the construction of a mental map is emotional attachment and its inverse, emotional stress or hostility. The distribution of names on a map may be a good way of judging which areas represent 'home' and which are 'foreign territory', with blanks often providing unconscious evidence of stress patterns in the perceived environment.[61] For most people, the known territory around the 'home' area looms disproportionately large on the mental map, in a way that can be rendered graphically by the 'information bump' caused by the larger number of local place-names to be fitted in. The effect is well illustrated in the Wallingford maps of the New Yorker's and the Bostonian's ideas of the United States. In the former, 'the northern borough of the Bronx is so far away that to all intents and purposes it is close to Albany and Lake George in the Adirondacks', while 'Connecticut is somewhere to the east, but it is mentally blurred with a place called Boston – obviously a mere village in the crook of Cape Cod'. For the Bostonian, on the other hand, 'brash, somewhat *nouveau,* towns like New York and Washington are put in their proper places in the hinterland, for it is clear that they are merely stopping points on the fringe of the West Prairies, where presumably other towns exist'.[62] In general, common sense would lead us to expect a simple correlation between information and distance from home, so that the more distant areas of the map appear as blanks, ready to be peopled with the monsters of the imagination: 'Here Be Dragons'.

Xenophon, as we have observed, exhibits a classic 'information bump' around his home territory of Ephesus, and the amount of geographical information shades off perceptibly as the narrative moves eastwards. Syria and Phoenicia, from this perspective, appear as virtual blanks, populated almost entirely by pirates and bandits. For Acts, by contrast, this is home territory, with a good distribution of local names (even more if we include Acts 1–12) and a chain of secure hospitality bases. Incidentally, the bandits are not entirely a figment of the novelistic imagination: there were bandits, both in Syria and in Cilicia. Paul mentions them, in passing, as a hazard of his travels (though he does not say where: 2 Cor. 11.26): but there is no sign of them in Acts.

---

61.   Gould and White, *Mental Maps*, pp. 12–17, 108: 'In cities of the United States people's spatial behaviour is shaped by the hills and valleys of the invisible information and environmental stress surfaces over them. One French newspaper…published a map of Manhattan in New York City, indicating what areas were safe to walk in day and night. The *New York Times* immediately responded with a similar cartographic guide to Paris, but both were making the same point: invisible stress surfaces lie over both cities, and influence people's paths and movements to a considerable extent.'

62.   Gould and White, *Mental Maps*, pp. 17–25.

This feature of the novelistic worldview is paralleled in the narratives' perception of where 'barbarians' are to be found. Both Chariton and Xenophon share a strongly Greek-centred perception of the Mediterranean world, in which the sea is 'the Greek sea',[63] and the exotic lands to east and south of its borders are full of 'barbarians'. This is a classic instance of 'the stifling parochialism, the boundary thinking, the Us-Themism'[64] which lies behind many mental maps, and which is unconsciously reflected even in the twentieth century in the North Atlantic attitude to 'the Oriental':

> In the ancient as in the modern world cultures and ideas have no frontiers. There were in the setting of Luke's stories many features that can be classified as neither Greek, Roman, Jewish, nor Christian. Some of these may be described as universally human, some as specifically ancient, while others belong to quite definite strands inside or outside the Roman Empire – Ethiopian, Arabian, Phoenician, Anatolian. For some of them we may apply the collective name oriental, but in doing so we should recall that it but imperfectly sums up them all, that they go back to very ancient migrations to the West and to indigenous cultures. In that melting pot it was not true that
> East is East and West is West
> And never the twain shall meet.
> In the time of Acts there was no oriental frontier either at the Euphrates or at the Bosporus. Even an imaginary frontier would have to place most of the Eastern Mediterranean on the oriental side. Scratch beneath the skin of the other cultures and you will find the Oriental still there.[65]

Despite his caution, Cadbury's words, written in 1955, betray an alarming disposition to what Edward Said calls 'Orientalism'.[66] More to the point, they display the way in which the mental maps of the novels may provide a window into worldviews less frankly displayed in other ancient texts. Chariton, in fact, does draw a clear frontier on his map at the Euphrates, beyond which lies the Persian Empire ('Asia' in its fullest sense), peopled by barbarians who are 'slaves' to the Great King and given to un-Greek habits like *proskynēsis*.[67] West of this line are the Greeks, who are correspondingly free, noble and democratic. But even among the Greeks there are degrees of nobility, matched by their position to east or west on the map. The whole area from Babylon up to and including the Ionian coast is (for the dramatic purposes of the story) subject to Persia (which is why Dionysius of Miletus has to take his case to Babylon to submit it to the arbitration of the Great King). These Ionian Greeks are therefore several degrees less free than the Athenians, who play an important role in the political geography of the story (though they play none at all in its action). The

63. Chariton: 4.7.8; 5.1.3. Cf. Alexander, 'Voyaging', pp. 34–35, (Chapter 4 in this volume, pp. 83–84).

64. Gould and White, *Mental Maps*, p. 151.

65. H.J. Cadbury, *The Book of Acts in History* (London: Adam & Charles Black, 1955), pp. 27–28.

66. E. Said, *Orientalism* (London: Routledge & Kegan Paul, 1978).

67. Euphrates: 5.1. Slaves: 6.4, 6.7, 7.1. *Proskynesis*: 5.3; cf. Reardon's note *ad loc.*, and Arrian, *Anabasis of Alexander* 4.9.9, 4.10.5ff.

Athenians, as Chariton frequently reminds his readers, had defeated the Persians at Salamis. The Syracusans, however, have just defeated the Athenians, which places them in the paradoxical position of being at one and the same time allies of the Persians in hatred of Athens, and supermen of the Mediterranean world as conquerors of the conquerors of the Great King.[68] Thus for Chariton the area which scores highest on his map in terms of '*Graecitas*' (especially seen in its democratic institutions) is not the author's own homeland in Caria but Sicily in the farthest west.

This background makes it easier to appreciate the force of Cadbury's observation. It is not true that 'in the time of Acts there was no oriental frontier either at the Euphrates or at the Bosporus', but it is true of Acts itself. Luke's worldview, as I have argued elsewhere,

> entails a reversal of the usual Greek perspective on the world: for Luke's hero, Syria and Phoenicia are home ground, while the Aegean is unexplored territory. The reversal is highlighted by occasional touches of regional characterisation. The only 'barbarians' in Acts are in the West, not in the East (28.2); and it is the Athenians, in the heartland of Greek culture, who are described as 'superstitious' (δεισιδαιμονεστέρους 17.22).[69]

Chariton, with his ambivalent attitude towards Athens, actually shares Luke's slightly ironic characterization of the Athenians as 'busybodies' – compare Acts 17.21 with 1.11.6–7:

> But Theron did not like the inquisitive ways of the town. 'Look, are you the only people who don't know what busybodies they are in Athens? They're a nation of gossips, and they love lawsuits. There'll be hundreds of nosey parkers in the harbor wanting to know who we are and where we got this cargo we're carrying. Nasty suspicions will seize hold of their malicious minds – and it's the Areopagus straightaway, in Athens, and magistrates who are more severe than tyrants.'

But Paul's perception that the city is 'full of idols' (17.16) expresses a viewpoint which no pagan Greek writer would share: this is the outsider looking in, the representative of an eastern religion coming to the centre of classical culture and finding it wanting[70]. This outside-in perspective on the Greek cities is reflected also in Acts' characterization of locality: where the novelists see temples, Luke foregrounds the meeting-places of the local Jewish community. These contrasting views of the urban landscape parallel the mental maps observed in a Los Angeles study, in which the maps of white, upper class respondents differed markedly from those other of ethnic groups. 'Most distressing of all was the viewpoint of a small Spanish-speaking minority in the neighbourhood of Boyle Heights...[which] includes only the immediate area, the City Hall and, pathetically, the bus depot – the major entrance and exit to their tiny urban world.'[71]

---

68.   5.8; 6.7; 7.5.
69.   Alexander, 'Voyaging', p. 36, (Chapter 4 in this volume, p. 84).
70.   Cf. also Acts' disparaging portrayal of the revered Greek cult of Artemis in Ephesus (19.23–41).
71.   Gould and White, *Mental Maps*, p. 17.

The Jewish community in fact creates both the social networks which support Paul and his associates and the location for their principal areas of environmental stress: for Acts, the boundary between 'us' and 'them' is to be found within the cities, not on the fringes of the map.

5. *Narrative Functions*

Finally, what of the narrative functions of the place-names in Acts? Narrative choice represents a further significant factor in the filtering of information for the implied map of any given text. The novels clearly provide a number of useful parallels here; but it is also important to notice significant differences.

First, geographical names have resonances of their own, and these can be exploited to build up the character of a distant locality. One result may be an inversion of the expected correlation between information and distance. In a literary text, the exotic may attract more place-names than the description of the homely and familiar. Chariton, as we have seen, uses 'secondary toponyms' in this way to give added topographical depth to his eastern and western locations, while the Ionian seaboard which he himself (presumably) knows best has a comparatively meagre ration of names. Xenophon's less sophisticated technique has a more even spread of place-names in the primary narrative. Here an 'information bump' of redundant toponyms around the Ionian seaboard seems to betray local knowledge of the 'home' region, but a second 'bump', in Egypt, is clearly used to evoke a sense of travel in a more exotic location. The names, though they do not appear to create a coherent itinerary, are real Egyptian names, some of them shared with Chariton's brief evocation of Egyptian topography:

> They gathered a large band of robbers and made for Pelusium; sailing on the Nile to the Egyptian Hermopolis and Schedia, they put in to Menelaus's canal and missed Alexandria. They arrived at Memphis, the shrine of Isis, and from there traveled to Mendes... Going through Tawa, they reached Leontopolis, and passing a number of towns, most of them of little note, they came to Coptus, which is close to Ethiopia. There they decided to do their robbing, for there was a great crowd of merchants passing through for Ethiopia and India... And when they had taken the heights of Ethiopia and got their caves ready, they decided to rob the passing travellers (4.1.2–5).

The brief description of the shrine of Apis (5.4.8–11) increases the sense of Egypt as an exotic location. If we look for the same techniques in Acts, it is the Aegean area, and the final voyage to Rome, which display the most striking use of redundant place-names (see the Appendix) – further confirmation of the observation made elsewhere, that from the Jerusalem-centred perspective of Acts, it is the Aegean, rather than the eastern Mediterranean, which is *terra incognita*.[72]

Place-names may also be used in a narrative to create an impression of geographical verisimilitude – the sense that the narrator (and hence the reader) was 'really there'. Here our study has shown that, despite the importance of travel for the novels, it is not really the case (as is so often assumed) that topographical verisimilitude is a major preoccupation in romance. Chariton is

---

72. Alexander, 'Voyaging', pp. 30–31 (= Chapter 4 in this volume, pp. 80–81).

extremely sparing in his use of geographical names, with the action focused overwhelmingly on three major locations. Even if we add in the names used in 'secondary' narrative, Acts has a far higher proportion of names to narrative.[73] Xenophon has a greater variety of locations than Chariton, with a correspondingly greater variety of names, and in general provides a better parallel to Acts.[74] But Xenophon's place-names are distributed more thinly over the Mediterranean area as a whole; despite the 'clusters' we noted in Ionia and Egypt, he cannot match the density of names which Acts displays for the relatively small area covered in Paul's mission (see Map 7).

When we add to this our earlier observation that Luke's narrative world is a contemporary one, we are left with a level of topographical factuality which recalls the *periplous* literature, with its pragmatic attention to detail, rather than the novels.[75] And the realism of this topography is enhanced by the noticeable use of redundant names which combine with the we-narration to create an impression of eyewitness participation: in fact, precisely of the *autopsia* which Luke promised his readers in the Gospel preface (see Map 8).[76]

And, finally, geographical names may play a significant role in a travel narrative in enhancing the sense of travel itself: they allow the reader to become a traveller by creating an illusion of movement in space (reading railway timetables can have the same effect). Here again, there is an immense variation in the narrative techniques of the novelists. For Chariton, as we have seen, most of the action is concentrated in major dramatic scenes in a limited number of locations. The process of travel between those locations, though itself part of the *pathos* of the hero (8.1.3), takes up a minimal amount of narrative space. Redundant names to mark the passage are few, and nautical 'business' – another way of foregrounding the travel process – seems to be deliberately eschewed. Callirhoe's first voyage is described in these terms:

> The ship put to sea and ran splendidly, since they were not struggling against sea and wind – they had no special course to follow; to their mind any wind was favorable, was a stern wind (1.11.1).

All the attention is focused on the emotions of the heroine, expressed in a touching soliloquy (1.11.2–3). The passage of the Ionian Sea passes almost unnoticed: 'While she was bewailing her lot in this fashion, the brigands were

---

73.   Reckoning a page of Greek in the Budé edition as roughly equivalent to a page in NA[26], Chariton has 76 pages with 56 different names; of these 28 occur in the primary narrative (19 regional names, 9 city or local names). Acts 1–28 has 51 pages with 70 different names, of which 65 occur in the primary narrative (16 regional, 54 city/local in all).

74.   On the same reckoning, Xenophon has 37 pages of text with 54 different names, of which 47 occur in the primary narrative (18 regional, 29 city/local).

75.   The *Periplus Maris Erythraei* provides a good example: cf. L. Casson, *The Periplus Maris Erythraei* (Princeton: Princeton University Press, 1989).

76.   I have argued elsewhere that *autoptai* are particularly associated with geographical information: cf. L.C.A. Alexander, *The Preface to Luke's Gospel* (SNTSMS, 78; Cambridge: Cambridge University Press, 1993), pp. 34–41, 120–23.

sailing past small islands and towns' (1.11.4). Chaereas' pursuit is treated even more brusquely: after the emotion and rhetoric of the embarkation scene (3.5.1–9), the description of the voyage itself takes no more than a couple of lines:

> A following wind caught the trireme, and it ran as if in the tracks of the cutter; they reached Ionia in the same number of days and moored at the same beach (3.6.1).

The return crossing, despite Callirhoe's rhetorically-heightened fears, is treated with equal insouciance:

> Meanwhile, Chaereas completed the journey to Syracuse successfully; he had a following wind all the time. Since he had big ships, he took the route across the open sea, terrified as he was of once more being a target for some cruel deity's attack (8.6.1).

Xenophon also presents most of his journeys in summary form; even the heroine's shipwreck (which occurs, oddly, on one of the book's shortest voyages, between Antioch and Tarsus) is decidedly short on nautical detail:

> They were caught by an adverse wind and the ship broke up; some of the crew survived with great difficulty and came ashore on planks with Anthia among them (2.11.10).

Habrocomes' voyage to Italy is equally curtly described:

> Meanwhile Habrocomes completed his voyage from Egypt but did not reach Italy itself; for the wind drove the ship back, blew it off course, and brought it to Sicily, and they disembarked at the large and splendid port of Syracuse (5.1.1).

Acts 27 achieves a very different effect, establishing a sense of journeying not only through the nautical details of the shipwreck but with the whole coastal voyage anchored in the contemporary world by the skilful use of geographical names – names of trading ports and the ships that ply between them, names of harbours and anchorages, names of winds. Not only does this create a sense of realism lacking (by and large) in the novels; it also makes it clear that, for this narrator, the journey itself is story.

Conclusions

The comparison between Paul, Acts and the novels, then, reveals both similarities and differences. Both may be illustrated from Xenophon's description of his lovers' honeymoon voyage, the passage cited by Conzelmann as a parallel to Acts.[77]

> And that day they had a favourable wind; they finished this stage and reached Samos, the sacred island of Hera. There they sacrificed and took a meal, and after offering many

77.   Cf. n. 50 above.

prayers they put out to sea the next night. Once more the sailing was easy, and they talked a great deal to each other. 'Will we be allowed to spend our whole lives together?' At this Habrocomes gave a loud groan, at the thought of what was in store for him. 'Anthia,' he said, 'more dear to me than my own soul, my fondest hope is that we live happily and survive together; but if it is fated that we suffer some disaster and be separated, let us swear to one another, my dearest, that you will remain faithful to me and not submit to any other man, and that I should never live with another woman.' When she heard this, Anthia gave a loud cry. 'Habrocomes', she said, 'why are you convinced that if I am separated from you, I will still think about a husband and marriage, when I will not even live at all without you? I swear to you by the goddess of our fathers, the great Artemis of the Ephesians, and this sea we are crossing, and the god who has driven us mad with this exquisite passion for each other, that I will not live or look upon the sun if I am separated from you even for a short time.' That was Anthia's oath; Habrocomes swore too, and the occasion made their oaths still more awesome. Meanwhile the ship passed by Cos and Cnidus, and already the great and beautiful island of Rhodes was coming into view; here they all had to disembark, for the sailors said that they had to take on water and rest in preparation for the long voyage ahead (1.11.2–6).

Acts does not share the 'luxury cruise' atmosphere of this description, nor its preoccupation with the thoughts and emotions of the protagonists. The religious underpinning is reversed: Artemis of Ephesus is supportive to this pair, hostile to the emissaries of the gospel. But what Acts and Xenophon do share is equally significant for our appreciation of the communication strategies of these texts. In this passage Xenophon displays, unusually for him, a relish for the details of travel (especially travel by sea) which we find in a rather more developed form in Acts 27, together with a narrative ability to turn the process of voyaging itself into story. In both cases the slow motion filming of the travel process has the effect of highlighting the narrative significance of this particular journey within the story as a whole.

But we should also note that in geographical terms, the selection of names gives this voyage a distinctively coastal perspective, controlled by the view from the sea: it is the viewpoint of the *periplous*, of merchant and explorer, but also (as Chariton reminds us) as old as Homer himself.[78] As we have seen, a high proportion of the redundant place-names in the Acts narrative are coastal, as are over half of the toponyms unique to Acts (20 out of 39). But of the 17 names shared by Acts with one or other of the novels and not with Paul, 12 are coastal, three being the Aegean islands and promontories named in this passage. This is one of the features which make the mental map of Acts look so different from that of Paul, despite the fact that almost all Paul's toponyms are included in Acts: and it is a clear point of overlap with the mental maps of the novels. It is an unusual perspective for a biblical writer, and one which links Acts, surprisingly, with a rather different geographical tradition:

For some unaccountable reason, says his friend, R.L. Stevenson's favourite line of Vergil from boyhood was
   Iam medio apparet fluctu nemorosa Zacynthos.

78.   4.1.5, citing *Odyssey* 24.83.

Was it unaccountable? Look at the last words; think of the sea and sea-faring; and there is Homer behind and Samoa to come; from Sertorius to Sancho it is in the Isle that men look for happiness.[79]

It is a tradition, we may suggest, which allows Luke, without losing his story's rootedness in the real contemporary world of the Roman empire, to link it in with the 'parallel epic' of romance:

> Generations of men, throughout recorded time, have always told and retold two stories – that of a lost ship which searches the Mediterranean seas for a dearly loved island, and that of a god who is crucified on Golgotha.[80]

Averil Cameron has observed that the creation of narrative is central to the early Christian enterprise of communicating with the Greco-Roman world:

> Christianity was a religion with a story. [It] built up its own symbolic universe by exploiting the kind of stories that people liked to hear... The better these stories were constructed, the better they functioned as structure-maintaining narratives and the more their audiences were disposed to accept them as true.[81]

The Greek novels provide one of the best means available to us of discovering what were 'the kind of stories that people liked to hear': they clearly liked adventures (as Richard Pervo has shown), and they liked them to occur within the framework of a travel-narrative. But it is hard to believe that anyone was ever disposed to accept these stories as true: and we may note it as significant in this regard that Luke's presentation of the travel element in detail is closer to the factual, pragmatic *periplous* tradition than to the novels, at least to Chariton and Xenophon. Paul's adventures, unlike those of Callirhoe or Anthia, happen in a realistic, contemporary landscape, a world of trading ships not of triremes. The hinted combination of romance and veracity is a seductive one.[82]

79.   T.R. Glover, in *The Cambridge Ancient History* (ed. S.A. Cook, F.E. Adcock, M.P. Charlesworth; Cambridge: University Press, 1st edn, 1934), X, p. 542. The line is from Virgil, *Aeneid* 3.270: 'Now amid the waves appear[s] wooded Zacynthus' (Loeb translation).

80.   N. Frye, *The Secular Scripture* (Cambridge, MA; London: Harvard University Press, 1976), p. 15, citing Borges, 'The Gospel according to Mark'.

81.   A. Cameron, *Christianity and the Rhetoric of Empire: The Development of Christian Discourse* (Sather Classical Lectures; Berkeley: University of California Press, 1991), pp. 89–93.

82.   J.R.R. Tolkien, *Tree and Leaf* (London: Unwin Books, 1964), pp. 62–63.

Appendix

Toponyms in the Pauline Travel Narrative

Note:　W = *we-passages*
　　　　S = *sea-voyages*
　　　　<u>Underlining</u> indicates redundant toponyms
　　　　CAPITALS *indicate regional toponyms*
　　　　(Brackets) *indicate secondary or decorative toponyms*

Scene 1: Antioch		13.1–3
Barnabas and Saul set apart, sent out on mission		

	Voyage A: 'First missionary journey':		13.4–14.28
	<u>Seleucia</u>		
S	CYPRUS		
	Salamis		
	Paphos		13.6–12
S	Perga in PAMPHYLIA		
	Antioch of PISIDIA		13.14–50
	Iconium		13.51–14.5
	LYCAONIA: Lystra and Derbe and *perichoron*		14.6
	Lystra	(Antioch, Iconium)	14.8–20
	Derbe		14.20
	Lystra		14.21
	Iconium		
	Antioch		
	PISIDIA		14.24
	PAMPHYLIA		
	Perga		14.25
	<u>Attalia</u>		
S	Antioch		14.26–28

Scene 2: Antioch and Jerusalem		15.1–40
Jerusalem conference; return to Antioch		

	Voyage B: 'Second missionary journey'		15.41–18.22
	SYRIA and CILICIA		15.41
	Derbe		16.1
	Lystra	(Iconium)	16.1–3
	PHRYGIA and GALATIA	(ASIA)	16.6–10
	<u>MYSIA</u>	(BITHYNIA)	
W	Troas	(MACEDONIA)	
W S	<u>Samothrace</u>		16.11
W S	<u>Neapolis</u>		
W	Philippi, city of MACEDONIA, colony		16.12–40

	(Thyatira		16.14)
	(Rome		16.21, 37–38)
	<u>Amphipolis</u>		17.1
	<u>Apollonia</u>		
	Thessalonica		17.1–10
	Beroea	(Thessalonica)	17.10–13
	to the sea		17.14
S	Athens	Areopagus	17.15–34
S	Corinth		18.1–18
	(PONTUS; ITALY; Rome		18.2)
	(MACEDONIA		18.5)
	(ACHAIA		18.12)
	SYRIA		18.18
	<u>Cenchreae</u>		
S	Ephesus		18.19–21
S	<u>Caesarea</u>		18.22
	'up to the church'		
	Antioch		

	Voyage C: Aegean Ministry		18.23–21.16
	<u>GALATIA and PHRYGIA</u>		18.23
	(Alexandria, Ephesus, ACHAIA		18.24–28)
	(Corinth		19.1)
	<u>upper country</u>		
	Ephesus	ASIA	19.1–41
	(MACEDONIA		19.21–22, 29)
	(ACHAIA, Jerusalem, Rome		19.21
	<u>MACEDONIA</u>		20.1
	GREECE		20.2
S	(SYRIA		20.3)
	<u>MACEDONIA</u>		20.3–6
	ASIA	(Beroea, Thessalonica, Derbe, ASIA)	
		(TROAS)	
W	<u>Philippi</u>		
W S	<u>Troas</u>		20.6–12
W S	<u>Assos</u>		
W S	<u>Mitylene</u>		
W S	<u>Chios</u>		
W S	<u>Samos</u>		
W S	Miletus	(Ephesus, ASIA, Jerusalem)	20.17–38
W S	<u>Cos</u>		
W S	<u>Rhodes</u>		
W S	<u>Patara</u>		
W S	(PHOENICIA)		
W S	<u>CYPRUS</u>		
W S	SYRIA		

W S	<u>Tyre</u>	(Jerusalem)	21.3–6
W S	<u>Ptolemais</u>		
W	Caesarea	(JUDAEA, Jerusalem)	21.8–14
W	Jerusalem	(Caesarea, CYPRUS)	21.15–16

<u>Scene 3: Jerusalem and Caesarea</u>   21.17–26.32
Paul's arrest and trials

	Voyage D: Jerusalem to Rome	27.1–28.15
W S	(ITALY	27.1)
W S	(<u>Adramyttium</u>, ASIA, Thessalonica	27.2)
W S	<u>Sidon</u>	27.3
W S	under lee of <u>CYPRUS</u>	27.4
W S	sea off <u>Cilicia and Pamphylia</u>	27.5
W S	<u>Myra,</u> city of <u>LYCIA</u>	
W S	(ship of Alexandria for ITALY	27.6)
W S	against <u>Cnidus</u>	27.7
W S	under lee of <u>CRETE</u> off <u>Salmone</u>	
W S	<u>Fair Havens</u> near <u>Lasea</u>	
W S	(<u>Phoenix)</u>	27.12
W S	under lee of <u>Cauda</u>	
W S	(<u>Syrtis</u>	27.17)
W S	up and down in <u>ADRIA</u>	27.27
W S	Malta	28.1–10
W S	(ship of Alexandria	28.11)
W S	<u>Syracuse</u>	28.12
W S	<u>Rhegium</u>	28.13
W S	<u>Puteoli</u>	
W	Rome	28.14
W	<u>Appii Forum</u>	28.15
W	<u>Tres Tabernae</u>	

Scene 4: Rome   28.16–31
Paul's address to Jewish leaders

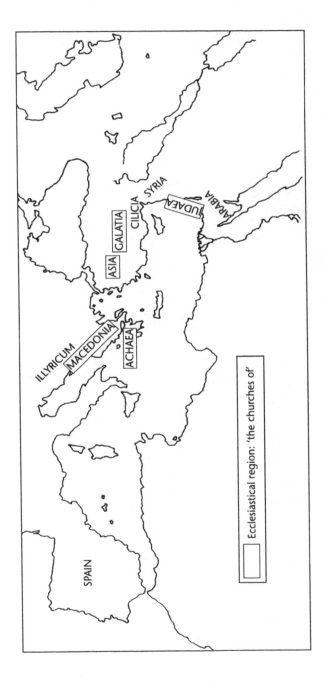

Map 1. *Regional Names in the Pauline Epistles*

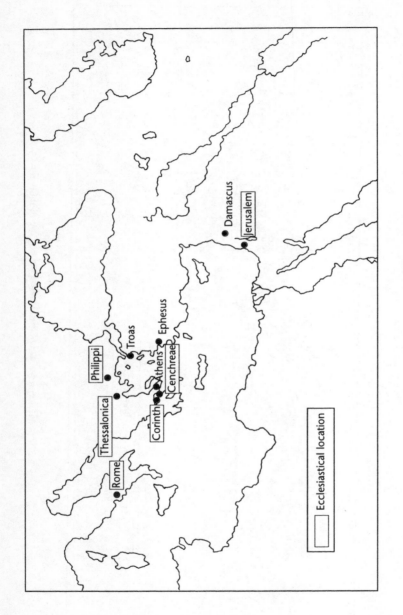

Map 2. City Names in the Pauline Epistles

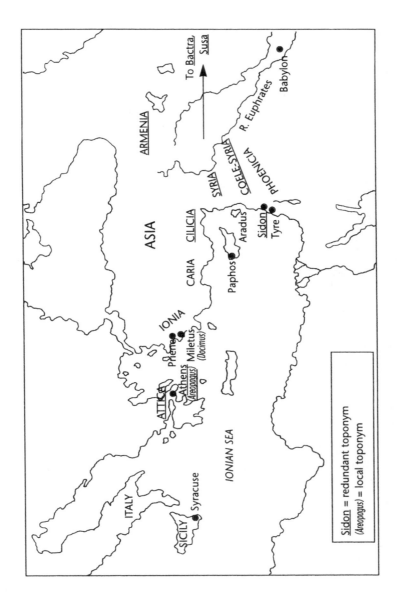

Map 3. *Chariton: Primary Toponyms*

Note: Small scale of map inevitably causes distortion in the placing of individual place-names

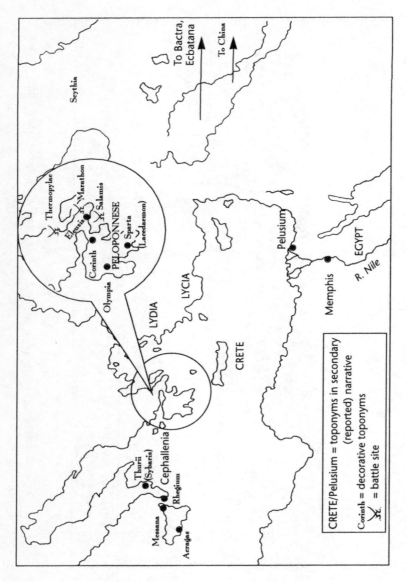

Map 4. Chariton: Secondary and Decorative Toponyms

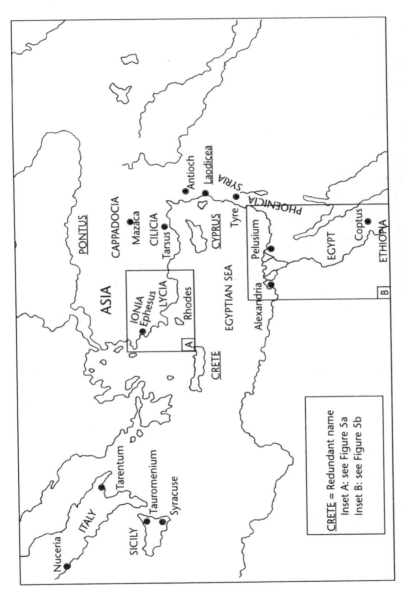

Map 5. *Xenophon: Primary Toponyms*

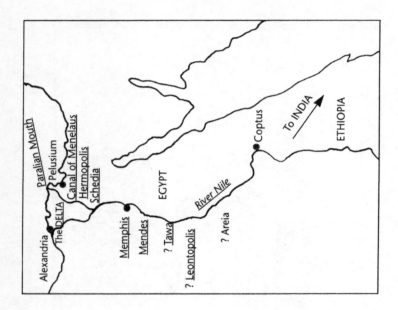

Map 5b. *Xenophon's Egyptian Toponymy*

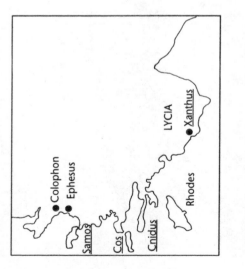

Map 5a. *Xenophon's Toponymy of Asia Minor*

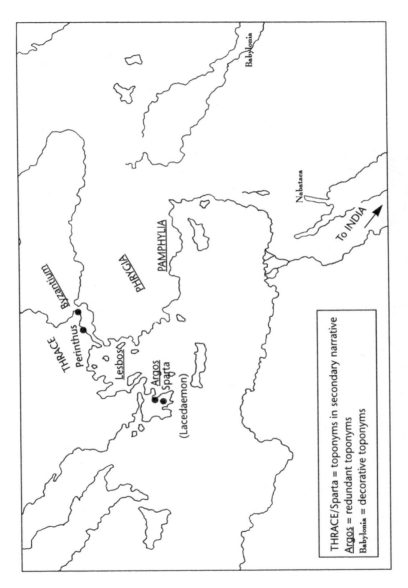

Map 6. *Xenophon: Secondary and Decorative Toponyms*

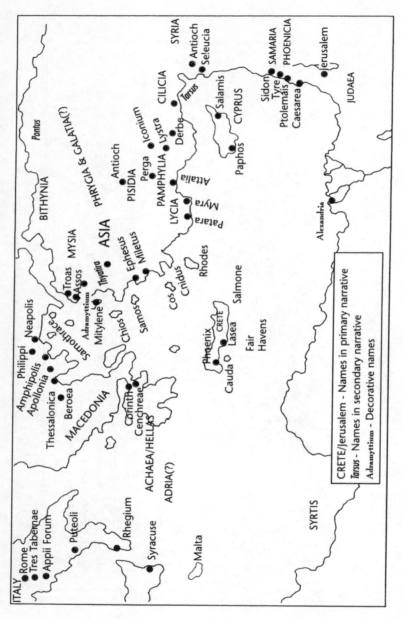

Map 7. Total Toponymy of Acts 13–28

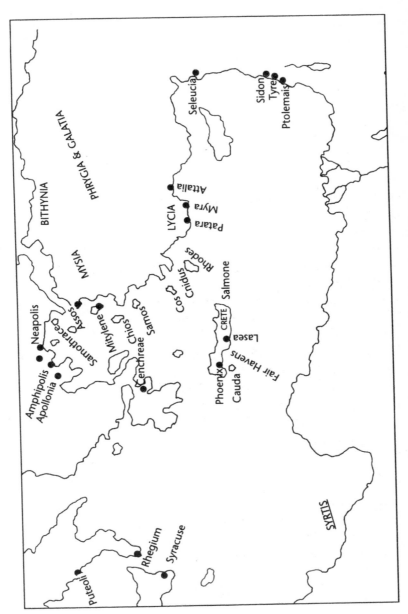

Map 8. *Redundant Place-Names in Acts 13–28*

Chapter 6

FACT, FICTION AND THE GENRE OF ACTS*

Ever since the revolutionary work of F.C. Baur and the 'Tübingen school', controversy has ranged over whether or not Acts should be read as 'history'.[1] The debate has, however, become more and more complex (not to say confused) over recent years, and one reason for this is the ambivalence of the word 'history' itself, which is commonly used both of a connected narrative of past events and of the events themselves: 'what actually happened', *wie es eigentlich gewesen...* In current scholarship, the debate about 'reading Acts as history' is readily taken as a debate about literary genre: does Acts fall into the genre 'history'? But for many readers the question is more obviously about the reliability of the narrative, that is, its relation to 'history' in the sense of 'the real events'. The underlying question here is: Does Acts give an accurate picture of the events it narrates? – or more simply, Is Acts true? This may be a naive way to put the question, but that is what most readers (at least outside scholarly circles) mean by it; and, as Colin Hemer points out, it is a perfectly right and proper question to ask of any narrative.[2] It raises the important issue of the relationship between the story told in the text and the external world which the text purports to describe. It is not, however, strictly speaking a question about the text at all: 'truth' is not a literary quality inherent in the text, but a function of the relationship between the text and something outside it. And the most obvious way to answer the question also involves looking outside the text for corroboration, by checking its story against external data (parallel narratives, documentary evidence, archaeological background). This has been a major concern of Acts scholarship during the twentieth century, from Ramsay to Hemer and beyond, and remains so: but it is not our prime concern in this paper.

*   This paper was first presented for discussion in the Luke-Acts seminar at the SNTS meeting at the University of Birmingham in August 1997, and I am grateful to members of that seminar for their helpful discussion. A shorter version of the paper was presented at the same meeting as a Short Main Paper and subsequently published in *NTS* 44.3 (July 1998), pp. 380–99, used here by kind permission of Cambridge University Press.

1.   For a helpful account of the 'Tübingen school', cf. William Baird, *History of New Testament Research*. I. *From Deism to Tübingen* (Minneapolis: Fortress Press, 1992), ch. 8, pp. 244–93.

2.   Colin J. Hemer, *The Book of Acts in the Setting of Hellenistic History* (WUNT, 49; Winona Lake: Eisenbrauns, 1990; [Tübingen: Siebeck-Mohr; 1989]), ch. 1, pp. 1–29.

There is, however, another dimension to the question of historicity. Checking a narrative against external data is not the only way readers assess its reliability: other factors within the text itself may be brought into play. These may be broadly divided into two categories, drawing on two different kinds of reader experience. The first rests on a philosophical judgement about the intrinsic probability (plausibility) of what is related, what we might call the 'fact-likeness' or realism of the narrative. This kind of judgement draws on the reader's wider experience of the world: human behaviour, geographical information, scientific or sociological theory may all be brought into play. This question typically arises for the reader of Acts in relation to the narrative's treatment of the miraculous and the supernatural: 'Such things do not happen, therefore the narrative is fiction (or fantasy, or wish-fulfilment)'.[3]

The second kind of assessment draws on the reader's experience of other texts, an experience which identifies certain literary phenomena as indicators of reliability: 'Is this the kind of literature to which we would normally give credence?' This kind of judgement forms a part of our reading equipment for a whole range of texts, and is widely exploited, as in the use of black-and-white film to give an impression of authentic newsreel or documentary, or in the use of the scientist (white coat, laboratory equipment) to lend credence to an advertisement for soap powder or toothpaste. In practice, these two kinds of experience – experience of the world, and experience of other texts – are often played off against one another to telling effect. Thus fantasy can use the 'documentary' technique to frame a narrative of the frankly unbelievable, like the use of the paraphernalia of the authentic travel narrative in Swift's *Gulliver's Travels*. There it is the improbability of the content which warns the reader to distrust the signals emitted by the genre. Conversely, the realistic film or novel, which has no such tell-tale improbability, was dogged for many years by the need to carry a conventional disclaimer warning the reader that 'no representation of any actual persons alive or dead is intended'.

Both these kinds of assessment, in their different ways, open up the possibility of exploring the textual factors which predispose a reader to accept or reject a narrative as 'true': and this brings us back to the question of genre. For many people, I suspect, this is the real (if undisclosed) justification for the lengthy debate over genre which has preoccupied Acts scholarship for much of this century.[4] Ever since Ramsay set out to give his 'reasons for placing the author of Acts among historians of the first rank',[5] scholars who have a high estimate of the accuracy of the Acts narrative have tended to align it with the literary

---

3.		As for example in the classic work of David Friedrich Strauss, cited in Baird, *New Testament Research*, I, pp. 252–53: 'We...distinctly declare that we regard the history of the resurrection of Lazarus as...in the highest degree improbable in itself'. For Strauss, the 'progression in the marvelous' found in the Gospels 'is at the same time, a gradation in inconceivability'.

4.		See on this now Todd Penner, *In Praise of Christian Origins: Stephen and the Hellenists in Lukan Apologetic Historiography* (Emory Studies in Early Christianity, 10; New York/London: T&T Clark International/Continuum, 2004), ch. 1, pp. 1–59.

5.		W.M. Ramsay, *St Paul the Traveller and the Roman Citizen* (London: Hodder & Stoughton, 1895), p. 4.

practice of contemporary Greek or Roman historiography. Conversely, it is often assumed that detaching Acts from the generic label 'historiography' inevitably means impugning its reliability as a record of past events. But all these inferences rest on the too-easy assumption that 'accurate reporting of past events' is co-extensive with the ancient literary genre 'history', as if each entails the other: which is not necessarily the case. First, it is much too simple to assume that identifying Luke's work on literary grounds with 'Greek historiography' is an automatic guarantee of reliability. In fact it has become fashionable to argue that the literary identification may actually militate against a high estimate of the text's accuracy.[6] One of the most famous examples of this kind of argument occurs in Dibelius' study of the speeches in Acts.[7] Fifty years on, the problem of the fictionality of speeches in Greek historiography is still hotly disputed, both in NT and in classical scholarship; but this is only a corner of the vigorous discussions now taking place about the practice of the Greek and Roman historians, especially the influence of rhetoric. Hence there is a need to place the Acts debate within the context of a well-informed discussion of history as an ancient literary genre and how it was actually practised.[8]

But there is another side to this question which is not always considered, and that is the converse assumption that 'accurate' necessarily means 'history'. Common-sense reflection suggests that a text can easily give an accurate account of past events without belonging to the literary genre 'history'. It could be a letter, for example, or a laundry-list, or any of the multitudinous documents which could rank as a source for the historian but would not normally be counted as a 'history' in its own right. Even if we restrict ourselves to a text structured as a narrative, it is not too difficult to think of stories about the past which might be accurate but are not 'history' – newspaper reports, diaries, court proceedings, minutes of meetings, popular story-telling. In the ancient world, which classified history-writing under the rather more formal literary code of rhetoric, the list would be even longer: ancient writers like Cicero and Lucian make it clear that the unadorned memoirs of a general or a soldier, however accurate, are not 'history' but the raw material of history, waiting to be turned into a proper history by the literary skill of the rhetorically-trained writer.[9] And, as Glen

6.   Cf. W.L. Knox, *The Acts of the Apostles* (Cambridge: Cambridge University Press, 1948), p. 4; C.K. Barrett, *Luke the Historian in Recent Study* (London: Epworth, 1961), pp. 9–12.

7.   M. Dibelius, 'The Speeches in Acts and Ancient Historiography', in H. Greeven (ed.), *Studies in the Acts of the Apostles* (trans. M. Ling and P. Schubert; London: SCM Press, 1956 = *Aufsätze zur Apostelgeschichte* [Göttingen: Vandenhoeck & Ruprecht, 1951], pp. 138–85; now reprinted in Martin Dibelius, *The Book of Acts: Form, Style, Theology* (ed. K.C. Hanson; Minneapolis: Fortress Press, 2004), pp. 49–86.

8.   This argument is now developed more fully in Penner, *In Praise of Christian Origins*, ch. 3; cf. p. 217, 'The holistic methodology employed by ancient writers differs categorically from the canons of modern historical enquiry'.

9.   Lucian, *How to Write History*, §16. On Cicero, cf. Penner, *In Praise of Christian Origins*, pp. 123–27, and on the whole subject, T.P. Wiseman, *Clio's Cosmetics* (Leicester: Leicester University Press, 1979), chs. 1, 2.

Bowersock has recently reminded us, classifying a text as 'fiction' does not necessarily rob it of historical value.[10]

Even from a cursory survey, then, it is clear that generic boundaries are not the same as the boundary between fact and fiction. We cannot hope to solve the question of the reliability of Acts simply by identifying its literary genre, and I shall not attempt to do so in this study. What I intend to do here is to sketch out an approach (no more than an agenda, for the subject is a vast one) to 'reading Acts as history' which focuses on the reader rather than the author, and particularly on the kind of readerly expectations associated with Greek historiography. This approach will allow us to explore some of the textual features, generic and otherwise, which form an essential component in the reader's expectations of a text's reliability, the likelihood of its being 'true'. What were the literary techniques which disposed ancient readers to accept a narrative as 'true'? Does Acts use any of these? Or does Acts (negatively or positively) use literary conventions which effectively align it with other types of narrative: fiction, paradoxography, fantasy? What is the effect on the reader of the substantial supernatural element of the narrative? Putting the question this way has the advantage at least of highlighting issues which often operate as hidden assumptions in the debate about the genre of Acts. It also reveals, of course, that these assumptions themselves raise even broader questions, much too broad to be answered in a short introductory study like this. It is a real question, for example, whether the concept of 'fiction' is appropriate at all in ancient prose literature: yet there are ancient narratives which are clearly fictitious, and which it is hard to believe any ancient reader would ever have accepted as 'true'.[11] All of these questions are currently being discussed in the broader debate on the nature of fiction in the ancient world which I shall attempt to address in this article.

History as Fact

The claim to factuality is bound up with the very origins of Greek historiography, indeed with the very origins of Greek prose. The oldest and most venerable genres in Greek literature are poetic: epic, lyric, drama; even the wisdom-literature of the Greeks uses didactic verse as its primary medium of expression. Prose, by contrast, has more utilitarian associations:

> The appeal of this early classical prose is to the intellect almost exclusively, rather than to the emotional or to the artistic sense, and it is not used, at least not consciously, as a medium by which to convey poetic or inspirational or sentimental values.[12]

10.   G.W. Bowersock, *Fiction as History, Nero to Julian* (Sather Classical Lectures, 58; Berkeley: University of California Press, 1994).

11.   See, besides Bowersock's *Fiction as History*, the stimulating collection of essays in C. Gill and T.P. Wiseman (eds.), *Lies and Fiction in the Ancient World* (Exeter: University of Exeter Press, 1993) [hereafter *Lies and Fiction*].

12.   B.E. Perry, *The Ancient Romances* (Sather Classical Lectures, 37; Berkeley: University of California Press, 1967), p. 55.

So when the first historians chose to write in prose, they were already implicitly making the point that the work of the historian was different from that of the poet. The distinction is made explicitly and polemically by Thucydides:

> It is safer to assume that the Trojan expedition surpassed its predecessors without attaining to modern dimensions – always supposing that the evidence of Homer may be taken as trustworthy. As a poet he presumably exaggerates, yet the inferiority remains, even on his showing.[13]

Herodotus makes a similarly disadvantageous comparison between 'what is said' of the Trojan War and 'what we know' of the magnitude of Xerxes' expedition (7.20.2–21.1).

But the historians' concern to distance themselves from the poets – despite their manifest similarities in subject-matter and purpose – goes far deeper than the occasional disparaging allusion. Herodotus' history begins with a resumé of rival accounts from Greek, Persian and Phoenician sources of the origins of the Persian Wars. This allows the historian, as J.L. Moles puts it,

> to begin his work in great style, to maintain the association between that work and Homer's *Iliad*, to entertain his readers, to suggest ideas dear to himself – yet he also distances himself from it and makes a distinction between myth and solid, verifiable history. Such ambiguity of attitude both to myth and 'things that are said' is character-istic of the ancient historian, yet rarely articulated with such flair.[14]

This distancing is suggested in the very first sentence of the history:

> Quite unhomeric, however, is the proud obtrusion of the historian's identity in the first two words – a pattern already set by Hecataeus and followed by Thucydides and many later historians. The effect is double: the naming suggests that Herodotus himself will be an important figure in his *History* (as indeed he is); the use of the third person suggests objectivity and detachment.[15]

The construction of this authorial *persona* is a crucial step in the development of Greek historiography. It allows Herodotus to maintain a sense of 'objectivity and detachment' throughout (even though the third person disappears after the preface) by introducing himself as observer and commentator on his own narrative. Sometimes this takes the form of first-person authentication for sights he himself has seen, for example on the sources of the Nile.[16] More distant

---

13.   Thuc. 1.10.3, trans. A.J. Toynbee, *Greek Historical Thought from Homer to the Age of Heraclius* (London: Dent, 1924).

14.   J.L. Moles, 'Truth and Untruth in Herodotus and Thucydides', in Gill and Wiseman, (eds.), *Lies and Fiction*, pp. 88–121 (96).

15.   Moles, 'Truth and Untruth'.

16.   2.29.1. This type of authentication tends to involve geographical rather than historical material, since Herodotus does not claim to have been a participant in the events narrated in his history. On the Herodotean narrative persona, see further Katherine Clarke, *Between Geography and History: Hellenistic Constructions of the Roman World* (Oxford: Clarendon Press, 1999), p. 34 and the literature there cited.

phenomena can also be authenticated at one remove: not 'I saw' but 'I heard from an informant' (2.32.1, 33.1). The use of the first person here implicitly provides a reassuring link in a chain of autopsy. The incredible data related have actually been 'seen', if not by the author himself, then by somebody he has met: the anonymous 'they say' becomes a series of real (if unnamed) informants.

But the authorial *persona* can also be used to create an (equally reassuring) buffer zone of scepticism between 'what is reported' and the reader. It speaks the language of reason, of conjecture and probability and calculation (e.g. 2.31). It proposes rationalistic, physical explanations for the marvellous phenomena of legend and travellers' tales (e.g. 2.24–28). Probability – 'what usually happens' – plays an important part in these explanations (e.g. 2.27). It is frank about the limits of autopsy: 'I have not seen a phoenix myself', Herodotus reassures his readers, 'except in paintings, for it is very rare and only visits the country (so at least they say in Heliopolis) only at intervals of 500 years, on the death of the parent-bird'.[17] The implication is that the equally incredible descriptions of the crocodile and the hippopotamus (2.68–71), which carry no such limitation, are trustworthy reports of real animals. Reassurance also lies in the way the historian-as-observer is careful to distinguish between observable and verifiable facts (paintings, places, animal bones, religious customs) and the stories told to explain them (e.g. 2.75). Having heard and relayed the most amazing variety of tales passed on by the scribes, priests, travellers and native inhabitants who cluster at the boundaries of autopsy, the authorial voice presents itself as one which can afford to select and discriminate on rational, common-sense principles: two witnesses are better than one, though rival traditions which do not agree may discredit one another. And in the last analysis, the historian reserves the right to an absolute scepticism: 'I give the story as it was told me,' he says of the phoenix, 'but I don't believe it' (2.72, cf. 2.28).

This self-deprecatory, faintly ironical authorial voice is the final assurance of reliability: a narrator who is so ready to confess the limitations of his knowledge must surely be trustworthy. It is the reader's companion throughout Herodotus' many geographical excurses, on a journey of investigation (*historia* in the Ionian sense) which ranges from the merely curious to the frankly fantastic. But there is no deceit, no compulsion to believe what is simply recorded as τὰ λεγόμενα, the things people say. The same voice provides an insidious running commentary on the events of the *Histories,* especially where they stray into the realm of the marvellous or the supernatural:

> There is a story that the Athenians had called upon Boreas – the north-east wind – to help them, in consequence of another oracle... I cannot say if this was really the reason why the fleet was caught at anchor by the north-easter, but the Athenians are quite positive about it: Boreas, they maintain, had helped them before, and it was Boreas who was responsible for what occurred on this occasion too. On their return they built him a shrine by the river Ilissus.[18]

17.　2.72; cf. 3.115.1; 4.16.1.
18.　7.189 (trans. A. de Selincourt; Harmondsworth: Penguin, 1954).

A similar technique is used to telling effect on the archaeological material in the preface, where Herodotus relays a selection of the stories told by different nations to explain the origins of the conflict between the Greeks and the Persians. Here the problem is not distance in space but distance in time: only myth and legend reach so far back into antiquity. Herodotus' solution is not to ignore this legendary material but to pass it on, framed in such a way that the historian is protected from the charge of gullibility by foregrounding his own impartiality (refusing to mediate between rival versions of the story) and scepticism:

> So much for what the Persians and Phoenicians say; and I have no intention of passing judgement on its truth or falsity. I prefer to rely on my own knowledge, and to point out who it was in actual fact that first injured the Greeks; then I will proceed with my history... (1.4–5, trans. de Selincourt).

The Herodotean authorial *persona*, a compound of the freethinking 'enquiry' of Ionian *historia* and Herodotus' own endlessly curious and slightly quizzical personality, is determinative for the characteristic voice of Greek historiography. Thucydides (who builds on Herodotus' work though without explicit acknowledgment)[19] has less curiosity about the world at large, and makes scarcely any space for geographical digression: but he is even more deeply imbued with the Ionian rationalism which was so fashionable among the intellectuals of Periclean Athens.[20] His preface sets the tone for the whole *History of the Peloponnesian War* with its humanistic, economic explanations for ancient enmities, its careful calculus of the 'probable' and its extensive use of the language of reason and evidence.[21] Like Herodotus, Thucydides begins his history with a long investigation into the prehistory of the conflict, which becomes the occasion for a more self-conscious and explicit formulation of the methodological difficulties of dealing with the mythical and legendary tales which are the only sources we have for the distant past:

> Still, it is safer to draw substantially the conclusions that I have drawn from the evidence that I have cited, as contrasted with the poets' exaggerated rhapsodies or the entertaining rather than accurate compositions of the genealogists [*logographoi*]. There is really no means of verification in a subject of such antiquity that it has won its way into the misty region of romance [*epi to muthodes*], and in this field it may be regarded as sufficient if the salient features are established (Thuc. 1.21.1, trans. Toynbee).

The poets' tales belong to the realm of *to muthodes* not because they are necessarily false (Homer can be cited as good historical evidence)[22] but because the early period provides the historian with no means of independent verification for their statements. The ideal subject for historical research, in Thucydidean

19.   Cf. Moles, 'Truth and Untruth', pp. 88–121.
20.   'Thucydides was deeply influenced by his association with the intellectual movement of Periclean Athens': H.D. Westlake, *Essays on the Greek Historians and Greek History* (Manchester: Manchester University Press, 1969), p. 19.
21.   Cf. Simon Hornblower, *Thucydides* (London: Duckworth, 1987), ch. 4; Westlake, *Essays, passim*, e.g. chs. 1, 2, 10.
22.   Thuc. 1.3.3; 9.4; cf. 10.3 cited above.

terms, is contemporary history which presents ample opportunity for first-hand experience and the rigorous questioning of eyewitness testimony:[23]

> As regards the material facts of the war, I have not been content to follow casual informants or my own imagination. Where I have not been an eyewitness myself, I have investigated with the utmost accuracy attainable every detail that I have taken at second hand. The task has been laborious, for witnesses of the same particular events have given versions that have varied, according to their sympathies or retentive powers.[24]

But for the early period, the historian must simply rely on a critical rationalism which refuses to accept any historical tradition at face value (1.20–21) and robustly prefers the pragmatic to the heroic in estimating historical causation.[25] Once again, the lengthy 'archaeology' section of Thucydides' preface (whose relevance was criticized[26] even in antiquity) allows him to project an authorial *persona* which inspires, if not affection, at least respect for its objectivity and commitment to accuracy:

> Possibly the public will find my unromantic narrative forbidding, but I shall be satisfied if it is favourably received by readers whose object is exact knowledge of facts which had not only actually occurred, but which are destined approximately to repeat themselves in all human probability. I have tried to produce a permanent contribution to knowledge rather than an ephemeral *tour de force* (1.22.4, trans. Toynbee).

Herodotus thus bequeathed to Greek historical tradition a barrage of techniques for distinguishing fact from fiction – or from unconfirmed report – within historical narrative. And by displaying their ability to use these techniques in their opening chapters, Herodotus and his successors could convince their readers that everything that followed had been subjected to the same careful, sifting process by a critical, analytical mind. The narrative itself tends to proceed with a minimum of authorial intervention: the ancient historians do not cite sources in the modern fashion, but leave the story to tell its own tale. But the use of the authorial voice in the preface, and the sensitivity to critical issues displayed there, has the effect of framing the whole story as the perception of a particular, rational – but not omniscient – narrator. The effect is reminiscent of mediaeval illuminations of the Apocalypse, which are careful to include the seer in the framework of his pictured visions – presumably as a reminder that the management takes no overall responsibility for what is, ultimately, a private vision.[27] And this effect is maintained within

---

23.   A.D. Momigliano, 'The Place of Herodotus in the History of Historiography', in *idem*, *Studies in Historiography* (London: Weidenfeld & Nicholson, 1969), pp. 127–42 [130]; but cf. a caution in Westlake, *Essays*, p. 2., n. 4.

24.   1.22.2, trans. Toynbee. But note that Thucydides (unlike Herodotus) does not use the word *autoptes*, here or anywhere else in his *History*: what he says is, 'where I was present (παρῆν) myself'. Cf. n. 50 below.

25.   E.g. on Agamemnon's naval power (1.9.1)

26.   Dionysius of Halicarnassus, *De Thuc.* 19–20.

27.   Cf. the *Biblia Pauperum* in the John Rylands Library, Manchester, described in M.R. James, *The Apocalypse in Art* (The Schweich Lectures of the British Academy, 1927; London: Oxford University Press for the British Academy, 1931).

the narrative by bracketing particular items as reports – *logoi* – passed on to them by others: we might compare the dissociative effect of *Private Eye*'s 'allegedly', or the quotation marks of the tabloid newspapers. Certain kinds of 'things said' seem to attract especial suspicion and thus a particular need for distancing: reports from distant places; tales of the distant past; and anything to do with religion. Here the Greek historians, like a modern anthropologist, tend to take the outsider's role: whatever their private religious viewpoint, they observe and record religious rite and monument as 'fact' but reserve judgement on the theological explanations offered by insiders. This careful distancing of the recording self from religious belief remains characteristic of Greek and Roman historiography.[28]

History as Fiction

From all of this it seems clear that Greek historical writing as a genre projects itself as 'fact' rather than 'fiction'. This is not to say, of course, that everything a Greek historian says is true. Any writer, whatever their commitment to fact, may be mistaken, or deceived, or simply fail to live up to their own standards. But the ideal *persona* of the historian, as created by Herodotus and Thucydides and perpetuated in the tradition which continued to revere them as classics,[29] is designed to encourage the reader to place history firmly on the 'Non-Fiction' shelves of the library. Lucian's ideal historian, six centuries after Thucydides, falls recognizably into the classical mould:[30]

> As to the facts themselves, he should not assemble them at random, but only after much laborious and painstaking investigation. He should for preference be an eyewitness (καὶ μάλιστα μὲν παρόντα καὶ ἐφορῶντα), but, if not, listen to those who tell the more impartial story, those whom one would suppose least likely to subtract from the facts or add to them out of favour or malice. When this happens let him show shrewdness and skill in putting together the more credible story... Above all, let him bring a mind like a mirror, clear, gleaming-bright, accurately centred, displaying the shape of things just as he receives them, free from distortion, false colouring, and misrepresentation. His concern is different from that of the orators – what historians have to relate is fact and will speak for itself, for it has already happened: what is required is arrangement and exposition (*How to Write History* §§49–50, trans. Kilburn LCL).

The surprising and even paradoxical result of all this is that the critical historical enterprise, in the very process of defining and delimiting an area which we would call 'fact' (i.e. that which can be verified by rational means), simultaneously

---

28.   J.S. Lown, 'The Miraculous in the Greco-Roman Historians', *Foundations and Facets Forum* 2 (1986), pp. 36–42.

29.   'The intuitions and methodological principles of Thucydides later became canons of interpretation for history': E. Gabba, *Dionysius and the History of Archaic Rome* (Sather Classical Lectures, 56; Berkeley: University of California Press, 1991), p. 102.

30.   On Lucian see esp. Gert Avenarius, *Lukians Schrift zur Geschichtsschreibung* (Meisenheim/Glan: Hain, 1956); Helene Homeyer, *Lukian: Wie man Geschichte schreiben soll* (München: W. Fink, 1965).

delimits an area of 'fiction' (or more properly, 'non-fact'), i.e. that which cannot be verified by rational means. History-as-fact, in other words, itself creates the possibility of fiction. This is a situation of which Greek and Roman writers in the first and second centuries are keenly aware. There is an extensive literature, both ancient and modern, on the potential for fiction within ancient historiography and in the literature that clusters around its edges. The Greek and Roman historians are frequently attacked as 'liars':

> For Seneca, in the first century A.D., it was axiomatic that historians are liars. There is a passage in his *Quaestiones Naturales* (7.16.1f.) where, discussing comets, he brushes aside the theory offered by Ephorus with a damning remark: 'It takes no great effort to refute him – he's a historian.'... Seneca justifies his paradox with a sardonic little digression on the practice of history as mere entertainment: 'Some historians win approval by telling incredible tales; an everyday narrative would make the reader go and do something else, so they excite him with marvels. Some of them are credulous, and lies take them unawares; others are careless, and lies are what they like; the former don't avoid them, the latter seek them out. What the whole tribe have in common is this: they think their work can only achieve approval and popularity if they sprinkle it with lies.'[31]

Even Lucian, that doughty champion of a proper Thucydidean devotion to 'fact', suggests on closer examination that this was a minority interest among the historians of his day. *How to Write History* makes it clear that the normal way to achieve success with the 'common rabble' was to provide eulogy, exaggeration, and 'complete fiction'.[32] This cynical view is matched by a widespread perception among modern scholars that by the first century CE history as a genre was as much concerned with fiction as with fact – or, more damaging still, that historians and their readers had lost the ability to distinguish between the two.[33]

The thrust of this debate is not to question how successful historians were in practice at achieving the ideal of objective, factual reporting of the past (or even the related but not identical ideal of objective, critical examination of reports about the past). Rather – and this is where it impinges on the debate about the genre of Acts – it suggests that historical writing in the first centuries of our era suffered from a fundamental failure to distinguish 'fact' from 'fiction'. Despite a continuing devotion to 'truth' as a historiographical ideal, the genre of history in the hellenistic and Roman periods laboured under a set of operating assumptions which effectively blurred the distinction between 'fact' and 'fiction'.

There are a number of reasons for this. The first, I would suggest, is an ambivalence which lies at the heart of the Herodotean critical methodology itself.

---

31.   T.P. Wiseman, 'Lying Historians: Seven Types of Mendacity', in Gill and Wiseman (eds), *Lies and Fiction*, p. 122. For the ancient (and modern) debate on Herodotus, cf. W.K. Pritchett, *The Liar School of Herodotus* (Amsterdam: Gieben, 1993).

32.   τὸ κομιδῆ μυθῶδες: *How to Write History* §10, LCL.

33.   Cf. Bowersock, *Fiction as History*, ch. 1; Emilio Gabba, 'True History and False History in Classical Antiquity', *JRS* 71 (1981), pp. 50–62; M.J. Wheeldon, 'True Stories: The Reception of Historiography in Antiquity', in *History as Text: The Writing of Ancient History* (ed. A. Cameron; London: Duckworth, 1989), pp. 33–63 (41ff., 149ff.); A.J. Woodman, *Rhetoric in Classical Historiography* (London/Sydney: Croom Helm, 1988), esp. chs. 1, 2 and Epilogue.

Herodotus made the distinctly postmodern discovery that beliefs and traditions are 'facts' in their own right, even if the things they report are not. The critical historian may doubt that X exists or Y happened, but it remains a fact that A believes – or that the story (*logos*) exists – that X exists or Y happened. The historian is therefore free to include any number of fanciful or marvellous reports of monsters and miracles, provided that they are bracketed with the ubiquitous 'so they say...'. The training of the rhetorical schools meant that Greek writers learnt early to be proficient in turning stories into *oratio obliqua*,[34] a proficiency that is not only a *tour de force* in itself but also an insistent reminder that the narrator is refusing to take full responsibility for the content of what is related. This is, of course, a wonderful method of having your cake and eating it, of enjoying all the pleasures of fiction without abandoning the respectability of fact. Herodotus exploits this duality to the full,[35] and it is abundantly clear that later readers found this one of the most rewarding and exciting aspects of historiography. But the recounting of marvels need not conflict in principle with a commitment to the pursuit of 'truth'. As Lucian cynically puts it:

> Again, if a myth comes along you must tell it but not believe it entirely; no, make it known for your audience to make of it what they will – you run no risk and lean to neither side (*How to Write History*, §60 LCL).

Dionysius of Halicarnassus displays a similar ambivalence. On the one hand, Thucydides is to be commended because 'he did not insert anything of the mythical into his history, and he refused to divert his history to practice deception and magic upon the masses, as all the historians before him had done, telling...about demi-gods, the offspring of mortals and gods, and many other stories that seem incredible and very foolish to our times'.[36] On the other hand, Dionysius himself was a collector of 'the fictions of myths' and openly used them in his *Antiquities* (*Ant.* 1.8.1). The solution is to issue a specific disclaimer:

> I have not been led to say these things by the desire to censure those writers, since, on the contrary, I have much indulgence towards them for mentioning the fictions of myths when writing national and local history. For among all men alike there are preserved some records of both national and local traditions of the kind that I have mentioned, which children have received from their parents and have taken care to hand down to their children in turn, and they have insisted that those who wished to publish them should record them as they have received them from their elders. These historians, then, were compelled to embellish their local histories by such mythical digressions. On the other hand, it was not suitable for Thucydides, who chose just one subject in which

---

34. ἀποφαντικὸν ἐγκεκλιμένον: Hermogenes, *Prog.* 2.18.
35. 'Herodotus has it all possible ways: he uses the sandwiched material to begin his work in great style, to maintain the association between that work and Homer's *Iliad*, to entertain his readers, to suggest ideas dear to himself—yet he also distances himself from it and makes a distinction between myth and solid, verifiable history': Moles, 'Truth and Untruth', p. 96.
36. Dionysius of Halicarnassus, *De Thuc.* §6, trans. W.K. Pritchett, *Dionysius of Halicarnassus: On Thucydides* (Berkeley: University of California Press, 1975), p.4.

he participated, to mix theatrical enticements with the narrative, or to practice deceit against readers which these compilations customarily exhibited, but to be useful, as he himself explained.[37]

I speak of a blurring of boundaries here (rather than a deliberate crossing from 'fact' to 'fiction') because I think it is clear from passages like those quoted that ancient historians were aware that a commitment to methodological truth (the historian's duty to pass on ancient tradition) might conflict with the truth of the narrative's content – especially where, as so often with the later antiquarians, the historian fails to subject the tradition to critical analysis. Dionysius himself, in the passage just quoted, uses words like ἀπάτη and πλάσμα, and praises Thucydides for leaving θεατρικὰς γοητείας out of his narrative: and it is clear that this passage is part of a wider debate in the first centuries BCE and CE about the relationship between history and 'myth': cf. the widespread castigation of Herodotus as a 'liar'.[38]

The ambivalence of the Herodotean methodology was not the only factor that contributed to a blurring of the boundaries between 'fact' and 'fiction' in ancient historiography. The Greek and Roman historians, at least in the Hellenistic and Roman periods, were also constrained by a rhetorical training which assigned a high value to dramatic truth in a historical narrative. A plain unvarnished account of events was not 'history' but, as Lucian puts it, merely the raw material for the historian to work on. The composer of 'a bare record of the events…such as a soldier or artisan or pedlar following the army might have put together as a diary of daily events' has merely 'cleared the ground for some future historian of taste and ability' (*How to Write History* §16 LCL). Real historians are like great sculptors or artists: they were not responsible for creating their raw material but 'confined themselves to fashioning it, sawing the ivory, polishing, gluing, aligning it, setting it off with the gold, and their art lay in handling their material properly. The task of the historian,' Lucian continues, is 'to give a fine arrangement to events and illuminate them as vividly as possible. And when a man who has heard him thinks thereafter that he is actually seeing what is being described and then praises him – then it is that the work of our Phidias of history is perfect and has received its proper praise' (*How to Write History* §51 LCL). Dionysius of Halicarnassus devotes the bulk of his treatise on Thucydides to questions of *exergasia* (vocabulary, style and arrangement), far more than he does to the question of accuracy in the collection and analysis of data.[39] Implicit in this process is a recognition that achieving a vivid and realistic portrayal of actual

---

37.   Dionysius of Halicarnassus, *De Thuc.* §7, trans. W.K. Pritchett. This kind of 'agnosticism' is evident throughout Dionysius' treatment of the mythical origins of Roman history: Gabba, *Dionysius and the History*, pp. 118–125.

38.   Cf. Pritchett, *Liar School*. A similar complaint is made in Josephus, *Apion* 1.12–14: but note how Thackeray's translation of *pseudomenon* here equivocates between 'lying' ('mendacity') and 'mistaken'.

39.   On history as a branch of rhetoric, cf. esp. Wiseman, *Clio's Cosmetics*, ch. 3; Woodman, *Rhetoric* with the bibliography there cited. Moles, 'Truth and Untruth', pp. 88–121 offers a useful critique. See now also Penner, *In Praise of Christian Origins*, ch. 3.

events may entail playing with the fact/fiction boundary in a different way: in Lucian's metaphor historiography, like sculpture, is a form of *plasma* (*plattein*, after all, is what sculptors do).

Probably the best-known example of this ambivalence is the famous Thucydidean dictum about the role of speeches in history (1.22.1). The whole concept of speech and dialogue in Thucydides is of course highly dramatic and must owe something to Thucydides' experience of the dramatic representation of argument and emotion in Periclean Athens. Thucydides at least seems to see no incoherence in the juxtaposition of his prime statement of commitment to accuracy with the much more equivocal statement about the speeches.[40] Thucydides' preface also provides a reminder that one of the more dubious planks of Thucydidean rationalism was the claim to be able to identify the real motives of the protagonists underneath the mask of speech (1.23.6). This highly sophistic form of analysis is essential to the task of the critical historian, and identifies him as an observer not easily taken in: but in strictly historiographical terms it allows Thucydides to go well beyond the bounds of evidence in attributing hidden motives to his characters.[41] This has the paradoxical effect of adding to the historian's *persona* an omniscience of the most irritating form, that of the psychoanalyst who always knows your motives better than you do yourself.

But even more widespread in hellenistic historiography was the rhetorical definition of the aim of history as producing *enargeia*, dramatic vividness in both the selection and the depiction of emotion-inducing scenes.[42] This is particularly asociated with the so-called 'tragic historians' against whom Polybius spent so much energy arguing, but Polybius was in a minority here. For Dionysius, this is one of the historian's most important skills: even Thucydides can be criticized when he fails to produce it on the right occasions:

> Having been often compelled to write of the capture, overthrow, and enslavement of cities, and other similar disasters, he sometimes makes the sufferings appear so cruel, so terrible, so piteous, as to leave no room for historians or poets to surpass him. And then again he represents them as so insignificant and so slight, that the reader receives not an inkling of the terrors (*de Thuc.* §15, trans. Pritchett).

Woodman aptly compares the task of the historian here to that of the documentary film-maker: the comparison highlights the potential conflict

---

40.   There is an extensive literature on speeches in ancient historiography: cf. Dibelius, 'The Speeches in Acts and Ancient Historiography', in Dibelius, *Studies*, pp. 138–191; C.W. Fornara, *The Nature of History in Ancient Greece and Rome* (Berkeley: University of California Press, 1983), ch. 4; Conrad Gempf, 'Public Speaking and Published Accounts', in Bruce Winter and Andrew D. Clarke (eds.), *The Book of Acts in its First Century Setting*. I. *Ancient Literary Setting* (Grand Rapids, MI: Eerdmans, 1993), pp. 259–303; Hornblower, *Thucydides*, ch. 3; Philip A. Städter, (ed.), *The Speeches in Thucydides* (Chapel Hill: University of North Carolina Press, 1973); Woodman, *Rhetoric*, pp. 11–15.

41.   Hornblower, *Thucydides*, p. 166.

42.   Gabba, 'True History and False History', p. 53; Wiseman, 'Lying Historians', esp. pp. 144–46; Woodman, *Rhetoric*, ch. 1, esp. p. 27; Penner, *In Praise of Christian Origins*, ch. 3.

between dramatic truth and documentary accuracy, and especially in the area of emotional realism, as discussion about some recent fact-based films in this country has made clear.[43]

A third kind of ambivalence (though one which concerns us less here) centres on the historian's commitment to present a story and characters which conform to a cultural ideal of moral truthfulness. This concept of truth is associated particularly with the Platonic critique of the poets as promulgating 'falsehood in the psyche':

> The claim that representative poetry is 'three degrees removed from the truth' and 'deceptive' (in *Republic* Ten) consists in the claim that poetry deceives people into thinking that it can convey knowledge of ethical truth, when it cannot, and when (by the nature of its form) it serves rather to propagate certain kinds of psychological and ethical falsehood. In the first discussion, the complaint about the falseness of most Greek poetry seems, initially, to take a form which, while controversial, is not unprecedented in Greek culture. This is the complaint that poets misrepresent gods by making statements about them and attributing actions to them which are out of line with what is claimed to be their true nature... But...Plato's complaint forms part of a distinctive, and innovative, line of thought, and ... in this context, the 'falseness' involved has an extended meaning... In Plato's view, the beliefs embodied in Greek poetry are, for the most part, false; they are wrong, for instance, about the extent to which death is an evil, or about whether justice brings happiness. Therefore, identification with such figures involves the absorption of false beliefs (and of the correlated patterns of aspiration and desire) into the personality, thus making up what Plato...calls 'falsehood in the psyche' or 'the lie in the soul' ([*Rep.*] 382b9–11).[44]

It is clear that this view of what is 'appropriate' will conflict with the high value placed on psychological realism in modern imaginative literature, and indeed in much of the poetry and tragedy of the ancient Greeks, which specialized in the vivid and realistic portrayal of a whole range of unedifying passions. But historians too could be called on to portray less than edifying events and emotions, and a similar unease seems to underlie some of the later criticisms of Thucydides and Herodotus. For Dionysius of Halicarnassus, Thucydides is seriously at fault for his selection of an unedifying subject:

> The first, and one may say the most necessary task for writers of any kind of history is to choose a noble subject and one pleasing to their readers. In this Herodotus seems to me to have succeeded better than Thucydides... Thucydides, on the other hand, writes of a single war, and that neither glorious nor fortunate; one which, best of all, should not have happened, or (failing that) should have been ignored by posterity and consigned to silence and oblivion... As clearly as the story of the wonderful deeds of the Greeks and barbarians is superior to the story of the sad and terrible disasters of the Greeks, so clearly does Herodotus show better judgement than Thucydides in his choice of subject (*Ad Pomp.* 3.767–8, trans. Rhys Roberts).

---

43.   Woodman, *Rhetoric*, pp. 197–212. Cf. the row that followed the release of such films as *Michael Collins* or *In the Name of the Father*.

44.   C. Gill, 'Plato on Falsehood—Not Fiction', in Gill and Wiseman (eds.), *Lies and Fiction*, esp. pp. 44–45.

A similar kind of distaste underlies much of Dionysius' critique in the *De Thucydide,* for example when he accuses Thucydides of using inappropriate words in the Melian Dialogue, that is 'words...appropriate to oriental monarchs addressing Greeks, but unfit to be spoken by Athenians to the Greeks whom they liberated from the Medes, to wit, that justice is the normal conduct of equals to one another, but violence is "the law" of the strong against the weak' (*De Thuc.* 38, trans. Pritchett). The concept of *to prepon* can also be used to critique the rhetorical appropriateness of words for a given occasion, as when Dionysius criticizes the words attributed to Pericles in §45:

> As I said at the outset, the historian, giving expression to his own views about the merits of Pericles, seems to have spoken these words contrary to the proprieties of the occasion (*topos*). The writer ought himself to have expressed whatever views he desired about the statesman, but ought not have put into his mouth, when he was in danger, words that were humble and calculated to conciliate the anger [of his audience]. Such a course would have been befitting a writer who was desirous of giving a picture of the truth (trans. Pritchett).

What offends Dionysius here is not that the historian is putting words into Pericles' mouth (which he seems to take as the norm), but that the words selected are *morally* bad rhetoric, in other words that they set a bad example to the students to whom Thucydides is recommended as a model for 'imitation' (*De Thuc.* 1). Clearly the 'truth' of the narrative in this sense has little to do with its factuality as we would understand it.

Border regions: Fiction in Geography, Paradoxography, and Biography
History is not the only Greek prose genre to exemplify this kind of blurring of the boundaries between fact and fiction. Plutarch sees the same processes at work in geography and in biography – not surprisingly, since both are closely related to history:

> As geographers, Sosius, crowd into the edges of their maps parts of the world they know nothing about, adding notes in the margin to the effect, that beyond this lies nothing but sandy deserts full of wild beasts, unapproachable bogs, Scythian ice, or a frozen sea, so in this work of mine, in which I have compared the lives of the greatest men with one another, after passing through those periods which probable reasoning can reach to and real history find a footing in, I might very well say of those that are farther off: 'Beyond this there is nothing but prodigies and fictions, the only inhabitants are the poets and inventors of fables: there is no credit, or certainty any farther'.[45]

Geography for the Greeks was a branch of *historia* at least as old as historiography, and many writers followed Herodotus in combining the two. But there is also a range of geographical writing in Greek treating geography as a distinct branch of knowledge in its own right.[46] Much of this work is intensely scientific,

---

45.   Plutarch *Life of Theseus* 1.1, trans. A.H. Clough, *Plutarch's Lives* (London: J.M. Dent [Everyman], 1910), I, p. 1

46.   On the relationship, cf. Clarke, *Between Geography and History*, esp. ch. 1 (though Clarke appears wrongly to identify *historikos* with 'historical' in her remarks on Ps.-Scymnus on p. 63).

using mathematical calculation as a basis for serious cartography: it culminated in the gargantuan achievement of Ptolemy, which was to dominate the geographical perspectives of Europe for more than a thousand years. But the work of the mathematical geographers was partly in tension with, partly reliant on a much broader base of travellers' reports, from the brief, pragmatic *periploi* of mariners and merchants[47] to the more grandiose reports of imperialistic fact-finding expeditions like the voyage of Nearchus or Arrian's report to Trajan on the Black Sea coasts.[48] Like the historians, Greek geographers probed and extended the traditional picture of the world inherited from the poets (Homer's *Odyssey* was a key text in Greek geographical education) by collecting and analyzing the reports of travellers from ever more distant lands.[49] Where their own experience ran out, they could cite the testimony of other travellers, *autoptai* in their own right, who collectively pushed the bounds of Greek geographical knowledge well beyond the the limits of the Mediterranean world.

The word *autoptai* and its cognates is in fact particularly associated with geography, as I have demonstrated at length elsewhere: that is, it tends to occur most often in association with items of information from or about distant lands.[50] It positions geographical writers firmly within the Herodotean discourse of critical rationalism, and opens up a similar range of ambivalence. On the one hand, a discourse which proclaims its dependence on *autopsia* (whether at first or at second hand) clearly affirms the value of personal experience as a testimony to 'fact' – and, incidentally, underlines its own critical awareness of the need to produce 'evidence' for its statements in the shape of first-hand testimony. Simultaneously, however, this discourse creates the possibility of a critical distance between narrator and narrated: one does not believe every traveller's tale.[51]

In fact, as Plutarch suggests, there was a widespread perception that the marvels which filled the blank spaces at the edge of the geographers' maps were simply fictions, poetic fantasies which did not call for serious belief: and it seems clear that writers who wanted to create geographical fiction could do so by

47.   The *Periplus* texts are collected in C. Müller, (ed.), *Geographi Graeci Minores* I and II (Paris: Didot, 1855, 1861), and are discussed in full in *RE* s.v. 'Periplus'; A. Diller, *The Tradition of the Minor Greek Geographers* (American Philological Association Monographs, 14; New York: Lancaster Press, 1952). Individual editions include: M.L. Allain, 'The Periplous of Skylax of Karyanda' (PhD, Ohio State University, 1977); J. Blomqvist, *The Date and Origin of the Greek Version of Hanno's Periplus* (Lund: Gleerup, 1979); G.W.B. Huntingford (ed.), *The Periplus of the Erythraean Sea* (London: Hakluyt Society, 1980); Lionel Casson (ed.), *The Periplus Maris Erythraei* (Princeton: Princeton University Press, 1989). Allain, 'The Periplous of Skylax', ch. 1 has a useful introduction to the Periplus literature, as does O.A.W. Dilke, *Greek and Roman Maps* (London: Thames & Hudson, 1985), ch. 9; Clarke, *Between Geography and History*, pp. 197–202.

48.   Arrian, *Anabasis of Alexander* Bk VIII (LCL); Arrian, *Periplus Ponti Euxini* (ed. Aidan Liddle; Bristol Classical Press; London: Duckworth, 2003).

49.   P. Pédech, *La Méthode Historique de Polybe* (Paris: Les Belles Lettres, 1964), pp. 582–86.

50.   On the geographical associations of *autopsia*, cf. L.C.A. Alexander, *The Preface to Luke's Gospel* (SNTSMS, 78; Cambridge: Cambridge University Press, 1993), pp. 34–41.

51.   Cf. Lucian, *How to Write History*, §29.

exploiting these spaces at the limits of *autopsia*.[52] Lucian parodies these 'incredible' (*apista*) travel-narratives in his *True History*, which contains, so he warns his readers, only one true statement:

> I think I can escape the censure of the world by my own admission that I am not telling a word of truth. Be it understood, then that I am writing about things which I have neither seen nor had to do with nor learned from others – which, in fact, do not exist at all and, in the nature of things, cannot exist. Therefore my readers should on no account believe in them. Once upon a time, setting out from the Pillars of Hercules and heading for the western ocean with a fair wind, I went a-voyaging... (Lucian, *A True Story*, 1.4–5, LCL).

Lucian takes Herodotus' 'framing' technique to its logical extreme here, by bracketing his whole narrative as a lie: but this was an unusual expedient. Most writers of geographical fiction were careful to maintain the 'credibility ethic'[53] by retaining the framework of traveller's report, bracketing their incredible tales in multiple layers of quotation marks. This emerges clearly from Photius' account of *The Wonders beyond Thule*:

> And so Dinias begins the narration of these things to an Arcadian named Cymbas, whom the Arcadian League sent to Tyre to ask that Dinias return to them and his homeland... He is represented as recounting what he himself had seen during his wandering or what eyewitness accounts he had heard from others; and what he had learned from Dercyllis' account while on Thule, that is, her already reported journey...and what she previously heard from Astraeus, that is, his account of Pythagoras and Mnesarchus – which Astraeus himself heard from Philotis...[54]

Diogenes, whom Photius calls 'the father of fictional stories of that time' (112a, Reardon p. 782), also takes care to give his story an air of antiquarian learning by citing earlier writers 'so that the incredible events would not seem to lack authority' (111a, Reardon p. 781); and the whole thing is placed in a pseudo-historical framework by the story of the discovery of Dercyllis' story written on cypress tablets in a vault opened in the presence of Alexander.[55]

---

52. J.S. Romm, *The Edges of the Earth in Ancient Thought* (Princeton: Princeton University Press, 1992), ch. 5.

53. 'Credibility ethic': cf. Romm, *Edges*, p. 174. But Romm misses this effect in Antonius Diogenes, *The Wonders beyond Thule* (Photius, *Bibl.* 166.109b), trans. Sandy; cited from *Collected Ancient Greek Novels* (ed. B.P. Reardon; Berkeley: California University Press, 1989).

54. Diogenes, *The Wonders beyond Thule*, p. 778.

55. 111b, Reardon, *Novels*, p. 782. The scholarly apparatus of the antiquarian tradition, with its constant references to ancient documents and archives, has the same potential for subversion and parody as the *autopsia*-convention. One of the most famous literary hoaxes of the first century CE was the 'discovery' and publication of a diary dating from the Trojan War: cf. Bowersock, *Fiction as History*, ch. 1 (esp. p. 23). On the fictional *hypomnemata* of Damis and the *Life of Apollonius of Tyana*, see E. Bowie, 'Philostratus, Writer of Fiction', in Morgan and Stoneman (eds), *Greek Fiction*, ch. 11, and *idem*, 'Apollonius of Tyana: Tradition and Reality', in *ANRW* 2.16.2 (1978), pp. 1652–99.

All of this means that the generic markers of factuality are not sufficient in themselves to help the reader distinguish between fact and fiction. The *autopsia-*convention, which is designed in the first place to provide reassurance about the factuality of a geographical narrative, can just as easily be subverted to encourage the reader to collude in the creation of fiction. And a similar fuzziness, as we have seen, pervades the whole related area of antiquarian history or 'archaeology'. Beyond the reach of 'probable reasoning' and 'real history', as Plutarch puts it, are 'nothing but prodigies and fictions, the only inhabitants are the poets and inventors of fables; there is no credit, or certainty any farther'. Plutarch does indeed go on to express the hope that 'the purifying processes of reason' may be able to reduce this legendary material to something like 'exact history': but even if it cannot, Plutarch sees no reason not to use such excellent material:

> Let us hope that Fable may, in what shall follow, so submit to the purifying processes of reason as to take the character of exact history. In any case, however, where it shall be found contumaciously slighting credibility and refusing to be reduced to anything like probable fact, we shall beg that we may meet with candid readers, and such as will receive with indulgence the stories of antiquity (Plutarch, *Theseus* §1, trans. Clough).

The readers, in other words, are being asked to accept the story of Theseus as largely fiction – but fiction sanctioned by being classified as a 'story of antiquity'.

Such 'stories of antiquity' were hugely popular in the first centuries of our era, and the period saw an explosion of more or less learned compilations of 'marvels' (*paradoxa, apista*), both ancient and contemporary, in a genre which modern scholarship has labelled '*paradoxography*': Gabba calls this 'one of the central concerns of middlebrow culture in the Hellenistic and Roman periods'.[56] This kind of compilation has been aptly compared to the bizarre 'news' stories which appear regularly in popular tabloid newspapers: talking heads, sex-changes, and two-headed babies figure among the 'Marvels' listed by Phlegon of Tralles in a collection published at the beginning of the second century CE.[57] But I would contest Gabba's statement that 'the problem of the truth or credibility of the phenomena or facts…was simply not raised, since the question of truth was not present in the minds of readers'.[58] Certainly there is no attempt at making a critical assessment of the credibility of the data recorded: but these writers place themselves firmly in the tradition of antiquarian erudition going back ultimately to Herodotus, and their stories are regularly bracketed as 'reports' or attributed to earlier sources ('as Isigonos says in the second book of his *Incredible Matters*'; 'Hieron of Alexandria or of Ephesos relates that a ghost also appeared in Aitolia').[59] Many of Phlegon's marvels are given precise dates in the not-so-distant past: ch. 9, for example, relates a sex-change which happened 'when

---

56.   Gabba, 'True History and False History', p. 53.

57.   Phlegon of Tralles, *Book of Marvels* (ed. and trans. W. Hansen; Exeter: University of Exeter Press, 1996). Cf. also Jacob Stern (ed.), *Palaephatus: On Unbelievable Tales* (Wauconda, IL: Bolchazy-Carducci, 1996).

58.   Gabba, 'True History and False History', p. 53; cf. Hansen, *Phlegon*, p. 9.

59.   Hansen, *Phlegon*, pp. 7, 29.

Makrinos was archon at Athens, and Lucius Lamia Aelianus and Sextus Carminius Veterus were consuls in Rome' – that is, 116 CE. This last phenomenon is further authenticated as an eyewitness report: 'I myself have seen this person', Phlegon states. Similarly in the case of the hippocentaur sent to Rome: 'anyone who is sceptical can examine it for himself, since as I said above it has been embalmed and is kept in the emperor's storehouse' (§35, Hansen p. 49). Like Herodotus, Phlegon has an eye to the possibility of disbelief and is prepared to disarm it by describing strictly observable phenomena (e.g. §15.1, Hansen p. 44). Fiction, in other words, still prefers to wrap itself in the generic trappings of fact.

It would be a mistake, however, to go to the opposite extreme and argue that all such claims should automatically be disbelieved. Not all travellers' tales are fact – but not all are fiction, either. Many of Phlegon's 'marvels' are physical freaks and abnormalities which do, in fact, occur and can be documented.[60] The point is that not all such tales are false, simply that it is hard to know which are true. Where personal experience gives out, the scientific observer can only fall back on a rational judgement of what is 'possible' within the limits of the physical world. But that plausibility-judgement is itself necessarily constrained by the limitations of the observer's own experience: and ancient geography contains a number of classic examples of travellers' tales which Mediterranean antiquity found implausible but which have been vindicated by a wider geographical knowledge. Herodotus tells the story (4.42) of the circumnavigation of Africa around 600 BCE by a Phoenician expedition sent out by Pharaoh Neco. The explorers reported that on the return leg the sun was on their right, a fact which Herodotus finds incredible. To the modern geographer, this apparently implausible detail is confirmation that the expedition had indeed gone beyond the equator.[61] Around 320 BCE, Pytheas of Massilia sailed out of the Pillars of Hercules and made a voyage north towards the 'Tin Islands' and the British Isles. His *Periplus* (which is now lost) was treated with varying degrees of scepticism in subsequent centuries by the scientific geographers of subsequent centuries. Among the 'implausible' details about these islands related by Pytheas are: the use of barns for threshing grain 'because they have so little sunshine that an open threshing-place would be of little use in that land of clouds and rain'; North Sea tides which could swamp low-lying country in minutes; and a mysterious fog-like substance which assails the sailor in these northern seas:

> In these regions obtained neither earth as such, nor sea, nor air, but a kind of mixture of these, similar to the sea-lung, in which…earth, sea, and everything else is held in suspension; this substance is like a fusion of them all, and can neither be trod upon nor sailed upon.[62]

Romm, who cites the above, professes himself unsure 'what pelagic phenomena (if any) lie behind this strange description', but to a native of these islands it is not too difficult to recognise a description of a good East Coast sea-fret or 'haar'.

---

60.   cf. Hansen's notes *ad loc.*
61.   Dilke, *Greek and Roman Maps*, p. 25.
62.   Pytheas frg. 7b (Polyb. 34.5.3–4; Strabo 2.4.1), cited from Romm, *Edges*, p. 22.

Biography also straddles this border region between fact and fiction. On one side, biography runs in parallel with historiography and shares many of its techniques and limitations. Plutarch, for example, though a devoutly religious man himself, is thoroughly committed to the classic stance of historiographical scepticism with regard to the supernatural. Signs and portents, like Brutus' eve-of-Philippi vision, are treated with just enough distancing to protect the narrator from the charge of gullibility:[63]

> About the time that they were going to pass out of Asia into Europe, it is said that a wonderful sign was seen by Brutus... Thus one night...he was all alone in his tent, with a dim light burning by him, all the rest of the camp being hushed and silent; and, reasoning about something with himself and very thoughtful, he fancied someone came in, and, looking up towards the door, he saw a terrible and strange appearance of an unnatural and frightful body standing by him, without speaking. As soon as the apparition vanished, he called his servants to him, who all told him that they had neither heard any voice nor seen any vision... (Plutarch, *Brutus* 36.1–37.1, trans. Clough).

> The same night, they say, the vision appeared again to Brutus, in the same shape that it did before, but vanished without speaking. But Publius Volumnius, a philosopher, and one that had from the beginning borne arms with Brutus, makes no mention of this apparition, but says... But the story of the Ethiopian is very famous, who, meeting the standard-bearer at the opening the gate of the camp, was cut to pieces by the soldiers, that took it for an ill omen (Plutarch, *Marcus Brutus,* trans. Clough, 48.1–5).

Similarly, Plutarch's account of Alexander's birth is a masterpiece of critical distancing, in which (if we read it carefully) only two pieces of information are given the narrator's unqualified approval: that a snake was once found lying by Olympias as she slept, and that Philip sent Chaeremon of Megalopolis to consult the oracle about this. Everything else is recorded as someone's dream, or someone's interpretation, or something that 'Eratosthenes says', or 'others say' (Plutarch, *Alexander* 1). This sceptical bracketing technique is entirely characteristic of biographical discourse, which reveals its roots in hellenistic erudition with every 'it is said' and every citation from learned authority.[64]

Yet, as we have already seen, Plutarch is prepared to use legendary material from the distant past when it suits him to do so (*Theseus* 1.3); and he will cheerfully sacrifice chronological accuracy if it conflicts with the biographer's need to find the perfect anecdote to summarize a subject's character. And there are other ways in which the biographer may be encouraged by the needs of the genre to stray into areas left untouched by critical historiography. The biographer's prime task is not describing the hero's deeds so much as revealing his character, and, as Plutarch points out, visible, public actions are not always the best indicator of character: 'sometimes a matter of less moment, an expression or a jest, informs us better of their characters and inclinations, than the most famous sieges, the

---

63.   J.S. Lown ('The Miraculous in the Greek and Roman Historians') points out that Plutarch uses the dialogue with Cassius to raise the credibility issue within the narrative. Visions in Plutarch are 'seen' and interpreted by the characters, not the narrator.

64.   This kind of erudition is a prominent feature of the narrative texture of Diogenes Laertius' *Lives of the Philosophers*. See further Chapter 3 in this volume, esp. pp. 55–56.

greatest armaments, or the bloodiest battles whatsoever' (*Alexander* §1 p. 463, cf. *Nicias* §3 p. 244). Even Thucydides, as we have seen, allowed himself at times a level of omniscience in the attribution of motive to his characters which he would have abjured in the description of public events. For the biographer, the temptation to probe beneath the surface is all the more pressing, and the means available all the more dubious: ancient biography, in its pursuit of the 'personal angle' on the great men of history, could be irredeemably 'gossipy and frivolous'.[65] Where their subjects were famed not for military or political prowess but for intellectual achievement, the biographers seem to have resorted to a wholesale process of psychologizing in order to extract insights into their authors' moral character – and even the events of their lives – from the poems or plays they wrote. Thus much of ancient literary biography can be characterized as 'fiction' simply because it is based on deduction from the literary works of the authors studied.[66]

The Greek Novel

It is now possible to see, I think, how fiction in Greek literature inhabits the empty spaces at the edges of the cultural map of Greco-Roman antiquity. In part, these spaces are created by the very success of the historical-critical enterprise which achieved classic status in the histories of Herodotus and Thucydides. It was their careful agnosticism about the regions beyond the reach of autopsy, and their distinction between the mythical past of the poets and the historical past accessible to reason and verification, that created the possibility of a narrative of 'non-fact' as well as a narrative of 'fact'. It is clear, as time goes on, that Greek writers begin to relish the narrative potential of creative fiction, but very few adopt Lucian's bold stance of labelling their own tales as 'lies'. Authors and readers prefer to collude in maintaining the credibility ethic by positioning their stories carefully within this equivocal territory on the edges of the area dominated by critical historiography, Plutarch's area 'which probable reasoning can reach to and real history find a footing in'.

This border territory is precisely the area occupied by the literary genre we now call 'Greek fiction', that is, the Greek novels (though it is important to remember that this group of texts was never identified with a single generic title in antiquity).[67] Many of the novels exploit the credibility-gap at the beginning

---

65.   A.D. Momigliano, *The Development of Greek Biography* (expanded edn. of 1971 *bis;* Cambridge, MA: Harvard University Press, 1993), p. 103: 'What we call Hellenistic biography, with its characteristic features of erudition, scholarly zeal, realism of details, and gossip, seems to be the creation of Aristoxenus rather than Aristotle... [It] fitted into the new Hellenistic fashion of care for details, erudition, elegant gossip. Rhetoricians and philosophers still wrote apologies and encomia. But what was now called *bios* was a detached, slightly humorous account of events and opinions characterizing an individual.'

66.   Janet Fairweather, 'Fiction in the Biographies of Ancient Writers', *Ancient Society* 4 (1974), pp. 231–75; Mary Lefkowitz, *The Lives of the Greek Poets* (London: Duckworth, 1981).

67.   Cf. John Morgan's remark: 'In antiquity the novel was drastically under-theorized' (J.R. Morgan, 'Make-Believe and Make Believe: The Fictionality of the Greek Novels', in Gill and Wiseman (eds), *Lies and Fiction*, pp. 175–229 [176]).

of historical time, picking as heroes great figures from the mists of national legend, like Ninus and Semiramis.[68] These tend also to be figures from non-Greek legend, and are thus doubly protected from critical investigation. Chariton, whose story belongs very definitely to historical time, exploits a different kind of gap in the Thucydidean concept of history. His heroine's father is Hermocrates, the famous Sicilian general who was instrumental in the defeat of the Athenian expedition in Thucydides Book 7. But Thucydides' general has no family life – indeed, women are conspicuous by their absence in Thucydides. So by attaching his romance to Hermocrates' daughter, Chariton is fitting it neatly into 'real history' while opening up a whole new area of personal experience – especially women's experience – which 'real history' preferred to ignore.[69]

The novels also exploit the spaces at the edge of the geographical map. The romantic novelists show little or no interest in the physical marvels which concerned the geographers, but they all make use, one way or another, of exotic settings and extensive travel as a background to their heroes' adventures. Many of the novels bear 'ethnographic' titles, like Heliodorus' *Ethiopika*, or Lollianus' *Phoinikika*. Achilles Tatius presents himself as an Herodotean ethnographer, relating the story behind a striking picture he discovers on his travels to the 'Phoenician' city of Sidon, beside the 'Assyrian sea': both epithets highlight Sidon's foreignness, as well as imparting an archaic air to the narrative.[70] Longus, too, though his travels take him no further than Lesbos, presents his story as the 'interpretation' of a picture spotted on a hunting trip – and his story (which manages to include the obligatory shipwreck) opens with a description of Mitylene romanticized as an exotic location.[71] Chariton and Xenophon, the two earliest of the extant novels, share a common pattern of voyaging which begins and ends in the familiar (Syracuse, Ephesus), but removes its protagonists for most of the plot to a series of exotic locations: Egypt, Syria, Babylon. The 'exotic', here, is largely a narrative construction. For Xenophon's readers (and his story carries no indication that it is dated anywhere but their present, i.e. the first or second century CE), Egypt and Syria were populous and prosperous Roman provinces; but in the narrative world of the novel, they are empty, desolate landscapes devoid of inhabitants apart from bandits and shepherds.

68.   Martin Braun, *History and Romance in Graeco-Oriental Literature* (Oxford: Basil Blackwell, 1938).

69.   *Joseph and Aseneth*, of course, does the same thing with biblical history. Cf. Lawrence M. Wills, 'The Jewish Novellas', in J.R. Morgan and Richard Stoneman (eds.), Greek Fiction: *The Greek Novel in Context* (London: Routledge, 1994), pp. 223–38; Lawrence M. Wills, *The Jewish Novel in the Ancient World* (Ithaca: Cornell University Press, 1995).

70.   Achilles Tatius I.1ff, Reardon, *Novels*, p. 175: cf. Winkler's note *ad loc.*

71.   *Daphnis and Chloe*, 1.1. Reardon, *Novels*, p. 289: cf. Gill *ad loc*. The travel element is at a minimum in Longus, but he still contrives a shipwreck: and his whole narrative has been described as 'a journey in time' (Reardon, *Novels*, p. 33).

Chariton reconfigures his own homeland of Caria as a Persian satrapy worked by chaingangs, and his Babylon is a fantasy city drawing on long-standing Greek constructions of the Orient, from Ctesias downward.[72]

The novels explore further uncharted waters on the margins of civic life. Their heroes belong by birth to a privileged elite within the Greek city, securely rooted in the communal life of gymnasium, assembly, and religious festival. All the action of the novels, however, takes place outside that cocoon of security – at sea (shipwreck, capture by pirates), in the countryside (capture by bandits), or in the hands of barbarians (Psammis, Mithridates, the Persian king). Even the more familiar Greek locations of Miletus or Sicily become alien territory as the protagonists are pushed into a temporary and catastrophic loss of social status, and experience life as slave, prisoner, prostitute or labourer.[73] One of the striking things about these novel-plots is the parity of status accorded to women: hero and heroine share equally in the adventures which test their chastity and fidelity to the *n*th degree. Chariton, interestingly, also allows women to feature prominently in the crowd scenes and democratic assemblies which punctuate the plot. This is almost a parody of the Thucydidean view of public life, and perhaps symptomatic of a commitment to take the narrative into areas of private life which the historian rigorously excluded. Chariton's story is introduced as a *pathos erotikon*, a very private affair played out across a huge public canvas. It is love, not war, that preoccupies the heroes and their cities – a striking reversal of the public values embodied in the classic historical texts. Herodotus, of course, is a better model than Thucydides here: his narrative does include some female characters, and there are some extended scenes of domestic life. But their setting is Persian, not Greek: for an exploration of private passion in a Greek setting, readers would look to drama (especially to comedy), not to history. And it is to the drama, in all probability, that we should look for the antecedents of the novels' highly stylized use of direct speech for the vivid portrayal of *pathos* on the lips of their characters.[74]

The novels also make an intriguing and unexpected use of the more disturbing and contested space created by religious discourse – or rather, by the historians' refusal to give it direct credence. The aetiological framework used by many of the novelists might well have been an invitation to elaborate on the tales of the marvellous such as were told at every Greek local shrine. The novels are certainly

72.   On the role of travel in the novels of Chariton and Xenophon, see further especially L.C.A. Alexander, '"In Journeyings Often": Voyaging in the Acts of the Apostles and in Greek Romance', in C.M. Tuckett (ed.), *Luke's Literary Achievement: Collected Essays* (Sheffield: Sheffield Academic Press, 1995), pp. 17–49 (Chapter 4 in this volume, pp. 69–96); and *eadem*, 'Narrative Maps: Reflections on the Toponomy of Acts' , in *The Bible in Human Society: Essays in Honour of John Rogerson* (JSOTSup, 200; ed. M. Daniel Carroll R., D.J.A. Clines, P.R. Davies; Sheffield: Sheffield Academic Press, 1995), pp. 17–57 (Chapter 5 in this volume, pp. 97–128).

73.   E.g. Xen. *Eph.* 5.8 (Reardon, *Novels*, p. 164); Chariton 2.2, 2.5 (Reardon, *Novels*, pp. 39, 43).

74.   Cf. Loveday Alexander, 'The Passions in the Novels of Chariton and Xenophon', in John T. Fitzgerald (ed.), *Passions and Progress in Greco-Roman Thought* (London: Routledge, 2005).

full of marvels (*paradoxa*), and their narratives are studded with expressions of religious awe and wonder – standard reactions to miraculous events – on the part of the bystanders. But there is something self-mocking and deprecatory about all this. There are no real miracles here, only good stage-management: all the novelists' marvels (including a series of 'resurrections' which verge on the grotesque)[75] turn out to have a rational explanation. Perhaps there is also something obscurely comforting in the way these narratives effectively screen out the supernatural from real life. Despite their religious trappings, the novels' plane of action remains resolutely human. The gods have their place, but it is a familiar and acceptable one: divine oracles, or Fortune, may be invoked on occasion to move the plot forward; people who offend against Love are punished; a troubled heroine prays to Isis or Aphrodite for protection. The only real miracle is the management of the plot, which turns far too often for modern tastes on unforeseen coincidence. But these coincidences are not themselves occasions for 'marvelling', either by the characters in the narrative, or by its readers: as Morgan points out, ancient readers do not seem to have been concerned about the plausibility of the overall plot provided each episode is 'plausible'.[76]

The Book of Acts: Fact or Fiction?

So where does all this leave us, finally, as readers of Acts? First of all, it now seems abundantly clear that we shall never resolve the question of Acts' historicity by solving the genre question. 'Fact' and 'fiction' are not generic categories at all, and in ancient literature it is clear that the conventional markers of factuality (in any genre) were easily – and regularly – subverted. Secondly, it is evident that the privileging of 'fiction' implied by the library category 'non-fiction' is a very modern phenomenon. For the public librarian of the ancient world, if we can posit such an anachronism, the categories would more appropriately be called 'fact' and 'non-fact', with the latter embracing a huge and undefined area of statements whose factuality must be doubted simply because it cannot be guaranteed. Nobody is quite sure what to call this dangerous territory, or where its limits are: the warning posts which mark the danger area bear a variety of names ('myth', 'lies', 'poetic tales', 'invention', *plasma*, *apista*…). But ancient readers attuned to the debate – and its key features are remarkably constant over the centuries – were well aware of the kind of terrain where fiction was likely to be found: distant times; distant places; ancient traditions, especially of non-Greek peoples; tales of the traveller and the shipwrecked mariner; tales of the marvellous and the supernatural. All these were topics which the reading public enjoyed for their entertainment value, but which the responsible historian

---

75.   Bowersock, *Fiction as History*, ch. 5.
76.   J.R. Morgan, 'Make-Believe and Make Believe: The Fictionality of the Greek Novels', in Gill and Wiseman (eds.), *Lies and Fiction*, pp. 175–229.

would take care to encircle with a ring-fence of authorial scepticism: 'This is what I was told, but I don't necessarily believe it – and you needn't either'. This prudent agnosticism acts as a disclaimer lest the unwary reader might claim to have been deceived: 'You have been warned'. The problem is not that all poets and travellers are liars, simply that there is no means of testing their veracity beyond the bounds of first-hand experience and 'probable reasoning'.

The narrative of Acts, in particular, inhabits many of the spaces allocated to 'fiction' on the Greco-Roman cultural map. It draws on the scriptures of an exotic race, alluding freely to a whole set of characters and stories from a distant, barbarian past inaccessible to the historians of the Greek world. Geographically, too, the story is located at the edges of the Mediterranean map. It begins in the 'exotic' regions of Syria-Palestine, with a whole series of barbarian place-names to add authentic local colour. Like the novels, it bursts the confines of the Mediterranean map by alluding briefly to travellers from even further afield – Parthians, Medes, Elamites; the treasurer of an Ethiopian queen. Its characters become travellers in their own right, with a series of dramatic encounters with Greek and non-Greek, culminating in a fully-fledged shipwreck scene recounted in technicolour detail.[77]

The narrative of Acts also occupies some of the same spaces at the edges of public life that were exploited by the Greek novels. Its characters experience travel, alienation, and constant conflict with the political authorities both at home and abroad in the cities they visit which leads to loss (or threatened loss) of civic status. As in the novels, there are dramatic imprisonments and trial scenes attended by the pomp of a (semi-) barbarian court (25.23). The story's heroes, however, are themselves 'private' characters, fishermen and tentmakers rather than the political and military leaders who tend to occupy centre stage in historical narrative. They interact with and challenge the political hierarchy, but their words and actions are significant in their own right. Women (who are also 'private' rather than public characters) play a secondary but significant role in this narrative, and their participation in group activity is highlighted at a number of points.[78] The conflicts in which the characters constantly find themselves also expose them to suffering and allow them (like the novels' heroes and heroines) to explore the private – but increasingly important – spaces at the limits of personal endurance.[79]

Not that everything in Acts can be paralleled in the novels.[80] The central force which powers its plot is not a *pathos erotikon* but a prophetic mission laid on the characters in the opening scene. *Eros* does not figure anywhere in the book, even negatively: contrast the role of celibacy in some of the later

---

77.   For a detailed and persuasive reading of Acts as novel, cf. R.I. Pervo, *Profit with Delight* (Philadelphia: Fortress Press, 1987).

78.   E.g. 1.14; 5.1–7, 14; 8.3, 12; 9.2; 13.50; 16.13f.; 17.4, 12, 34; 18.2; 21.5, 9; 24.24; 25.13, 23.

79.   On the interface between *eros* and *pathos*, see further Alexander, 'Passions', and *eadem*, 'St. Paul and the Greek Novel', in Ron Hock (ed.), *Ancient Fiction and Early Christian Narrative* (SBL Symposium Series; Atlanta: Scholars Press, 1998), pp. 235–256.

80.   Both the similarities and the differences argued in this paper are set out more fully in Alexander, 'Voyaging' (Chapter 4 in this volume) and 'Toponymy' (Chapter 5 in this volume).

apocryphal acts.[81] But the characters have their own deity, who communicates his purposes through a variety of divine agents: and here, too, the book fails to confine itself to the approved limits of rationalistic history. Religion is not something that can be screened out of the narrative of Acts, and the author makes no attempt to do so. There is a glimpse of the detached authorial voice at the beginning of the book (Acts 1.1), but this reassuring frame collapses almost immediately into the relentlessly supernatural scene of the Ascension. The authorial voice never returns: Acts contains no authorial comment, no 'they say' or 'it is said' to bracket its many reports of miraculous events and divine guidance. Whatever the function of the first person in the 'we-passages', it is not used in the Herodotean fashion to provide comment on the narrated from the perspective of a detached observer. On the contrary, this author projects himself as a participant in the action who explicitly shares the religious perspectives of his characters: cf. 16.10, where the narrator identifies himself with the group which shares both in the theological interpretation of Paul's vision and in the commission which it implies. A narrative which so openly espouses a particular religious ideology as Acts does certainly risks being classified by the educated ancient reader as 'myth', though it may be recognized as an edifying one.[82]

All of this suggests that, from the perspective of at least one group of ancient readers (readers, that is, attuned to this Greek literary debate), Acts might well be classed at first sight as fiction. Nevertheless, there are disturbing features about the construction of Luke's narrative which make it difficult to sustain this classification. The exotic setting does not quite live up to the expectations of the novel-reader. Syria-Palestine turns out to be neither bandit-infested wilderness nor pastoral countryside, but a network of cities and streets which exhibit much the same humdrum features as the rest of the Mediterranean world.[83] Travel takes place not in the archaic fantasy landscape of Greek romance but in the real, contemporary world of the Roman empire, and it is described in intensely (even boringly) realistic terms: unlike the novelists, this narrator takes the trouble to find out about winds and harbours, cargoes and ports of call. The shipwreck (and there is only one, as against Paul's three: 2 Cor. 11.25) is described in dramatic but realistic terms – and there is no divine intervention, only a private vision to reassure the hero that the ship's passengers will survive. The miracles which punctuate the narrative also have unusual features for the Greek reader. Unlike the 'marvels' of the Greek novels, they are presented as real events of supernatural origin, not coincidences or dramatic

---

81.   Contrast also the treatment of *eros* in Philostratus' *Life of Apollonius*: Bowie, 'Philostratus', p. 193.

82.   Cf. Galen's description of the Gospel narratives as *parabolai,* that is stories which are morally useful in encouraging a philosophical attitude to death, but 'true' only in a Platonic sense: Richard Walzer, *Galen on Jews and Christians* (London: Oxford University Press, 1949), p.15; further, Loveday Alexander, 'The Four among Pagans', in M. Bockmuehl and D. Hagner (eds.), *The Written Gospel* (Cambridge: Cambridge University Press, 2005), pp. 235–36.

83.   Paul apparently feared bandits (2 Cor. 11.26) but there are none in Acts.

fakes. In this respect Luke is perhaps closer to the 'strange but true' world of Phlegon of Tralles – except that Phlegon's *paradoxa* have no significance beyond the creation of a momentary sense of 'wonder', whereas Luke's are part of a religiously-charged narrative in which every event is seen by the characters as part of a divine plan. This narrative determinism has some parallels in the Greek novels, where an apparently random sequence of adventures can be interpreted as part of a divine schema:

> But now that Chaereas had made honourable amends to Love, in that he had wandered the world from west to east and gone through untold suffering, Aphrodite took pity on him; having harassed by land and sea the handsome couple she had originally brought together, she decided now to reunite them... So I shall tell you how the goddess brought the truth to light and revealed the unrecognized pair to each other.[84]

Unlike the novels, however, Acts provides no final resolution for its characters' *pathe*. It has an open-ended character which dissipates any feel of romantic fantasy: suffering and conflict are part of the agenda for the foreseeable future (Acts 20.29–30, 14.22), and Paul's trial narrative has no happy ending.[85]

The more ethnographic aspects of Acts exhibit a similar ambivalence. Within the discipline, as I have explained above, ethnographic material was always open to suspicion: Dionysius of Halicarnassus protects himself when using 'myth' by the claim that the historian's task is simply to transmit traditions in the form in which he has received them. But even this claim may be deceptive: and the Greek reader of Acts might well seek some reassurance about the genuine antiquity of the ancient writings which are so often cited by the book's characters. We, of course, know that they are genuine – the Hebrew Scriptures are not fictitious inventions on Luke's part but real ancient documents (even if they are not as old as Luke thought they were). But, without prior knowledge of the Jewish community and its scriptures, how was the Greek reader to recognize this?

Josephus shows a keen awareness of this dilemma in the introduction to *The Antiquities of the Jews*. He has to demonstrate his credentials as a rationalistic historian by showing that he shares the general distrust of 'mythology' and 'the poets', and that he recognizes the potential for 'inventing fictions' (*pseudon plasmaton*) in any history which deals with 'ages so long and remote' (*Ant.* 1.15–16, LCL). In other words, Josephus implicitly acknowledges that his subject-matter takes him into the area of 'fiction', but he energetically refuses to be bound by the designation. His defence is twofold: the Jewish scriptures are reliable, first, because they constitute a reliable written record going back 1000 years, which depends on accurate principles of transmission (*Ant.* 1.5, 10–12, 17); and, second, because the content of Moses' writings – specifically, his concept of the Deity – is much more 'worthy' of its subject than the 'unseemly'

---

84.   Chariton, *Callirhoe* 8.1 (Reardon, *Novels*, p. 110); cf. the (less clearly-defined) role of the oracle of Apollo in Xenophon, *Ephesian Tale* 1.6 (Reardon, *Novels*, pp. 131f.).

85.   On the ending of Acts, cf. Chapter 9 in this volume.

mythology of the Greeks (*Ant.* 1.15) – in other words, he buys into the Platonic concept of *moral* truth (cf. above, pp. 146–47). The first of these arguments is developed in the preface to the *Contra Apionem*, where Josephus goes on the offensive and launches a wholesale attack on the methods of Greek historiography. Unlike the Egyptians, Chaldeans and Phoenicians, the Greeks do not have reliable written records of their ancient past, partly because they developed literacy relatively late in their history (*Apion* 1.19–23). As a result, they are forced to rely on 'conjecture' (*Apion* 1.15) and produce contradictory accounts of the same events (*Apion* 1.16). Even their own critics castigate Greek historians as 'liars' (*Apion* 1.16–18) and their works as 'mere stories (*logoi*), improvised according to the fancy of their authors' (*Apion* 1.45 LCL). One of the principal reasons for this (besides their lack of *autopsia*, 1.45–56) is the rhetorical nature of Greek historiography, which is written 'not so much to discover the truth, notwithstanding the profession which comes always readily to their pen, as to display their literary ability (*logon dunamin*)' (*Apion* 1.24–27 LCL).

Josephus' attitude to documentary evidence here is radically different from that of Herodotus and Thucydides, for whom written documentation is always 'marginal'.[86] But there is more to this than a difference of cultural background. Josephus is forced to attack the presuppositions of the historical-critical enterprise (scepticism about ancient traditions, comparison of divergent stories, 'plausible' conjecture on rational grounds) precisely because it is this enterprise which pushes his own national history into the dubious border region of 'fiction'. The mere assertion that Jewish history is based on ancient texts in a foreign language is not a sufficient defence against the imputation that it is fiction – especially not in Rome, at the end of a century which had seen a remarkable flurry of historical forgeries and fictions.[87] Jews and other non-Greek peoples in the Mediterranean world shared an interest in redefining the boundaries of fact and fiction which was also to prove important for the emergent polemics of Christian apologetic and historiography.[88]

Does Luke share these interests? It might be more appropriate to ask, does Luke show any awareness at all of this debate? At one level, it is remarkable how little of the paraphernalia of historiographical methodology surfaces in Luke-Acts, especially when we compare Luke's work with Josephus's.[89] Cadbury comments on 'the absence in Luke of the familiar parade of proofs from the official archives'[90]. No sources are cited, and there is no attempt to create a critical distance between the narrator and the narrated by citing parallel versions or rival interpretations of events. Even in the preface, where Josephus ducks and

---

86.   Momigliano, 'Historiography', p. 214.

87.   Cf. n. 55 above.

88.   For polemic against Greek historians, cf. Theophilus of Antioch, *Ad Autol.* III; on the use of documents in ecclesiastical history, cf. Momigliano, 'Historiography', p. 217. Further, E.A. Judge, 'Christian Innovation and its Contemporary Observers', in B. Croke and A.M. Emmett (eds.), *History and Historians in Late Antiquity* (Sydney: Pergamon Press, 1983), pp. 13–29.

89.   On Acts as apologetic literature, see further Chapter 8 in this volume.

90.   H.J. Cadbury, *The Making of Luke-Acts* (New York: Macmillan, 1927), p. 191.

weaves expertly to avoid flying shrapnel, Luke seems scarcely to be aware that he has strayed into a battle-zone.

Nevertheless, there is the preface, and Luke does assume there (however briefly) the authorial persona which is largely lacking in biblical narrative. He acknowledges the existence of 'many' other accounts of the business he is about to relate – though he does not accuse them of being deficient or contradictory, or signal any wish to correct them.[91] He designates this material carefully as *paradosis* (tradition), handed down by an anonymous group who share the joint distinctions of antiquity (*ap' arches*) and autopsy (*autoptai*). The author's role in all this is limited to the orderly arrangement (*kathexes*) of material which he has carefully 'followed' (*parekolouthekoti*) – and by implication understood – 'from way back' (*anothen*), and his object in doing all this is to establish the 'reliability' (*asphaleian*) of the 'stories' (*logon*) in which the inscribed reader has already received instruction (*katechethes*).

All of this breathes a measured air of moderate rationalism which the ancient reader must have found deeply reassuring. To some readers, indeed, Luke's stress on *akribeia* and *autopsia* might recall the language used by historians, and the effective bracketing of the whole narrative as *paradosis* is reminiscent of the historians' caution in introducing ethnographic or aetiological traditions.[92] But the appeal is much broader. All Luke's buzzwords can be paralleled across a much wider spectrum of Greek writing on technical subjects which valued fidelity and accuracy in the transmission of ancient tradition as much as first-hand experience.[93] The language of the final clause (Lk.1.4) is business-like rather than academic, paralleled most closely in official letters and reports, and even the seemingly-technical *autoptes* is found in a soldier's letter of the first century CE, where it seems to mean little more than 'an experienced traveller'.[94] This more pragmatic tone may in the end contribute as much to the reassurance of the reader as any amount of historiographical protestation.[95]

So what, in the end, can we conclude about the status of Luke's work in the eyes of the ancient reader? Would it be taken as fact, or as fiction? 'Ancient readers' of course, are not a homogenous group: and readers who shared Josephus' background knowledge of the Hebrew Scriptures would probably have no difficulty in recognizing Acts as a historical narrative in scriptural style. But for readers educated in the Greek classics, much of the narrative content of Acts

---

91. My interpretation of the detailed wording of the preface is argued fully in Alexander, *The Preface* (esp. chapter 6); more briefly in Chapter 3 of this volume.

92. Like Plutarch, too, Luke tends to leave it to his characters in Acts to supply (and debate) the supernatural implications of the visions they have seen: cf. Daniel Marguerat, *The First Christian Historian: Writing the 'Acts of the Apostles'* (trans. by Ken McKinney, Gregory J. Laughery and Richard Bauckham; SNTSMS, 121; Cambridge: Cambridge University Press, 2002), ch. 5.

93. Alexander, *The Preface*, chs. 4–5.

94. Alexander, *The Preface*, pp. 122, 138.

95. Contrast Philostratus' use of his Damis source, which Bowie sees as consciously novelistic: Bowie, 'Philostratus', p. 195.

would place it in the danger-area of fiction – though with a disturbing under-current which suggests that it might after all be fact. It deals with many of the topics which were pushed into the convenient no-go areas at the edges of the map of verifiable 'fact' by Greek historians – distant places, non-Greek traditions, private beliefs, supernatural events. Weighing against this are the realistic contemporary setting in a thoroughly Roman world, the lack of a fantasy happy ending, and the sober, business-like tone of the preface. But ultimately I suspect that the ancient reader knew too much to rely solely on literary signals to assess whether a narrative was 'fact' or 'fiction'. Generic signals of factuality could too easily be mimicked or subverted, and writers of the first and second centuries CE were exploring ever more ingenious ways of 'playing with the ontological status of a narrative'.[96] Like ourselves, ancient readers had to fall back on something outside the text to assess the veracity of what they read.

They might, like the readers of Philostratus, be able to draw on sufficient prior knowledge of the book's main characters to establish a shared presumption of the story's historical core.[97] Or they might, following the venerable tradition of Herodotus and Thucydides, choose to subject the stories they heard to the common-sense critique of 'probable reasoning' – which essentially means assessing the plausibility of the new by reference to a world already known. Rationalism, of course, has its limitations: proceeding from the known to the unknown is a sound enough principle, but it can create a scholasticism which makes it impos-sible to accommodate any new data (as in the case of the circumnavigation of Africa). The habitual scepticism of the historical-critical *persona* created particular difficulties (then as now) for any narrative of religious phenomena, a difficulty to which both Plutarch and Josephus, in different ways, bear testimony. Interestingly, however, our earliest testimony to the reception of Christian narrative among pagans at the end of the second century seems to have no real difficulty in accepting the plausibility of the miraculous deeds that pepper the pages of the Gospels and Acts – in fact, Celsus treats the NT miracles as simply not up to the standards set by the pagan deities.[98] What is disturbing – and ultimately unacceptable to Celsus – is the mismatch between these deeds of power and the ignominious life and death of the founder of Christianity: 'How is it anything but blasphemy,' asks Celsus, 'to assert that the things done to Jesus were done to God?'[99]

Alternatively – and this is perhaps the most likely scenario – readers could rely on the social context in which a narrative was first encountered to help them assess its factuality: 'only on a written or printed page, torn of its context,' as Bowie points out, 'does its reader have to resort to its content to establish its real status'.[100] Luke's prefaces effectively collapse the distinction between outsider

96. Bowie, 'Philostratus', p. 195.
97. Bowie, 'Philostratus', p. 193. E.P. Sanders makes a similar point about Paul: E.P. Sanders, *Paul* (Past Masters; Oxford: Oxford University Press, 1991), p.15.
98. Origen, *Contra Celsum* 1.67: see now Loveday Alexander, 'The Four among Pagans', pp. 237–38.
99. Origen, *Contra Celsum* 7.15: Alexander, 'The Four among Pagans', p. 234.
100. E.L. Bowie, 'Lies, Fiction and Slander in Early Greek Poetry', in Gill and Wiseman (eds.), *Lies and Fiction*, pp. 1–37.

(observer) and insider (believer) which was so important in the construction of the historian's critical *persona*. This author is not only the receiver and arranger of traditions, but one of the group (*hemin*) which has witnessed the 'accomplishment' of the momentous 'business' he describes (Lk. 1.1) – and, as he makes clear in the second half of Acts, he has no scruple in aligning himself with the insider-viewpoint of his main character. His inscribed reader, Theophilus, is one who has already had some instruction in the book's subject-matter, and must therefore himself count in some sense as an insider.[101] Within the epistemological space created by Luke's preface, then, there is no real room for doubt as to the broadly factual status of his narrative. This is committed narrative of a type unusual in Greek prose literature. Whether or not Luke was aware of the more sophisticated historiographical debates in which Josephus participates (and there is nothing to indicate that he was), he chose a different vehicle for expressing what to him was evidently a new and significant viewpoint on the world. Acts is a narrative which both implies and creates the presumption of a shared religious experience: and that is something difficult to accommodate within the standard fact/fiction grid of Greek literature.

---

101. On Theophilus, cf. Alexander, *The Preface*, pp. 139–42, 191–92.

Chapter 7

NEW TESTAMENT NARRATIVE AND ANCIENT EPIC*

There is a need for our culture to have a myth, like the Greeks had. Star Trek is Greek storytelling all over again.

William Shatner, aka Capt. James T. Kirk

Dorothy L. Sayers gives a classic example of a paradigm-shift in her 1946 essay 'A Vote of Thanks to Cyrus'.[1] She first encountered Cyrus, diverting the course of the Euphrates so that he could march into Babylon, in a children's magazine called 'Tales from Herodotus'. He remained, she says, securely 'pigeon-holed in my mind with the Greeks and Romans' until 'one day I realised with a shock as of sacrilege that on that famous expedition he had marched clean out of Herodotus and slap into the Bible', just at the point where

Belshazzar's feast had broken up in disorder under the stern and warning eye of the prophet Daniel. But Daniel and Belshazzar did not live in 'the classics' at all. They lived in church, with Adam and Abraham and Elijah, and were dressed like Bible characters, especially Daniel. And here was God – not Zeus or Apollo, or any of the Olympian crowd, but the fierce and dishevelled old gentleman from Mount Sinai – bursting into Greek history in a most uncharacteristic way, and taking an interest in events and people that seemed altogether outside His province. It was disconcerting.

It was this paradigm shift, she says, that 'prodded me into the belated conviction that history was all of a piece, and that the Bible was part of it'.

That conviction – that history is all of a piece, and that the Bible is part of it – is one I would share: indeed I have spent much of my academic life exploring its implications. Nevertheless, I have to admit to a rather similar sense of being disconcerted by a number of recent studies which argue for significant affinities between New Testament narrative and the classical epics of Homer and Vergil. Marianne Bonz, in her recent study on Luke-Acts and Ancient Epic, says this:

---

*   This paper was first presented in the Ancient Fiction and Early Christian Narrative Section at the SBL Annual Meeting in Toronto in November. It was later published in two parts: in TLZ 129 (2004), pp. 381–83, as a review of Marianne Bonz's *The Past As Legacy*; and as 'New Testament Narrative and Ancient Epic', in Emmanuelle Steffek and Yvan Bourquin (eds.), *Raconter, interpréter, announcer: Parcours de Nouveau Testament. Mélanges offerts à Daniel Marguerat pour son 60e anniversaire* (Le Monde de la Bible, 47; Labor et Fides, 2003), pp. 239–249, used here with the kind permission of both publishers.

1.   Dorothy L. Sayers, *Unpopular Opinions* (London: Gollancz, 1946), pp. 23–28.

It is my contention that the author known to us as 'Luke' was one of those authors on whom Vergil's epic of Roman origins and divinely guided destiny had a profound influence. Accordingly, the analysis of the *Aeneid* that follows serves not only to illustrate the major themes of Vergil's work but also to isolate a number of the dramatic devices that he employed so effectively and that can also be discerned in the later prose epic, Luke-Acts.[2]

Luke-Acts as ancient epic? Isn't epic, of all ancient genres, the furthest removed from the narrative world of the NT? What possible connection can there be between NT *koine* and the archaic diction of Homer, between Luke's straightforward prose and Vergil's hexameters, between Solomon's Portico and the Scaean Gate? Dennis MacDonald makes a similar claim for Mark as 'a prose epic modeled largely after the *Odyssey* and the ending of the *Iliad*',[3] while admitting that this kind of comparison flies in the face of received wisdom. New Testament writers are widely perceived to be either ignorant of or indifferent to the pre-eminent literary classics of the Greco-Roman world: 'After all, those who had studied the role of epic in the early church observed that no Christian author referred to Homer or quoted from the epics before Justin Martyr, and have concluded from this silence that he in no way influenced the New Testament or other early Christian texts. When later Christian authors mentioned the bard, they did so to lambaste his gods for adulteries, murders, lies, and thefts.'[4] Of all the ancient literary genres that we might invoke in comparative studies with New Testament narrative, epic is surely the most remote, the most difficult to conceive. Is this a paradigm shift too far? Or is it simply, like all paradigm shifts, a truth which once seen becomes so obvious that it is hard to imagine it was ever questioned?

The topic is, of course, a huge one. In this paper I want simply to explore in a very brief and programmatic fashion some of the ways we use the term 'epic', and to highlight what I believe to be some important distinctions, so that we can move towards asking how it might or might not be useful to read Luke's work as a 'prose epic of Christian origins'. For reasons of space I focus here on Acts, though much of the argument could be extended (*mutatis mutandis*) to the Gospels.

What Do We Mean by Epic?

First, what do we mean by 'epic'? For Bowra, writing in 1944, the task of definition was remarkably unproblematic:

2.　Marianne Palmer Bonz, *The Past as Legacy: Luke-Acts and Ancient Epic* (Minneapolis: Augsburg Fortress, 2000), p. 39; cf. p. 130, 'He conceived of his project as a prose epic of Christian origins'.

3.　Denis R. MacDonald, *The Homeric Epics and the Gospel of Mark* (New Haven: Yale University Press, 2000), pp. 2–3: 'My faint suspicions turned into convictions that the author of the earliest gospel indeed used the *Odyssey* as his primary literary inspiration but also imitated Books 22 and 24 of the *Iliad* for narrating Jesus' death and burial. Sometimes the similarities obtain even at the level of word-choice and minor plot elements. Furthermore, I have come to conclude that Mark wanted his readers to detect his transvaluation of Homer.'

4.　MacDonald, *Homeric Epics*, p. 2.

In the disputable and usually futile task of classifying the forms of poetry there is no great quarrel about the epic. An epic poem is by common consent a narrative of some length and deals with events which have a certain grandeur and importance and come from a life of action, especially of violent action such as war. It gives a special pleasure because its events and persons enhance our belief in the worth of human achievement and in the dignity and nobility of man.[5]

The question is rather more contested among today's literary theorists, but the working definition put forward in a recent collection of cross-cultural studies, though very different in language, is recognizably close to Bowra's:

What is the epic?… A first reaction of many scholars of the classical or Renaissance epic to an account of contemporary performed oral poetry might be to argue that it is not really the epic as they know it. Similarly, scholars doing fieldwork who can measure their epics by the number of days it takes to perform them might question whether strict formal limits can produce an adequate definition of the genre. Our working definition for this volume itself has a polemical or at least limiting edge: the epic is defined here as a poetic narrative of length and complexity that centers around deeds of significance to the community. These deeds are usually presented as deeds of grandeur or heroism, often narrated from within a verisimilitudinous frame of reference.[6]

For both, epic is a poetic genre involving a long and complex verse narrative, with an agonistic focus and a heroic value-system. The term 'epic', in other words, embraces at least three sets of correlatives: literary form (verse narrative); scale and scope (length; complexity; 'a certain grandeur'); and values ('heroic').

The underlying reason for this complex pattern is evident from a cursory glance at the more pragmatic definitions of the dictionaries. These tend to move outward from the particular (the classical poems to which the word originally applied) to the general (similar narratives in a different culture or genre). Thus the *Oxford English Dictionary* (2nd edition, 1989, s.v.) moves from 'Pertaining to that species of poetical composition represented typically by the *Iliad* and the *Odyssey*' to 'A composition comparable to an epic poem' to 'A story, or a series of events, worthy to form the subject of an epic'. Other dictionaries extend the last category: 'heroic, majestic, impressively great; of unusual size or extent';[7] 'full of grandeur; majestically impressive; heroic; grandiose';[8] 'something that is described as *epic* is considered to be very impressive or ambitious, e.g. *the beginning of that epic 6000 mile retreat; his triumphant return after his epic voyage*'.[9] Thus epic is defined first

5. C.M. Bowra, *From Virgil to Milton* (London: Macmillan, 1965 [1st edn 1945]), p. 1.
6. M. Beissinger, J. Tylus, S. Wofford, (eds.), *Epic Traditions in the Contemporary World: The Poetics of Community* (Berkeley: University of California Press, 1999), Introduction, p. 2. For the genre debate, see further this Introduction and Gregory Nagy's essay 'Epic as Genre' in the same volume, pp. 21–32.
7. *Random House Dictionary of the English Language* (New York: Random House, 1966), s.v.
8. *The Reader's Digest Great Encyclopedic Dictionary* (New York: Reader's Digest, 1966), s.v.
9. *Collins Cobuild English Language Dictionary* ('Helping learners with *real* English'; London and Glasgow: Collins, 1987), s.v.

and foremost in relation to its classic literary exemplars, then extended to parallel literary forms in other cultures or genres, then more broadly to narratives (or even events) which in some way resemble the classic exemplars in scale, scope, or values.

Epic as Cross-Cultural Genre

In this sense there is no problem in principle in the increasingly common habit of describing the foundational narratives of the Hebrew Bible as 'Israel's national epic'.[10] This description recognizes the fact that epic, as a generic label, can cross cultural boundaries: if we can speak of Beowulf or Gilgamesh as epic heroes, why not David or Moses? Working out the precise degree to which the Hebrew Bible narratives, so conceived, might or might not be comparable to the classical epics is a valuable and potentially revealing exercise, of which notable exemplars can be found in Auerbach's *Mimesis* and Frank Cross' *From Epic to Canon*.[11] For such a cross-cultural definition to work, however, there has to be a minimal degree of generic fit. There is a recognizable generic affinity between the heroic lays of the Anglo-Saxon Beowulf poet and the epic poems of Homer and Vergil, an affinity that works at all three levels: in their common use of a particular mode of verse narrative (even though the details of poetic construction are very different), in the values of the heroic worlds they depict, and in the more indefinable sense that epic demands a certain level of poetic seriousness and grandeur of conception. Even if we ignore the first, most precise level of generic analogy (there is no extended, heroic verse narrative in the Bible), a cross-cultural comparison would look for epic features in the broader senses of the term, something conveying the values of a heroic world-view, or something with that 'majestic' or 'grandiose' quality that epic seriousness seems to require. And this creates our first problem: for while some of that quality might plausibly be claimed for parts of the Hebrew Bible, few (if any) readings of New Testament narrative have claimed them as 'epic' in any of these senses. Even Auerbach, an acute reader of narrative, used the comparison between Homer and the Hebrew Bible principally to point up the differences between them at the narrative level.[12]

10.   E.g. Bonz, *Legacy,* p. 87 and ch. 1.

11.   Erich Auerbach, *Mimesis: The Representation of Reality in Western Literature* (trans. Willard R. Trask; Princeton: Princeton University Press, 1953). Frank Moore Cross, *From Epic to Canon: History and Literature in Ancient Israel* (Baltimore: Johns Hopkins, 1998), esp. pp. 22–52, 'Traditional Narrative and the Reconstruction of Early Israelite Institutions'.

12.   Auerbach, *Mimesis*, p.11: 'It would be difficult, then, to imagine styles more contrasted than those of these two equally ancient and equally epic texts'. Cross identifies a body of ancient Israelite tradition as fitting the following 'epic' criteria: '1. oral composition in formulae and themes of a traditional nature, 2. narrative in which acts of god(s) and men form a double level of action, 3. a composition describing traditional events of an age conceived as normative, 4. a "national" composition, especially one recited at pilgrimage festivals' (*From Epic to Canon,* p. 29). But Cross regards this oral traditional material as many stages removed from 'the great conflate amalgam of many ages we call the Pentateuch' (*From Epic to Canon,* p. 52).

Epic as National Foundation Myth

More often than not, however, the description of biblical narrative as 'epic' is making a functional rather than a generic statement. It reflects the widely-accepted perception that the cultural role played by the biblical narratives for Jewish and Christian groups at the beginning of the Common Era was comparable to that played by the classical epics of Homer and Vergil in Greco-Roman culture. Using the term 'epic' for texts that play such a role within a national culture has a longer pedigree than might be suspected. The *Oxford English Dictionary*[2] (s.v.) adds the following note under sense B. (Sb.) 2.b. *transf.* ('A composition comparable to an epic poem'):

> The typical epics, the Homeric poems, the *Niebelungenlied*, etc., have often been regarded as embodying a nation's conception of its own past history, or of the events in that history which it finds most worthy of remembrance. Hence by some writers the phrase national epic has been applied to any imaginative work (whatever its form) which is considered to fulfil this function. Carlyle, *Heroes* (1858): 'Schlegel has a remark on his Historical Plays, Henry Fifth and the others, which is worth remembering. He calls them a kind of National Epic.'

In this sense any biblical narrative, including Acts, could be labeled 'epic' insofar as it embodies the community's conception of its own past.

It must be recognized, however, that this functional description is distinct from a generic one, and that the one does not necessarily imply the other. When William Shatner declares that 'Star Trek is Greek storytelling all over again', we may be happy to concede that this particular piece of Hollywood mythmaking has epic qualities. But if (for the sake of argument) we were to argue that Harry Potter had usurped this mythic role for moviegoers of the twenty-first century, that would not make Harry Potter an epic: even with the added frisson of the fantasy element, its genre is the classic boarding-school story of a type very familiar to English schoolchildren between the wars. Equally, while the functional analogy (as is clear in this case) may be illuminating to us as readers, it tells us nothing whatever about what was in the author's mind at the time of composition. In this sense, reading the biblical narratives alongside the Greek and Roman epics (like reading them alongside the myths of Hollywood) is a valuable imaginative exercise which has a lot to teach us, not least about the mythic patterns that resonate with the human spirit. Such readings can be exciting and illuminating in their own right, but they are essentially a-historical: they tell us nothing of deliberate imitation or conscious evocation.

Epic as Cultural Hypotext

In inviting us to read New Testament narrative in conjunction with Homer or Vergil, however, Bonz and MacDonald are making a claim which is much more specific than this, and potentially much more significant for the socio-historical understanding of New Testament narrative. The claim is not that biblical narrative belongs to the epic genre in scale or scope, or even that it serves the same function as classical epic in its society, but that the biblical writers themselves are consciously adopting the classical epics as intertexts. Here the first point to establish is accessibility: an intertext (in this sense) must be a text that is accessible to both author and readers. For Homer, this is not difficult to establish. Early Christian discourse is formulated in a cultural world in which the classical epics held a pre-eminent position in education and the production of literature. The papyri make it abundantly clear that Homer was the most widely-read Greek text in antiquity, outstripping all other literary texts by a considerable margin; actively taught in schools from the elementary level upwards, actively edited, imitated, and quoted, Homer underpins the cultural and educational systems of the Greek East. This is an essential and important point for understanding the cultural worlds of the first century, and it gives a strongly persuasive force to the insistence that we must reckon with the stories and characters of Homer as part of the cultural script of the New Testament writers and their first readers.

Vergil's *Aeneid*, more recent but no less influential, performs the same function for Romans, energetically promulgated by the Julio-Claudian dynasty as a foundation myth to undergird the political systems of the Empire. How well the Latin epic of Vergil was known among the Empire's Greek-speaking inhabitants is less clear, however. Bilingual cribs have turned up in Egypt, and there was a Greek prose version of the *Aeneid*, but we do not know how far these circulated outside the immediate environs of the Roman military and administrative elite.[13] It is perhaps more important to point out that the story of Aeneas was portrayed in visual and concrete form, not only in Rome[14] but in the Asian city of Aphrodisias, so that at least some inhabitants of the Greek East could have known the story of Aeneas without having to acquire the dubious skill of reading Latin hexameters. Doug Edwards points out that any visitor to the forum of Aphrodisias would see Aeneas depicted there in visual form:

> The niches of the monumental propylon (outer gateway) of the imperial cult complex at Aphrodisias offered additional displays of power for the viewer. There, the viewer saw busts or statues of Aphrodite Prometor, Aeneas, and various members of the Julio-Claudian family. The busts and statues stress the connection between the goddess Aphrodite and the founding (or power) of the Julio-Claudian line. For Aphrodisias, the power of Aphrodite defines and legitimates the power of Rome, a point made clearer when one enters the complex. There one saw at the far end of the complex a temple dedicated to Aphrodite and the emperors and a series of panels along the two porticoes that displayed mythic scenes (including Aphrodite and Aeneas) and scenes of imperial victory.[15]

This highlights a further important distinction we need to bear in mind when thinking about the classical epics and their role in Greco-Roman culture. The *story* of the *Aeneid*, the story which links an apparently insignificant survivor of the Trojan war with the foundation of Rome, must be distinguished from the *discourse* in which it finds literary expression in Vergil's epic poem. The connection between

---

13.   Bonz, *Legacy*, p. 64. But was Polybius' prose version ever any more than a crib, designed to accompany and ease the reading of an unfamiliar Latin text for Greek readers?

14.   Bonz, *Legacy*, pp. 62–63.

15.   Douglas R. Edwards, *Religion and Power: Pagans, Jews, and Christians in the Greek East* (New York: Oxford University Press, 1996), p. 55.

Aeneas and Rome is nowhere made in Homer, but it was not Vergil's invention: Hellenistic and Roman traditions had completed the loop by the third century BCE, bringing Aeneas and the Trojan remnant to Italy and combining the post-Homeric story with Latin and Roman foundation myths.[16] The story, the myth, in other words, could be known independently of the epic poem which became its most famous and successful carrier. To put it another way, the cultural hypotext may not be a text (in the obvious literary sense) at all: a point confirmed by a study of the Stoic allegory of Cornutus, in which the underlying point of comparison is not the text of Homer (despite the usual peppering of Homeric quotations), nor even in many cases a narrative at all, but the mythological attributes of the gods as depicted in poetry, ritual practice, and the visual arts.[17] And conversely, the hypertext need not be a 'text' either, much less a text belonging to the particular literary genre 'epic'. The figure of *polutlas dios Odysseus*, 'much-suffering divine Odysseus', provides a key typological motif for Cynic philosophy: but that does not turn the Cynic writings into epics.[18]

Epic and imitatio
The argument that classical epic could have functioned as a cultural hypotext for New Testament writers is frequently linked with the widely-recognized fact that the role of the foundational epics as 'classics' for allusion, mimesis and trans-valuation in their societies forms an exact and illuminating analogy to the role of the Hebrew Bible in Jewish and Christian discourse. Thus, for Bonz, 'the use of literary allusion to add complexity and ambiguity to the surface level of the narrative' in Acts is treated as one of 'the specific elements from contemporary Greco-Roman epic tradition'.[19] But it is surely a non-sequitur to treat literary allusion *per se* as an epic feature.

Three distinct points need to be made here. First, there are many different ways of paying homage to a cultural classic (quotation, allusion, parody, pastiche, to name but a few), and most of them fall a long way short of generic *imitatio*, that is the attempt to emulate a classic text by producing something in the same genre. Homer is the most widely-quoted author of classical antiquity, but very few of the writers who quote him are themselves claiming (or even remotely aspiring) to write epic poems. In fact a measure of the awed esteem in which Homer was held is precisely the mockery with which someone like Lucian treats contemporary historians who try to write in Homeric fashion.[20] It is partly the temerity of Vergil's ambition to write a modern epic poem in Latin that gives us the measure of his astonishing achievement.

Moreover, *imitatio* (in either the broad or the narrow sense) is not a specific characteristic of epic but a widespread cultural phenomenon fundamental to

16.   J. Perret, *Les Origines de la légende troyenne de Rome* (281–31) (Paris: Les Belles Lettres, 1942).
17.   This observation arises out of many fruitful conversations engendered by the 'Stoic allegory' project of the SBL Hellenistic Moral Philosophy and Early Christianity group.
18.   MacDonald, *Homeric Epics*, pp. 15–19.
19.   Bonz, *Legacy*, p. 95
20.   Lucian, *How To Write History* §14.

ancient Mediterranean society. And it is part of an educational pattern that placed a high value on sensitivity to linguistic register.[21] Studying Homer meant training both in *historia* and in *lexis*, both getting to know the story of epic – immersing yourself in the names, the places, the actions, the values of the heroic world – and understanding its *lexis*, the way its language works: epic diction, epic accidence and syntax, epic rhythm and metre all had to be mastered and absorbed. With prose literature, *imitatio* was primarily focused on *lexis*, on being able to reproduce the distinctive style of Demosthenes or Thucydides – and that in itself meant a heightened sensitivity to the difference between prose and verse, seen for example in the avoidance of verse rhythms and vocabulary in a prose composition. To any reader trained in this system, the distinctive features of epic discourse, so easily dismissed by modern readers, could not be ignored.

In such a society, what is important, what labels you and gives you your cultural identity, is not the fact of *imitatio* but the choice of model: if you like, the question is not whether you are interested in football but which team you support.[22] What is culturally significant about Luke's work, then, is precisely the fact that the model he chooses as his 'classic' is not Homer or Vergil but the Greek Bible. Our growing awareness of the cultural dominance of the classical epics merely throws this choice into relief as a conscious decision to inhabit an alternative narrative world. Luke's work proclaims at every level that it belongs to a 'different story', to the narrative world of the Bible: people and places, style and language, allusion and quotation, narrative management, plot devices, symbolic repertoire, ideology and values all proclaim a distinctive cultural location within the Greco-Roman world,[23] much as the choice of an Egyptian decorative motif betrays the alternative cultural world of the Isis-devotee who once live in the port area of Roman Lausanna.[24] Not that the world of the Bible and the world of epic are necessarily mutually exclusive: as Dorothy L. Sayers' story demonstrates, children (and adults) are quite capable of sustaining a number of distinct cultural scripts, without making the connections that seem obvious to outsiders. Indeed, it could be useful to have more than one cultural script to draw on when straying outside the narrative register of one's own tradition: and (as we shall see) there may well be subtle allusions to the classical epic in Luke's work. But this scattered and allusive cultural cross-referencing is very different from the explicit and obvious *imitatio* that we see in Luke's treatment of his main hypotext, the Greek Bible.

---

21.   Cf Loveday Alexander, 'Intertextualité et la question des lecteurs', in D. Marguerat and A. Curtis (eds.), *Bible et Intertextualité* (Geneva: Labor et Fides, 1999), pp. 201–14.

22.   Further on this Loveday Alexander, 'IPSE DIXIT: Citation of Authority in Paul and in the Jewish and Hellenistic Schools', in Troels Engberg-Pedersen (ed.), *Paul beyond the Judaism-Hellenism Divide* (Louisville: Westminster John Knox, 2001), pp. 103–27.

23.   On the significance of this cultural decision for understanding Luke's world, see further Chapter 10 in this volume and the literature there cited.

24.   The Musée romain Lausanne-Vitry displays a Roman-era 'Fragment de relief en terre cuite' depicting a 'divinité égyptienne (Anubis ou Horus) portant un autel ou une table d'offrande'.

A Prose Epic?

All of these considerations contribute to my sense of unease at the description of Acts as a 'prose epic'. Epic may be defined broadly as something on the grand scale, or as national foundation myth: but these senses are essentially a-historical, and offer no way of making connections with Luke's social and cultural location. Functional and cross-cultural comparisons are valuable in their own right, but do not automatically entitle us to move from the perceptions of readers to historically-located deductions about the processes of authorship. The important distinction between story and discourse cuts two ways. On the one hand, it increases the accessibility of a particular mythic story (e.g. the story of Aeneas) to a wider audience than the readers of Vergil's Latin epic poem, and thus makes it more likely that this story could be part of Luke's cultural script. But on the other hand, it also drives a wedge between story and text: one could know and allude to the story without necessarily being trained in reading or imitating the particular literary genre which Vergil chose as his vehicle. And the literary training in *imitatio* that was integral to the Greek and Roman educational systems heightened sensitivity to distinctive patterns of discourse – a factor that leaves a nagging feeling of unease as to whether the concept 'prose epic' would make any sense in Greco-Roman culture. The whole point about writing prose is that it turns into something different: Greek history, for example, eschews the mythological element inextricably linked with poetry but retains the heroic subject-matter and ideology; Greek novels return to a mythological framework closer in some ways to the epic originals, but subvert the heroic ideology.

Epic and New Testament Narrative

So is there any value in pursuing the comparison between New Testament narrative and ancient epic? Given the pivotal role of epic in the cultural systems of antiquity (a role to which studies such as those of Bonz and MacDonald bear eloquent and valuable testimony), I believe that we have little choice: we simply cannot ignore an element so important in the cultural script of the first Christian centuries. But reading New Testament narrative alongside epic has enormous pitfalls as well as huge potential: what is essential is a close and sensitive reading that is as alert to differences as to similarities. At the surface levels of discourse and narrative management, Acts is not an epic, and no ancient reader would mistake it for one. The story of Aeneas, with his divine mission to journey to Rome and found a new people, does not lie on the surface of Luke's narrative. Nevertheless, there are sufficient clues to bring the comparison readily to mind for at least some readers of Luke's story, and to make it possible if not probable that Luke saw some of them himself.

Acts and the Story of Epic

A bald narrative summary of the story of Aeneas suggests a number of similarities – as well as a number of obvious contrasts – with the story-line of Acts:

Aeneas flees from the flames of Troy, bearing on his shoulders the stricken Anchises with the Penates, leading his boy Ascanius and followed by his wife Creusa (who is lost on the way), till he comes to Mount Ida. There he gathers the remnants of the Trojans in twenty ships, and sails by way of Thrace and Delos to Crete, imagining that to be the destination assigned him by Apollo. But driven thence by pestilence, and warned in a dream that Italy is his goal, he is first carried out of his course to Epirus, and then makes his way to Sicily, where his father dies. He has just set out to cross to the mainland, when a hurricane raised by his enemy Juno casts him on the coasts of Carthage. Here Juno and Venus have agreed that he shall marry Dido; but at Jupiter's command he secretly quits Africa, and, having touched at Sicily, Cumae, and Caieta, arrives after seven years' wandering at the Tiber's mouth. Latinus, king of Latium, gives him leave to build a town, and betroths him to his daughter Lavinia. Turnus, king of the Rutuli, to whom she had been promised before, takes up arms in alliance with Mezentius of Caere: in twenty days the war is ended by Aeneas defeating both.[25]

The most obvious point of comparison here is with the final westward voyage of St Paul, destined by divine decree to visit Rome, travelling from Troas down the Aegean coast, by-passing Crete and narrowly escaping disaster on the coasts of North Africa, then swept by storm-winds to Sicily before finally making landfall in Italy. Tenuous enough, perhaps: but these superficial geographical parallels (to a story whose general outline was energetically propagated by the Julio-Claudian dynasty via the imperial cult) could be sufficient to entice the reader to explore the much more profound theological parallels between the destiny of Aeneas and the sense of divine mission which underlies the whole plot of Acts.[26] For Luke himself, as Bonz argues, the relationship with the Roman foundation myth should probably be seen in terms of transvaluation[27] rather than simple adoption: what Luke provides is 'a rival vision of empire, with a rival deity issuing an alternative plan for human salvation... Furthermore, Luke-Acts names a very different sort of hero as the primary instrument for the implementation of that plan, a different concept of the chosen people, and a very different means by which conquest leads to inevitable victory.'[28] Setting the two texts together in this way allows us to highlight their ideological differences, and thus to explore some of the ways in which the Christian story was able to challenge and ultimately subvert the dominant grand narratives of the Empire.

Acts and the Language of Epic

Epic was easily recognizable to readers in antiquity because of the very specific discourse mode associated with the genre (epic metre, epic diction, epic similes, epic vocabulary); and these are entirely absent in Luke's work. Nevertheless, Luke does show a keen sensitivity to a variety of alternative linguistic registers, and this often becomes apparent precisely where his biblical model has least to offer him. Within the story of Acts, some episodes are much closer to the narrative

25.   H. Nettleship and J.E. Sandys (eds.), *A Dictionary of Classical Antiquities* (London: Wm. Glaisher, 3rd edn, 1894), p. 10.

26.   Bonz, *Legacy*, p. 128.

27.   For the term, cf. MacDonald, *Homeric Epics*, p. 2.

28.   Bonz, *Legacy*, p. 182.

worlds of Greco-Roman literature than others: and it is perhaps hardly surprising that in these episodes Luke should slip with apparent ease into the linguistic register appropriate to a particular narrative location. Thus in Athens, in the heartland of Greek philosophical territory, he cannot resist slipping in an allusion to Socrates and the charge of bringing in *kaina daimonia*, strange gods whom the city does not believe in.[29] Similarly, in the voyage around the Aegean coastline and across to Rome the language becomes nautical – mostly prose nautical, with all the correct terms for 'embarking' and 'beating against the wind' and 'the open sea' (e.g. Acts 27.2–5); but at one point Luke clearly slips into the nautical language of epic. Susan Praeder has convinced me that there is a conscious linguistic echo of Homer, in the distinctive phrase ἐπέκειλαν τὴν ναῦν at Acts 27.41.[30] And once this is identified as a piece of conscious intertextuality, it opens the door to recognizing other, less genre-specific, linguistic features of the shipwreck account (such as the 'we-narrative') as literary hyperlinks which for some ancient readers at least will almost inevitably evoke antiquity's most famous sea-voyage.[31]

Acts and the Symbolism of Epic

Precisely because of its universality, epic can also provide an invaluable index to the symbolic grammar of Greco-Roman antiquity. As an example, I would cite the classic epic simile at *Aeneid* 1.148–56:

> And as, when oft-times in a great nation tumult has risen, the base rabble rage angrily, and now brands and stones fly, madness (*furor*) lending arms; then, if haply they set eyes on a man honoured for noble character and service (*pietate gravem ac meritis*), they are silent and stand by with attentive ears; he with speech sways their passion and soothes their breasts; even so, all the roar of ocean sank, soon as the Sire, looking forth upon the waters and driving under a clear sky, guides his steeds and, flying onward, gives reins to his willing car. (trans. Fairclough, LCL)

This simile, as Brookes Otis observes, works at two levels. At the individual level, it sets up a moral antithesis between *furor* and *pietas* as the two poles of Aeneas' personal struggle in the first half of the *Aeneid*:

29.   Cf. Loveday Alexander, 'Acts and Ancient Intellectual Biography', in Bruce W. Winter and Andrew D. Clarke, (eds.), *The Book of Acts in its First Century Setting*. I. *Ancient Literary Setting*, (Eerdmans: Grand Rapids, 1993), pp. 31–63, esp. pp. 57–63, (Chapter 3 in this volume, pp. 43–68); Karl Olav Sandnes, 'Paul and Socrates: The Aim of Paul's Areopagus Speech', *JSNT* 50 (1993), pp. 13–26.

30.   Susan M. Praeder, 'Acts 27:1–28:16: Sea Voyages in Ancient Literature and the Theology of Luke-Acts', *CBQ* 46 (1984), pp. 683–706.

31.   V.K. Robbins, 'By Land and by Sea: The We-Passages and Ancient Sea Voyages', in C.H. Talbert (ed.), *Perspectives on Luke-Acts* (Edinburgh: T&T Clark, 1978), pp. 215–42; Susan M. Praeder 'The Problem of First Person Narration in Acts', *NovT* 29.3 (1987), pp. 193–218. For a critique, cf. Stanley Porter, 'The "We" Passages', in David W. Gill and Conrad Gempf, (eds.), *The Book of Acts in its First Century Setting*. II. *Graeco-Roman Setting* (Eerdmans: Grand Rapids, 1994), pp. 545–74.

The moral contrast is not simply external, between the pious on the one hand and the impious on the other. *Furor* and *pietas* lurk in the same breast and the problem is quite as much to achieve the internal victory of *pietas* over the emotions and motivations that weaken or oppose it. The symbolic contrast of storm and calm is centred, as it were, on a psychological contrast between two moods of Aeneas.[32]

But the simile also introduces an overtly political dimension to what is otherwise a purely mythological scene:

> The contrast between the *vir pietate gravis ac meritis* and the *ignobile volgus* reveals at a stroke the human meaning of the storm and thus makes quite clear its essential symbolism. The shock effect of the simile comes from its inversion of a quite common-place comparison. The likening of an agitated assembly or mob to an agitated sea or to stormy waves was familiar enough: Homer so described the assembly called by Agamemnon in *Iliad* 2 (144f.) and Cicero in his *Pro Milone* (2) talked of the 'tempests and storms of Assemblies'. But only Vergil reversed the simile and compared the storm to a human, political reality. Thus he laid the ground-work for his overtly historical use of the *furor-pietas* theme at the end of the Jupiter prophecy: after the deification of Julius, the gates of the Janus temple will be closed; peace and Roman *pietas* will prevail (I.294ff). The victory of *pietas* over *furor* is here finally and definitively related to the moral superiority of Rome to the *impii* and *furiosi* (1.294ff).

By comparing the storm-tossed waves to a strife-torn civic body, Vergil anticipates Jupiter's prophecy at 1.286–96, where Augustus' closing of the Temple of Janus at the end of the republican civil wars marks the final defeat of *impius furor* (1.294). The wise statesman who calms the *ignobile volgus* with a few well-chosen words is thus by implication an evocation of Augustus himself.

Reading Luke's narrative within this symbolic framework gives added depth to the storm which brings Paul to Rome. Luke is no friend of civic disorder, and Paul has his own share of trouble with the *ignobile volgus* on his travels (cf. e.g. Acts 17.5, 19.28–41, 21.27–40). Paul's own behaviour on the storm-tossed ship bears all the marks of the Augustan *pietas* that Aeneas so signally lacks in Vergil's more dramatic portrayal, as he calms the panic-stricken sailors with a word, while retaining an unshakeable trust in his own personal destiny (Acts 28.21–26, 30–32). Luke's Paul is not a particularly epic hero, but he is a very Roman one, and the symbolic grammar of Vergil's shipwreck provides one possible key to the way Luke's scene might be read by Roman readers.[33] But the commonplace equation of stormy sea and civic discord has a double resonance for readers of the Psalms, where the roaring waves of the sea are regularly used as a symbol for the *furor* of the pagan nations opposed to God's rule.[34] For a hero who is being transported to Rome to 'stand before Caesar' (Acts 27.24), the ability of Paul's God to 'still the raging of the seas' provides a forceful reminder of a power that is greater than Caesar's.

---

32. Brooks Otis, *Virgil: A Study in Civilized Poetry* (Oxford: Clarendon Press, 1963), p. 230.

33. The fate of Theron the pirate in Chariton's novel *Callirhoe* provides another: cf. Chariton, 3.4.7–18.

34. Cf. e.g. Psalms 46; 65; 93.124; 135.5–12; 144.7.

Acts and the Discourse of Epic

But slipping into pseudo-Homeric diction in a shipwreck story is a long way from writing a prose epic, and any comparative study must also give full weight to those characteristic features of epic discourse that are missing from Acts: the Homeric epithets; the epic similes; the vivid set-piece descriptions; the grandeur and seriousness of the language. The shipwreck narrative in *Aeneid* Bk 1 provides a vivid demonstration of the astonishing linguistic virtuosity entailed in Vergil's bold project of creating a Latin epic. Vergil's metrical rhythms (famously described by Tennyson[35] as 'the stateliest measure ever moulded by the lips of man') are too easily ignored by those who read the poem only in prose translation: but even in translation, the poetic texture of the language is evident through and through. Vergil begins by showing us Aeneas and his companions 'spreading their sails seaward, and merrily ploughing the foaming brine with brazen prow'.[36] The storm is not a natural phenomenon, but comes direct from the storehouse of the wind-god Aeolus:

> Here in his vast cavern, Aeolus, their king, keeps under his sway and with prison bonds curbs the struggling winds and the roaring gales. They, to the mountain's mighty moans, chafe blustering around the barriers. In his lofty citadel sits Aeolus, sceptre in hand, taming their passions and soothing their rage; did he not so, they would surely bear off with them in wild flight seas and lands and the vault of heaven, sweeping them through space (1.52–59).

When at Juno's instigation, Aeolus is persuaded to release the storm, the effect on the fleet is described in vivid and grandiose terms, with the focus on aural, visual, and emotional effects:

> So he spoke and, turning his spear, smote the hollow mount on its side; when lo! The winds, as if in armed array, rush forth where passage is given, and blow in storm-blasts across the world. They swoop down upon the sea, and from its lowest depths upheave it all – East and South winds together, and the South-wester, thick with tempests – and shoreward roll vast billows. Then come the cries of men and creaking of cables. In a moment clouds snatch sky and day from the Trojans' eyes; black night broods over the deep. From pole to pole it thunders, the skies lighten with frequent flashes, all forebodes the sailors instant death (1.81–91).

Everything is painted on a larger-than-life canvas. Aeneas reveals his emotional reactions like a tragic actor in an anguished soliloquy (1.92–101), only to be cut short by the horrifying vision of the storm's dramatic climax:

> As he flings forth such words, a gust, shrieking from the North (Aquilo), strikes full on his sail and lifts the waves to heaven. The oars snap, then the prow swings round and gives the broadside to the waves; down in a heap comes a sheer mountain of water. Some of the seamen hang upon the billow's crest; to others the yawning sea shows ground beneath

35.   Tennyson, *To Virgil* (1889).
36.   1.35. The mannered and archaic language of Fairclough's translation in the *Loeb Classical Library* (London: Heinemann, 1916; revised edn. 1935) gives a fair impression of Vergilian diction.

the waves; the surges seethe with sand. Three ships the South-wind catches and hurls on hidden rocks – rocks the Italians call the Altars, rising amidst the waves, a huge ridge topping the sea. Three the East (*Eurus*) forces from the deep into the shallows and sand-banks (*syrtis*), a piteous sight, dashes on shoals and girds with a mountain of sand (1.102–112).

Vergil heightens the tragic effect by subsuming the whole scene under the horrified gaze of Aeneas, watching helpless as friends and faithful followers (names and epithets reminders of a shared past) are devoured by the voracious sea *ipsius ante oculos*, before his very eyes:

One, which bore the Lycians and loyal Orontes, before the eyes of Aeneas a mighty toppling wave strikes astern. The helmsman is dashed out and hurled head foremost, but the ship is thrice on the same spot whirled round and round by the wave and engulfed in the sea's devouring eddy. Here and there are seen swimmers in the vast abyss, with weapons of men, planks, and Trojan treasure amid the waves. Now the stout ship of Iloneus, now of brave Achates, and that wherein Abas sailed and that of aged Aletes, the storm has mastered; with side-joints loosened, all let in the hostile flood and gape in every seam (1.113–123).

Paul's ship, we might observe, is harried by the same winds (*Euraquilo* 27.14) and narrowly escapes disaster on the same sand-banks (*Syrtis* 27.17); but despite the superficial parallels, Vergil's storm is poles apart from the restrained and realistic depiction of nautical manoeuvres that characterizes Luke's shipwreck description in Acts 27. This is not a judgement of historicity but of literary mode. Even if Luke's account is fiction, it is realistic fiction, while Vergil's evokes the majesty of epic with every grandiloquent phrase.

Acts and the Narrative Management of Epic

When we turn to narrative management, too, a detailed comparison highlights some fundamental differences. The opening scenes of the *Aeneid* provide examples of some of the characteristic narrative structures of epic, including the use of prophecy to provide the link between the present and the mythic past, and the 'use of supernatural beings as a narrative device employed at critical junctures to shape the direction and further the movement of the plot' (cf. 1.223–304).[37] Both of these devices stem from the mythological setting which, in classical literary theory, was one of the fundamental distinctives between the poetic narrative of epic and the prose narrative of history.

'Homeric' epic was myth or mythos in pure, narrative form. It was thus the direct opposite of prose *historia*, which was non-poetical narrative applied to a non-mythical, non-mythologized subject-matter. Even in comparison with other poetic forms that used myth, epic was archaic since it was after all narrative and could not, by its very nature, subject myths to the symbolic and dramatic transformations of lyric and tragedy.[38]

---

37.   Bonz, *Legacy*, p. 164.
38.   Brooks Otis, *Virgil*, p. 8.

And the point about myth is precisely that that is where you can talk about the gods intervening in human affairs: Homer's legacy, 'which largely determined the character of all later ancient poetry', was 'his mythical subject-matter – more exactly, his limitation of poetry's proper content to a cycle of heroic myths in which men were almost inextricably mingled with gods and other divinities'.[39] That is one of the things that distinguishes poetry from history.[40]

But that same fact creates a problem, an irreducible incongruity, for anyone setting out to write an epic poem about contemporary historical events. Vergil's solution, and part of the reason for his success, is that the story he tells is unimpeachably poetic, precisely because it is set in the mythological past. The Augustan present appears in the poem only in the guise of prophecies, forays into the future, freely discussed among the gods (e.g. 1.257ff), and revealed to the human characters by a variety of prophetic devices. This was perfectly possible in biblical literature too: compare Daniel, or Jubilees. But it is the reverse of what Luke does, which is to tell a story set very firmly in the mundane present and linked backwards to the nation's mythic past by prophecies recalled and interpreted. Luke's way of relating his contemporary story to the foundational 'epic' of his own faith community is thus the exact opposite of Vergil's: and it makes the mingling of divine and human figures within Luke's narrative problematic for the ancient reader in a way that it is not in Vergil.

This may be one reason why Vergil is actually much freer than Luke (more 'poetic', in fact) in including in his narrative scenes which give a pure and unmediated divine viewpoint: cf. the description of Jupiter at 1.223ff:

> Now all was ended, when from the sky's summit Jupiter looked forth upon the sail-winged sea and outspread lands, the shores and people far and wide, and, looking, paused on heaven's height and cast his eye on Libya's realm [Loeb].

There is no parallel in Acts to this privileged bird's-eye viewpoint: Luke never tells us, as narrator, what God is thinking or how God views the events unfolding in the human realm, much less of heavenly conspiracies and debates like those between Juno and Aeolus or Venus and Jupiter. This is not simply because Luke's belief-system is monotheistic: apart from the book of Job, the closest structural approximation we get to this kind of episode in the Bible is in apocalyptic literature. But even within the world of biblical narrative, Luke is unusually restrained in his refusal to exploit the privileged position of the narrator to convey the supernatural significance of the events as they unfold: almost invariably he leaves it to his characters to give the (sometimes conflicting) theological interpretations of events in the speeches which pepper the narrative.[41] The closest we get in Acts to

---

39.   Brooks Otis, *Virgil*, p. 6.
40.   See further on this in Chapter 6 in this volume.
41.   'Visiblement, Luc répugne à décrire un Dieu se métamorphosant et se mêlant incognito aux affaires des hommes, à la manière de la Genèse ou de l'Odyssée': Daniel Marguerat, *La première histoire du christianisme (Les Actes des Apòtres)* (Lectio divina, 180; Paris/Geneva: Cerf/Labor et Fides, 2nd edn, 2002), p. 132. See now also Daniel Marguerat, 'The God of Acts', in *The First Christian Historian: Writing the 'Acts of the Apostles'* (SNTSMS 121; Cambridge: Cambridge University Press, 2002), ch.5, pp. 85–108.

a heavenly perspective is in the opening chapter, the high point of Luke's composition, where the walls between earth and heaven are reduced to the thickness of a cloud, and the view from the mountain reaches (in a sense) to the ends of the earth (1.8). But even so, the Jesus who gives the apostles their mission plan still has his feet very firmly on the ground: and we have only Peter's and Stephen's word for it that he ever reached his heavenly destination.[42]

The opening of *Aeneid* Bk 1 illustrates some other ways in which Luke's narrative management differs from Vergil's. There is the tragic, subjective presentation of character, with the foregrounding of emotion in a way that never happens in Acts: Luke is actually closer to Homer here, or perhaps we should say that Homer in this respect is generally closer to biblical narrative than Vergil. And there is the complex structuring of the narrative itself, with the characteristic epic expansion of the action of significant episodes within the larger narrative (cf. the *Iliad*'s concentration on fifty-one days at the end of the ten year of the Siege of Troy) to achieve dramatic tension and unity, with the main story-line assumed or told in flashbacks. Luke, by contrast, follows the standard biblical approach to narrative management: he may select significant episodes to develop,[43] but chronologically he follows a straightforward, linear narrative line.

One often-forgotten result of this characteristic feature of epic style is that it is actually quite hard to get hold of the simple narrative outline of 'the story of Aeneas' summarized above. That is an extrapolation from the poem, combined with other versions of the legend from tradition: the hypotext, perhaps, but not the text. Students of contemporary oral epic have observed a similar disjunction between 'the notional totality of epic as oral tradition and the practical limitations of epic in actual performance':

> Thus, although scholars have spent considerable energy recording epic stories 'from the beginning to the end,' counting the number of hours and pages required to do so, this is not how the epic is received by indigenous audiences. Further, certain episodes of the epic are performed more frequently than others; and there may be episodes that exist only in the oral tradition and not in performance at all.[44]

And this has consequences for the way we read the text itself. The prologue to the *Aeneid* is not the prologue to his whole story (which will be told in flashback in Bk 2); Vergil's narrative actually starts in the middle of Aeneas' story, and an unschooled reader would have quite a job to work out what is happening and to whom. Gilbert Murray's fascinating meditation on how a Homeric bard might have tackled the book of Judges highlights some of the differences between Epic and the Bible in terms of narrative management:

---

42.   Acts 2.33; 7.56.

43.   E.g. the shipwreck itself, which does not correspond to any of the three times Paul says he was shipwrecked in 2 Cor. 11.25.

44.   Gregory Nagy, 'Epic as Genre', p. 28, citing J.B. Flueckiger, *Gender and Genre in the Folklore of Middle India* (Ithaca: Cornell University Press, 1996), pp. 133–34. Cf. also Nagy, *Homeric Questions* (Austin: University of Texas Press, 1996), pp. 77–82.

He would, we may suppose, select a hero and a centre for his poem... [H]e would probably choose Gideon. Then he would consider how to draw into his poem as much as possible of the rest of the book. He certainly must not lose the Song of Deborah, for instance. Looking through the record, he would find that at a certain point (vi.34f) 'Gideon blew a trumpet...and he sent messengers throughout all Manasseh...and unto Naphthali.' There is an opening. When the herald went to Naphthali, we should be told, he spoke to the men of Naphthali, and the men of Naphthali wavered, and did not wish to join in the war. They feasted and bade their minstrel sing to them. And an old minstrel – in Greek saga he would be a blind minstrel – came and smote his harp and sang the Song of Deborah, how Jabin the Syrian had oppressed Israel; how Barak awoke and led his captivity captive; how Deborah arose, a mother in Israel; how the river Kishon swept them away, the ancient river, the river Kishon. So the princes of Naphthali were reminded of the great deeds of their forefathers and came in their strength to fight for Gideon. All the Song of Deborah will come straight in.[45]

Murray's flight of fancy is illuminating in showing that while the raw material of Judges, the story itself, is certainly susceptible of epic treatment, the biblical narrator has chosen a different path: and it is this much more straightforward structure, not the convoluted narrative lines of epic, that Luke chooses to follow.

Conclusions

We are left, then with a hermeneutical conundrum. Studies like those of Bonz and MacDonald perform a valuable service in alerting us to the importance of epic (both Greek and Roman) in the cultural worlds of the New Testament writers. But describing Luke's work as a 'prose epic' written in generic imitatio of Homer or Vergil remains, for me, a paradigm shift too far. Detailed narrative comparison with the classical Epics suggests rather that Luke is writing a prose narrative that is not epic in genre or language, not (in classical terms) mythological, and for which his dominant narrative model is the Greek Bible. Even in the broadest cross-cultural sense, Luke's work resists classification as 'epic' in terms of the three correlatives (literary form, scale and scope, or heroic values) listed above. Nevertheless, at certain points in his narrative, there are subtle linguistic and symbolic clues which create hyperlinks with alternative cultural scripts: and I would include under this head both the Socratic paradigm evoked in ch.17, and the narrative world of epic, evoked especially in Paul's final voyage to Rome. Significantly, both of these may be regarded as cultural hypotexts whose influence pervades the culture as story rather than through generic imitatio of a particular text.

Daniel Marguerat has been a significant contributor to the advances made by New Testament scholarship in recent decades, moving away from the simplistic search for 'sources' or influences' into a greater appreciation of the way our texts work as narrative. Reading the Bible alongside other narratives from the Greco-Roman world is an essential part of that process: but too often the sophisticated

---

45.   Gilbert Murray, *The Rise of the Greek Epic* (Oxford: Oxford University Press, 4th edn, 1934), pp. 170–72.

reading sensitivities we have developed for the biblical texts are left out of account when dealing with classical writers. We need to refine the blanket concepts of genre and *imitatio* and to work towards finding a more nuanced and sophisticated language for articulating the ways narrative works in different cultural worlds, and the modes of connection between them: an enterprise to which I am sure Daniel will continue to contribute as he has done so signally in the past.

Chapter 8

THE ACTS OF THE APOSTLES
AS AN APOLOGETIC TEXT*

The author of Acts has a right to....be recognised as the first Christian apologist. The
great age of Christian apologetic was the second century, but of the three main types of
defence represented among the second-century Christian apologists Luke provides first-
century prototypes: defence against pagan religion (Christianity is true; paganism is false),
defence against Judaism (Christianity is the fulfilment of true Judaism), defence against
political accusations (Christianity is innocent of any offence against Roman law).[1]

Of all the books of the New Testament, the one which has most persistently
attracted the label 'apologetic' is the Acts of the Apostles. This designation seems
to go back at least to 1721, when Heumann suggested that Luke's work was an
apologia, written in defence of Christianity to a pagan official named
Theophilus.[2] Since then, the label has recurred in a wide variety of guises, many
of which, as Bruce observes, prefigure the three major concerns of the second-
century Christian apologists. But the enthusiasm with which the term has been
adopted masks a huge area of disagreement as to how exactly the apologetic
situation of Acts is to be construed. The book has been described variously as
a defence of the church against political charges, as a defence of Christianity
against Judaism or Greek religion, as a defence of Paul against rival theological
interests within the church, or even as a defence of the Roman Empire to the
church.[3] Part of the problem here is the wide range and fuzzy definition of the
term 'apologetic' itself, which threatens to undermine its descriptive usefulness
altogether: and since this fuzziness constitutes one of our primary difficulties in
exploring apologetic within the New Testament, it will be as well to begin by

* I am indebted to Todd Klutz and Andy Reimer for their valuable assistance with the
bibliographical research for this article, and to the members of the Oxford seminar for helpful
discussion. The faults which remain are of course my own. This article was originally published
as 'The Acts of the Apostles as an Apologetic Text', in Mark Edwards, Martin Goodman, Simon
Price and Christopher Rowland (eds.), *Apologetics in the Roman Empire* (1999), pp. 15–44, and
is used here by kind permission of Oxford University Press.
1.   F.F. Bruce, *The Acts of the Apostles* (Grand Rapids: Eerdmans, 3rd edn, 1990), p. 22.
2.   As cited by H.J. Cadbury, 'The Purpose Expressed in Luke's Preface', *The Expositor*
21 (1921), pp. 431–41 (437): 'The suggestion that Luke's expressed purpose is *apologia* was made
two hundred years ago by C.A. Heumann in *Bibliotheca Bremensis* [Class. iv., fasc. 3 (1721)],
and no sufficient argument seems to have been brought against it'.

constructing a rough typology of apologetic readings which will make it clear just how far the Acts debate does and does not relate to the broader topic of ancient apologetic.

One essential feature of any attempt at defining a given discourse as apologetic is the question of its implied audience. Even where the implied audience is clearly different from the text's real audience (and this is a problem of which more recent studies have become increasingly aware), most critics seem to expect an apologetic discourse to be one which adopts a particular stance (self-defence) in relation to a particular challenge or charge and before a particular audience. Accordingly, the simplest way to construct a rough working typology is to classify the apologetic options for Acts by audience, in ascending order of remoteness.

TYPE I: Acts as internal apologetic: apologia as inner-church polemic. This reading focuses on the large amount of inner-church debate embodied within the narrative, a point made forcefully by Barrett:

> [Acts] was not addressed to the Emperor, with the intention of proving the political harmlessness of Christianity in general, and of Paul in particular; a few passages might be construed to serve this purpose, but to suggest that the book as a whole should be taken in this way is absurd. No Roman official would have filtered out so much of what to him would be theological and ecclesiastical rubbish in order to reach so tiny a grain of relevant apology.[4]

On this kind of reading, the book's primary purpose is the defence of Paul against rival theological interests ('the circumcision party'), or of apostolic orthodoxy against Gnosticism, and it is addressed not to outsiders but to readers within the church.[5]

TYPE II: Acts as sectarian apologetic: apologia as self-defence in relation to Judaism. It is not always easy to determine at what point inter-factional polemic within a fragmenting movement becomes inter-sectarian polemic between rival religious communities. In this sense it is not a great step from reading Acts as a defence of Pauline Christianity against Jewish Christianity to reading it as a defence of Christianity *tout court* before the tribunal of the wider Jewish community. This reading rests on the sound literary observation that a large part

---

3.   A useful survey of apologetic readings of Acts may be found in Philip F. Esler, *Community and Gospel in Luke-Acts* (SNTSMS, 57; Cambridge: Cambridge University Press, 1987), pp. 205–19. The typology I use here follows and develops that proposed by Stephen E. Pattison, 'A Study of the Apologetic Function of the Summaries of Acts' (PhD thesis, Emory University, 1990; Ann Arbor: University Microfilms), pp. 10–35.

4.   C.K. Barrett, *Luke the Historian in Recent Study* (London: Epworth Press, 1961), p. 63.

5.   For recent examples of the former position, building on and refining the classic view of the Tübingen school that Acts is an 'apology' for Paul, cf. J.T. Sanders, *The Jews in Luke-Acts* (London: SCM Press, 1987), pp. 315–17; for the latter, C.H. Talbert, *Luke and the Gnostics* (Nashville: Abingdon Press, 1966), p. 115: 'The purpose of Luke-Acts is anti-Gnostic. Luke-Acts was written to serve as a defense against Gnosticism.'

of Acts deals with the question of the relationships between emergent Christian groups and the parent Jewish community. Jervell points out that Paul's defence speeches (many of which deal with his relationship with his ancestral faith) take up as much time in the narrative as his missionary activity; any subsidiary elements of political apology are 'weak and inconsistent' in comparison with the book's main purpose, which is the defence of Paul as faithful to the Law.[6]

TYPE III: *Acts as an apologetic work addressed to Greeks: apologia as propaganda/evangelism*. On this view, Luke, like the second-century apologists who addressed their work 'to the Greeks', is writing for a pagan audience with a philosophical and cultural interest in eastern religion. Acts on this reading lies in a line of continuous development from the apologetic narratives of hellenistic Judaism through to the Christian apologists of the second century.[7] The book's argument is not defensive but evangelistic; the success of the church boosts its claim to be the only true religion, as does the frequency of Gentile conversions. Christianity is presented as 'an ancient and honourable monotheism', admired by respectable citizens and 'eminently worthy of their allegiance'.[8] Apologetics and missionary propaganda, on this view, 'functioned like two sides of the same coin':[9] Droge, indeed, offers a definition which makes it almost impossible to distinguish between the two:

> Apologetic in the New Testament comprises a study of the 'art of persuasion' employed by the early Christians. Such persuasion evolved in a context of Jewish and Hellenistic thought and laid a foundation for the second century apologists... Much of early Christian literature, including the New Testament, was written to promote and defend the Christian movement. As the early Christians attempted to appeal to the inhabitants of the Greco-

---

6.   Pattison, 'Apologetic Function', pp. 30–32, following J. Jervell, 'Paul: The Teacher of Israel: The Apologetic Speeches of Paul in Acts', in *Luke and the People of God: A New Look at Luke-Acts* (Minneapolis: Augsburg, 1972), pp. 153–83.

7.   Cf. Pattison, 'Apologetic Function', pp. 393–94: 'It is better to speak of a stream of tradition running from the Jewish apologists, through Luke, extending to the Christian apologists of the second century, a tradition which at all points interacts intimately with its environment'. Acts, on this view, is a refutation of a series of well-documented pagan charges against the Christians: 'superstition; sorcery; political agitation; misanthropy; atheism; reckless courage; lower-class [status]; love of money; credulity; immorality; new religion; ritual murder'. To counter these, 'Luke...chose themes which would be widely accepted as admirable by all noble and objective outsiders, themes which in many cases had already been used for a similar purpose by the Jewish apologetic tradition'.

8.   J.C. O'Neill, *The Theology of Acts in its Historical Setting* (London; SPCK, 1961), p. 173.

9.   Cf. E. Schüssler Fiorenza, 'Miracles, Mission and Apologetics: An Introduction', in *eadem* (ed.), *Aspects of Religious Propaganda in Judaism and Early Christianity* (Notre Dame: Notre Dame University Press, 1976), pp. 1–25 (2–3): 'Jews as well as Christians appealed to the Greco-Roman world and used the means and methods of Hellenistic religious propaganda... The appropriation of such missionary-propagandistic forms was necessary if Judaism as well as Christianity were to succeed in the face of competition from other religions, especially those of Oriental origin, as well as competition from the philosophical movements of the time.' Cf also Fiorenza, *Aspects of Religious Propaganda*, p. 19.

Roman world at large, use was made of the strategies and methods of hellenistic religious propaganda. The appropriation of such apologetic-propagandistic forms was essential if Christianity was to succeed in the face of competition from other religions.[10]

TYPE IV: *Acts as political apologetic: apologia as self-defence in relation to Rome*. By far the commonest reading of Acts as apologetic is the view that the book was written to provide a defence against political charges brought before a Roman tribunal. It has indeed been argued quite specifically that Acts was written as a defence brief for Paul's trial before Nero: hence the narrative's repeated stress on Paul's acquittal by successive governors encountered on his travels, and the favourable view of Roman justice presented in the narrative.[11] More generally, many Acts commentators would see the book as a defence of the political innocence of the Christian movement within the Roman Empire. Both Jesus and Paul are presented as innocent of any charges touching Roman interests; Paul, in addition, is presented as a Roman citizen, moving confidently around the eastern Empire, enjoying the support of the best elements in provincial society, and advocating a politically harmless message with faintly philosophical overtones.[12]

TYPE V: *Acts as apologetic addressed to insiders: apologia as legitimation/self-definition*. More recent discussion has effectively created a fifth category with a rather more nuanced perspective on the role of apologetic discourse in creating group identity. Greg Sterling places Acts alongside Manetho, Berossos, and Josephus' *Antiquities* in a tradition which he labels 'apologetic historiography'. Despite the use of such well-known apologetic motifs as the antiquity and political innocence of the movement, the book is addressed to Christians, not to Romans, and offers 'examples and precedents to Christians so that they can make their own *apologia*. Luke-Acts is like the Hellenistic Jewish historians who addressed their works to Jews in an effort to provide them with identity in the larger world.'[13] Philip Esler gives a sociological twist to this perspective. Acts is addressed to second-generation sectarians, and represents 'a sophisticated attempt to explain and justify Christianity to the members of his own community

---

10.   Arthur J. Droge, art. 'Apologetics, NT' in *ABD* I, pp. 302–307. Cf. also *idem, Homer or Moses? Early Christian Interpretations of the History of Culture* (Hermeneutische Untersuchungen zur Theologie, 26; Tübingen: Siebeck-Mohr, 1989).

11.   E.g. J.I. Still, *St. Paul on Trial: A New Reading of the History in the Book of Acts and the Pauline Epistles* (London: SCM Press, 1923), p. 11: 'Of course the defence of Paul involved the defence of Christianity, but the book aims at more in particular. The whole story is seen to be planned, with great care and with consummate skill, for one definite end.'

12.   Cf., e.g., H.J. Cadbury, *The Making of Luke-Acts* (London: Macmillan, 1927), ch. 20 and 'The Purpose Expressed in Luke's Preface', *The Expositor* 21 (June 1921), pp. 431–41. This position is well summarized in R.J. Cassidy, *Society and Politics in the Acts of the Apostles* (Maryknoll: Orbis, 1987), ch. 10.

13.   G.E. Sterling, *Historiography and Self-Definition: Josephos, Luke-Acts and Apologetic Historiography* (NovTSup, 44; Leiden: Brill, 1992), pp. 382, 385–86. Cf. Pattison, 'Apologetic Function', p. 392: 'Although most apologetic is written to bolster the confidence of insiders, it is written using topics which would be persuasive to outsiders'.

at a time when they were exposed to social and political pressures which were making their allegiance waver. Luke re-presents traditions…in such a way as to erect a symbolic universe, a sacred canopy, beneath which the institutional order of his community is given meaning and justification.'[14] This reading allows Esler to encompass virtually all the insights of earlier scholarship: Luke's downplaying of the Peter–Paul divisions, his stress on continuity with Judaism, and his assurance that faith was not incompatible with loyalty to Rome can all be accommodated under the umbrella of 'legitimation'.

Apologetic as Dramatic Fiction

It is evident at the outset that these various readings are operating with widely different understandings of the meaning of 'apologetic'. One thing which they have in common, however, is an underlying assumption that the term presupposes some kind of dramatic situation. Reading a text as apologetic seems to mean, for most people, reading it as some form of self-defence against a charge or charges perceived as coming from a particular quarter. This minimal disposition conforms, of course, to the original usage of the Greek word-group from which the modern term is derived: an *apologia* is a speech in one's own defence (following the ancient Greek forensic practice whereby defendants had to present their own defence in court). The word thus evokes the essentially dramatic situation of the law-courts: an *apologia* presents a first-person defence of a particular character (the defendant), against a specific charge, and before a specific tribunal – which could vary from the large 500-citizen jury panels of classical Athens to the single examining magistrate more typical of Roman practice. This tribunal, whether a group or an individual, constitutes the primary audience of a defence speech, and is by convention frequently apostrophized. But the forensic scenario also allows for the presence of a wider 'public gallery' of supporters and spectators, to whom the defendant may covertly appeal, and these too may legitimately be considered as part of the dramatic audience presupposed by the apologetic scenario.

Within the conventions of classical Greek rhetoric, this dramatic situation already contains an accepted element of necessary fiction in that the speech itself might well have been written by a professional *logographos* on the defendant's behalf: nevertheless, it was delivered in the first person, and therefore written in the character of the defendant (as opposed to the Roman legal convention in which the advocate speaks in his own person on behalf of the accused). It is not a great step from this forensic fiction to the creation of literary *apologia*, that is a written composition which presents arguments in defence of an individual or group against certain charges (the most famous, in Antiquity as today, being the Socratic *Apologies* of Plato and Xenophon). Whether or not the underlying apologetic situation is a real one (as it was in the case of Socrates), it becomes a dramatic fiction for the purposes of the written *apologia*, which creates a gap not only between the author and the inscribed speaker (the 'I' of the speech) but also between the

---

14.   Esler, *Community and Gospel*, p. 222.

actual audience of the written text (the 'readers') and the inscribed audience (tribunal and/or public gallery) to whom the speech is nominally addressed. This kind of dramatic fiction was of course bread-and-butter to an educated Greek or Roman readership brought up on the multi-layered fictions of rhetoric: it provides a useful reminder that the distinctions we have drawn between implied audience and real audience were always a *de facto* possibility present to the ancient reader.

The dramatic situation remains a crucial defining factor in the composition of literary apologetic, even though there may be a shift from the defence of an individual to the defence of a group, and from a defence against specific legal charges to a more generalized defence of a religious or philosophical way of life. First-person discourse is still the most obvious and appropriate speech mode for apologetic, though it may change from singular to plural; and the necessary dramatic interlocutor can be created in a variety of ways, whether by direct apostrophe or by casting the discourse into the form of a dialogue (as for example with the *Octavius* of Minucius Felix). Josephus' *Contra Apionem* evokes this dramatic fiction quite clearly in the preface, which makes copious use of the language of charge and counter-charge. Apion is inscribed into the text as the fictional *kategoros* against whom Josephus musters his arguments; its inscribed audience, behind the representative figure of Epaphroditus, is an educated, sympathetic jury of non-Jews. It is in this sense that we may sensibly conceive of apologetic as addressed to 'outsiders': whatever the real audience of the text, it is essential that its dramatic audience, the judges before whom the case is presented, are not members of the community under attack. The texts which most clearly merit the label 'apologetic', in other words, rely on a transparent fiction: they presuppose a dramatic situation whose elements can readily be reconstructed from the text, even though the readers, then and now, will be perfectly well aware that the text's real situation may be quite different.

'Apologetic' readings of Acts almost all conform to this pattern. In positing that Acts is addressed to the Jewish community, to the Romans, or to the 'Greek' world of educated paganism, they configure the text as a defence (of the Pauline gospel, or of the church), against certain charges (e.g. disturbing the peace of the empire), before an identifiable dramatic audience who fill the dramatic role of tribunal and/or spectators. Those who suggest that the real audience of Acts is actually different from the audience implied by the dramatic situation are simply showing a proper awareness of the essentially fictive nature of the apologetic situation, or (more simply) of the potential, in literary apologetic, for a gap to open up between the text's inscribed audience and its real readers: a gap well described by Greg Sterling in relation to Artapanus:

> The fragments presume an imaginary audience which consists of outsiders. On the other hand, there is no evidence that Greeks read works written by nationals except for collectors like Polyhistor. The real-world audience of the work is therefore Jews. The Jews who read this would have to deal with the fragments' imaginary audience in the real world.[15]

---

15.   Sterling, *Historiography and Self-Definition*, p. 184

In this sense we can dispense with the fifth category proposed in our tentative typology. Any kind of literary apologetic may also function as legitimation or self-definition for the group which it sets out to defend: to recognize that some apologetic functions as self-definition is not to identify a distinct 'type' of apologetic, but simply to recognize the always latent disparity between the dramatic audience of apologetic and its real readers.

Most of the apologetic scenarios proposed for Acts configure the dramatic audience as an external one: Greeks or Romans or Jews. This brings the definition into line with the standard modern usage, in which the term 'Apologetics' means 'that branch of theology devoted to the defense of a religious faith and addressed primarily to criticism originating from outside the religious faith; esp. such defense of the Christian faith'.[16] It also allows for a degree of continuity with the standard understanding of the second-century Christian apologists as 'the Christian writers who (c. 120–220) first addressed themselves to the task of making a reasoned defence and recommendation of the faith to outsiders'.[17] It is of course another question how far it makes sense in the first century to describe the Jewish community as an 'external' audience: nevertheless, there is an undeniable continuity of interest here between the intra-communal tensions explored in Acts and the concerns of much second-century apologetic.

This definition, however, would exclude readings of Acts which see the book primarily as a defence of Paul (and/or his Gospel) before the wider tribunal of catholic Christianity. Here neither the dramatic audience nor the actual audience can be construed as 'outsiders', and it might be simplest to dispense with Type I on the grounds that it is not apologetic but theological polemic.[18] On the other hand, such readings do presuppose an 'apologetic' scenario in the wider, more classical sense of the term, in that they create opportunities for self-defence. The New Testament contains many such opportunities within a context of inner-church polemic: Paul is happy to use the Greek word *apologia* and its cognates in this context – for example in connection with his 'defence' of his own apostolic status (1 Cor. 9.3; 2 Cor. 12.19).[19] The classic *locus* for this apostolic apologia is of course the Epistle to the Galatians (although the term is not used there). Whether or not we choose to call this material 'apologetic', may in the end simply be a matter of personal choice.

---

16.   *Webster's Third New International Dictionary* (1986), s.v. 'apologetic': '1. a formal apology or justification; 2. the systematic defense and exposition of the Christian faith addressed primarily to non-Christians'. 'Apologetics' yields a fuller, more technical definition: '1. systematic argumentative tactics or discourse in defense; 2. that branch of theology devoted to the defense of a religious faith and addressed primarily to criticism originating from outside the religious faith; esp. such defense of the Christian faith'.

17.   *Oxford Dictionary of the Christian Church* (ed. F.L. Cross and E.A. Livingstone; Oxford: Oxford University Press, 3rd edn, 1997), p. 87, s.v. 'Apologists'.

18.   As Sanders prefers: *Jews in Luke–Acts*, p. 305.

19.   Cf. 2 Cor. 7.11 (of the Corinthians), where the RSV translates 'eagerness to clear yourselves'.

Acts Is Not an Apologetic Discourse

This brings us within sight of one of the crucial problems for the whole enterprise of reading Acts as apologetic. There is, as we have seen, abundant testimony
to the popularity of the label 'apologetic' among critics of Acts: but equally significant for our purposes is the high level of disagreement as to the precise linea-
ments of the text's apologetic situation. For literary apologetic to work, the key
elements of the fictional scenario (audience, charge, defendants) should be easy
to pick off the surface of the text, even if its real audience and purpose may be
less transparent. Some of the readings proposed for Acts are complementary (for
example, the demonstration that Christianity is a legitimate development of
Judaism may serve equally well for apologetic addressed to the Roman authorities). But many of them are mutually contradictory: Walaskay and Cassidy, for
example, have identified a number of counter-apologetic elements which appear
to undermine the consensus view that Acts is conciliatory towards the Roman
authorities.[20] The fact that two hundred years of Acts scholarship have failed to
produce a consensus on the text's purpose and audience need not, of course,
occasion either surprise or concern in these postmodern days; but it is particularly damaging to the attempt to configure the text as apologetic, which must
above all make its fictional situation clear. Any apologetic reading which aims
to give a reasonably coherent view of the text as a whole must find a way to
account for those features which suggest a counter-reading. The fact that so many
mutually contradictory viewpoints can be argued from the same text with equal
plausibility suggests at the very least that, if Luke's aim was apologetic, he has
failed in his task: a defence speech which provides equally convincing arguments
for the prosecution is clearly not achieving its purpose.

One reason for this lack of clarity, I would suggest, is that, in the quest to
uncover the text's deepest motivations, insufficient attention has been paid to
surface matters of genre and discourse mode. This may be because apologetic
itself is not an ancient genre-description: but the apologetic scenario, as we have
described it, belongs squarely within the larger, and very familiar, generic
framework of forensic rhetoric. Within this framework the dominant mode of
discourse is direct speech, in which the inscribed speaker (the 'I' of the discourse)
makes a direct address to an inscribed audience (the 'you' of the discourse).[21]
As we have noted, these elements can be transmuted in a number of ways in

20.   P.W. Walaskay, *'And So We Came to Rome': The Political Perspective of St Luke*
(SNTMS, 49; Cambridge: Cambridge University Press, 1983) argues that Luke–Acts contains
too many counter-apologetic features to impress a Roman reader (Zealot disciple/ 'buy swords'/
Kingdom/ ambiguous ending of Acts), and therefore proposes a reverse reading of the narrative
as an *apologia pro imperio*: it embodies a pro-Roman perspective addressed to 'a church
harboring anti-Roman sentiment, anxiously awaiting the Parousia, and pondering the Romans'
crushing of the Jewish revolt'. For Cassidy even this pro-Roman perspective has been
exaggerated: R.J. Cassidy, *Jesus, Politics and Society: A Study of Luke's Gospel* (Maryknoll,
NY: Orbis Books, 1987), esp. pp. 145–55; *idem*, 'Luke's Audience, the Chief Priests and the
Motive for Jesus' Death', in R.J. Cassidy and P.J. Scharper (eds.), *Political Issues in Luke Acts*
(Maryknoll, NY: Orbis Books, 1983), pp. 146–67.

21.   Athenian speeches also allow for direct address to the prosecutor.

literary apologetic (including the occasional transposition to the more overtly dramatic form of dialogue): but the dominant speech mode (as we would expect in this highly rhetorical world) is argumentative speech. Narrative has a part to play in this discourse, as it does in any forensic speech, in the formal statement of the facts of the case *(diegesis/narratio)*; but the authorial voice of the inscribed speaker will always be there to explain the narrative and drive home the conclusions the audience should draw from it.

This pattern can be seen clearly in Josephus, *Contra Apionem*, which contains long narrative sections (for example, in the refutation of Manetho), but where the apologetic significance of the narrative is always explained and rammed home by an insistent authorial voice.[22] It is precisely the lack of this authorial voice in Acts which leaves the narrative so open to diverse interpretations. Acts, on the other hand, is uniformly narrative except for the opening half-sentence (Acts 1.1), which takes the form of a conventional first-person recapitulation of the contents of the first volume.[23] Apart from this, the narrator of Acts never intervenes in the text: Luke simply leaves himself no space to explain how the text's dramatic situation is to be constructed. Sterling notes the difference clearly:

> It is hard not to compare Josephos and Luke–Acts in this regard. Each pleads for their respectability and uses precedents in the form of *acta* or trials to argue their case. There is, however, a difference: Josephos makes its case *directly* to the Hellenistic world; Luke–Acts makes its case *indirectly* by offering examples and precedents to Christians so that they can make their own apologia.[24]

But this difference of surface texture is actually a crucial factor in the determination of literary genre: and it raises the question whether Acts can in any meaningful sense be placed in the same generic category as the second-century apologies.

Sterling in fact provides one of the few readings of Acts to tackle the genre question directly. He proposes that Acts belongs to a specifically narrative genre which he calls 'apologetic historiography'.[25] This is defined as 'the story of a sub-group of people in an extended prose narrative written by a member of the group who follows the group's own traditions but Hellenizes them in an effort to establish

---

22. e.g. 1.227–53; 2.8–19; and *passim*.

23. On the preface to Acts, cf. my 'The Preface to Acts and the Historians', in B. Witherington III (ed.), *History, Literature and Society in the Book of Acts* (Cambridge: Cambridge University Press, 1996) (= Chapter 2 in this volume), and on the Gospel preface my *The Preface to Luke's Gospel*, (SNTSMS, 78; Cambridge: Cambridge University Press, 1993). Where the first person does reappear in Acts, in the famous 'We passages' (e.g. Acts 16.10–17), it is used (mysteriously) not of the author , but of a character within the narrative: there is no explicit direction to the reader as in Josephus. See on this phenomenon J. Wehnert, *Die Wir-Passagen der Apostelgeschichte: Ein lukanisches Stilmittel aus jüdischer Tradition* (Göttingen: Vandenhoeck & Ruprecht, 1989).

24. Cf. Sterling, *Historiography and Self-Definition*, p. 386.

25. Cadbury (*Making of Luke–Acts*, pp. 299–300, 316) notes that the narrative form of Acts may be an objection to reading it as 'a form of defense', but simply retorts, 'one must admit that on such matters of fitness opinions differ. *De gustibus non disputandum.*'

the identity of the group within the setting of the larger world'.[26] Other examples of the genre are Manetho and Berossus, the lost Hellenistic Jewish historians, Philo of Byblos, and Josephus' *Antiquities*. This generic description is a useful one, and it may well be helpful to place Luke's work in this broader literary context. How far it illuminates the specifically 'apologetic' aspects which concern us here, however, is another question. On the one hand, because these texts are predominantly narrative, the imputation of apologetic intent rests to a large extent on the assumption that any text written in Greek in the eastern empire around the turn of the eras and describing non-Hellenic cultural or religious traditions was in some sense seeking to 'Hellenize' non-Greek material for a 'larger' (and by implication unitary) cultural world. I have no quarrel with that as a description of the literary activities of Manetho and Berossos: but it does not seem to me self-evident that all such texts had such an 'apologetic' intent. The Greek reading public was far from homogeneous, and it seems to me perfectly conceivable, at least in principle, that some texts were written in Greek for a much smaller cultural world which happened to use Greek (as so many did) as a *lingua franca*. Clearly such language-users cannot be isolated altogether from the larger cultural networks to which the language gives access: but it is a large assumption that the use of the Greek language necessarily commits a writer to wholesale cultural propaganda. (Using computer software does not necessarily mean becoming a computer buff: even the Internet, a recent newspaper article lamented, is turning out to be a nexus of small communication groups rather than the 'global' audience which the propaganda promised.)

And secondly, the identification of Acts' genre as 'apologetic historiography' raises problems of its own. Oden's study of Philo of Byblos lists five or six typical features of 'hellenistic historiography...composed by those living in lands subjected to the full force of Hellenism' (p. 118) – that is, of 'apologetic histori-ography'.[27] These are euhemerism; a universal scale, with 'vastly extended' chronological and geographical limits, combined with 'special pleading on behalf of the great and unparalleled antiquity of [the historian's] nation'; 'patriotic cultural history', in which 'each historian claims [humanity's] cultural benefactors as his own nation's ancestors'; 'a belligerent and defensive stance with respect to Greek civilization and particularly Greek mythography', expressed 'without resorting to circumlocution and without searching for subtlety'; and a claim to have access to recently-discovered archives of unimpeachable provenance and antiquity. I find it hard to parallel most of this in Acts: if Luke does share some of the aims of this kind of historiography, it seems to me that the narrative strategies he employs to fulfill them are rather more subtle.[28]

I would suggest that if we are to make any progress in understanding the rhetorical strategies of this text we must begin by paying more serious attention

---

26. Cf. Sterling, *Historiography and Self-Definition*, p. 17.

27. R.A. Oden Jr, 'Philo of Byblos and Hellenistic Historiography', *PEQ* 110 (1978), pp. 115–26. Sterling would class Philo with 'apologetic historiography', although he does not analyze this work because of its date: Sterling, *Historiography and Self-Definition*, p. 11 n. 55.

28. As Sterling implicitly concedes when he notes that Luke's action of 'writing the Christian story in this genre...altered the definition [sc. of the genre] itself': *Historiography and Self-definition*, p. 388. On the definition of 'apologetic historiography' see further Chapter 2 in this volume, p. 40.

to the details of structure and surface texture. As we have seen, Acts lacks the formal structure of an *apologia* in that it is not presented as direct rhetorical discourse addressed to an identifiable audience. Luke's work must first of all be taken seriously as a narrative; but it is not in any primary sense an antiquarian account of Judaeo-Christian historical traditions. It is a relatively short description of recent historical events, set in the real world of the eastern Empire in the middle of the first century CE. This narrative construct is much too substantial to be called merely a framework, like the narrative frameworks to the great dialogues of the classical tradition. Nevertheless, it is a narrative which creates a great number of dramatic opportunities for formal speech: and these are the most obvious place to look for apologetic in Acts.

Acts is Built around a Series of Apologetic Scenarios

The language of *apologia*, of charge and counter-charge, is a prominent feature of the textual surface of Acts.[29] This one book contains six out of ten occurrences in the NT of the verb *apologeomai* (two others being in Luke's Gospel), two out of eight NT occurrences of *apologia*, and a high proportion of the NT usages of forensic terms like *katēgoreō*.[30] The more philosophical language of debate and discussion (e.g. *dialegomai*) is also prominent (e.g. Acts 18.4; 19.9). And the reason for this is simple: like the Greek novelists, Luke uses narrative to create a whole series of dramatic situations which call for apologetic speech.[31] Public assemblies and trial-scenes form a significant feature of the narrative, and this dramatic presentation allows the author to present his characters in inter-action with a succession of audiences and to elaborate various kinds of self-defence (*apologia*) against a variety of charges.[32] In this way, in fact, all the imaginary situations presupposed in the various apologetic readings outlined

---

29.   Sterling, *Historiography and Self-definition*, p. 385; cf. A.A. Trites, 'The Importance of Legal Scenes and Language in the Book of Acts', *Novum Testamentum* 16 (1974), pp. 278–84: 'There is a wealth of legal terminology in Acts referring literally to actual courts of law and courtroom procedure' (p. 279).

30.   ἀπολογέομαι: Lk. 12.11; 21.14; Acts 19.33; 24.10; 25.8; 26.1, 2, 24; ἀπολογία: Acts 22.1; 25.16; κατηγορέω: Acts 22.30; 24.2, 8, 13, 19; 25.5, 11, 16; 28.19 (there are five further occurrences in Luke's gospel and ten elsewhere in the NT); κατήγορος (Acts 23.30, 35; 24.8; 25.16, 18) is found nowhere else in the NT.

31.   The parallel with the novels is explored at some length in R.I. Pervo, *Profit with Delight: The Literary Genre of the Acts of the Apostles* (Philadelphia: Fortress Press, 1987), ch. 2, esp. pp. 34–50.

32.   For analysis of the speeches in Acts in terms of forensic rhetoric, cf. Trites, 'Importance'; J. Neyrey, 'The Forensic Defense Speech and Paul's Trial Speeches in Acts 22–26: Form and Function', in C.H. Talbert (ed.), *Luke-Acts: New Perspectives from the Society of Biblical Literature* (New York: Crossroads, 1984), pp. 210–24; and Bruce W. Winter and Andrew D. Clarke (eds.), *The Book of Acts in its First Century Setting*. I. *Ancient Literary Setting* (Grand Rapids: Eerdmans, 1993), ch. 11 (Winter) and ch. 12 (Satterthwaite). Luke has an intriguing fondness for the formal rhetorical address (even in a Jewish context) which irresistibly recalls the classical orators: cf. 1.16; 2.14, 22, 29, 37; 3.12; 5.35; 7.2; 13.16, 26; 15.7, 13, 22; 19.35; 22.1; 23.1, 6; 28.17.

above are actually embedded in the text as dramatic scenes. Generically speaking, this means that it is the characters, not the narrator, who make these apologetic speeches, and that the narrator never intervenes in his own person to drive home the point to the text's inscribed audience. But this is one reason why the proposed apologetic scenarios all carry some degree of conviction. They are all represented dramatically within the narrative; and this is the obvious place to begin to explore its apologetic agenda.

Inner-church debate (Type I apologetic) takes up a relatively small proportion of the narrative as a whole. Luke's brief allusions to ecclesiastical disagreement are on the whole merely tantalizing, giving little hint of the impassioned debates which lie behind Paul's letters. The dispute between 'Hebrews' and 'Hellenists' is depicted only briefly in 6.1 as a background to the election of Stephen. Traces of conflict with a Christian group identified as 'those of the circumcision' (11.2) emerge at intervals during the later narrative, especially at 21.18–22, where they play a crucial role (here carefully distinguished from that of James) in Paul's fateful decision to visit the Temple. But on the whole Luke is at pains to stress the internal unity of the church rather than its dissensions, and there is relatively little direct speech that could be classified as belonging to this apologetic type.

There are however two paired formal scenes in the Jerusalem church which create an apologetic scenario right at the centre of the narrative. The 'apostolic decree' of 15.23–29 is intentionally presented as a formal document, using the well-known language of civic deliberation, issued by a curial body within the church and defining the religious obligations of Gentile converts.[33] This scene forms a closure to one of the pivotal episodes in the book, Peter's encounter with the God-fearing centurion Cornelius (10.1–48) and his subsequent interrogation by the Jerusalem apostles (11.1–18). Here we have a charge (eating with Gentiles), a defence speech, and a verdict (v. 18): 'Then to the Gentiles also God has granted repentance unto life'. It is interesting (and a testimony to Luke's eirenic purpose) that it is Peter, not Paul, who delivers this key defence of the Pauline position that Gentiles who have received the Spirit are thereby placed on the same footing as Jewish believers. But the substance of Peter's defence is a thousand miles away from the elaborate display of exegetical argument which occupies so much space in the Pauline letters dealing with this issue, Galatians and Romans. Peter's speech in Acts is simply a reiteration of key points from the narrative: first the divinely-inspired vision which sent him to Caesarea (already told twice in great detail),[34] then the meeting with Cornelius and the visitation of the Holy Spirit.[35] The speech, in other words, provides essentially

---

33.   Cf. the use of ἔδοξε (15.22, 25), ἐπειδή (15.24), both common in formal civic decrees: Alexander, *The Preface*, pp. 108–109, 127. Luke is elsewhere curiously silent about this 'apostolic council'.

34.   Cf. R.D. Witherup, 'Cornelius over and over and over again: "Functional Redundancy" in the Acts of the Apostles', *JSNT* 49 (1993), pp. 45–66.

35.   Note that the reception of the Spirit also forms a part (though a less significant one) of Paul's argument in Gal. 3.2–5.

an intensification and a more focused theological interpretation of what the narrative has already told us,[36] sharpened by a quotation from 'the word of the Lord' (that is, Jesus: 11.16) and by Peter's explicit theological conclusion: 'Who was I that I could withstand God?' (11.17). The essential force of the argument, revealingly, is the conviction produced in the characters by the supernatural events which the narrative describes. Paul, by contrast, though he does give great weight to his own visionary experience as the foundation for his mission (Gal. 1.10–17), spends far more time in Galatians and Romans developing a theological and exegetical rationale for his procedures in an extended argument which could with some justice be labeled (in the classical sense) 'apologetic'.[37]

Disputes with the Jewish community (Type II apologetic) take up a much larger proportion of the Acts narrative, with a number of formal trial scenes providing opportunity for apologetic speeches of this type. Chapters 4 and 5 find Peter and John on trial before the Sanhedrin, where they are able to demonstrate their own *parrhēsia* ('right to free speech') and the powerlessness of the authorities to intimidate them. Here the judicial framework is much more elaborate. The first hearing is represented as a judicial inquiry into the apostles' religious credentials: 'By what power or by what name did you do this?' (4.7). This is not an accusation but a question, and it invites not so much a defence as a theologically-charged assertion of the supernatural status of Jesus (4.8–12), which illustrates how hard it is in practice to maintain a hard-and-fast distinction between *apologia* and religious propaganda, and between speech and narrative. The claim that Jesus is now an exalted heavenly figure is both a precise answer to the council's question and an essential part of Peter's message. But an indispensable subtext to this assertion is the supernatural event which triggers the whole episode, the miraculous healing of the lame man (4.9), and it is this event, rather than any skill in speech, which in the end silences the opposition (4.14, 21–22).

This first hearing issues in a warning injunction 'not to speak or teach at all in the name of Jesus' (4.18), and it is this injunction – and the apostles' refusal to obey it – which forms the basis for subsequent judicial proceedings (5.28). Such an affront to free speech provides a classic *locus* for the display of apostolic *parrhēsia* before a Council pushed neatly into playing the role of tyrant.[38] In refusing to obey the Sanhedrin, Peter implicitly questions its moral authority and lays claim, as so many philosophers had done from Socrates onward, to a higher allegiance: 'We must obey God rather than men' (5.29, cf. 4.19–20). But it is characteristic of Luke's work that despite its philosophic resonances, the

36.   Cf. Daniel Marguerat, 'Le Dieu du Livre des Actes', in Alain Marchadour (ed.), *L'Évangile Exploré: Mélanges offerts à Simon Légasse* (Lectio Divina, 166; Paris: Cerf, 1996), pp. 301–31.

37.   For a broader understanding of the role of exegetical argument in early Christian apologetic cf. B. Lindars, *New Testament Apologetic: The Doctrinal Significance of the Old Testament Quotations* (London: SCM Press, 1961); R.B. Hays, *Echoes of Scripture in the Letters of Paul* (New Haven: Yale University Press, 1989).

38.   On Luke's propensity for this kind of role-determination, cf. John Darr, *On Character Building: The Reader and the Rhetoric of Characterisation in Luke-Acts* (Westminster: John Knox Press, 1992).

framework of this scene remains resolutely theological, its roots most obviously in the late and post-biblical tradition of bold prophets or martyrs encountering wicked tyrants.[39] Theological commentary on the scene is given, in a nicely ironic touch, by the figure of Gamaliel, who warns the council (in an unusual *in camera* addendum to the more public drama of the trial) that it could be dangerous to interfere with a movement which just might prove to have God on its side (5.33–39): 'You might even be found to be opposing God!'

These early chapters also illustrate an important subsidiary theme in the apostolic *apologia*, the counter-charge that the tribunal which is examining the apostles was responsible for Jesus' death (4.10, 5.28). As in Luke's Gospel, this charge is directed primarily at specific holders of authority in Jerusalem, not at 'the Jews' as an ethnic group. The responsible group is identified particularly with the Temple hierarchy and the high-priestly family,[40] and is implicitly distinguished from 'the people' (*laos*), which is represented as broadly sympathetic (4.21). Even for the hierarchy, this is not a final condemnation: the Jerusalem crowd has already been challenged with its own responsibility in the events of the previous few weeks (3.13–15), and has been offered the chance of repentance and blessing (3.19, 26). Both rulers and people acted 'in ignorance' (3.17), and the whole event was also part of a greater divine plan.[41] Once again, it is difficult to draw clear distinctions here between *apologia* and religious propaganda: the offensive charge of responsibility for Jesus' death is in fact the obverse of the apostles' defensive response to a challenge to their own religious authority, and the trial narrative effectively dramatizes two irreconcilable theological interpretations of the same key event.[42]

Stephen's encounter with the Sanhedrin (6.8–7.60) produces the longest defence speech in the book and the movement's first martyr. This secene is set up to echo the trial of Jesus, with a trial before the religious council and 'false witnesses' who bring a charge of speaking 'blasphemous words against Moses and God' and 'words against this holy place and the law' (6.11, 13). Stephen's speech in reply (ch. 7) adds another familiar dimension to the apologetic of Acts, the ransacking of biblical history for archetypes and precedents to add weight to the apostolic interpretation of current events. For Stephen, it is the prophets of the biblical tradition who provide the most striking template for the persecuted

39.   H.A. Fischel, 'Martyr and Prophet', *Jewish Quarterly Review* 37 (1946/47), pp. 265–80, 363–86; A. Ronconi, 'Exitus illustrium virorum', in T. Klauser (ed.), *Reallexikon für Antike und Christentum* (Stuttgart: Hiersemann, 1966), VI, cols. 1258–68.

40.   Acts 4.6; 5.17, 21 – though a broader list (in a church context: 4.27) includes 'both Herod and Pontius Pilate, with the Gentiles and the peoples of Israel'. Cf. also 13.27 'those who live in Jerusalem and their rulers'.

41.   3.18 etc. On the role of this theme in 'apologetic polemic', cf. J.T. Squires, *The Plan of God in Luke-Acts* (SNTSMS, 76; Cambridge: Cambridge University Press, 1993), esp. pp. 190–94.

42.   For an extended treatment of the theme of 'the Jews' in Luke-Acts, cf. Sanders, *Jews in Luke-Acts*, with the response by J.D.G. Dunn, 'The Question of Anti-Semitism in the New Testament', in J.D.G. Dunn (ed.), *Jews and Christians: The Parting of the Ways A.D. 70 to 135* (WUNT, 66; Tübingen: Siebeck-Mohr, 1992), pp. 177–211, esp. 187–95.

church (7.52), and a judicious quotation from Deuteronomy allows him to enrol Moses among their number (7.37). Paul, when we find him a few chapters later presenting a similar re-reading of biblical history in the synagogue at Antioch-of-Pisidia, focuses more on the figure of David (13.16–40). Significantly, it is not easy in practice to maintain a firm distinction in terms of apologetic content between Stephen's formal defence speech and Paul's synagogue sermon, though the dramatic scenario in the latter case is evangelistic rather than judicial.

The presentation of the Christian case to a 'Greek' audience (Type III apologetic) is much less prominent in the narrative. Despite Acts' interest in the Gentile mission, only two of Paul's reported sermons are addressed to a non-Jewish audience: the short exhortation at Lystra to a Lycaonian-speaking crowd who want to treat Paul and Barnabas as gods (14.11–18) and the more famous speech on the Areopagus in Athens (17.16–34). There is a hint of the judicial in this last case, with the Areopagus setting which (whatever the actual legal situation in the first century) was popularly associated with the trials of philosophers:[43] it is surely no accident that the Epicureans and Stoics who bring Paul to the Areopagus echo the Socratic accusation of being 'a preacher of strange divinities' (17.18).[44] But Paul's defence, as much propaganda as *apologia*, is a fine example of philosophical rather than judicial argument, showing continuity both with the Hellenistic-Jewish tradition of philosophical debate with paganism and with the later Christian Apologists.[45] Far from introducing 'foreign' deities, Paul is speaking about a God already worshipped in the city, though hidden under the ascription 'To an unknown God' (17.23). This conciliatory opening might be dismissed as a preacher's play on words, but the whole tone of the sermon, though uncompromising in its condemnation of the practice of 'idolatry' (17.29), tends towards the recognition that the Zeus of the Greek poets and philosophers is the same as the creator whom Paul proclaims (17.24–28). The negative side of this debate surfaces in Ephesus, where the town clerk cheerfully defends Paul and his friends against the charge of being 'sacrilegious and blasphemers of our goddess' (19.37), despite Paul's reputation as a scourge of idolatry (19.26).

Finally, Luke's narrative presents numerous opportunities for self-defence before Roman magistrates (Type IV apologetic). These scenes show a well-honed awareness of the complexities of civic life in the Greek East, and especially of the potential advantages (for all concerned) of playing off one set of opponents against

---

43. Diogenes Laertius 2.101; 2.116; 7.169.

44. This is the only place in the NT where the term *daimonion* (whose close association with Paul is never disavowed) does not have the negative connotation 'demon'. For a detailed exploration of the Socratic parallels in this passage and elsewhere in Acts cf. Karl Olav Sandnes, 'Paul and Socrates: the Aim of Paul's Areopagus Speech', *JSNT* 50 (1993), pp. 13–26; L.C.A. Alexander, 'Acts and Ancient Intellectual Biography', in Winter and Clarke (eds.), *The Book of Acts in its Ancient Literary Setting*, pp. 31–63, esp. pp. 57–63 (= Chapter 3 in this volume).

45. Bertil Gärtner, *The Areopagus Speech and Natural Revelation* (Acta Seminarii Neotestamentici Upsaliensis, 21; Uppsala: Almqvist & Wiksell, 1955). Paul's Aratus quotation (17.28) already appears in a fuller form in Aristobulus, frg. 4 *ap.* Euseb. *Praep. Ev.* 13.13 (ed. and trans. A.Y. Collins; in J.H. Charlesworth [ed.], *The Old Testament Pseudpigrapha* [New York: Doubleday, 1983], II, p. 841).

another. At Philippi, Paul is accused before the colony's magistrates (16.19) both of being Jewish and of propagating 'customs which it is not lawful for us Romans to receive or to observe' (16.20–21). At Thessalonica, it is 'the Jews' and the urban rabble (17.5) who lay charges before the city authorities[46] (17.6) that the apostles are 'turning the world upside-down' and 'acting against the decrees of Caesar, saying that there is another king, Jesus' (17.6–7). Corinth sees Paul formally indicted before the tribunal of Gallio (18.12) on a charge of 'persuading men to worship God contrary to the law' (18.13). Precisely whose law is being flouted is not stated: Gallio chooses to believe that it is Jewish law, not Roman law, and dismisses the case. The riot at Ephesus is successfully defused by the town clerk (19.35) without direct recourse to Roman authority, but the potential presence of that authority is felt in his speech both as judicial safety-valve and as threat (19.38, 40). And it is the Roman judicial system which in the book's dramatic final scenes hears Paul's case in Caesarea (chs. 24–26), allows his appeal to Caesar (25.11), and dispatches him to Rome for trial (25.12; 26.32; 27–28), though in the end we never get to hear whether the case did come before the emperor and what the issue was.

For most readers, this is the most prominent apologetic scenario in the book, and the one which has most claim to determine its overall purpose. Here there is a clear intention to stress the political innocence of the story's protagonists, with Paul finally dispatched to Rome for his own protection, but publicly judged by the Roman authorities to be 'doing nothing to deserve death or imprisonment' (26.31). Yet, as we have seen, there is a distinct ambivalence in Acts' presentation of the Christian case before a Roman tribunal. Paul, certainly, is presented as innocent of the particular charge on which he was tried in Caesarea (which was in fact an offence against Jewish law). But he and his associates have incurred a number of other charges along the way which have never in so many words – that is, in the explicit terms we would expect of apologetic speech – been refuted. Mud has a disturbing tendency to stick, and it is a dangerous strategy for an apologetic writer to bring accusations to the reader's attention without taking the trouble to refute them. At Philippi, for example, the charge is: 'These men are Jews and they are disturbing our city. They advocate customs which it is not lawful for us Romans to accept or practise' (16.20–21). There is no defence speech: Paul is beaten and imprisoned by the colony's magistrates, and saved only by the (implicitly supernatural) intervention of an earthquake. Paul's tardy claim to be a Roman citizen (16.37) serves only to embarrass the magistrates, and their plea that he should leave the city immediately (16.39) tacitly implies that at least the first part of the charge is true. Despite a minor act of defiance in visiting Lydia before leaving (16.40), there is to be no more missionary activity in Philippi.[47] Thessalonica produces further

---

46.   On this term, see now G.H.R. Horsley, 'The Politarchs', in David W.J. Gill and Conrad Gempf (eds.), *The Book of Acts in its First Century Setting*. II. *Greco-Roman Setting* (Grand Rapids: Eerdmans, 1994), pp. 419–31.

47.   RSV 'apologized to them' (16.39) is more than the Greek says: Johnson better translates 'implored'. The Western Text, clearly feeling something lacking in Luke's account, inserts a more robust declaration of innocence by the magistrates. Cf. L.T. Johnson, *The Acts of the Apostles* (Sacra Pagina, 5; Collegeville: Liturgical Press, 1992), p. 302.

accusations (17.6–7), this time involving the Christian group in the serious charge of 'acting against the decrees of Caesar, saying there is another king, Jesus'.[48] Again, there is no defence and no verdict: the charge of trouble-making is implicitly admitted, and the missionaries are asked to leave. Neither Paul's irresponsible use of his own citizenship, nor the riots which inevitably accompany his activities, are calculated to impress the reader that the new movement offers potential enhancement to civic life. On the contrary, the overall effect of the whole narrative section from ch. 13 to ch. 19 is to leave the damaging impression that Paul's mission causes trouble wherever it goes (17.6): prudent magistrates might well conclude that any well-regulated city would be better off without it.

The other noticeable fact about these forensic or semi-forensic encounters on Paul's missionary journeys is that Paul himself gets very little opportunity to speak in his own defence: even when the apologetic opportunity is there, the narrator does not give Paul any apologetic speeches. If there is an apologetic agenda here, then, its strategies are those of dramatic narrative rather than of rhetorical speech. At Philippi and Thessalonica, there is no defence at all. In Ephesus, Paul tries to address the crowd, but his friends beg him not to (19.30–31). The closest he gets to making his own *apologia* in this section of the narrative is in Corinth, where Gallio interrupts the proceedings just as Paul is 'about to open his mouth' (18.14). Significantly, however, the proconsul's intervention makes it clear that the real issue is not one of Roman law but of 'questions about words and names and your own [that is, Jewish] law' (18.15).

Paul's surprising silence in the journey section is more than compensated, however, by a flood of direct speech on his final visit to Jerusalem, which culminates in his removal to Caesarea and the two court appearances before Felix and Festus (chs. 21–26). This is the section of the narrative which most clearly depicts the apostle on trial before a Roman tribunal, culminating with the famous 'appeal to Caesar' and the journey to Rome (chs. 27–28). This is the most obviously 'apologetic' section of the book: five of Acts' six occurrences of the verb *apologeomai*, and both its occurrences of the noun *apologia*, appear in these chapters. Paul is given three substantial speeches (22.3–21; 24.10–21; 26.2–23) and a short but trenchant declaration of his own innocence (25.8), as well as significant amounts of dialogue with assorted Roman officials. The trial takes place before two named and identifiable Roman magistrates, Felix and his successor Festus, and we even have a formal speech from a rhetor hired to present the case for the prosecution (24.1–8).

It is easy to forget, however, that although Paul's final speech is made before a Roman tribunal, the bulk of the defence is addressed to a Jewish audience and answers charges which are specifically stated to be concerned with matters of Jewish rather than Roman law. Paul is allotted four defence speeches in these last chapters, all except the second explicitly identified (by noun or verb) as *apologia* (22.1; 24.10; 25.16; 26.1–2, 24). The first is not made in a formal trial

---

48.   Cf. E.A. Judge, 'The Decrees of Caesar at Thessalonica', *Reformed Theological Review* 30 (1971), pp. 1–7.

scene at all but to the hostile crowd in the Temple (22.1–21), and the second is before the Sanhedrin (23.1–10). The formal defence before Felix in Caesarea is clearly presented as an answer to the charges brought by the high-priest and his party (24.1): Felix has been brought in as arbitrator, not as prosecutor. And Paul's final defence before Festus (26.1–32) is actually addressed to Agrippa, who has expressed an interest in hearing Paul and is hailed by Paul as one who is 'especially familiar with all customs and controversies of the Jews' (26.3). The charge is originally described as the serious one of bringing Gentiles into the Temple beyond the permitted limits (21.28), which would, if proved, have merited the death penalty; the narrator, unusually, makes sure that the readers know that this accusation was unfounded (21.29). But it is the more general charge of 'speaking everywhere against the people and the law and this place' (21.28, cf. 21.21) which sets the tone for the subsequent series of hearings: Paul's defence speeches make no kind of answer to specific charges, but present an extended narrative reprise of his whole career, and especially of the divine inspiration for the Gentile mission (22.3–21; 26.2–23). The Sanhedrin hearing is deliberately highjacked by Paul into a theological debate on the resurrection (23.6–8). Only in passing, and without allowing his subject the luxury of an extended speech, does the narrator mention that Paul also thought it necessary to defend himself against Roman charges: 'Neither against the law of the Jews, nor against the temple, nor against Caesar have I offended at all' (25.8).

In the light of all this, it becomes rather hard to maintain the traditional view that it is the Roman tribunal which is the definitive one in determining the rhetorical thrust of the apologetic in Acts. Only one of the final defence speeches is explicitly addressed to a Roman, and in all of them the serious work of *apologia* addresses Jewish, not Roman issues. Paul's last substantial speech, in ch. 26, (like Peter's in ch. 11) repeats material which the readers have already heard twice, once in the narrative (ch. 9) and once in an earlier speech (ch. 22): again, Luke uses apologetic speech both to break down the generic barriers between speech and narrative and to sharpen up the theological focus of the debate. The crucial point at issue in Paul's trial, as it emerges from the speech, is not legal but theological:

> And now I stand here on trial for hope in the promise made by God to our fathers, to which our twelve tribes hope to attain, as they earnestly worship night and day. And for this hope I am accused by Jews, O king! Why is it thought incredible by any of you that God raises the dead? (26.6–8).

If this is *apologia*, it has quickly lost any sense of limitation to legal issues and become the defence of a religious belief-system in the most general possible terms: its arguments rest as much on the supernatural sanction supplied by Paul's vision (26.12–19) as on the more general testimony of the subject's character (26.4–11). *Apologia*, in fact, has become testimony based on a personal religious vision backed up by the assertion that its roots lie in the common tradition: 'To this day I have had the help that comes from God, and so I stand here testifying (*marturoumenos*) both to small and great, saying nothing but what the prophets and Moses said would come to pass' (26.22). The speech closes with an emotional appeal to Agrippa: it is hardly surprising that Festus' intervention is politely dismissed as an irrelevancy. The closing interchange is a revealing one (26.24–29):[49]

> Festus: Paul, you are mad; your great learning is turning you mad.
> Paul: I am not mad, most noble Festus, but I am speaking the sober truth. For the king knows about these things, and to him I speak freely (*parrhēsiazomenos*); for I am persuaded that none of these things has escaped his notice, for this was not done in a corner. King Agrippa, do you believe the prophets? I know that you believe.
> Agrippa: In a short time [or: almost] you think to make me a Christian!
> Paul: Whether short or long, I would to God that not only you but also all who hear me this day might become such as I am – except for these chains.

This is an appeal addressed specifically and very directly to a leading and highly-placed patron of Diaspora Judaism, and its object is not to exonerate Paul but to bring the hearer – any hearer – to share his religious worldview. It is not perhaps too fanciful to suggest that this may be the point at which the dramatic audience of the speech approaches most closely to the real-life audience of the book.

Apologetic in Acts and the New Testament

Is it possible to determine any more precisely how the varied dramatic scenarios of Acts relate to one another and to the text's overall rhetorical strategy? We might prefer more simply to maximize the variety and richness of the narrative world which Luke has created, stressing the open-endedness of narrative as opposed to the purposive closures of rhetorical discourse. Luke's account of Jesus' ministry begins with the formal synchronism of 3.1: but the event so portentously introduced is not the coming of Jesus, or even of John the Baptist, but in true prophetic fashion the coming of 'the Word of the Lord' (Lk. 3.2). Arguably it is this divine Word, rather than any of its human propagators, which is the true hero of Acts, and its progress in the world certainly provides one of the narrative's most prominent agendas (Acts 1.8). By creating so many dramatic opportunities for speech, we might argue, Luke is simply giving maximum coverage to this Word and its impact on a succession of audiences. This is a record which has a strong exemplary force for a Christian readership: as Cassidy puts it, Acts provides Christian readers with 'perspective and guidance' to inform their own apologetic witness.[50] Luke's Jesus has already predicted (twice)

---

49. The dramatic layout highlights a potential parallel with the *Acta Alexandrinorum* (H. Musurillo [ed.], *Acts of the Pagan Martyrs: Acta Alexandrinorum* [Oxford: Clarendon Press, 1954]), a parallel further explored by Cheol-Won Yoon in his unpublished PhD thesis 'Paul's Citizenship and its Function in the Narratives of Acts' (Sheffield, 1996). Parallels noted by Yoon include the lively and provocative dialogue; the inclusion of Agrippa and Berenice as characters; and the charge of 'turning the world upside down'.

50. Cassidy, *Society and Politics*, ch. 11 (p. 159).

in the gospel that Christians will find themselves in situations where they will be called upon for an *apologia* before 'synagogues and rulers and authorities'.[51] Acts simply dramatizes this prospect by providing a whole repertoire of opportunities for the apostles to proclaim the Word with *parrhēsia* in every conceivable situation. Moreover, apologetic speech in this context is more than mere dramatized pathos (an essential difference from the superficially similar narrative construction of the Greek novels, where speech serves largely to dramatize the characters' emotions in any given situation). In Acts speech is an important event in its own right, transcending the boundaries of narrative to exert persuasive force directly on the readers.[52]

Looked at in this light, the apologetic speeches embedded in Acts tell us a good deal about the apologetic strategies of the New Testament period. They demonstrate how easy it is to slide from *apologia* in the strict sense (self-defence against a specific charge) to propaganda in a much broader sense. This slide (which is particularly clear in the speech before Agrippa in ch. 26) is tacitly endorsed by Paul's own use of the word in the Epistle to the Philippians, where the *apologia* of the imprisoned apostle is effectively interchangeable with 'the confirmation of the Gospel' (Phil. 1.7), and its expected outcome is the spread of faith (Phil. 1.12–14). Similarly, when 1 Pet. 3.15 urges its readers, 'Always be prepared to make a defence (*apologia*) to anyone who calls you to account for the hope that is in you, yet do it with gentleness and reverence…', the word belongs quite properly in a context where the believer may be called upon at any time to 'suffer as a Christian' (4.16): yet there is an underlying assumption that the correct Christian response may serve not so much to deflect persecution as to win over the opposition (2.13; 3.1). In this sense the apologetic of Acts, and of the New Testament in general, tends to corroborate Schüssler Fiorenza's observation that apologetic and missionary propaganda 'functioned like two sides of the same coin'.[53]

This is a feature of the apologetic scenario which anticipates the propaganda opportunities seized by Christians (and noted by their opponents) in the later accounts of Christian trials and martyrdoms; but it also draws on the older traditions of Jewish martyrology. The speeches of the Maccabean martyrs[54] provide an opportunity to defend not merely themselves but a whole way of life – a form of *parrhēsia* which also figures in the defiant deathbed speeches of philosophers and of the so-called 'pagan martyrs' of Alexandria.[55] It is against this background, I believe, that we should understand the rather puzzling vagueness of the apologetic scenarios in Acts. Despite their careful dramatic construction and characterization, it is not always easy to tell what the precise charge is and how (if at all) it is rebutted.

51.   Luke 12.11; cf also 21.14, which adds 'kings and governors' to the list.
52.   Averil Cameron, *Christianity and the Rhetoric of Empire* (Sather Classical Lectures, 55; Berkeley: University of California Press, 1991), pp. 94–95 notes a similar phenomenon in the apocryphal *Acts*.
53.   cf. n. 9 above
54.   2 Macc. 6.18–7.42.
55.   Cf. Musurillo (ed.), *Acts of the Pagan Martyrs,* Appendices 2 and 3 (pp. 236–58).

The apologetic speeches in Acts also exemplify other important features of early Christian apologetic in the New Testament period. The formal distinction between speech and narrative is largely deconstructed by Luke himself, in that the speeches he gives to his characters constantly refer back to narrative, repeat narrative, and reinforce and interpret narrative. Two pools of narrative resource inform this interpretative activity: stories and characters from the Hebrew Bible and miraculous and charismatic events from the narrative of Acts itself. The former was a hallmark of early Christian apologetic, from the pre-New Testament testimonies through to the second-century apologists: in this sense, Luke's narrative dramatizes (and probably over-simplifies) a flurry of exegetical activity which must have occupied quite a lot of somebody's time in the first decades of the church, and which is presupposed by the already developed use of Scripture in the epistles.[56]

The latter, however, takes us out of the study and onto the streets. Time and again, it is the activity of the Spirit (tongues, healings, visions) which is appealed to as the decisive argument in apologetic speech. Gamaliel's warning (5.39) is picked up by character after character: 'Who was I that I could withstand God?' (11.17); 'What if a spirit or an angel spoke to him?' (23.8); 'Wherefore, O king Agrippa, I was not disobedient to the heavenly vision' (26.19). Two visions above all – Peter's and Paul's (each repeated three times),[57] – hold a pivotal place in the book's cumulative argument. This is a type of apologetic which does not really rely on demonstrative argument (even exegetical argument) at all for its persuasive force, at least not in any sense Galen would have recognized:

> Most people are unable to follow any demonstrative argument consecutively; hence they need parables and benefit from them – and he [Galen] understands by parables tales about the rewards and punishments in a future life – just as now we see the people called Christians drawing their faith from parables [and miracles *alii*] and yet sometimes acting in the same way as those who philosophize.[58]

In its reliance on the demonstrative force of 'signs' – miracle and vision – Acts falls almost entirely on the 'parable' side of this division: and this was a position which later Christians were quite happy to accept.[59] It places Acts' apologetic squarely within the broader context of early Christian missionary

---

56.   Lindars, *Apologetic* is the classic treatment of this material. Birger Gerhardsson's picture (*Memory and Manuscript: Oral Transmission and Written Transmission in Rabbinic Judaism and Early Christianity* [*Acta Seminarii Neotestamentici Uppsaliensis*, 22; Lund: Gleerup, 1961]) of the *collegia apostolorum* in Jerusalem busily engaged in exegesis may be oversimplified, but (as Lindars shows) Paul's letters show that there undoubtedly was intensive exegetical activity going on somewhere in the church's first few decades.

57.   On the significnance of the repetition, cf. Witherup, 'Cornelius over and over and over again'; D. Marguerat, 'Saul's Conversion (Acts 9, 22, 26) and the Multiplication of Narrative in Acts', in C.M. Tuckett (ed.), *Luke's Literary Achievement: Collected Essays* (JSNTSup, 116; Sheffield: Sheffield Academic Press, 1995), pp. 127–55.

58.   R. Walzer, *Galen on Jews and Christians* (London: Oxford University Press, 1949), pp. 15, 57.

59.   Cameron, *Christianity and the Rhetoric of Empire*, ch. 2.

activity described by MacMullen, with its heavy dependence on miracle and prophecy.[60] In this sense, the apologetic of Acts must be differentiated from the more philosophical stance of the second-century apologists (and, for that matter, of 4 Maccabees). Despite the Areopagus speech, Luke's interest in Stoic philosophy is minimal (though it is undoubtedly significant that he mentions it at all: Acts 17 in this sense represents the first glimmerings of a philosophical strain in Christian apologetic which was to become much more important in the second century). But Luke's apologetic strategy belongs firmly on the 'story' side of early Christian discourse.[61] Aratus' philosophical poem proclaimed the universal indwelling of Zeus in all human life:

> Let us begin with God, whom men never leave unspoken: full of God are the streets, and all the marketplaces of humanity, and full the sea and the harbors; and we are all in need of God everywhere. We are all his children...[62]

Luke's narrative, by contrast, inscribes his God into the Mediterranean landscape of street and harbour, city and sea, just as Chariton's novel inscribes the power of Aphrodite into the same landscape.[63]

Nevertheless, it is tempting to try to decide which, of all the book's apologetic scenarios, has the most claim to represent the author's real interests: and in purely numerical terms, it is not difficult to see which it should be. Types I and III (inner-church debate and presentation of the Gospel to the Greeks) take up relatively little narrative time: Luke's purpose in the former seems to be eirenic rather than apologetic, showing a reluctant Peter convinced by supernatural means to accept the 'Pauline' position (only Acts does not so identify it) on Gentile converts. Similarly, the theme of preaching to the Greeks has surprisingly little prominence in terms of direct speech: important though the theme is, it would seem a little unbalanced to identify philosophically-minded Greeks as the book's primary audience. Of all the reported sermons in Acts, only two are addressed to pagans, and Paul's synagogue discourse to the Jewish community in Antioch-in-Pisidia (13.16–41) is longer than the two put together. Even more striking is the relative weighting accorded to Types II and IV (self-defence to the Jewish community, and self-defence to the Romans). Maddox points out that Luke devotes more narrative time to Paul's arrest and imprisonment than to his missionary journeys: 'when we read Acts as a whole, rather than selectively, it

60.   Ramsay MacMullen, *Christianizing the Roman Empire, A.D. 100–400* (New Haven: Yale University Press, 1984).

61.   Cameron, *Christianity and the Rhetoric of Empire*, ch. 3.

62.   Aratus, *Phaenomena* 1–9, as cited by Aristobulus: trans. Collins, in Charlesworth, Old Testament Pseudepigrapha, II, p. 841.

63.   For the comparison, see further Douglas R. Edwards, *Religion and Power* (New York: Oxford University Press, 1996), and Loveday Alexander, '"In journeyings often": Voyaging in the Acts of the Apostles and in Greek Romance', in Tuckett (ed.), *Luke's Literary Achievement*, pp. 17–49 (= Chapter 4 in this volume); and *eadem*, 'Narrative Maps: Reflections on the Toponymy of Acts', in M. Daniel Carroll R., D.J.A. Clines, P.R. Davies (eds.), *The Bible in Human Society: Essays in Honour of John Rogerson* (JSOTSup, 200; Sheffield: Sheffield Academic Press, 1995), pp. 17–57 (= Chapter 5 in this volume).

is Paul the prisoner even more than Paul the missionary whom we are meant to remember'.[64] Even more significant for our purposes, however, is the observation that, over both kinds of speech in Acts (sermons and defence speeches), by far the greatest number of verses are addressed to a Jewish audience.[65] Even where the dramatic audience is Roman (as in the hearings before Felix and Festus), the accusers and the charges are essentially Jewish; and by bringing on Agrippa as an interested observer in the final court scene (ch. 26), Luke effectively turns Paul's last and fullest apologetic speech into a restatement and defence of his whole theological standpoint before a figure who can be identified as a symbolic spokesman for Diaspora Judaism. It is the cynical, worldly-wise Agrippa to whom Paul addresses his most impassioned and direct appeal, and it is arguably this powerful Jewish patron who has the best claim to be identified as the ideal (and doubtless idealized) target audience for the apologetic in Acts.[66] The Romans, on this view (as so often in the first century) are simply brought in as external arbitrators in a dispute which is really (as Gallio declares in 18.15), 'about words and names and your own law'. The success of the mission among pagan audiences provides divine confirmation of its effectiveness, and of Paul's prophetic destiny: but it does not follow that Luke's primary readership is Gentile. Acts is a dramatized narrative of an intra-communal debate, a plea for a fair hearing at the bar of the wider Jewish community in the Diaspora, perhaps especially in Rome. It may be that one of the most significant pointers to the apologetic scenario of the book as a whole is the neutral, uncommitted, stance of the community leaders in Rome in the final scene: 'We have received no letters from Judea about you, and none of the brethren coming here has reported or spoken any evil about you. But we desire to hear from you what your views are; for with regard to this sect we know that everywhere it is spoken against' (28.21–22).

Will this work as a setting for the apologetic of Acts? If so, it must be placed somewhere within the ongoing debate between church and synagogue which went on well into the second century:[67] it would be interesting (though it is beyond the scope of this study) to try to pin it down to a more precise date. But

64.   Robert Maddox, *The Purpose of Luke-Acts* (Edinburgh: T&T Clark, 1982), pp. 66–67.

65.   A rough hand count of verses gives the following result: Type I = 33 verses; Type II = 84 (defence) + 70 (sermon); Type III = 12 verses; Type IV = 40 verses, of which 25 are spoken in Festus' presence, but addressed to Agrippa.

66.   On Agrippa, cf. 'Excursus: Agrippa II', in E. Schürer, *The History of the Jewish People in the Age of Jesus Christ* (rev. G. Vermes and F. Millar; Edinburgh: T&T Clark, 1973), I, pp. 470–83; Tessa Rajak, 'Friends, Romans, Subjects: Agrippa II's Speech in Josephus's Jewish War', in L.C.A. Alexander (ed.), *Images of Empire* (Sheffield: Sheffield Academic Press, 1991), pp. 122–34. On the role of the Herodian dynasty as mediators and patrons for Diaspora Judaism (especially in Rome), cf. Tessa Rajak, 'Was There a Roman Charter for the Jews?', *JRS* 74 (1984), pp. 107–23; John Barclay, *Jews in the Mediterranean Diaspora* (Edinburgh: T&T Clark, 1996), pp. 72, 294–95, 302–303, 308–309, 328–29; and Musurillo (ed.), *Acts of the Pagan Martyrs*, pp. 119, 124–28, 168–72.

67.   P.S. Alexander, '"The Parting of the Ways" from the Perspective of Rabbinic Judaism', in J.D.G. Dunn (ed.), *Jews and Christians: The Parting of the Ways A.D.70 to 135* (Tübingen: Siebeck-Mohr, 1992), pp. 1–25.

any solution must take into account the essential literary observation that the dramatized apologetic of Acts is also embedded within a complex narrative. Generically, Luke's choice of vehicle brings him closer to the world of 'popular'[68] narrative and pamphlet than to the 'higher' forms of rhetorical discourse which were adopted by the later apologists: closer, let us say, to the novels, the martyrologies, the idealized philosophical biographies, or even the *Acta Alexandrinorum*, than to the *Contra Apionem*. But narrative imposes its own disciplines, one of which is the need to bring the story to an end. Whatever its ambiguities, the final scene of Acts does appear to place some kind of closure on the appeal to the Jewish community: 'Let it be known to you then that this salvation of God has been sent to the Gentiles; they will listen' (28.29). The 'most chilling prophecy'[69] quoted here from Isa. 6.9–10 (28.26–27) already has a long history in early Christian apologetic, and will continue to figure in the patristic debate.[70] It provides a biblical explanation for Judaism's failure to respond to the Gospel, and a prophetic model for the theological puzzle of a divinely-inspired message which fails to convince its target audience.[71] On this view, the ending of Acts, with its puzzling failure to narrate the outcome of Paul's appeal to Caesar, is entirely consistent with the prominence of the Jewish apologetic scenario throughout the narrative:

> Absolutely nothing hinges on the success or failure of Paul's defense before Caesar, for Luke's apologetic has not been concerned primarily with Paul's safety or even the legitimacy of the Christian religion within the empire. What Luke was defending he has successfully concluded: God's fidelity to his people and to his own word.[72]

Whether this conclusion would be acceptable to any readers outside the church is another question: apologetic, as we have seen, often fails to reach the dramatic audience to whom it is ostensibly addressed. That does not make it any the less apologetic.

---

68.   I use the word in full awareness of its pitfalls, on which see Cameron, *Christianity and the Rhetoric of Empire*, pp. 107–113.

69.   Johnson, *Acts*, p. 476.

70.   Lindars, *Apologetic*, pp. 159–67.

71.   Though the use of these verses does not necessarily imply a final rejection on either side: even Paul treats the 'hardening' as a temporary precursor to the ultimate salvation of Israel in Rom. 11.25–32. Cf. Dunn, 'The Question of Anti-Semitism', pp. 191–92.

72.   Johnson, *Acts*, p. 476.

Chapter 9

READING LUKE-ACTS FROM BACK TO FRONT*

In literary-critical terms, the ending of Acts is a notorious puzzle. Many readers would query (and have queried from earliest times) whether it can even be regarded as a fitting end to Acts as a single volume.[1] After the drama of the repeated trial scenes in Jerusalem and Caesarea, it is odd – to say the least – that we never find out what happened to Paul. Why do we have no grand climactic trial before Caesar? Why, if Paul is being presented as a proto-martyr (as I believe in some sense he is),[2] do we not have the narrative of his death? Most readers would agree that the narrative of voyage and shipwreck (27.1–28.15) is conceived on the grand scale, but after this Paul's story seems in a curious way to meander to an unsatisfactory and provisional close, living 'at his own expense' in a hired lodging, waiting for a denouement which never happens. The ending is equally unsatisfactory for the presentation of Paul the missionary, for although in the final verses Paul is portrayed as preaching the Gospel 'unhindered', he has lost the dynamic freedom of movement which so characterizes his missionary voyages, and in any case Luke has made it clear that there is already a church in Rome before Paul arrives. More to the point, the emphasis in ch. 28 is not on missionary preaching but on community conflict: it is the disturbing encounter with the leaders of the Jewish community in Rome, with its harsh and menacing ending, which dominates the final chapter of Acts. My question here is, Is it possible that this puzzling ending actually makes as much sense – maybe even more sense – as an ending to Luke-Acts as a two-volume work? Is Acts ch. 28 actually intended to provide a closure for the longer story which began in Luke ch. 1? If so, that would give us a rather powerful argument in favour at least of a retrospective narrative coherence for Luke's two-volume composition.

---

*   Originally published as 'Reading Luke-Acts from Back to Front', in Jos Verheyden (ed.), *The Unity of Luke-Acts*, (BETL; Leuven: Peeters, 1999), pp. 419–46, used here with kind permission of Peeters Publishers.

1.   Cf. D. Marguerat, '"Et quand nous sommes entrés dans Rome": L'énigme de la fin du livre des Actes (28,16–31)', in *RHPR* 73 (1993), pp. 1–21, esp. 2–6, citing Chrysostom, *Hom. Act.* 15. L.T. Johnson, *The Acts of the Apostles* (Sacra Pagina, 5; Collegeville, MN: Liturgical Press, 1992), p. 474 traces this sense of unfinishedness back to the Muratorian canon.

2.   L.C.A. Alexander, *Acts and Ancient Intellectual Biography,* in B.W. Winter and A.D. Clarke (eds.), *The Book of Acts in its First Century Setting*. I. *Ancient Literary Setting* (Grand Rapids: Eerdmans, 1993), pp. 31–63, esp. 62–63 (Chapter 3 in this volume).

Whether this is sufficient to establish the 'unity' of the two volumes is a different question, however: and that is the question with which I shall begin.

1. *Beginnings and Endings*

In an earlier paper on the preface to Acts,[3] I have suggested that there are two ways in which readers of Acts tend to approach the unity question. The first is prospective: we ask the question, Is the story of the apostles envisaged right from the start of Luke's Gospel? Gospel critics often ask this question in terms of the author's intention: Did Luke have the second volume in mind when he wrote the first? Was Acts part of Luke's conception from the outset? But it can just as well be asked from the point of view of the reader: Can the reader predict the end of the story (or at least its development in the second volume) from the beginning? This question in itself raises issues about the creation of suspense and the maintenance of narrative tension, to which we shall return.

The second question is retrospective, and likewise can be asked in terms of the readers as well as of the author. Does the second volume provide a coherent continuation to the first? Here we are on slightly firmer ground. We do know at least that the Gospel is part of the reading experience expected of the readers of Acts. Luke tells us so much in his opening verse (Acts 1.1): Acts is clearly intended to be read as a sequel to the Gospel story. But this does not of itself tell us the answer to the first question (a sequel may still be an afterthought); and the question of coherence still remains. Does Luke carry through his narrative programme in a coherent way? When we reach the end of volume two, do we feel that we have reached a proper closure to the work as a whole, or is it simply the end of a discrete episode within an ongoing series? Can we as readers spot connections which link the end of the story to its beginning, and if so are these connections contrived by the narrator, or are they simply the result of readerly hindsight? And either way, what is their function? What effect does it have on the reader if the entrance to the text is recalled just as she or he reaches the exit?

How many of these different types of coherence do we have to have in order to substantiate the claim to have discovered the 'unity' of Luke-Acts? Writers do not always know exactly where they are going to end up when they begin their work: and without the benefit of the word-processor, they may not have either the inclination or the capacity to go back to the beginning and adjust their opening to fit their closing scene. What they may do instead is to write a sequel which contains a sufficient number of retrospective connections to create a convincing sense of narrative coherence. This kind of coherence, *ex hypothesi*, would not have been envisaged at the start and could not be predicted from the start: but I see no reason in principle why it should not count as 'unity'. There

---

3.　　L.C.A. Alexander, *The Preface to Acts and the Historians*, in B. Witherington III (ed.), *History, Literature and Society in the Book of Acts*, (Cambridge: Cambridge University Press, 1996), pp. 73–103 (= Chapter 2 in this volume).

is however one kind of indication which might allow us to move from a retro-spective coherence (readerly or authorial) to a prospective coherence intended by the author from the start of the work, and that is the significant omission or holding over of narrative detail from the first volume to the second. This of course takes us back into the sphere of redaction-critical analysis, and is only possible within the matrix of a broad consensus on the Synoptic Problem (something which it would be dangerous to assume). Nevertheless, it would be foolish for the literary critic to ignore this perspective, precisely because of its potential importance for the question of unity. I shall return to this point in my final section.

What signals were available to the ancient reader for determining the narrative unity of a sequence of texts? For modern authors, there is a whole barrage of extra-textual devices for giving the reader directions about sequence and coherence in a multi-volume narrative: this is one of the functions of what Genette calls the 'paratexte', that is,

> titre, sous-titre, intertitres; préfaces, postfaces, avertissements, avant-propos, etc.; notes marginales, infrapaginales, terminales; épigraphes; illustrations; prière d'insérer, bande, jaquette, et bien d'autre types de signaux accessoires, autographes ou allographes, qui procurent au texte un entourage (variable) et parfois un commentaire, officiel ou officieux, dont le lecteur le plus puriste et le moins porté à l'érudition externe ne peut pas toujours disposer aussi facilement qu'il le voudrait et le prétend.

This 'paratexte', Genette goes on, 'est sans doute un des lieux privilégiés de la dimension pragmatique de l'oeuvre, c'est-à-dire de son action sur le lecteur – lieu en particulier de ce qu'on nomme volontiers … le *contrat* (ou *pacte*) générique'.[4] An important aspect of this pragamatic function is to assist the reader's entry into and exit from the narrative world: that is, to facilitate the transitions between the readers' real world(s) and the world of the text.[5]

In the absence of the exterior apparatus available to modern authors (ancient books did not have bookjackets, spines, blurbs, or page headers, and titles were rudimentary and easily lost), ancient authors made extensive use of prefaces, transitional summaries, and epilogues for these purposes. In Genette's words, 'une simple mention comme *Premier volume* ou *Tome I* a force de

---

4.   G. Genette, *Palimpsestes: la littérature au second degré* (Paris: Seuil, 1982), p. 9; cf. *Seuils*, (Paris: Seuil, 1987), pp. 376–77. 'Le paratexte n'est qu'un auxiliaire, qu'un accessoire du texte. Et si le texte sans son paratexte est parfois comme un éléphant sans cornac, puissance infirme, le paratexte sans son texte est un cornac sans éléphant, parade inepte. Aussi le discours sur le paratexte doit-il ne jamais oublier qu'il porte sur un discours qui porte sur un discours, et que le sens de son objet tient à l'objet de ce sens, qui est encore un sens. Il n'est de seuil qu'à franchir.'

5.   'Le début d'une oeuvre (comme sa fin d'ailleurs) veut assister (conduire) le lecteur dans son passage du monde du texte au monde réel, l'aider à prendre position et à lire correctement le récit et veut programmer une réponse particulière de sa part' (Claire-Antoinette Steiner, 'Le lien entre le prologue et le corps de l'évangile de Marc', in D. Marguerat and A. Curtis (eds.), *Intertextualités: La Bible en échos* (Geneva: Labor et Fides, 2000), pp.161–84. Cf. M.C. Parsons, *The Departure of Jesus in Luke-Acts* (JSNTSup, 21; Sheffield: JSOT Press, 1987), p. 173.

promesse – ou, comme dit Northrop Frye, de "menace"'.[6] I could cite plentiful examples of clear and explicit authorial guidance to the reader from ancient authors (especially authors of technical handbooks) indicating exactly how one volume is related to another in a multi-volume work, and I have shown elsewhere how Luke's prefaces match the conventional language used in these recapitulatory prefaces.[7] However, the preface to the Gospel does not by itself contain sufficiently precise indications of content to decide the question of unity.[8] As it stands, it makes perfect sense either as the preface to the Gospel alone or as the preface to both volumes. The preface to Acts, by contrast, does indicate clearly that there is some kind of link between the two volumes, i.e. that Acts is to be read as a sequel to the Gospel (Acts 1.1). But there are no further explicit authorial guideposts (that is, passages in which the author speaks in his own voice) either in transitional passages such as were common in ancient texts, or at the end of either volume.[9] This is one reason why we still have a debate about the unity of Luke-Acts, and why we have to look for more subtle narrative clues to the coherence of the composition as a whole.

But there are other means readers can use to determine the overall narrative coherence of a text. 'Paratext' is not limited to formal, externally bounded prefaces of the type we find in Lk. 1.1–4.[10] Some at least of the pragmatic functions associated with the authorial or editorial apparatus which constitutes the 'peritext' of the modern book[11] can in antiquity be found in the narrative itself, especially in its opening and closing scenes. A number of recent studies have analysed the pragmatic functions of Gospel beginnings along these lines,

---

6.   Genette, *Seuils*, p. 16.

7.   Cf. L.C.A. Alexander, *The Preface to Luke's Gospel*, (SNTSMS, 78; Cambridge: Cambridge University Press, 1993), esp. pp. 143–44; and further in *The Preface to Acts and the Historians* (Chapter 2 in this volume).

8.   Cf. *The Preface to Acts and the Historians*, pp. 76–82 (= Chapter 2, pp. 23–27).Presumably because of the uncertainties of roll-length (and of handwriting), most ancient authors do not indicate the precise distribution of contents between rolls at the beginning of the first volume, since it was not at that stage possible to determine exactly how much the first roll would hold. Precise description of the contents of a given roll is normally made retrospectively, at the beginning of the next: cf. Josephus, *Contra Aponiem* 1.59, where the final topic promised in the opening volume actually spans the last section of the first roll and the first section of the second: the roll-break presumably could not have been predicted at the outset. Dioscorides, *De Simplicibus* 1 pref., speaks of τὰ βιβλία, but only in the second volume does he commit himself to 'two books': M. Wellmann (ed.), *Dioscoridis Anazarbei De Materia Medica Libri V* (Berlin: Wiedmann, 1907–1914), III, pp. 151, 13 and 242, 317.

9.   Cf. Parsons, *Departure*, p. 177: the authorial voice and the dedication help to manage the move from the real world to the story world, but neither reappears at the end.

10.   Even in antiquity, as Genette insists, 'il n'existe pas, et...il n'a jamais existé, de texte sans paratexte' (*Seuils*, p. 9). Much of this 'paratext' was supplied for ancient books by the social context in which they were encountered: L.C.A. Alexander, 'Ancient Book-Production and the Circulation of the Gospels', in R.J. Bauckham (ed.), *The Gospels for All Christians: Rethinking the Gospel Audiences* (Grand Rapids, MI: Eerdmans, 1997), pp. 71–111.

11.   Genette, *Seuils*, p. 8.

and have stressed the importance of the interpretative framework provided by the narrative prologues and epilogues to the Gospels.[12]

In this sense, we could look not to the authorial *preface* to Luke's work (Lk. 1.1–4) but to its narrative *prologue*, by which I mean the first four chapters of the Gospel. In his important 1987 study of the Ascension narratives, Mikéal Parsons has explored the links between the ending of the Gospel and Luke's narrative prologue (Lk. 1–4) in terms of Uspensky's analysis of the 'framing' patterns created by the beginnings and endings of narratives.[13] Joseph B. Tyson also uses Uspensky's analysis to examine the relationship of the birth narratives (Luke 1–2) to the rest of the Gospel narrative.[14] Neither of these has attempted to read the end of Acts as a framing device in relation to the narrative prologue of the Gospel, however: most important in this respect is the study of J. Dupont,[15] in which Dupont notes a number of links between Acts 28 and Lk. 3–4. I hope here to build on and extend Dupont's insightful analysis.

2. *The Ending of Acts*

Dupont supplies a detailed narrative analysis of the ending of Acts, and makes the following useful points: (a) Acts 28.30–31 should be treated as summary, not climax; (b) The core scene of ch. 28 runs from 28.17 to 28.28 and consists of a staged debate between Paul and the members of the Jewish community in Rome, ending with Paul's 'last words' at 28.26–28; (c) 28.11–16 is a narrative link passage describing the final stages of the journey to Rome and introducing the dramatic location for the book's final scene.

I would argue, however, that Acts 27.1–28.16 cannot be left out of account in any consideration of the ending of Acts. The shipwreck and Melita narative is of course a substantial 'scene' in its own right,[16] and contains many significant

12. Cf. the articles in D.E. Smith (ed.), *How Gospels Begin* (Semeia, 52; Atlanta, GA: Scholars Press, 1991); F.J. Matera, 'The prologue as the Interpretative Key to Mark's Gospel', in *JSNT* 34 (1988), pp. 3–20; A. Steiner, 'Le lien'.

13. Parsons, *Departure*, ch. 3. He also examines the links between the ending of Acts and Acts ch. 1, but notes that, while numerous, these links are 'rather weak' (p. 159).

14. J.B. Tyson, 'The Birth Narratives and the Beginning of Luke's Gospel', in D.E. Smith (ed.), *How Gospels Begin* (Semeia, 52; Atlanta, GA: Scholars Press, 1991), pp. 103–20.

15. J. Dupont, 'La conclusion des Actes et son rapport à l'ensemble de l'ouvrage de Luc', in J. Kremer (ed.), *Les Actes des Apôtres: Traditions, rédaction, théologie* (BETL, 48; Leuven: Leuven University Press – Gembloux, 1978), pp. 359–404. Subsequent to the presentation of this paper I was alerted to the important study of G. Wasserberg, *Aus Israels Mitte – Heil für die Welt. Eine narrative-exegetische Studie zur Theologie des Lukas* (BZNW, 92; Berlin: de Gruyter, 1998). Wasserberg highlights the significance of Acts 28.16–31 'als hermeneutischer Schlüssel zum Gesamtverstandnis von Lk-Act' (ch. 4), and notes hermeneutical links with Simeon's prophecy (ch. 6) and the Nazareth episode (ch. 7).

16. For the terminology, cf. T. Hägg, *Narrative Technique in Ancient Greek Romances: Studies of Chariton, Xenophon Ephesius, and Achilles Tatius* (Skrifter Utgivna av Svenska Institutet i Athen, ser. 8, VIII; Uppsala: Almqvist & Wiksell, 1971), ch. 2. Travel can form either a significant 'scene' in its own right or function simply as a 'summary' link between scenes in a narrative. The shipwreck of Acts 27–28 clearly falls into the former category.

narrative details which cannot be brought into consideration in this article. However, it is above all else a journey *to Rome*, and as such adds to the decided effect of closure – not necessarily climax – which marks the ending of Acts. In this sense I would designate the last two chapters of Acts (27–28) as a narrative epilogue, culminating in a final scene in Rome (28.17–28) and topped off by a two-verse summary (28.30–31)

In this final scene of Acts, four obvious narrative features can be identified: its geographical location is Rome; its dramatic scenario is a debate within the Jewish community; its hermeneutical framework is provided by a long quotation from Isaiah; and it foregrounds the act of proclamation (witness) and the person of the proclaimer himself.

2.1. *The Geographical Location of Acts 28*

The geographical framework of Acts is one of its most striking features: the story ends in Rome, emphatically not where it started, either in the Gospel or in Acts itself. The start of ch. 27 signals a distinctive new direction within the complex journeyings of Acts, marked by a formal decision (ἐκρίθη), by the sudden reappearance of Paul's journeying companions (27.1 'we'), and by the solemn evocation of the nautical ceremonies of embarkation and coastal voyaging (27.2–5). The whole pace of the narrative changes as the cerebral cut and thrust of forensic drama is left behind and the narrator (and perforce the reader) becomes immersed in the slow details of cargoes and harbours, of wind directions and sails, dinghies and anchors, and finally drawn into the nightmare of storm and shipwreck. Parsons notes how the final scene of Acts has 'a static texture which may assist the reader in entering into and exiting from a story which is momentarily stationary',[17] but Luke has been slowing his narrative down all through ch. 27, as Paul's ship tacks laboriously against the wind along the coast of Asia.[18] The original motivation for the voyage is almost forgotten in all this, except by Paul himself, who reports the assurance of an angelic vision to the effect that 'you must stand before Caesar' (27.24).

This superbly (and realistically) detailed voyage description adds to a real sense of climax when the party finally, after a three-month delay in Melita, set out for the last stages of the journey to Rome (28.11). Once again the redundant detail of ships, winds, ports of call, and intermediate stages on the road (three days 28.12; two days 28.13; seven days 28.14) slows the narrative down and builds the tension. There is a real sense of arrival in 28.14–16, with the double announcement (28.14 'And that's how[19] we got to Rome'; 28.16 'When we entered Rome') separated by the emergence from the city of a church delegation which ceremoniously escorts Paul along the final stages of the Via Appia.[20]

17.   Parsons, *Departure*, p. 159.

18.   27.4; cf. 27.7 βραδυπλοοῦντες ... μὴ προσεῶντος ἡμᾶς τοῦ ἀνέμου.

19.   Note the emphatic (and summative) force of καὶ οὕτως 28.14: I would translate not simply 'And so', but 'And that's how...' Taken this way, there is no redundancy with ὅτε δὲ εἰσήλθομεν εἰς Ῥώμην in 28.16.

20.   'Ἀπάντησις appears to have been a sort of technical term for the official welcome extended to a newly arrived dignitary by a deputation which went out from the city to greet him and escort him for the rest of his way': F.F. Bruce, *The Acts of the Apostles: Greek Text with Introduction and Commentary* (Grand Rapids, MI: Eerdmans, 3rd edn, 1990), p. 536.

The narrative significance of this westward voyage is not always appreciated. Luke has been at pains up to this point to centre his story on Jerusalem even against the grain (so far as we can conjecture) of his source-material. Jesus' story is given an additional Jerusalem focus in the opening chapters of the Gospel,[21] and Luke's Paul visits Jerusalem more often than we would have expected from the Epistles.[22] Luke uses Jerusalem to create a novel-like outward-and-return pattern to the journeys of Peter, Paul, and the other apostles in Acts, culminating in Paul's long-drawn-out final journey to Jerusalem (Acts 20–21), which so strikingly parallels Jesus' final journey to Jerusalem to imprisonment and death.[23] Structurally, then, the last two chapters of Acts form an odd, almost anti-climactic coda to the narrative, an additional voyage outside the expected *nostos*-pattern which gives the book an unexpectedly open-ended structure. Luke has of course been at pains to stress that this ending, though it might be unexpected to the reader, was by no means unexpected to Paul – and, more importantly, that it was part of the divine plan for the apostle.[24]

But in what sense is Rome the proper ending for the narrative as a whole? Many generations of exegetes[25] have taken the narrative's ending in Rome as a fulfilment of the task laid on the apostles at Acts 1.8: though Rome can at best be only a representative symbol for 'the end of the earth', alongside the implied voyages of the Ethiopian of Acts 8 and the other unnamed travellers of Acts 2. But does it make sense to regard Rome as 'the end of the earth' at all? Acts provides some evidence that Luke is working, at least in part, with a mental map which entails a reversal of the geographical perspectives of the Greco-Roman reader: cf. especially Acts 2.9–11, where Rome is one of the most distant points on the circumference of a Jerusalem-centred compass rose.[26] PsSol. 8.16 suggests that for some first-century readers at least, Rome was at 'the end of the earth'. In this sense the voyage of Acts 27 can be read within the genre of exotic voyages, but with a reversal of the usual Greco-Roman perspective which tends to locate the exotic in the east. It takes Paul and his companions decisively away from Syria-Palestine and the coastlands of the Aegean, narrowly escaping the legendary terrors of Syrtis (27.17) and driven by the forces of nature across the

21.   Lk. 1.5–23; 2.22–38, 41–51.

22.   Cf. R. Jewett, *Dating Paul's Life* (London: SCM Press, 1979), p. 86: 'Luke's insertion of extra Jerusalem journeys causes irreducible pressures…the traditional compromises between the ascertainable data and the Lukan framework of Jerusalem journeys are all unworkable'.

23.   L.C.A. Alexander, '"In Journeyings Often": Voyaging in the Acts of the Apostles and in Greek Romance', in C.M. Tuckett (ed.), *Luke's Literary Achievement: Collected Essays* (JSNTSup, 116; Sheffield Academic Press, 1995), pp. 17–49, esp. 23–24 and fig. 3 (Chapter 4 in this volume, esp. pp. 73–74).

24.   Acts 19.21; 23.11.

25.   Cf. Bengel's representative comment, cited in Bruce, *Acts*, p. 543: 'Victoria Verbi Dei: Paulus Romae, apex evangelii, Actorum finis… Hierosolymis coepit, Romae desinit. Habes, Ecclesia, formam tuam: tuum est, servare eam, et depositum custodire.'

26.   Alexander, '*Voyaging*', p. 30 and fig. 9 (Chapter 4 in this volume, p. 80); J.M. Scott, 'Luke's Geographical Horizon', in D.W.J. Gill and C. Gempf (eds.), *The Book of Acts in its First Century Setting*. II. *Graeco-Roman Setting* (Grand Rapids, MI: Eerdmans, 1994), pp. 483–544, esp. 496–99.

stormy and chaotic wastes of the Ionian sea.[27] Landfall, after such a voyage, is predictably exotic: a bay, a beach, an island unrecognizable even to the experienced sailors (27.39). Given the symbolic significance of 'the islands' in biblical geography, it is not unreasonable to suggest that readers might see this as a rather subtly-hinted fulfilment of the commission of Acts 1.8. This island turns out rather prosaically to have a name (28.1), but it is still peopled by 'barbarians' (28.2: the only βάρβαροι in the whole of Acts), who, like the Lycaonians of 14.11, show a satisfying readiness to attribute divine status to the apostle (28.6).

But it is not so easy to be confident that the voyage's final destination, Rome, has this symbolic significance. After the romantic thrills of the shipwreck it is almost an anti-climax to find that Melita has a 'first man' with the very Roman name of Publius (28.7) and that one can pick up an Alexandrian grain-ship wintering on the other side of the island (28.11). And the onward journey to Rome breathes an atmosphere which is progressively less, rather than more, exotic: 'brothers' greet the party at Puteoli (28.14), more 'brothers' come out to meet them from Rome, and the naming of the final, local stages of the road, *Apii Forum* and *Tres Tabernae*, has almost an air of homecoming (28.15).[28] The names themselves (well known on the itineraries of the Roman road system) are a reminder that from a Roman perspective, Rome was not the end but the centre of the earth, with a central milepost from which all the roads of the empire radiated out.[29]

2.2. *The Community Setting of Acts 28*

The central dramatic scenario of the final chapter of Acts, however, is not the city of Rome but the divided Jewish community. I have already noted Dupont's important distinction here between the two-verse 'summary' of 28.30–31 and the carefully-constructed final 'scene' of 28.16–29. These two elements point in different directions, one forward, one back.

The *final summary* of vv. 30–31 points forward to some unnarrated and undefined conclusion beyond the bounds set by the narrative. It leaves a number of questions unanswered: What happened after 'the whole two years'? How long did Paul remain in the essentially transitional phase implied by verse 30?[30] How

---

27.   The fearsome reputation of this stretch of sea can be gauged from the novelists: cf. Chariton, *Callirhoe*, 3.3.9–12; 3.5.1–9; 8.4.10; 8.6.1; Xenophon of Ephesus, *Ephesiaca*, 5.1.

28.   Contrast Athens (Acts 17), where Paul visits the city like a tourist.

29.   The Antonine Itinerary (107.3–4) lists *Tres Tabernae* and *Apii Forum* as the second and third stations on the *Via Appia*, working outwards from the city (O. Cuntz, *Itineraria Romana*, I (Stuttgart: Teubner, 1990). There are other 'Three Taverns' elsewhere in the system: cf. 318.3 and 329.9 (Macedonia); 617 (Gallia Cisalpina). Dio Cassius 54.8.4 records that a golden milestone was erected in the Forum in 20 BCE symbolizing '[Rome's] position as centre of the world: it was engraved with the distances from the principal cities of the empire to the gates of Rome': M.T. Griffin, 'Urbs, Plebs and Princeps', in L.C.A. Alexander (ed.), *Images of Empire* (JSOTSup, 122: Sheffield: Sheffield Academic Press, 1991), pp. 19–46, here 20. Scott, 'Luke's Geographical Horizon,' p. 541, also argues that Rome is not 'the end of the earth' for Luke.

30.   Ἐν ἰδίῳ μισθώματι: Luke's choice of words here emphasizes that Paul's residence in Rome was 'at his own expense', i.e. not in a public prison; but the noun (which normally means 'contract', 'hire', or 'rent') also underlines the transitional nature of the residence.

long did the lack of opposition (negatively construed: ἀκωλύτως) last? These unanswered questions create a forward-looking cluster in the reader's mind along with certain events anticipated in earlier stages of the narrative, like Paul's standing before Caesar (27.24) and his death (implied in 20.25 and 20.38). As unfulfilled prophecies, these are themselves an important factor in the open-ended effect of the conclusion of Acts. But the final summary is doubly open-ended in that it leaves the apostle, despite the uncertainties surrounding his personal future, engaged in 'unhindered' evangelization which implies (although it does not narrate) the future fulfilment of Paul's last prophecy in 28.29: 'They will listen'.

But the more substantial *final scene* which precedes this (28.17–29) is harder to configure as a climax to the career of Paul the missionary. Paul is certainly not a church-founder in this scene: Luke has taken pains to tell the readers (quite unnecessarily) that there are already 'brothers'[31] in Italy, both in Puteoli and in Rome. The stress in ch. 28 is not so much on preaching the Gospel to the Romans (contrast the Athens scene of Acts 17) as on an ongoing debate within the divided Jewish community. This is the forum before which Paul presents his own last *apologia* and a final exposition of the Gospel message before turning decisively 'to the Gentiles' (28.28). The dramatic scenario of the Jewish community is of course familiar throughout Acts, but it is formalized in an unusually careful and explicit manner in 28.17–22. Note especially the neutral, objective tones of the community leaders in 28.21–22: 'But we desire to hear from you what your views are; for with regard to this sect, we know that every-where it is spoken against'. Paul's own relationship with this community is under-lined in his own opening words (ἄνδρες ἀδελφοί v. 17), a formula which has occurred throughout Acts[32] and which also hints at the formal address to a civic assembly familiar from Greek rhetoric. Note also that the final state of the community which Luke chooses to highlight (using the classical οἱ μέν...οἱ δέ formula, another classic device for describing tensions within the body politic) is not simply disbelief but division: 'Some were convinced by what he said, while others disbelieved. So they departed, in a state of disharmony' (vv. 24–25 ἀσύμφωνοι δὲ ὄντες).

2.3. *The Hermeneutical Matrix of Acts 28*
The hermeneutical framework for understanding this scene is provided by Paul himself in an extended quotation from Isaiah ch. 6 (Acts 28.26–27). The foregrounding of this quotation in the final scene of Acts (where, significantly, it forms the core of Paul's last recorded words) is part of a coherent pattern throughout the two-volume work which establishes the Jewish Scriptures (Luke

---

31.   Most commentators assume these were Christians, though Paul also addresses his fellow-Jews as 'brothers' in 28.17 and elsewhere (see next note). More significant, I suspect, is that Luke takes no trouble to clarify the point: either it is not important, or perhaps better the ambivalence of the relationship between the Nazarene sect and the parent body is precisely what he needs to maintain at this stage in the book.

32.   Acts 1.16; 2.29, 37; 7.2; 13.15, 26, 38; 15.7, 13; 22.1; 23.1, 6. The formula is used indiscriminately in address to audiences within the church and within the Jewish community.

quotes the text here in its LXX-form) as the hermeneutical framework for understanding not only the Jesus-story itself (cf. Lk. 24), but also the vicissitudes of those who fulfil Jesus' command to act as 'witnesses'.

This particular text from Isaiah ch. 6 figures prominently in early Christian hermeneutics as a key to understanding the Gospel's lack of success within the Jewish community.[33] It is already firmly embedded in the synoptic tradition as part of what Barnabas Lindars calls the 'apologetic of response', and is quoted at some length in the interpretation of the Parable of the Sower at Mk 4.12 (// Matt. 13.14–15, Lk. 8.10), more briefly at Mk 8.17–18 (applied to the disciples' failure to understand), and again in a more general context at Jn 12.39–40, where it is part of an extended editorial reflection on the unbelief of 'the Jews'. What is interesting for our purposes is that Luke, although he includes the citation in his Sower narrative (Lk. 8.14–15) cuts it down to the briefest possible compass (unlike Matthew, who gives it in a longer form than Mark). Acts 28.25b, moreover, in Lindars' words, 'bears a close similarity to the way Mark has introduced another quotation which is very relevant to the same issue (Mk 7.6)' (p. 165). In both cases it is not unreasonable to conclude (as Lindars does) that 'Luke has been saving up this quotation as the climax to the repeated theme that Paul was opposed by the Jews, but found a better hearing amongst the Gentiles.'[34] If it is the case that the citation has been 'saved up' for the end of Acts (i.e. displaced from its synoptic context), we have a *prima facie* reason for taking very seriously the idea of a *prospective* unity for Luke's two volumes (authorial intent): though it should also be noted that, in Lindars' analysis, the Marcan application of the text to the parables is almost certainly the latest in the hermeneutical sequence, and Luke's use of the text in Acts corresponds to a logically earlier stage.[35]

2.4. *The Act of Proclamation Foregrounded in Acts 28*

Although the implied focus of the debate (and of Paul's preaching) is Jesus and 'the Kingdom of God' (28.23, 31), the actual topic foregrounded in the text is the act of proclamation itself and the person of the proclaimer (28.17 ἐγώ). It is no accident, I believe, that Luke uses a variety of words to describe the content of Paul's preaching in ch. 28: 'the kingdom of God' (28.23 and 28.31); 'about Jesus from both the law of Moses and the prophets' (28.23); 'the things to do with the Lord Jesus Christ' (28.31). These terms underline the catholicity

---

33. B. Lindars, *New Testament Apologetic: The Doctrinal Significance of the Old Testament Quotations* (London: SCM Press, 1961), *passim*, esp. pp. 159–167, 254–255.

34. Lindars, *Apologetic*, pp. 164, 166. Cf. J. Dupont, 'Le Salut des Gentils et la signification théologique du Livre des Actes', in *NTS* 6 (1960), pp. 132–55.

35. Lindars, *Apologetic*, p. 18: 'This example is especially instructive, because the sequence of interpretation is the direct opposite of the presumed order in which the books themselves were written. John preserves the oldest application, Acts the second, and Mark the latest! This does not mean that our estimate of the dates when these books were written must now be radically revised. But it does provide a warning not to evaluate a book by its date alone, for a later book may preserve more primitive ideas. The shift of application shows the logical sequence in the development of thought.'

of Paul's preaching, and also its continuity with the preaching of the Jerusalem apostles and of Jesus himself: cf. esp. Acts 1.3; Lk. 24.27; 24.44. The verbs used are equally varied. Within the Jewish community, verbs of debate and persuasion are used: (28.23 διαμαρτυρόμενος, πείθων), recalling the many scenes in Acts where the apostles (and especially Paul) have been depicted in argumentative mode: neither of these terms is used in an evangelistic sense in the Gospel.[36] In the final summary, however, κηρύσσων τὴν βασιλείαν τοῦ θεοῦ (28.31) takes us right back through Paul's own summary of his life's work (20.25) to the Gospel directives to the apostles (Lk. 9.2; 24.47; cf. Acts 10.42) and behind them to the proclamation of the Baptist (Lk. 3.3; Acts 10.37) and of Jesus himself (Lk. 4.18 and 19; 8.1). Διδάσκων (28.31) also echoes terminology used earlier of Paul himself (often in a church or synagogue context), but even more of the activities of the Jerusalem apostles in the early part of Acts, and very characteristically of Jesus (cf. Acts 1.1).[37] There seems to be a deliberately resumptive air about this terminology, drawing together the threads of the proclamation right back through Paul's argumentative career to the preaching of the apostles and ultimately to Jesus and the Baptist.

But although the last chapter of Acts has quite a lot to *tell* us about Paul's proclamation of Jesus, it does not *show* us much of the content of that proclamation. Paul's recorded words in the final scene (there are none in the final summary) are not about Jesus but about the message and its reception (28.26–27) and about the messenger himself (28.17–20). It is Paul who is the focus of vv. 17–20, right from the opening ἐγώ: 'I have done nothing against the people or the ancestral customs; I was handed over bound into the hands of the Romans; they judged me to have done nothing worthy of death; I was compelled to appeal to Caesar; I had no accusation to bring against my race; it is for the hope of Israel that I am bound like this'. This is an extension of Paul's lengthy *apologia* before the bar of the Jewish community, an appendix to the debate which has occupied most of chs. 21–26: it is surely significant that this is the apologetic message Luke chooses to record in Rome, rather than an *apologia* before a Roman tribunal.[38] The reply of the community leaders has the same focus (περὶ σοῦ twice in v. 21; παρά σοῦ ἀκοῦσαι ἅ φρονεῖς in v. 22), and then moves on to the messenger's group affiliation: 'for about this sect, it is known to us that it

---

36. Διαμαμαρτυρόμενος: cf. Acts 2.40 (Peter); 8.25 (Peter and John); 10.42 (Peter and the other apostles); 18.5 (Paul); 20.21, 24 (Paul); 23.11 (Paul). The only occurrence of the verb in the gospels is at Lk. 16.28, where it is used of the brothers of Dives. πείθων: cf. Acts 18.4; 19.8; 26.28. The passive (which has a wide semantic range) also occurs in the very Lukan parable of Dives and Lazarus (Lk. 16.31).

37. Διδάσκων: cf. Lk. 4.15, 31; 5.3, 17; 6.6; 13.10, 22, 26; 20.1; Acts 4.2, 18; 5.21, 25, 28, 42. Missing in Acts 28 are the 'gospel'-words common elsewhere in Acts (εὐαγγελίζομαι, ευάγγέλιον: cf. 5.42; 8.4; 14.7; 17.18).

38. L.C.A. Alexander, 'The Acts of the Apostles as an Apologetic Text', in M.J. Edwards, M. Goodman, C. Rowland (eds.), *Jewish and Christian Apologetic in the Graeco-Roman World* (Oxford: Oxford University Press, 1999), pp. 15–44, esp. 36–38 (= Chapter 8 in this volume, esp. pp. 195–97).

is spoken against everywhere' (v. 22). As in the forensic speeches, the messenger's self-defence slides neatly into an exposition of the message (v. 23); but what Luke foregrounds, by the direct speech he assigns to Paul's final "word" (v. 25 ῥῆμα ἕν) is not the discourse of salvation itself but a debate about that discourse and its reception. This is the phenomenon on which Paul invokes the authority of the Holy Spirit expressed in the words of the prophet (v. 25). It is not only the Jesus event that can be persuasively argued from Scripture (v. 23), but the events of its proclamation and reception: and this is the focus with which Luke chooses to close his two-volume work.[39]

3. *The Prologue to the Gospel*

All of these features are foreshadowed in the extended narrative prologue with which Luke begins his Gospel (by which I mean not the preface but the first four chapters of the Gospel).

3.1.*The Geographical Location of the Gospel Prologue*
The introduction of the city of Rome as a geographical location for the proclamation of the Word is, as we have seen, a markedly new feature of the end of Acts (§2.1), and in this sense signals a new theatre of action for the sect whose activities begin in Jerusalem (Acts 1) and which traces its origins back to the even more provincial setting of Galilee (Acts 1.11; 2.7; 10.37; 13.31). In a sense, Luke has already created a broader spatial frame for his story by highlighting the role of Jerusalem in the Gospel prologue (Lk. 1.8; 2.22–39; 2.41–50; 4.9). But the importance of the Roman framework in which the whole narrative operates is also highlighted at the beginning of the Gospel. Not the city, but the empire and its interlocking hierarchies are foregrounded in the prologue, which includes the names of two reigning emperors: by contrast, only one reigning emperor is named in Acts.[40] This is seen most obviously in the formal multiple dating of Lk. 3.1–2, which establishes a spatio-temporal location for the Gospel narrative by placing it within a series of Chinese boxes: the principate of Tiberius, the governorship of Pontius Pilate, the tetrarchates of Herod, Philip and Lysanias, and the highpriesthood of Annas and Caiaphas. It is worth noting that the event dignified with this ceremonial date – to which there is no parallel in Acts – is not (or not directly) the coming of Jesus but the coming of the prophetic Word: 'the word of God came to John the son of Zechariah in the wilderness'. But Luke has already (ironically, as I believe) created an imperial setting for the whole Jesus event by linking Jesus' birth with the empire-wide census of Augustus at

---

39.   cf. Dupont, 'La conclusion', p. 371; Parsons, *Departure*, p. 158: 'Jesus is no longer the teacher, but the subject matter, no longer the proclaimer, but the proclaimed'.

40.   The Caesar to whom Paul appeals at 25.10–11 must be Nero, but he is never named. Claudius is named at 11.28 (prospectively) and at 18.2 (retrospectively): whatever chronological deductions we may make from these texts, neither sets out to provide a formal temporal framework for the narrative of Acts in the way that Lk. 3.1–2 does for the Gospel.

2.1ff. Note again that an awareness of regional and imperial hierarchies is assumed (2.2).

3.2. *The Community Setting of the Gospel Prologue*

The Gospel Prologue already highlights the fact that the proclaimer of God's word may not find ready acceptance within the Jewish community. The Jewish community forms the dramatic scenario against which the whole action of Luke-Acts is played out: even on the 'missionary voyages' in Acts, preaching to the Gentiles is subordinated to preaching and debates within the Jewish community. This element of internal dispute – the fact that the proclaimers of God's word may find themselves at odds with the leaders of God's people – is already foreshadowed in the narrative prologue to the Gospel. It is evident in the preaching of John the Baptist (more extensively reported in Luke than in Mark), which causes 'debate' (3.15) and includes a warning against relying on descent from Abraham (3.7–9). It is evident again in the Nazareth scene (a Lukan creation: Lk. 4.16–30), where Jesus incurs the wrath of his compatriots (and narrowly escapes death) by reminding them that God's word and God's healing power have in the past by-passed Israel and 'been sent' (4.26) to Gentiles. For Dupont, who devotes several pages to an extensive analysis of this passage, 'En esquissant le programme du ministère public de Jésus, cette page fait en même temps pressentir toute la suite du récit jusqu'à la conclusion que lui donne l'épisode de Rome'.[41] The crucial move here, as Dupont rightly notes, is the progression from Capernaum[42] as a potential object of local resentment in Lk. 4.23 to the introduction of Naaman the Syrian and the widow of Sarepta as much more potent objects of patriotic resentment in vv. 25–27:

> Il est clair que ces versets font passer d'un horizon à un autre: d'une querelle de clocher, où les gens de Nazareth estiment que, comme πατρίς de Jésus, leur village a plus de droits que Capharnaüm, à la grosse question théologique de la situation privilégiée d'Israël par rapport aux nations païennes. Et on peut se demander si ce n'est pas précisément en raison de cette perspective plus large que Luc a voulu placer l'épisode de la synagogue de Nazareth au point de départ de la ministère de Jésus. Le texte-programme d'Is 61,1–2 aurait pu être cité dans n'importe quelle synagogue; mais c'est Nazareth qui fournissait l'occasion de jouer sur le double sens du mot πατρίς et de faire pressentir dans un incident local le sens d'un évolution dont le Livre des Actes racontera les grands étapes.[43]

The Nazareth episode can thus be read as a direct counterpoint to Paul's final word in Acts 28; and the echo is intensified by Paul's use of 'Israel' in 28.20.[44] But the apostle's striking phrase 'the hope of Israel' has even stronger echoes in an earlier episode in the Lukan narrative prologue, bringing to mind the

---

41. Dupont, 'La conclusion', pp. 396–402, here 396.
42. The introduction of Capernaum is itself an oddity: 'une maladresse littéraire' (p. 397).
43. Dupont, 'La conclusion', p. 400.
44. Other possible narrative echoes: Lk. 4.30 and Acts 28.31 (Dupont, 'La conclusion', p. 397); Lk. 4.17–18 and Acts 28.25 (linkage of Isaiah quotation with the Spirit).

description of Simeon in Lk. 2.25 as 'waiting for the consolation of Israel'. Even more clearly than the Nazareth episode, Simeon's song (Lk. 2.29–32) also prefigures the proclamation to the Gentiles. There is no prediction here of final rejection: the hymns of Luke's first two chapters clearly configure the coming of Jesus in terms of 'salvation' for 'Israel' (both terms figure prominently in the hymns: cf. Lk. 1.47, 54, 68–69, 77; cf. also 24.21) and as a fulfilment of the promises to Abraham (1.55, 73). Simeon holds out the hope that the light of God's salvation will produce the simultaneous effects of 'revelation' for the Gentiles and 'glory' for Israel. But there is a clear warning of pain and conflict to follow the revelation, both personal pain for Mary and conflict within the community ('Israel'). In this context it is surely significant, as Dupont observes, that the rare septuagintal word σωτήριον occurs only four times in the New Testament in all, and that three of those occurrences are in the narrative prologue and epilogue to Luke-Acts: here in Simeon's song (Lk. 2.30), in the extended Isaiah quotation at Lk. 3.6 (see below), and in Paul's final word at Acts 28.28.

3.3. *The Hermeneutical Matrix of the Gospel Prologue*

The Gospel prologue, like the ending of Acts, is dominated by the hermeneutical framework provided by the Jewish Scriptures, and assigns a particularly important role to the prophet Isaiah. The link between the prophecies of Isaiah and the beginning of the Gospel goes back to Mark (Mk 1.2–3) and is clearly deeply embedded in the hermeneutical tradition of the early church.[45] Luke extends the use of this crucial intertext in two obvious ways in his Gospel prologue. In his account of the Baptist in ch. 3 he extends the Markan quotation from Isaiah 40 to include the implicitly universalist promise 'All flesh shall see the salvation (τὸ σωτήριον) of our God' (Lk. 3.6). He also introduces a further Isaiah quotation (Isa. 61.1–2) in the Nazareth scene at 4.18–19, in a position which assigns the prophecy a controlling role in the reader's interpretation of the Jesus event (see above). It thus comes as no surprise to find that an equally substantial quotation from Isaiah 6 (apparently 'held over' from its Markan context) is used to create an effective 'last word' for Paul in Acts 28.27–28, completing the 'framing' effect.[46] By using this text here, in other words, Luke establishes a line of continuity which links Paul's activities in Rome right back to the Baptist's proclamation.

But the hermeneutical matrix which links the ending of Acts with the beginning of the Gospel is also established in more subtle ways. There are several significant lexical choices in Acts 28 which tie the final scene of Paul's life – despite its Roman setting – firmly into the framework of biblical history which has dominated Luke's narrative from the beginning. The link between Jesus and 'Moses and the prophets' is stated explicitly at Acts 28.23 (echoing

---

45.   Cf. K. Stendahl, *The School of St. Matthew and its Use of the Old Testament* (Philadelphia: Fortress Press, 2nd edn, 1968; repr. Ramsey, NJ: Sigler, 1991), pp. 47–54.

46.   Note that although there are other implicit allusions to Isaiah in Luke's work, the only places where the prophet is named are at the end of Acts (Acts 28.25), in the Gospel prologue (Lk. 3.4; 4.17), and in Acts 8.30.

Luke 24); the importance of the prophets (cf. also 28.25) has been a consistent thread throughout the two-volume work. Paul's allusion to 'the hope of Israel' (28.20) introduces an openly theological tone[47] which contrasts oddly with the studiedly neutral language of 28.17–22 (τῆς αἱρέσεως ταύτης). At one level, as I have argued, the use of 'Israel' underlines Paul's links with the Jewish community; but as a political term (especially in Rome) it is anachronistic. 'Israel' is essentially a theological term, tying Luke's story into biblical history: there is no place for it in the imperial hierarchies of Lk. 3.1–2. It is common, however, in the early chapters of Acts, and especially in the first four chapters of the Gospel, where it occurs nine times;[48] cf. also 24.21, which underlines its hermeneutical role.

And there are also more subtle intertextual echoes, both with Isaiah and with other scriptural texts. Paul's use of the rare word τὸ σωτήριον at 28.28 sets up multiple intertextual links with a cluster of texts which speak of the 'knowledge' of God's salvation 'among the Gentiles' and at 'all the bounds of the earth': cf. Ps. 66.3 LXX and 97.3 LXX. The citation of Isa. 49.6 at Acts 13.47 reinforces the links between 'salvation' (here σωτηρία) and 'the end of the earth' with 'light to the Gentiles' (φῶς ἐθνῶν). This latter is a key concept for the self-understanding of the apostle as it is presented in Acts: cf. especially 26.18, which picks up the theme of 'light to the Gentiles' from Isa. 42.7, where it is combined with the 'eyes of the blind' motif: (ἔδωκά σε εἰς διαθήκην γένους, εἰς φῶς ἐθνῶν ἀνοῖξαι ὀφθαλμοὺς τυφλῶν). But, as we have seen, both terms, 'salvation' and 'light to the Gentiles', are anticipated in the Gospel prologue in Simeon's song (Lk. 2.32).[49] In this context it is not without significance, I would suggest, that Luke stresses the perspicuity of Simeon's spiritual eyesight by the apparently redundant phrase οἱ ὀφθαλμοί μου in Lk. 2.30. What after all would one use eyes for but to 'see' (εἶδον)? This spiritual vision is something achieved by 'all flesh' in Isa. 40.5 (Lk. 3.6) καὶ ὄψεται πᾶσα σὰρξ τὸ σωτήριον τοῦ θεοῦ. But the Isaiah 6 passage cited at the end of Acts makes it clear that it is possible to have 'eyes' and yet fail to 'see': and this is indeed the tragedy of the story Luke unfolds.

3.4. *The Act of Proclamation Foregrounded in the Gospel Prologue*

There is no question that Luke is committed to telling the story of Jesus at length and in detail in his two-volume work: even in Acts, the story is repeatedly retold in summary form in the apostolic witness. The bulk of Acts, though, focuses not so much on the story of Jesus as on the persons of the witnesses and on the act of witness itself, with all its dangers and internal contradictions. It is not difficult to read Luke-Acts as a diptych for which the Ascension narrative provides the hinge: before it comes the Gospel, predominantly devoted to Jesus;

---

47. For 'hope', cf. esp. Acts 26.6–7: but is this really about resurrection? See also Lk. 24.21. The noun does not occur in the Gospel.

48. Lk. 1.16, 54, 68, 80; 2.25, 32, 34; 4.25, 27. All of these are Lukan uses without synoptic parallel, as is 24.21. The only occurrence of the term in Mark (apart from the scriptural quotation at 12.29) is at 15.32 (which Luke omits). Luke's other two uses are Q passages: Lk. 7.9 // Mt. 8.10; Lk. 22.30 // Mt. 19.28.

49. Note also that ἄφεσιν ἁμαρτιῶν is echoed in Lk. 1.77.

after it comes Acts, predominantly devoted to the apostles. This focus on the person of the proclaimer and the act of proclamation itself is, as we have seen, accentuated in the ending of Acts, where the overt focus of the text is very much on the person of Paul (vv. 17–22) and on the Gospel message itself and its reception (vv. 23–31).

But it is in many ways too simple to treat Luke-Acts as a diptych. If it is a diptych, it is at least a diptych with a substantial frame. We have already seen how Luke uses the prologue of the Gospel (partly building on Mark and Q, partly introducing his own material) to create a 'framing narrative' for the whole two-volume story: and this focus on the person of the proclaimer is in many ways foreshadowed here too. This is most obvious in the enhanced role given to John the Baptist in Luke 1–4. First of all, Luke concentrates his Baptist material in this section by moving back the story of John's imprisonment and telling it prospectively (but without explanation) before the baptism of Jesus (Lk. 3.19–20). This creates some narrative oddities (e.g. Lk. 9.7–9), but it allows Luke to telescope John's career and cast him as the 'forerunner' to Jesus (Lk. 7.28; 16.16) rather more effectively than the other evangelists: Luke's story implies that there is no overlap between the active career of John and that of Jesus. Yet it is hard to read this as a downgrading of John. Luke's Jesus gives him extensive coverage and warm commendation as 'more than a prophet' (7.18–35; cf. 20.3–8); and the narrator adds his own comment, in words which imply that rejection of John's baptism is tantamount to rejecting 'the purpose of God' (7.29–30). And although John's action of baptizing Jesus is downplayed in the baptism narrative itself (Lk. 3.21), his preaching (dignified with the term εὐηγγελίζετο: 3.18) is given increased coverage in 3.7–18; and by juxtaposing this immediately with John's imprisonment (3.19–20), Luke creates another typological parallel between the witness of the forerunner and that of the apostles who suffer a similar fate.

Most remarkably of all, John has his own birth narrative in Luke, culminating in a hymn which highlights his role as 'prophet' (1.76–79); and this prophetic role is emphasized by the full prophetic formula which marks the start of his ministry and begins the Gospel narrative proper: 'The word of God came to John the son of Zechariah in the wilderness' (Lk. 3.1–2). His status as proclaimer is authenticated by his miraculous birth (told in as much detail as the birth of Jesus: Lk. 1.5–25, 57–80) and by an angelic announcement (Lk. 1.13–17). It is also authenticated by the witness of the Holy Spirit, whose activity is prominent in these opening chapters but not elsewhere in the Gospel narrative. It is the Spirit who fills John 'from his mother's womb' (Lk. 1.15), and who inspires Elisabeth to recognize the nature of John's relationship with his cousin (Lk. 1.41–45). It is the Spirit who inspires Zechariah to describe John's future role as forerunner (Lk. 1.67–79).

John is not the only prophetic character in the prologue to Luke's Gospel. Zechariah and Elisabeth, Simeon and Anna are all in different ways singled out as inspired by the Holy Spirit (Lk. 1.41, 67; 2.25–26, 36) to recognize and testify to the significance of Jesus' birth. These minor characters too can be seen as foreshadowing the prophetic witness to Jesus which is the main subject of Acts, and which receives its final vindication in Paul's last debate in Rome.

This focus on the messengers rather than the message is already hinted at in the Gospel preface (Lk. 1.1–4). As I have noted elsewhere,[50] it is remarkable how little Luke manages to convey, when speaking *in propria persona* in his explanatory peritext, about the subject-matter of his discourse. The name of Jesus is not mentioned in Luke's Gospel until 1.31 (contrast Mt. 1.1; Mk 1.1); the preface never speaks of God (contrast Jn 1.1). Instead we have the opaque and coded phrase 'the business fulfilled among us' (Lk. 1.1), grammatically and pragmatically subordinated to the activities of the 'many' who have drawn up an account of this business (1.1 ἐπεχείρησαν ἀνατάξασθαι διήγησιν) and the 'eyewitnesses and ministers of the word' who have passed it on in the form of tradition (1.2 παρέδοσαν). This second-order discourse ('un discours qui porte sur un discours', as Genette would put it; cf. above n. 4) is framed in its turn by a third-order discourse which foregrounds the activities of the observing and recording authorial self (1.3 παρηκολουθηκότι, γράψαι) and of the inscribed reader (1.4 ἐπιγνῷς, κατηχήθης). None of this constitutes either a promise or a programme to narrate the story of the discourse alongside the discourse itself; but it does give us a hint that Luke has his attention fixed from the outset on the frame of Jesus' story (potentially, on its multiple frames) as well as on the story itself.

4. Conclusion: Acts 28 as Epilogue to Luke-Acts

How should we assess the significance of these echoes? In particular, what do they mean for the question of unity? I would suggest three or four points for further consideration.

4.1. Unity: Authorial and Prospective?
Somewhat to my surprise, this study has convinced me that a case can be made out for the proposition that Luke conceived his work from the outset as a two-volume set in which the Gospel story would be balanced and continued with stories of the apostles. I say, 'at the outset' with reference purely to the text as we have it: I do not pretend any privileged insight into the processes of composition, and would not presume to enter the debate about when and how the various parts of the narrative prologue to the Gospel assumed their present shape. It is not difficult to trace the development of this narrative prologue in reverse, as it were, working backwards from the core of the Markan prologue which Luke expands into chs. 3–4, and then into the birth narratives – a development which makes sense as a logical progression quite apart from any source-critical theories.[51] But what is important from my perspective – at least if I am right about the narrative echoes between the prologue and in the ending of Acts – is that the first four chapters of the Gospel have strong elements of narrative

---

50. Alexander, *The Preface*, pp. 113–14; 'The Preface to Acts and the Historians', pp. 92–93 (Chapter 2 in this volume, pp. 35–36).
51. For a useful summary cf. Tyson, 'Birth Narratives', pp. 106–109.

coherence with the ending of Acts, and that the two passages together may be thought of as a narrative frame, providing a prologue and epilogue to the whole two-volume work. If the prologue was added at a secondary stage in the composition of the Gospel, in other words, it was added with Acts in mind. But if these narrative links make any sense, we should also be prepared to allow the real possibility of strong *narrative* reasons for precisely some of the elements in the prologue which have been read as evidence for a source-critical view. This is especially true of the role of the Baptist, which I am arguing makes sense as a foreshadowing of the role of the proclaimers of the Gospel in Acts.

Whether we can move beyond the prologue to the Gospel as a whole is a different question. It is beyond the scope of this short paper to explore further links between Acts and the Gospel, and I have deliberately restricted myself in this study to trying to make sense of the beginning and ending of the two volumes. But, given the importance of beginnings and endings in narrative, it is worth remembering that the paratextual 'threshold' (as Genette reminds us; cf. n. 4) is simply that, a point of no significance in itself except as the entry point to a narrative world: the more we can make unified sense of the narrative as it stands, the less need we have to resort to source-criticism. In this context, the phenomenon of details which are apparently 'held over' from the Gospel to Acts assumes a particular importance (though that can only be assessed fully in the context of a larger analysis of the phenomenon). The fact that Luke appears to have held over the full quotation of Isaiah 6 from Luke 8 to the conclusion of Acts must at least be taken into consideration in that wider debate.

4.2. *Unity: Readerly and Retrospective?*

What is the effect of these narrative connections on the reader? Oddly enough, despite my (reluctant) conversion to authorial unity, I would argue that the nature of the echoes and foreshadowings I have identified precludes a strong view of *prospective* unity for the reader. There is no way the reader could predict the plot of the second volume from the prologue to the first as it stands: there are warnings of conflict and a hint of 'light to the Gentiles', but these are slight indications in a complex narrative which is enthralling and colourful in its own right. The hints of conflict and tragedy in the prologue are hidden among its many prophetic utterances: they are there to be discovered with hindsight, but the prologue (like real life) is not constructed in such a deterministic way that the outcome could be predicted in advance.

Nevertheless, I would argue that this kind of retrospective narrative coherence does entitle us to speak of Luke's two-volume work as a unity from the reader's point of view. It is over-simple to equate coherence with predictability, especially within a complex literary narrative: we might in fact ascribe the greater literary art to a narrative whose outcome is not totally predictable in advance. In the ancient world, moreover (certainly with early Christian texts), we need to reckon with reading strategies rather more complex than that of the critic's 'ideal reader', approaching the text *tabula rasa* and reading from front to back. The actual readers of Luke's work were almost certainly Christians themselves, reading in Greek, and knowing full well (whatever their own ethnic background) that the Gospel had in fact been preached to Gentiles as well as to Jews. Their prior knowledge of this state of affairs will inevitably rob the ending of Acts of some of its suspense: to paraphrase Acts 28.14, their reaction will be not so much, 'What happened in the end?' as 'So that's how it happened!' The same prior knowledge may of course also account for Luke's failure to narrate what happened to Paul. The existence of such readers is in fact already presupposed by the preface, with its ambiguous ἡμῖν and its 'retrospective' address to the already-instructed reader Theophilus.[52] Readers starting from this position are, we might say, already starting from the end of Acts: even without knowing the details of the story, they will read the beginning of the Gospel with the benefit of some kind of hindsight and may well therefore pick up some of Luke's hints at the outset.

The possibility of prior knowledge is, we might say, borrowing Genette's terminology, an aspect of the text's 'epitext', now inaccessible to us but none the less real for that.[53] Its importance for the readers of ancient texts (who rarely expected the kind of detective-story suspense that is taken for granted by the readers of fiction today) has been underlined in a number of studies of classical and biblical texts.[54] But there is another important aspect of retrospective narrative coherence which needs to be taken into account here, and that is the phenomenon of re-reading. 'Most readers of the gospels', as Elizabeth Struthers Malbon points out, 'are re-readers'; and (whether or not they are actually written last), this is one reason why beginnings as well as endings have a deeply retrospective nature: 'The prologue represents a *Metareflexion*... "a deeply retrospective gesture", a "postface". Only from the perspective of the ending are the implications of the beginning fully understood – if they are ever fully understood.'[55] So for Matera, the privileged information given to the reader in the prologue to Mark's Gospel is still not sufficient by itself to unlock the mystery of Jesus' identity, but 'must be supplemented by what is told in the rest of the narrative. Thus, by the end of the narrative the readers discover that they must integrate their knowledge of Jesus learned in the prologue with their knowledge

52.   A point made by Boris Uspensky, *A Poetics of Composition* (Berkeley: University of California Press, 1973), p. 149 (cited from Tyson, 'Birth Narratives', pp. 110–11): 'Temporal framing may be realized by the use at the beginning of a narrative of the retrospective point of view...as an example we may cite the Gospel of Luke, which begins from a retrospective position with a direct address to Theophilus.'

53.   Genette, *Seuils*, pp. 10–11, 316–17: 'Est épitexte tout élément paratextuel qui ne se trouve pas matériellement annexé au texte dans le même volume, mais qui circule en quelque sorte à l'air libre, dans un espace physique et sociale virtuellement illimité. Le lieu de l'épitexte est donc *anywhere out of the book*, n'importe où hors du livre.'

54.   Cf. Marguerat, 'L'énigme', p. 4, n. 12; J.L. Magness, *Sense and Absence: Structure and Suspension in the Ending of Mark's Gospel* (Semeia Studies; Atlanta, GA: Scholar's Press, 1986). A similar point is made by E. Bowie on readers' knowledge of Apollonius of Tyana: E. Bowie, 'Philostratus: Writer of Fiction', in J.R. Morgan and R. Stoneman (eds.), *Greek Fiction: The Greek Novel in Context* (London: Routledge, 1994), pp. 181–99, esp. 193.

55.   E.S. Malbon, 'Ending at the Beginning: A Response', in D.E. Smith, *How Gospels Begin*, pp. 175–184, here 184, citing Kelber's essay in the same volume.

of him learned in the light of the cross and resurrection.'[56] A more recent study of the Markan prologue makes the point well:

> Le prologue de l'évangile de Marc se présente comme un pacte de lecture qui donne les moyens au lecteur[trice] de se situer dans la narration. Toutefois, le prologue et la suite de la narration entretiennent un rapport dynamique et doivent toujours à nouveau être relus l'un par l'autre.
>
> Ce système de renvoi semble comporter une forte dimension stratégique. Il invite à le lecteur[trice], dans une seconde lecture du texte, à porter une grande attention, au jeu d'échos et d'annonces implicites que l'on peut percevoir entre le prologue et le corps du récit, et invite à l'interprétation.[57]

The links between the prologue to Luke and the ending of Acts seem to work very much in this way: what we have here is not prediction, certainly not a 'table of contents',[58] but the creation of a paratextual framework whose full significance will only emerge on re-reading.

4.3. *The Theological Script*

This invitation to re-read the prologue in the light of the ending of Acts – and vice-versa – has, it seems to me, potentially important implications for our reading of the theology of Luke's work, especially his view of the theological relationship between Jew and Gentile at the end of Acts. I would concur with R. Tannehill's view that the tone in Acts 28 is properly understood as tragic rather than triumphalistic.[59] If the reader is sent back from Acts 28 to re-read the prologue to the Gospel, it seems to me, this awareness of tragedy can only be enhanced. There is no hint there of triumphalism: even where Simeon's vision encompasses the prophecy of 'revelation to the Gentiles', it is still paralleled with the promise of 'glory to your people Israel'. And what is the reader to make, on such a re-reading, of all the promises held out in Luke's opening chapters of 'salvation' to Israel? Are these simply unfulfilled predictions? If so, it is to say the least inartistic of the narrator to redirect the reader's attention to them at the end of the story. I would suggest rather that Luke, writing in full awareness of the tragic dimension of the story of Israel's rejection of the Gospel, invites the reader both to contemplate the tragedy for what it is and to read it as a warning of the possibility of having eyes, yet failing to 'see'. There is also, perhaps, an invitation to do some theological reflection of the kind Paul undertakes in Romans 9–11: one solution to the problem of unfulfilled predictions may be to change the definition of God's people (cf. Rom. 9.24–26).[60] But Luke is writing narrative, not argument, and he does not present the reader with a single, unified solution to the problem. The mere fact that Luke's Paul, despite constant 'last words' to 'the Jews',[61] keeps going back to the Jewish community right up

---

56. Matera, 'Prologue', p. 4.
57. Steiner, 'Le lien', p. 10.
58. Steiner, 'Le lien', p. 7 and n. 15.
59. R. Tannehill, 'Israel in Luke-Acts: A Tragic Story', in *JBL* 104 (1985), pp. 69–85.
60. J.T. Sanders, *The Jews in Luke-Acts* (London: SCM Press, 1987), pp. 48–49.
61. Acts 13.45–48; 18.6.

to the book's final scene, seems to dramatize the kind of ambivalence that Paul himself shows in Romans and elsewhere (cf. e.g. Rom. 11.1–32). A similar ambivalence is implicit in Luke's use of texts from Isaiah to provide a hermeneutical framework for the Gentile mission. And by redirecting the reader to the prologue, especially to the hymns of the infancy narrative (which are after all Lukan *Sondergut:* there was no traditional imperative to include this material), Luke seems deliberately to heighten the tension between the high hopes of his story's opening and the downbeat tragedy of its conclusion.

4.4. *Climax or Closure?*

To approach Luke's work, we have argued, the reader has to unwrap two successive layers of paratext: first the preface (Lk. 1.1–4), then the lengthy and engrossing narrative prologue (Lk. 1.5–4.30). One of the most important functions of paratext is to assist the passage of the reader from the real world to the textual world at the beginning of the narrative, and back again to the real world at the end (cf. above n. 5). The preface addresses this problem formally and directly: the author speaks in his own voice to the inscribed reader, using the conventions of academic prose to externalize his own project and describe it in neutral, objective third-order discourse. At Lk. 1.5 he slips into the role of narrator, enveloping the Gospel story in thick swaddling-bands of biblical narrative style. The ἐγένετο ἐν ταῖς ἡμέραις Ἡρῴδου βασιλέως of Lk. 1.5 is the equivalent of the 'Once upon a time' of English folktale, a formal marker of the start of narrative time, while the multiple dating of Lk. 3.1–2 marks a second beginning of a different kind, recalling the formulae used to tie the biblical prophecies into the events of world history. It is a slowly-paced opening which draws the reader gently into the narrative world of the Gospel, introducing a whole series of secondary characters who point up the significance of the main character well before he appears on the scene: only at 4.1 do we encounter the adult Jesus in person, and he does not speak until 4.4. But the effect of these preliminary encounters is similar to that of the Markan prologue: before getting to the main text, the reader is forearmed with privileged information (much of it imparted with the divine sanction of vision, prophecy or angelic visitation) about the identity of the story's protagonist.[62]

In what sense does the ending of Acts provide a counterpart to this framework, and how does Luke ease the reader's transition back to the world outside the text? The third-level discourse of the preface reappears briefly at the beginning of Acts, but it has no match at the end of either volume: in this sense (not unusually for ancient texts) the paratextual frame is incomplete. But if, as we have argued, the last two chapters of Acts form a kind of epilogue to the whole narrative, there is a complete narrative framework of prologue + epilogue, and we should be able to identify in the ending of Acts similar transitional effects (either parallel or inverted) linking back into the real world of the reader.

In one way we might say that the whole of Acts forms a narrative bridge between the story of Jesus and the world of the reader. Acts begins on a

---

62. Tyson, 'Birth Narratives', pp. 107, 115–16.

mountain-top outside Jerusalem, with Jesus just departed into the clouds and two angels telling the disciples to turn their attention away from heaven (Acts 1.11) and (by implication) to get on with the earthly task they have been given (Acts 1.8). All the movement of the narrative from this point is downwards (from the mountain) and outwards (from Jerusalem), and whatever the timescale of the book's composition, the end point of Paul's journeys must be considerably closer to the time of the readers than its beginning. In strictly linear terms, of course, the beginning of the Gospel is even further away from the time of the readers (and the biblical style of the temporal markers at Lk. 1.5 and 3.1–2 reinforces the impression of distance). In this sense the whole movement of Luke-Acts is from the unknown to the known, from the distant to the near: and this sense of temporal movement is strongly reinforced by the geographical movement of the book of Acts. The final chapters of the book, as we have seen combine a strong outward movement with an odd sense of homecoming: outward, towards the periphery of the narrative map, crossing the uncharted and storm-tossed Ionian Sea to landfall on a barbarian island; and homecoming, back to familiar territory, as the party pick up the regular shipping lanes again and make their way up the Appian Way to be greeted by 'brothers' in Rome. Whatever the actual location of Luke's readers, it seems likely that the book's final scenario in Rome is closer to their world than its opening scenes; and the bridging effect of this epilogue can only be aided by the ruthlessly pragmatic vocabulary of the final voyage.[63]

The closest approach to the world of the reader, as I have argued above, comes in the preface, where the author addresses a representative reader directly and makes it clear that what he narrates is tradition received (Lk. 1.2). There is reassurance in this claim:[64] but there is also distancing, for Luke's words makes it clear that he himself stands at one remove from the 'business' he reports. Luke's story is mediated by tradents (reliable tradents, but tradents none the less), the 'eyewitnesses and minsters of the word' who passed on the tradition to 'us' (Lk. 1.2). It is this intermediate group, the proclaimers, who form the subject of Acts: another bridge between the narrative world of the Jesus story and the world of the readers ('us'). This shift, as we have seen, is intensified in the final scene of Acts, and is foreshadowed in the prologue to the Gospel with the figure of the Baptist. But there is a difference. The Gospel prologue, like the prologue to Acts, is a place of vision, peopled with angels and open to direct revelation from God. In this sense too the movement of Acts is downward and outward, constantly further away from the mountain of revelation where Jesus speaks clearly and is visible (until the intervention of the cloud) to the disciples' eyes (Acts 1.9). It is, as so often in biblical narrative, a movement from clarity to unclarity, from a moment of public vision to an ongoing journey into darkness. Here, too, the

---

63.   Cf. further L.C.A. Alexander, 'Narrative Maps: Reflections on the Toponomy of Acts', in M.D. Carroll R. , D.J.A. Clines and P.R. Davies (eds.), *The Bible in Human Society: Essays in Honour of John Rogerson* (JSOTSup, 200; Sheffield: Sheffield Academic Press, 1995), pp. 17–57, esp. 43–45 (= Chapter 5 in this volume, esp. pp. 117–19).

64.   Cf. further Alexander, *The Preface*, pp. 118–25.

epilogue to Acts functions as a bridge back into the mundane realities of the readers' world: no angels, no heavenly voice, just the ongoing task of teaching and proclamation, and the tragedy of eyes and ears that fail to perceive the salvation sent by God (Acts 28.26–27). Paul invokes the authority of prophecy as a hermeneutical key to what is happening: but we have only Paul's word for it that the prophecy was inspired by the Holy Spirit (Acts 28.25), and no consoling angel or heavenly voice sounds out from behind the cloud to tell us whether he was right.

In this sense Acts is indeed an open-ended narrative, opening out into the readers' world where even the words of apostles are the subject of doubt and debate. On the one hand, the attentive reader has already had sufficient reassurance from the previous chapter as to Paul's right to speak on the Spirit's behalf. Nothing in the shipwreck narrative, strictly speaking, is miraculous: storms, winds, waves and the behaviour of the ship's crew are all natural phenomena. Yet one character stands out clearly from the narrative as a man whose courage and vision are vindicated by events. Paul predicts the storm, keeps his nerve, and advises the ship's captain – all in obedience to his own angelic vision (27.23). This is still in the world of private vision, carefully contextualized for a pagan audience: but it cannot but impress us as readers, just as it impresses the characters, when everything turns out just as Paul predicts. To readers well-versed in the grammar of hellenistic shipwreck narratives, the moral is clear: this is a man unjustly accused, vindicated by the God whom he serves (28.4–6).[65] To readers who can place Luke's story within its biblical matrix, the episode has another dimension. The only comparable sea-story in the Hebrew Bible is the story of Jonah, who runs away from God (and from his missionary vocation) and gets his ship into trouble as a result. Paul, travelling in obedience to his own missionary calling, has the opposite effect: the ship on which he is a passenger owes its salvation to him (27.24). So Paul's vindication, for all its naturalistic clothing, cannot really be in doubt; yet it is subordinated, in the final scene, to a Paul immersed once again (as his readers will be) in the entirely human and open-ended activities of debate and 'persuasion'.

I began with a citation from Genette, the last words in fact, of his *Seuils*: 'Aussi le discourse sur le paratexte doit-il ne jamais oublier qu'il porte sur un discourse qui porte sur un discourse , et que le sens de son objet tient à l'objet de ce sens, qui est encore un sens. Il n'est de seuil qu'à franchir' (see above n. 4). Luke's paratext, I am now convinced, provides with the opening chapters of the Gospel a carefully constructed *entrée* into the narrative world, a world where prophets and angels are always on hand to point up the significance of the encounter with Jesus. But his epilogue suggests that he has taken equal care to negotiate the voyage back to the everyday world where the rest of us live, a world where prophets and angels have receded back into a mythical past, but where the more mundane and open-ended tasks of teaching and persuasion continue 'unhindered'.

---

65.   Cf. the plea of the pirate Theron in Chariton, *Callirhoe* 3.4.9–10, 'I alone was saved because never in my life have I done anything wrong'; or Lucian's shipwrecked sailors, 'not only unfortunate but dear to the gods' (*On Salaried Posts in Great Houses*, 1).

Chapter 10

SEPTUAGINTA, FACHPROSA, IMITATIO:
ALBERT WIFSTRAND AND THE
LANGUAGE OF LUKE-ACTS*

'You talk like the Bible: but I was born here, and I know that that is not the right way to speak.' So, with all the confidence of a five-year-old, a young *sabra* addressing an eminent Polish professor visiting Israel some years ago.[1] The conversation neatly encapsulates the dilemmas of linguistic study of the Bible. Most of our knowledge of the languages we study, like that of the visiting professor, is derived entirely from ancient texts. We are aware that there are different ways of speaking and writing the same language, and different occasions for using them; but we will never get the chance to meet a young native speaker to tell us definitively how the archaic languages we know and love relate to the everyday spoken vernacular, and we can never share the child's unerring self-confidence in matching speech to situation.

Nevertheless, there are certain scholars in whose company we begin to feel a little less like foreigners as we navigate our way around the complexities of language and situation. One such is Eckhard Plümacher, whose *Lukas als hellenistischer Schriftsteller* (1972) has played a major role in drawing our attention to the importance of stylistic variation in ancient Greek culture.[2] In this well-deserved tribute to Plümacher's work it is appropriate to remember the work of another eminent classical philologian who, like Dr Plümacher, has made notable contributions to the study of the New Testament in its Greco-Roman context, and whose work intersects to a significant extent with Dr Plümacher's. Like Plümacher, Albert Wifstrand was a classical philologian who considered the New Testament an entirely appropriate subject of study for any

*   This article was originally published in Cilliers Breytenbach and Jens Schroter (eds.), *Die Apostelgeschichte und die hellenistische Geschichtsschreibung: Festschrift fur Eckhard Plumacher zu seinem 65. Geburtstag* (AGAJU, 57; Leiden: Brill, 2004), pp. 1–26, and used here with the kind permission of Brill Academic Publishers.

1.   The story was told me by Mrs Maria Strelcyn about her husband, the distinguished Ethiopic scholar Stefan Strelcyn.

2.   E. Plümacher, *Lukas als hellenistischer Schrifsteller* (Göttingen: Vandenhoeck & Ruprecht, 1972).

student of Graeco-Roman antiquity; both have thereby enriched our understanding, not only of the New Testament, but of classical antiquity as well.[3]

In this article I intend to review two papers of Wifstrand on the language of
Luke-Acts, papers which, though published in Swedish in the 1940s, have
exerted (and continue to exert) a surprising – though not inappropriate –
amount of influence on Lukan studies – so much so that they are about to receive
their first publication in English. An invitation to review these classic papers for
the SNTS meeting in Durham in 2002[4] provided a welcome opportunity to revisit
the whole question of Lukan language, and of the theoretical framework we use
to locate it in the many Greek-speaking cultural worlds of the first-century
Roman Empire. In this paper I want to explore some of the theoretical implications of Wifstrand's two articles, and in particular the sociolinguistic significance of Luke's decision to 'talk like the Bible'.

Luke and Greek Classicism (1940)[5]

The starting-point for Wifstrand's work on the language of Luke-Acts – and in
many ways the fundamental observation around which both these studies
revolve – is Eduard Norden's observation that 'in the many passages where Luke
alters the wording in Mark, Mark's terminology belongs to that denounced by
the Atticists, whereas Luke himself selects from among the words and phrases
recommended or at least tolerated by them'. Wifstrand refers here to the well-
known synoptic comparison between Mark and Luke in Norden's *Antike
Kunstprosa*, which concludes 'daß Lukas an einer überaus großen Anzahl von
Stellen das vom klassizistischen Standpunkt aus Bessere hat (besonders
bemerkenswert sind die von mir in den Anmerkungen angeführten Stellen der
attizistische Lexika), während die gegenteilige Fälle quantitative und qualitative
kaum in betracht kommen'.[6] From this observation the conclusion is readily

3.   For an appreciation of Wifstrand's work, see the eulogy by J. Palm in *Gnomon* 13.6
(1964), pp. 1–4.
4.   I am grateful to Lars Rydbeck and Stanley Porter for their invitation and to the
members of the 'Greco-Roman World of the NT' seminar group for a stimulating and helpful
discussion. I am also grateful to members of the AHRB Greek Bible Project in the Dept of Classics
at the University of Reading (especially to Dr James Aitken) for further fruitful interaction with
this paper, and to other correspondents including Dr David Mealand (University of Edinburgh)
and Joe Fantin (University of Sheffield). It goes without saying that any faults that remain are
my own.
5.   Albert Wifstrand, 'Lukas och den grekiska klassicismen', *Svensk Exegetisk Årsbok* 5
(1940), pp. 139–51. Citations are from the English translation by D. Searby, 'Luke and Greek
Classicism', in Albert Wifstrand, *Epochs and Styles* (WUNT 179; Tübingen: Mohr Siebeck,
2005), pp. 17–27. See also L. Rydbeck, '3. Sprache des Neuen Testaments', *RGG*[4] 1.1424–26
s.v. 'Bibel III: Neues Testament' (Tübingen: Mohr-Siebeck, 1998).
6.   Eduard Norden, *Antike Kunstprosa vom VI. Jahrhundert v. Chr. bis in die Zeit der
Renaissance* (Stuttgart: Teubner, 1983; based on the text of the 2nd and 3rd edns., Leipzig 1909,
1915), II, pp. 479–512, esp. p. 485.

drawn (not by Norden, but by a number of influential scholars such as Wendland and Lietzmann) that Luke was 'an Atticist in his Greek'.[7]

It is worth pausing at this point to clarify exactly what is going on here. The argument actually involves two distinct propositions. Norden's fundamental observation is a redaction-critical one. It depends on minute analysis of linguistic differences between Luke and Mark, leading to the conclusion that Luke consistently alters his underlying source in the direction of a more refined and elegant (though possibly also blander and more boring) type of Greek.

Redaction-critical Proposition 1.1A (Norden)

**Luke consistently adapts Mark
in the direction of a more refined and elegant Greek.**

Wifstrand does not contest the validity of this observation; in fact he amplifies it to include syntax as well as vocabulary, and observes that it is consistent with what can be observed of Lukan language where we have no known sources for comparison. Thus the observation can be restated in a form independent of any particular source-critical hypothesis: Luke's language, whether editorial or authorial, is consistently more refined and elegant – that is, closer to the 'Atticist' end of Norden's spectrum – than Mark's.

Linguistic Proposition 1.1B (Wifstrand)

Luke's Greek is consistently more refined and elegant than Mark's.

However, Norden does not treat this linguistic phenomenon as an isolated phenomenon in NT Greek, but seeks to plot it onto the broader map of contemporary Greek usage. The conclusion that Luke's Greek is influenced by Atticism is a logically distinct proposition which introduces a socio-cultural dimension to the linguistic observation. A more recent study describes Atticism as 'the process whereby the style and language of authors writing in the dialect of classical Athens became the foundation for virtually all *belles-lettres* in this (and later) periods. Atticism looked to an ideal of correct Greek within an already widely polarized language situation with clearly established differences between educated and non-educated Greek.'[8] It is a linguistic differentiation which also has clear social and cultural implications. The ability to 'atticize', to make correct (though not over-pedantic) use of this archaic (and largely artificial) language, is one of the distinguishing markers of the educated elite:

---

7. Wifstrand, 'Classicism', p. 17.

8. S. Swain, *Hellenism and Empire: Language, Classicism, and Power in the Greek World, AD 50–250* (Oxford: Clarendon Press, 1996), p. 7. On Atticism, cf. also G. Horrocks, *Greek: A History of the Language and its Speakers* (Longman Linguistics Library; London & New York: Longman, 1997), pp. 79–86.

The aim of *attikismos*, stylistic and linguistic, was to differentiate the leaders of Greek letters and speech from the broad mass of Greek speakers in order to signal clearly that they had command of the best sort of Greek. It was the expression of a certain sort of consciousness, a distinction to do with the maintenance of cultural superiority.[9]

The difficulty of defining this slippery concept effectively added to its mystique:

The maintenance of language standards needed leisure and wealth which allowed continuous study of the classics. Atticizing Greek depended upon a battery of rhetorical and grammatical or lexicographical aids. For this reason it acted in its social aspect as a sure means of advertising membership of the elite, the multiplication of rule books reflecting on the one hand scholarly rivalries and the genuine difficulty of isolating and reproducing an ideal, and on the other the very great value attached to its possession and reproduction. Linguistic differentiation from the mass is another side of the same political function.[10]

To be a person capable of atticizing, therefore, in fact or in aspiration, was to be a person of a high level of education – which meant by implication a high level of wealth and leisure.[11] But the choice of an atticizing style also has implications for the cultural status of any given composition. Even those who could atticize did not do so on every occasion:

Atticizing Greek was not used at all times, but was rather a refinement of educated speech for certain sorts of prestige literary and speech occasions. All Greeks continued to use a *koine* (reflecting their class and education) in non-belletristic writing and, so far as we may surmise, in their conversation.[12]

Attributing this kind of language to Luke, then, has far-reaching implications both for his own social status (he would have to have been sufficiently leisured or wealthy to have acquired the necessary level of education) and for the cultural status of his work (it would have to belong – or aspire to belong – to a 'prestige occasion').

Socio-cultural Proposition 1.2A (Norden)

Luke was an Atticist in his Greek.

It is worth pausing at this point to restate this socio-cultural proposition in socio-linguistic terms. The phenomenon of 'Atticism' in Greek of the early

---

9.   Swain, *Hellenism and Empire*, p. 21.
10.   Swain, *Hellenism and Empire*, p. 410.
11.   We should not forget, however, that within Roman society it was possible to find highly-educated Greek slaves who had the level of linguistic expertise necessary to teach correct 'Attic' Greek. Education (even literacy) is in this sense the 'property' of the elite – something they may own and deploy – without necessarily being exhibited in their own persons.
12.   Swain, *Hellenism and Empire*, pp. 21, 29; cf. also p. 410: 'It should be remembered that atticizing Greek was only employed for particular prestige occasions in speech and writing. It never supplanted the educated Hellenistic standard in general communication.'

imperial period reflects a distinctive pattern found in a variety of language-systems.[13] In sociolinguistic terms, this can be defined as a general pattern in which a 'high' (H) form of language is used for public, formal and official speech situations, while a 'low' (L) variety of the same language, which in some speech communities may be spoken only (or at least is not normally in written form), is used for informal and especially private speech situations involving intra-community conversation. The high form is generally associated with religion and traditional texts...while the low form is considered the language of the collective soul, so to speak. The terms 'variety', 'code' and 'form' are typically preferred over 'language' and 'dialect' so as to allow maximum flexibility in the accommodation of the paradigm to different linguistic communities.[14]

In a now classic article, Charles Ferguson labelled this phenomenon *diglossia*, citing Arabic, Modern Greek, Swiss German, and Haitian Creole as examples.[15] As defined by Ferguson,

> *Diglossia* is a relatively stable language situation in which, in addition to the primary dialects of the language (which may include a standard or regional standards), there is a very divergent, highly codified (often grammatically more complex) superposed variety, the vehicle of a large and respected body of written literature, either of an earlier period or in another speech community, which is learned largely by formal education and is used for most written and formal spoken purposes but is not used by any sector of the community for ordinary conversation.[16]

Ferguson identifies nine typical features of diglossia, most of which can be paralleled in the Greek linguistic situation of the early Empire.[17]

1. Function. 'In one set of situations only H is appropriate and in another only L, with the two sets overlapping only very slightly... The importance of using the right variety in the right situation can hardly be overestimated.' Typical H situations include: sermon; political speech; lecture; poetry; personal letter (Ferguson, 'Diglossia', pp. 328–29).
2. Prestige. 'In all the defining languages the speakers regard H as superior to L in a number of respects.' H (which is often connected with religion) is somehow believed to be 'more beautiful, more logical, better able to express important thoughts and the like' (Ferguson, 'Diglossia', pp. 329–30).

---

13. Wilamowitz himself spotted the parallel with the position of *Hochdeutsch* in Germany in the first half of the twentieth century: Ulrich von Wilamowitz-Moellendorff, *Geschichte der griechischen Sprache* (Vortrag gehalten auf der Philologenversammlung in Göttingen am 27. Sept. 1927; Berlin: Weldmann, 1928): Rydbeck, 'Sprache des NT', *RGG*⁴ 1.1425.

14. J. Watt, 'The Current Landscape of Diglossia Studies: The Diglossic Continuum in First-Century Palestine', in S.E. Porter (ed.), *Diglossia and Other Topics in New Testament Linguistics* (JSNTSup, 193; Studies in NT Greek, 6; Sheffield; Sheffield Academic Press, 2000), pp.18–36 (19).

15. C. A. Ferguson, 'Diglossia', in *Word: Journal of the Linguistic Circle of New York* 15 (1959), pp. 325–40.

16. Ferguson, 'Diglossia', p. 336.

17. Horrocks, *Greek*, p. 81: 'The resultant dichotomy between an unchanging Attic ideal and the Koine in all its heterogeneity quickly established a formal state of diglossia that became steadily more problematical with the passage of time, and which was not to be finally abandoned until the late twentieth century.' Cf. Swain, *Hellenism and Empire*, pp. 35–40 on similarities and contrasts with the Modern Greek situation.

3. Literary heritage. There is a sizable body of written literature in H which is held in high esteem by the speech community. This literature may have been produced in the distant past, but 'contemporary writers – and readers – tend to regard it as a legitimate practice to utilize words, phrases, or constructions from this past phase of the language' (Ferguson, 'Diglossia', pp. 330–31).

4. Acquisition. L is the normal means of communication between parents and children, and is thus the form of the language first learned by children. The acquisition of H is heavily dependent on the formal school system. (Ferguson, 'Diglossia', p. 331).

5. Standardization. The tools for grammatical study of the language tend to cluster around H, and are often scarcely existent for L. (Ferguson, 'Diglossia', pp. 331–32). This is another way of saying that for many native speakers L does not really 'exist' (Ferguson, 'Diglossia', p. 330).

6. Stability. Diglossia typically persists over several centuries (Ferguson, 'Diglossia', pp. 332–33).

7. Grammar. Typically, 'H tends to have grammatical categories not present in L and has an inflectional system of nouns and verbs which is much reduced or totally absent in L' (Ferguson, 'Diglossia', pp. 333–34).

8. Lexicon. Both varieties include technical or localized terms absent in the other; but 'a striking feature of diglossia is the existence of many paired items, one H one L, referring to fairly common concepts frequently used in both H and L, where…the use of one immediately stamps the utterance or written sequence as H or L' (Ferguson, 'Diglossia', pp. 334–35).

9. Phonology. The relative closeness of H and L phonologies diverges widely from one language-system to another, but on the whole 'the sound systems of H and L constitute a single phonological structure of which the L phonology is the basic system' (Ferguson, 'Diglossia', pp. 335–36).[18]

Since Ferguson's article, the concept of diglossia has been attacked, refined, and re-defined by linguistic theorists,[19] but it remains in my opinion a helpful way of codifying a situation where distinct linguistic codes exist side-by-side within a single language system, as in modern Arabic and in Modern Greek.[20] And one

---

18.   This last point is of limited relevance to the study NT Greek, since we do not have direct access to the spoken language. We do however have some indications of the increasing rate of phonological change in the Koine from the papyri: cf. Swain, *Hellenism and Empire*, pp. 30–31; Horrocks, *Greek*, §4.10 and ch. 6.

19.   Cf. the useful discussion in S.E. Porter (ed.), *Diglossia and Other Topics*, especially J. Watt, 'The Current Landscape of Diglossia Studies', (pp. 18–36) with bibliography there cited. More broadly, cf. R.A. Hudson, *Sociolinguistics* (Cambridge: Cambridge University Press, 2nd edn, 1996), esp. §2.4.2.

20.   I follow Ferguson in distinguishing diglossia from bilingualism (which I take to be a situation where two distinct languages co-exist, like Greek and Aramaic in first-century Palestine, or French and Arabic in North Africa) – though some of the same social patterns may occur in the relationship between the two languages, i.e. one language, typically the colonial language, may function as H in this situation. In this I differ from Greg Horsley, who somewhat confusingly uses diglossia of 'a community which uses two languages – or more – for intra-society communication' ('The Fiction of Jewish Greek', in G.H.R. Horsley, [ed.], *New Documents Illustrating Early Christianity* [Ancient History Documentary research Centre, Macquarie University, 1989], V, pp. 5–40, esp. 7–8). See further S.E. Porter, 'The Functional Distribution of Koine Greek in First-Century Palestine', in *idem* (ed.), *Diglossia and Other Topics*, pp. 53–78, esp. pp. 54–55; Watt, 'Current Landscape'; C.B. Paulston, 'Diglossia in First-Century Palestine', in Porter (ed.), *Diglossia and Other Topics*, pp. 79–89), esp. pp. 86–88.

of its most helpful aspects, paradoxically, is Ferguson's reluctance to define precisely what is meant by 'linguistic codes' in this context.[21] Hallidayan sociolinguistics works with two broad categories of linguistic variation in terms of dialect ('the way you speak determined by who you are') and register ('the way you speak determined by what you are doing at the time').[22] Dialect can be further sub-divided (in principle, almost infinitely): thus geographical dialect indicates 'the way you speak determined by where you come from' and social dialect 'the way you speak determined by your social class'. But Atticism seems to straddle the point where register and social dialect intersect on the linguistic map of Roman-era Greek culture. Attic Greek was originally a geographical dialect, but by the second century CE it had evolved, like 'standard English' or 'BBC English' into something much more like a social dialect. Galen captures perfectly the social snobbery implicit in the ability to employ Atticizing language:

> I had a father who was rigorously correct in the language of the Greeks, and my teacher and *paedagogus* were Greeks too. I was reared on these words. I do not recognize yours. Don't quote me the usage of merchants or tradesmen or tax-collectors – I haven't mixed with such people. I was brought up on the books of the men of antiquity.[23]

But there is also a significant degree of overlap with 'register': even for competent language users (as we have seen), Atticism is not appropriate on every occasion or for every kind of literature.[24] It has been argued, in fact, that the variation between codes in diglossia is best understood as 'a special instance of register variation'.[25] But the phenomenon of Atticism, considered as an example of

21.   Watt, 'Current Landscape', p. 19, cf. Ferguson, 'Diglossia', p. 325 n. 2: 'The terms "language", "dialect", and "variety" are used here without precise definition. It is hoped that they occur sufficiently in accordance with established usage to be unambiguous for the present purpose.' Ferguson's whole paper is a sustained plea for 'the careful study of the mixed, intermediate forms [of language] often in wider use' rather than the 'detailed descriptions of "pure" dialects or standard languages' often preferred by linguists (Ferguson, 'Diglossia', p. 340). Hudson, *Sociolinguistics*, ch. 2 offers a sustained discussion of the conceptual difficulties of producing precise definitions of 'language varieties' and 'speech communities'.

22.   M.A.K. Halliday, *Language as Social Semiotic* (London: Edward Arnold, 1978), pp. 31–35, 110–11, 185: 'A dialect is "what you speak" (habitually); this is determined by "who you are", your regional and/or social place of origin and/or adoption. A register is "what you are speaking" (at the given time) determined by "what you are doing, the nature of the ongoing social activity".' For more recent literature, see S.E. Porter, 'Dialect and Register in the Greek of the New Testament: Theory', in M. Daniel Caroll R., *Rethinking Contexts, Rereading Texts* (JSOTSup, 299; Sheffield: Sheffield Academic Press, 2000), pp. 190–208.

23.   Galen, De diff. puls. 2.5 (Kühn VIII, p. 587), my trans. See further L.C.A. Alexander, *The Preface to Luke's Gospel* (SNTSMS, 78; Cambridge: Cambridge University Press, 1993), ch. 8, esp. p. 182, from which the citation is taken.

24.   Cf. Galen, *De ordine librorum suorum* 5 (K XIX 60–61= SM II 89): 'It is not necessary (as some believe) that everyone should atticize, even if they are doctors, musicians, lawyers, philosophers, geometers, or simply rich people or *euporoi*' (Alexander, *Preface*, p. 183 n. 27). On the ambivalence of Galen's position *vis-à-vis* Atticism, see Swain, *Hellenism and Empire*, pp. 56–62.

25.   Porter, 'Functional Distribution', esp. pp. 61–62, based on R.A. Hudson, 'Diglossia as a Special Case of Register Variation', in D. Biber and E. Finegan (eds.), *Sociolinguistic Perspectives on Register* (Oxford: Oxford University Press, 1994), pp. 294–314.

diglossia, seems at the very least to embody a peculiarly intensified and well-formalized sensitivity to register. One of the interesting features of Atticism is precisely the large-scale stabilization of the linguistic repertoire, and thus the increased variety of conscious linguistic choice, it offers its consumers. All human language-use incorporates an instinctive ability to vary linguistic code in response to situation. In a bilingual or multilingual situation, the repertoire includes codes from different language-systems.[26] In contemporary Britain and America, as Hudson observes, 'the "varieties" concerned [are] social dialects, not registers'.[27] But in a diglossic language-system, competent language-users have both a heightened sensitivity to the importance of using the appropriate code and an unusually well-formalized repertoire of linguistic codes to choose from. As Hudson puts it, one significant difference between Ferguson's diglossia and what Hudson calls 'social-dialectia', (sc. register variation between social dialects) is that 'the varieties concerned are more sharply distinguished in the former. Whereas social dialects turn out to dissolve into a myriad of independently varying items, the items involved in diglossia all vary together so that their variations can be generalised satisfactorily in terms of large-scale varieties.'[28] The other major difference is that in these situations the prestige code, typically, is neither the native language of a colonizing power nor the home dialect of a social or tribal elite, but what we might call a *literary* dialect, a code derived from and reinforced by study of the key literary 'classics' whose religious or literary prestige gives them a unique position of linguistic authority.[29] The key to its acquisition is not birth but education – a factor which makes it in principle open to the outsider and the social climber, even though the educational system has its own intrinsic social limitations.[30]

Returning to Norden's argument, then, we could restate socio-cultural proposition 1.2A in Fergusonian linguistic categories:

---

26.   Cf. Paulston, 'Diglossia in First-Century Palestine', p. 87: 'It is quite clear that the notion of functional complementary distribution can include separate languages (and language families) as well as varieties of the same language'. More complex, 'polyglossic' situations can also be documented: cf. J.T. Platt, 'A Model for Polyglossia and Multilingualisim (with Special Reference to Singapore and Malaya)', *Language in Society* 6 (1977), pp. 361–78. For further studies, cf. J.B. Pride and J. Holmes, *Sociolinguistics: Selected Readings* (Harmondsworth: Penguin, 1972).

27.   Hudson, *Sociolinguistics*, p. 51.

28.   Hudson, *Sociolinguistics*, p. 51. Hudson, adds, however, 'Even in diglossic communities, it would be surprising if there were no intermediate cases, and the distinction between the types of community is probably less clear than this discussion implies'.

29.   Hudson, 'Special Case', p. 309.

30.   Cf. Hudson, *Sociolinguistics*, p. 50: 'The way to acquire a High variety in such a society is not by being born into the right kind of family, but by going to school'. Lucian would provide a good example of an outsider who acquired a high level of competence in Atticism – with all the attendant social insecurities. Cf. Swain, *Hellenism and Empire*, pp. 298–329, and 46: 'Lucian was worried about making mistakes in his Greek to an extent that verges on paranoia and he was intensely aware of the rules which guaranteed respect in second sophistic society'.

Socio-cultural Proposition 1.2B *(restated)*

In a language-system characterized by diglossia, Luke operates towards the high (H) end of the linguistic spectrum.

But what Wifstrand does very forcefully (and I believe correctly) in this paper is to help us to move forward from Norden's original (and rather too simple) observation by refining and re-defining what is going on at the H end of the linguistic spectrum – specifically, by rethinking how we relate the linguistic data (about which there is little dispute) to the social data. Norden placed Luke's Greek on a simple linguistic spectrum running from 'Atticism' at one end to 'popular everyday language' or colloquial *koine* at the other. But he was relying extensively on the second-century lexicographers, who tend to see all Greek usage in black and white polarities of 'right' (i.e. a 'mythically pure' Attic) and 'wrong' (contemporary popular usage).[31] Clearly if there is only one spectrum, then Luke must be closer to the 'Attic' end than Mark, wherever we put him on the spectrum. But one of Wifstrand's significant achievements in this paper is to refine this oversimplistic model by introducing a diachronic element. This is developed (somewhat confusingly) in two stages in the opening pages of 'Classicism'.

First, Wifstrand argues, 'Atticism' in its full prescriptive force (especially as articulated in the lexica Norden relied on) is a second-century phenomenon. More appropriate for Luke's first-century environment is the broader concept of 'classicism', which Wifstrand describes as 'an aesthetic movement of a more pliant nature and a deeper aim',[32] which set out to 'restore power and dignity to Greek prose' by *imitatio* of 'the great authors of the fifth and fourth centuries BC', but without condemning 'every single Hellenistic innovation in vocabulary, semasiology, phraseology and grammar'.[33] To talk of 'Atticism' in the first century, in other words, is simply anachronistic.[34]

First Diachronic Modification 1.3.1 *(Wifstrand)*

'Classicism' is a broader and earlier phenomenon than the high Atticism of the second century.

But Wifstrand then moves on to a second point, and one which is actually distinct:

31. On the lexicographers, see Horrocks, *Greek*, pp. 83–86; Swain, *Hellenism and Empire*, pp. 51–56, esp. 52: 'It is in the way of texts like these to reduce a complex linguistic situation (where varying shades of literary and non-literary Greek co-exist) to a simple binary antithesis between right ("Attic") and wrong (non-"Attic") usage'.

32. Wifstrand, 'Classicism', p. 18.

33. Wifstrand, 'Classicism', p. 18.

34. For the distinction, see e.g. Swain, *Hellenism and Empire*, p. 409; and for the terminology, cf. Th. Gelzer, 'Klassizismus, Attizismus, und Asianismus', in H. Flashar (ed.), *Le Classicisme à Rome aux I^{ers} Siècles avant et après J.-C.* (Entretiens sur l'Antiquité Classique, 25; Vandoeuvres-Genève: Fondation Hardt, 1978), pp. 1–55.

> Luke's language is unquestionably much closer to Attic than is that of the Gospel of
> Mark. This is due, however, not to his being an Atticist or a classicist but to his repre-
> senting a cultivated written style, in contrast to Mark who is more representative of the
> popular everyday language. Further more, the educated written language he adopted is
> one which had been untouched by classicism and was a direct continuation of that
> standard Hellenistic prose which itself was significantly closer to 'Attic' than everyday
> spoken Hellenistic Greek.

This point is vital and involves a nuanced and sophisticated understanding of
the development of the Greek language which I believe to be fundamental for
our understanding of the social and cultural location of New Testament Greek.
It can be formulated succinctly as a second diachronic modification of the basic
linguistic observation:

Second Diachronic Modification 1.3.2 (Wifstrand)

**Luke's language is a direct continuation of standard Hellenistic prose (SHP),
which was untouched by classicism but was itself significantly more 'Attic' in
character than everyday spoken Hellenistic Greek.**

This is in essence the point that Wifstrand sets out to prove in 'Luke and Greek
Classicism', and to my mind he does so very successfully. His argument has been
amplified and endorsed by later studies, which consistently show that Luke's
language (especially in Acts, where he is not adapting Mark) is consistently closer
to the Hellenistic prose writers untouched by classicism (Polybius, Diodorus
Siculus),[35] and to the imperial-era writers still using this pre-classicistic 'default'
Greek prose ('*Fachprosa*'),[36] than it is for example to Josephus (himself clearly
influenced by classicism) or to the Greek novelists.[37] The point, as Lars Rydbeck
observes, is not that Luke is writing *Fachprosa* as such, simply that Luke shares
with *Fachprosa* the distinction of preserving a language untouched by classicism,
a language once standard but more and more forced underground in an era when
literature was coming more and more under the sway of classicism, developing
into the full-blown Atticism of the second century.[38] A glance at the defining

---

35. Cf. D. Mealand, 'Style, Genre, and Authorship in Acts, the Septuagint, and Hellenistic
Historians', *LLC* 14.4 (1999), pp. 479–505; *idem*, 'Luke and the Verbs of Dionysius of
Halicarnassus', *JSNT* 63 (1996), pp. 63–86; 'Hellenistic Historians and the Style of Acts',
ZNW 82 (1991), pp. 42–66.

36. L. Rydbeck, *Fachprosa, vermeintliche Volkssprache und Neues Testament* (Acta
Universitatis Upsaliensis: Studia Graeca Upsaliensia, 5; Uppsala: Berlingska Boktryckeriet,
Lund, 1967).

37. On Josephus, see A. Pelletier, *Flavius Josèphe, adaptateur de la Lettre d'Aristée: une
réaction atticisante contre la koinè* (Études et Commentaires, 45; Paris: Librairie C. Klincksieck,
1962). For the novelists, cf. Swain, *Hellenism and Empire*, pp. 101–31.

38. Rydbeck's conclusions are summarized succinctly in *idem*, 'Sprache des NT', *RGG*[4]
1.1424–26.

characteristics of Atticist usage listed by Horrocks makes the point clearly. 'Important hallmarks of the best Attic usage', he says, 'included the following':[39] Attic spelling (e.g. –tt- for –ss-; *xun* for *sun*); regular use of the dual; extensive use of the dative in all its traditional functions; contracted forms of certain nouns where Koine (following Ionic) preferred the uncontracted; Attic declensions, e.g. λεώς for λαός; γίγνομαι, γιγνώσκω for γίνομαι, γίνωσκω; synthetic rather than periphrastic perfect; extensive use of middle verb forms; use of the optative in its full range of classical functions; use of perfect forms with 'stative/present' rather than simple past meaning. In all of these Luke follows the practice of the Koine rather than the hyper-correct usage of the Atticists.[40]

But there is a logical consequence to this move which is less often articulated. Although Wifstrand does not make this point explicitly himself in 'Luke and Greek Classicism', it follows inevitably from his argument that the diachronic dimension will make a significant difference to the perceptions of the H-code in the Greek of different periods. To put it bluntly, though we may say that Luke's language is closer to the kind of Greek that counted as H in the second or first century BCE, the fact is that by the first century CE that perception had changed. 'Standard Hellenistic Prose' (SHP) had slipped in the ratings: it was no longer what you were trying to write if you had serious literary or cultural aspirations (as Josephus shows very well). Under the growing influence of classicism, SHP was no longer the prestige language: it had become willy-nilly a kind of '*Zwischenschichtsprosa*',[41] still widely used for administrative purposes, a 'default' Greek prose style accepted as appropriate for non-belletristic writing even by writers who cultivated a more Atticizing style for literary composition (like the rhetoricians) as well as by writers who had no such aspirations, like the writers of *Fachprosa*.[42] So the second century CE witnesses the gradual dominance of various forms of literary classicism (mostly Atticism, but occasionally Ionicism),[43] and an increasing self-consciousness among those who continued to use SHP as their default Greek style (e.g. Galen).[44]

---

39. Horrocks, *Greek*, p. 8.

40. Cf. also Horrocks, *Greek*, §5.10.2, pp. 92–95 on the language of the NT.

41. Rydbeck, 'Sprache des NT', *RGG*⁴ 1.1425.

42. Horrocks, *Greek*, p. 83: 'A more practical, non-Atticizing Koine was, however, retained for everyday purposes in the Chancery, although even this "simple" administrative style, despite making concessions to change in the interests of communicative efficiency, became increasingly conservative, irrespective of sporadic Atticist infiltration, through the rigorous training of clerical offcials (and indeed all who learned to read and write at a basic level) in the conventions of traditional "business Greek"'.

43. Ionic tends to appear in ethnographic, 'Herodotean' compositions like Arrian's *Anabasis Alexandri* Bk VIII, or Lucian's *De Dea Syria*.

44. Swain, *Hellenism and Empire*, ch. 2 'The Practice of Purism' (pp. 43–100); Horrocks, *Greek*, §§5.5–5.10, pp. 79–95.

1.4 Socio-cultural Consequences

SHP, though it may have belonged originally to the H code, had moved down
the scale by the 1st century CE under the emergent influence of classicism.

But we should note that if we shift SHP downmarket, then we also shift Luke
downmarket. Luke shows no signs even of the incipient awareness of classicizing
norms that we see in Josephus or Chariton, much less what we find in Plutarch,
Arrian or Cassius Dio. Like the writers of *Fachprosa*, Luke uses a style of
Greek which signally fails to match up to the newly-defined standards of an ever
more rigorous literary language, a language designed as much to keep people
out as to include them. Luke's Greek, though it may have belonged to the H-
code of the Hellenistic era, falls well short of the standards of the prestige code
of the first and second centuries CE.

Luke and the Septuagint (1940)[45]

Wifstrand's second paper deals with the other essential element that has to be
factored into any understanding of Luke's language: the Jewish element of
Luke's Greek. This too is part of a long-running debate, and at the beginning
of the paper, Wifstrand briefly summarizes the issues and dichotomies that had
driven the discussion up to 1940. He argues concisely that any Semitic features
in Luke's Greek are Hebraisms rather than Aramaisms, reflecting the translation
Greek of the Septuagint; are apparent across both syntax and vocabulary; and
result from intentional, stylistic choice on the part of the author (especially
evident in redactional passages), rather than the unconscious influence of
Hebrew or Aramaic sources. The paper thus presents a succinct and forceful
statement of a position now widely accepted in Lukan studies,[46] namely that

> Luke, in contrast to the other synoptics, sought to give his narrative a more elevated and
> dignified style by consciously and deliberately associating it with the peculiar style of
> Greek prevalent in the LXX which, so often reflecting the phraseology of a different
> language, had acquired a sacred status in the eyes of Hellenized Jews and proselytes as
> well as of the first Christians.[47]

I do not propose to examine again the details of this position. What interests me
is how it relates to the propositions set out in Part I above. What happens when
we introduce this Jewish or 'biblical' element into the linguistic equation we have

---

45.   Albert Wifstrand, 'Lukas och Septuaginta', *STK* 6 (1940), pp. 243–62. Citations are
from the English translation by D. Searby, 'Luke and the Sepuagint', in Wifstrand, *Epochs and
Styles*, pp. 28–45.
46.   Notably in Plümacher's *Lukas als hellenistischer Schriftsteller*; and in the contemporary
(but apparently independent) studies by the English scholar H.F.D. Sparks, 'The Semitisms of
St. Luke's Gospel', *JTS* 44 (1943), pp. 129–38; *idem*, 'The Semitisms of Acts', *JTS* n.s. 1 (1950),
pp. 16–28.
47.   Wifstrand, 'Septuagint', p. 41.

already established on the basis of Luke's lack of 'classicism'? How do Wifstrand's first and second papers relate? Again, this is not an issue Wifstrand addresses directly: but I believe it is important that we push forward the conclusions reached independently in these studies, and there are some indications as to how he might have made the link.

Once again, there are two elements to the argument as set out in the conclusion just quoted. The first, as the reference to the other synoptic Gospels makes clear, is redaction-critical. It starts with Mark (assumed to be Luke's major source for the Gospel), and reveals something both interesting and unexpected. Both Mark and Luke display a variety of Greek with a strongly Semitic flavour; but there are significant differences between the two. Mark contains more Aramaisms, is more open to loan-words, more 'vulgar', probably closer to the spoken language.[48] Luke's is a more literary Semitism, a conscious adoption of biblical style influenced not so much by patterns of spoken Aramaic as by the 'translation Greek' of the LXX. This could be stated simply as a redaction-critical proposition:

Redaction-critical Proposition 2.1

Luke, in contrast to the other synoptics, gives his language a more elevated and dignified style associated with the peculiar style of Greek prevalent in the Greek Bible.

On this model, the comparison between Mark and Luke introduces a further level of linguistic complexity along the vulgar-refined or high-low axis: Wifstrand seems to imply a linguistic category of 'Semitized Greek' which contains its own 'high' and 'low' varieties and thus exhibits a form of diglossia parallel to that which we have already observed within the larger language-system.[49]

The second, and logically distinct, element of the argument here again introduces a socio-cultural twist. The reason for Luke's adoption of this heavily semitized variety of Greek, Wifstrand suggests, is a conscious and deliberate authorial decision to imitate the language of the Greek Bible. Moreover, Wifstrand here makes the imaginative suggestion that Luke's use of the Greek Bible as his literary model is analogous to the attitude of writers in other cultures to their own literary classics: 'He was deeply versed in his Bible and knew it like the Greek rhapsodes knew Homer or Dante knew Vergil'.[50] This is a bold analogy in terms of social function. It implies that in the classicizing world of the first century CE, Luke has his own 'classic' texts which he treats in the same way as the pupils of Dionysius of Halicarnassus were trained to treat

---

48.   For more recent analysis of Mark, cf. E.C. Maloney, *Semitic Interference in Marcan Syntax* (SBLDSS, 51; Chico: Scholars Press, 1981). On loan-words (especially Latin) as a feature of the vulgar Koine, cf. Horrocks, *Greek*, pp. 73–74.

49.   Wifstrand, 'Septuagint', p. 31.

50.   Wifstrand, 'Septuagint', p. 41.

Demosthenes or Xenophon. It involves a further refinement of the H end of the linguistic spectrum, which we should perhaps now begin to see not simply in diachronic terms but also in terms of communal or cultural differentiation: within certain social contexts, there were other 'classics' which served the same literary function as the Greek classics did in the dominant literary culture.

Sociolinguistic Proposition 2.2

Luke's use of biblical Greek represents a form of *imitatio* analogous with the use made of the literary classics by Greek and Roman authors.

The identification of the Greek Bible as Luke's 'classic' has unexpected consequences (the same consequences as we noted above for SHP) at least with regard to outsider perceptions of Luke's Greek. The Greek Bible may have achieved 'classic' status within its own community context.[51] But on the broader spectrum of first-century CE Greek, where the prestige code is defined by classicism, it belongs unequivocally with SHP. In fact, of course, the language of the Greek Bible, apart from the semitic elements derived from its Hebrew *Vorlage*, is at bottom a variety of SHP, a partly fossilized form of standard Koine based in all probability on the language of Alexandria in the second century BCE.[52] That is why there are so many congruences with documentary language from the Ptolemaic period, and why so many of the peculiarities of Lucan language can be paralleled *both* in the Greek Bible *and* in SHP. Biblical Greek, in other words, like *Fachprosa*, should be regarded as a partly-fossilized subset of SHP preserved within the Jewish communities of the Greek-speaking Diaspora. Thus the recognition of the 'septuagintal' (or 'biblical') aspect of Luke's language adds a further complication to our understanding of the H codes of first-century Greek. If 'biblical Greek' functioned as the H-code within the Jewish communities of the Greek-speaking Diaspora, its role within those communities forms a functional parallel with the role of Atticizing Greek among the Greek elite.

---

51. Cf. Ferguson's observation (*idem*, 'Diglossia', p. 330) that the superiority of the H-codes is often connected with religion.

52. The 'semitic' element of biblical Greek must not be overestimated: extensive study of the papyri has shown that many linguistic features once attributed to semitic interference can be paralleled in contemporary secular documents (Horsley, 'Fiction of Jewish Greek', pp. 26–30). Cf. Horrocks, *Greek*, p. 57: 'While it is undeniable that, as a close translation of a sacred text, it embodies Hebraisms (especially where the obscurity or formulaic language of the original led to literalness), the analysis of the language of contemporary documents from Egypt has demonstrated conclusively that its general grammatical and lexical make-up is that of the ordinary, everyday written Greek of the times. It therefore constitutes an important source of information for the development of the language in the Hellenistic period.'

Sociolinguistic Proposition 2.3

Within the Jewish communities of the Greek-speaking Diaspora, 'biblical Greek' functioned as the prestige H-code.

But it also has the same diachronic effect as under 1.4 above: 'biblical Greek', like *Fachprosa*, is a partly fossilized subset of SHP which, while it may have had classic status within its own community, would be ranked rather lower down the code spectrum by outsiders.

Sociolinguistic Proposition 2.4

But in the wider world of Greek culture, 'biblical Greek' would rank with SHP, lower down the code spectrum than Atticizing Greek.

The functional parallel with Atticism raises another set of questions about the social location of Luke's language. As long as we regard Luke's use of biblical Greek solely as a form of *imitatio*, we shall be treating it purely as a literary phenomenon, an unusually intensive form of intertextuality. I have no wish to deny that it is a literary phenomenon *inter alia*; but I do wonder increasingly whether this can account for all the data. Luke is past master of the art of 'code-switching'.[53] He commands a wide range of linguistic registers, which he matches adroitly to the different topics, genres and dramatic settings of his narrative. But there is an obvious factor that is often overlooked here. In order to code-switch effectively, you need to know the codes; and you need to know them well to be able to use them as confidently and creatively as Luke does. This is a point Swain makes repeatedly with regard to Atticism. Classicism cannot be read simply as a cultural phenomenon: 'Since the chief beneficiaries of it were the same people who advertised their superiority through language, it would certainly be right to hold that internal social divisions were entrenched by identification with the classics'. And access to the prestige language was controlled (with a clear interest in 'establishing a coherent and recognizable identity for the Greek elite') by education: 'we may imagine that it would not have been too difficult for the educated to incorporate Atticisms in their Greek, as they wished. But for others it would have been very difficult or impossible.'[54]

So where did Luke acquire his facility with this 'biblicizing Greek'? Wifstrand, along with the majority of Lukan scholars, assumes that Luke is not Jewish,[55] but that he adopted the Greek Bible as his classic on conversion. The more I work

---

53. The classic study of the phenomenon is still H.J. Cadbury, *The Style and Literary Method of Luke* (Harvard Theological Studies, 6; Cambridge, MA: Harvard University Press, 1920).

54. Swain, *Hellenism and Empire*, pp. 410–11.

55. Wifstrand, 'Septuaginta', p. 31. I am fast becoming convinced that the consensus needs to be challenged on this point: cf. my forthcoming commentary, *The Acts of the Apostles* (Black's NT Commentaries; London: Continuum).

with Luke's language, however, the more I find that this stretches credulity. It is hard to understand in social terms where Luke could have learned to write 'biblicizing Greek' as well as he does as an adult Gentile convert to Christianity. Even if we suppose him to have been a God-fearer before his conversion, with a long-standing prior attachment to the synagogue, the extent to which he has absorbed this language is remarkable. Matthew's use of proof-texts, by contrast, is much easier to account for, especially if we were to accept the now increasingly plausible hypothesis of some kind of Christian *testimonia*-collection.[56] But Luke's use of biblical language goes much deeper than mere quotation or explicit allusion. The obvious locus for acquiring such deeply-embedded linguistic patterns is a school. It was after all the schools that were the chief institutional means of promoting *imitatio* of the Greek classics; and this raises the question of the role of the Greek Bible in Jewish education in the Greek-speaking Diaspora.[57] Moreover, there is a substantial element of Luke's language that is *not* clear biblical allusion, but simply shares lexical and/or syntactic features with Jewish Greek texts which were never read in synagogue and did not hold the halakhic authority of the Torah or the prophets – texts like the books of the Maccabees and Ben Sira. Much of this is clearly clustered in the same linguistic domain as other Jewish Greek texts – though it does not necessarily reflect clear 'semitisms'. We must also factor in here our earlier observation that other features of Luke's 'default' language are common to pre-classicistic SHP across a wide range of literary and documentary types, from Polybius and Diodorus at one end to the documentary papyri at the other. The fact that this is also true of the Greek Bible suggests that Luke is drawing directly on the same linguistic pool as the Greek Bible, as well as (sometimes) fishing deliberately in the Greek Bible itself.

It seems to me that the hypothesis of LXX-*imitatio*, considered purely as a literary phenomenon, does not account for enough of the linguistic data. We need, therefore, an alternative and rather more complex model to factor in the social aspects of this linguistic phenomenon. One possible route is to describe Luke's Greek not only as 'biblical Greek' but also as 'Jewish Greek', with the former considered as a subset of the latter. 'Biblical Greek', so defined, would be a particular register (elevated, solemn, literary) operating within a broader variety of the Greek language (exhibiting some semitized syntax and distinctive vocabulary) found among Greek-speaking Diaspora Jews. Like other sectors of

---

56.   On which see now M.C. Albl, *'And Scripture Cannot Be Broken': The Form and Function of the Early Christian Testimonia Collections* (NovTSup, 96; Leiden: Brill, 1999).

57.   The classic study of the role of the classics in Greek and Roman education is still H.-I. Marrou, *History of Education in Antiquity* (ET; New York: Sheed & Ward, 1956; from the 3rd French edition of his *Histoire de l'Education dans l'Antiquité*, Paris: Ed. du Seuil). For the role of education in promoting Greek classicism, cf. Swain, *Hellenism and Empire*, p. 39: 'In the second sophistic period, the education system was totally and unashamedly elitist. In this system Attic language and literature were dominant and inescapable as the high standard. That does not mean that all those who had gone through the system were atticists *tout court*. But education in Attic texts cannot have failed to inculcate a strong bonding among those who had it and a sense of superiority over those who did not.'

SHP (e.g. *Fachprosa*), we could see this as a social dialect, often preserving 'Hellenistic' forms and vocabulary from a pre-classicistic era (including some Attic forms which had always survived in SHP). The Greek Bible is its classic and most influential text, but it also preserves wider elements drawn from the language-pool of Hellenistic Alexandria. It is a living variety of Greek, not simply a literary language, and its range is much wider than the LXX alone. This seems to be Wifstrand's vision: 'It was easy for [Luke] to come up with the idea of basing his style on LXX: the style was flourishing around him in Jewish Greek literature as well as in Christian preaching which through its constant use of the prophecies of the OT also absorbed a good deal of its language'.[58] Rydbeck draws a similar conclusion: 'Die Wurzeln dieses Sprachstils findet man in der erbaulichen Sprache der helleniserten Diasporasynagoge. Daher könnte man das synagogale griechisch als ein biblisches od. jüdisches Griechisch bezeichnen.'[59] This hypothesis seems on the face of it the neatest way to account for all the linguistic observations made in both Wifstrand's studies, and also for Luke's affinities with *Fachprosa* (a parallel variety of SHP surviving in technical treatises) and with pre-classicizing literary texts of the Hellenistic era.

But do we need the concept of 'Jewish Greek' at all? Greg Horsley, in a celebrated and indispensable study, dismisses the whole concept of 'Jewish Greek' as a fiction.[60] He argues that there is no evidence for 'Jewish Greek' as 'a coherent grammatical subsystem of a language…with consistent syntax, morphology and phonology', and that the varied phenomena which seem to point in that direction are all explicable in terms of 'the expected phenomenon of interference which manifests itself in varying degrees in the speech and writing of bilinguals'.[61] This approach suggests an alternative model, in which all NT writers employ varying forms of standard Koine. Thus we could say that Matthew and Mark exhibit more vernacular varieties of the Koine, influenced more closely by Aramaic, more open to Latin loan-words – perhaps more Palestinian, less Alexandrian than Luke, but simply reflecting the normal regional diversity which did exist (as Horrocks insists) within standard Koine.[62] Luke's Greek, on this model, is also Koine, but emanating from a more uniform and educated sector, consistently closer to the H-end of SHP – perhaps a little old-fashioned by the standards of emergent classicism, pragmatic and businesslike rather than literary, but well within the range of the standard educated Koine

58.   Wifstrand, 'Septuaginta', p. 42. Similarly, Sparks speaks of 'the Semitic-Greek *patois* current among so many of his co-religionists' (*idem*, 'Luke's Gospel', p. 131). Horsley, 'Fiction of Jewish Greek', p. 29 gives further examples.

59.   Rydbeck, 'Sprache des NT', RGG^4 1.1426.

60.   Horsley, 'Fiction of Jewish Greek'.

61.   Horsley, 'Fiction of Jewish Greek', pp. 31, 40.

62.   Note that Horrocks argues strongly (contra Horsley, 'Fiction of Jewish Greek', pp. 36–37) for regional diversity within standard Koine: Horrocks, *Greek*, §4.10, pp. 60–64: 'The Koine was, in its more popular registers, far from being a "uniform" language; its considerable heterogeneity, both in old Greece and in the new kingdoms, is already clearly apparent from documents of the later Hellenistic period, with local differences deriving from both ancient dialectal/foreign-language substrate effects and language-internal developments within particular regions'.

which remained (despite classicism) the default language for business and administrative purposes across the Empire.[63] Attempting to relate Mark's Greek to Luke's – say, as L and H varieties within the same diglossic continuum of 'Jewish Greek' – is on this reading merely an excess of tidy-mindedness: both can be well described with sufficient accuracy as distinct idiolects within the broader linguistic pool of SHP.

But can this simplified model account for Luke's use of 'biblical Greek'? Horsley's explanation of bilingual interference will not help us here (and it must be noted that Horsley's discussion is concerned chiefly with the linguistic situation in Palestine). There is no indication that Luke is himself bilingual, or that he is writing in a bilingual society. Yet he shares with other Jewish Greek texts of the period a remarkable ability to deploy this distinctive 'biblicizing' Greek as a productive, living language. It is here that I would suggest that the analogy with Atticism, seen in sociolinguistic terms as a form of diglossia, may help us to move forward. Even at its height, the Atticism of the Second Sophistic falls well short of Horsley's definition of 'a coherent grammatical subsystem of a language'. As Horrocks notes, the language of the Atticists is essentially 'a grammatically antiqued Koine...with vocabulary and phraseology randomly excerpted to meet the needs of the moment'.[64] When compared with the language of the classical Attic writers, Atticizing prose contains 'Koineisms, analogical hyper-Atticisms, and straight grammatical mistakes...in even the most carefully contrived compositions, a natural product of attempts to employ a form of language which was, by definition, imperfectly controlled and understood':[65]

> 'Mistakes' of this kind are so common that it is more constructive to look at the Atticist programme less as an attempt to recreate the language of the past, and more as a commitment to forge a contemporary written style which, while employing the grammatical and lexical resources of the past, also allowed these to be developed in unclassical ways, the primary objective being to distance the literary language from the Koine. Atticism might then be seen as a learnèd, and learned, 'living' language rather than strictly as a 'dead' one, and we should not then be surprised, given the relative freedom from constricting associations with the contemporary vernacular, to see evidence of purely internal developments that conflict with, or at least display a freedom of usage that goes well beyond, the 'rules' of the classical language.[66]

This description of Atticism contains a number of suggestive parallels with biblical Greek which would well repay more detailed analysis (though – so far as we know – biblical Greek never developed quite the degree of regulation and articulation that the Atticists possessed in the lexical and grammatical rule-books). But what should we call this 'semi-living language'? As we have seen, Ferguson carefully resists the temptation to over-define precisely what is meant

---

63.   Horrocks, *Greek*, p. 81.
64.   Horrocks, *Greek*, p. 81. Cf. *idem*, p. 82, 'a state of mind that equated a surface dressing of "hallmarked" items with learning and good taste'.
65.   Horrocks, *Greek*, p. 85.
66.   Horrocks, *Greek*, p. 86.

by the linguistic 'codes' or 'varieties' found within a diglossic society; and it is easy to see why. Yet, however we define it, Atticism is a real and easily identifiable sociolinguistic phenomenon, which persisted up to the modern period, and which allowed 'the educated minority to maintain its Greco-Roman identity through cultural and linguistic continuity with the classical (and later Christian) tradition'.[67] It is not difficult to posit a similar social function for 'biblical Greek' within the scattered Jewish communities of the Diaspora, where the formation and maintenance of cultural and religious identity was just as important as it was to the Greeks of the Second Sophistic. Like Atticism, 'biblical Greek' may be difficult to define: but that is no reason to deny its existence. Like Atticism, it manifests itself in surface decoration (e.g. in biblical vocabulary, and in the use of obviously biblical idioms) rather than in deep-seated grammatical structure.[68] Like the Atticists, writers of biblical Greek may well create false 'classicisms' which clearly reflect the syntax or semantics of the Hebrew Bible, yet which cannot be paralleled in the Greek Bible itself.[69] And like Atticism, Luke's 'biblical Greek' seems to fall somewhere at the intersection between register and social dialect, though it is almost certainly more helpful here to think in terms of 'social network' rather than 'social class'.[70]

At bottom, much of the debate about 'Jewish Greek' seems to rest on a confusion over the definition of terms. Here there is much to be said for Ferguson's readiness to retain a certain terminological fluidity in discussing linguistic phenomena. Atticism, as we have seen, can be helpfully analysed as a form of diglossia, and this provides a fruitful and productive framework for analysing a recognizable cluster of linguistic and social phenomena. The debate about what to call the phenomenon – whether we are talking about 'dialect' or 'register' – is in large part a debate about how to configure the relationship between the linguistic and the social, between the linguistic phenomenon and its social context and/or effects. And here, it seems to me, some remarks of Halliday's on the intersection of register and social dialect may provide the key to our problem:

67.   Horrocks, *Greek*, p. 86.

68.   Cf. Rydbeck, 'Sprache des NT': 'Man muß sich dabei aber bewußt sein, daß sich das bibl.-jüd. Element allein auf Phraseologie und Satzstruktur beschränkt, während Phonologie, Formenlehre, Normalsyntax, Wortbildung und die meisten Wortbedeutungen ganz der Standardkoine unterstellt sind' (*RGG*[4] 1.1426).

69.   Horsley's example of the NT coinage *prosopolemptês* (Acts 10.34), should not be seen as indication that 'the actual influence of [LXX] on the vocabulary of the NT is small' (*idem*, 'Fiction of Jewish Greek', p. 28): on the contrary, it is precisely the kind of pseudo-classicisistic coinage that we find in Atticism, and which indicates the profound and creative influence of LXX idiom on language-formation.

70.   Recent interest among sociolinguists in studying language in social networks could have much to offer us here: cf. S. Romaine, *Language in Society: An Introduction to Sociolinguistics* (New York: Oxford University Press, 1994), pp. 81–83: 'The notion of network is more useful than social class'. Cf. Hudson, *Sociolinguistics*, p. 29; Joan Russell, 'Networks and Sociolinguistic Variation in an African Urban Setting', in S. Romaine (ed.), *Sociolinguistic Variation in Speech Communities* (London: Edward Arnold, 1982), pp. 125–40; Lesley Milroy, 'Social Network and Linguistic Focusing', in Romaine (ed.), *Sociolinguistic Variation*, pp. 141–152.

A particular register tends to have a particular dialect associated with it: the registers of bureaucracy, for example, demand the 'standard' (national) dialect, whereas fishing and farming demand rural (local) varieties. Hence the dialect comes to symbolize the register... In this way, in a typical hierarchical social structure, dialect becomes the means by which a member gains, or is denied, access to certain registers.[71]

Register and social dialect are not the same thing; but they interact in two important ways, both of which impact on the way we view Luke's language. In many societies, social dialect controls access to particular registers; and – precisely as a consequence of this limited access – certain registers become associated with certain social dialects.

We have already seen how this interaction works with Atticism. If dialect means 'the way you speak depending on your social class', Atticism cannot strictly be described as the social dialect of elite educated Greeks, because even the elite did not speak and write atticizing Greek on all occasions; as in other diglossic situations, the prestige language is not the mother-tongue of any single social group. Elite education and Atticism are not co-extensive. You can be educated without atticizing: that freedom is one of the privileges of education.[72] But the converse does not apply: you cannot atticize without being educated, because you do not have the necessary competence. Thus if a writer shows a high level of skill in atticizing, we have to deduce a high level of education (and thus almost certainly a high social status). But, conversely, a lack of atticizing does not necessarily imply a lack of education: even in the second century, some highly educated writers (like Galen) chose to write a non-atticizing prose, because full-blown Atticism was not the appropriate register for what they were writing. Nevertheless, because certain registers tend to be associated with certain dialects this choice always carried the risk that readers would make the illegitimate assumption that a failure to atticize indicated an inability to atticize, i.e. marked one out as 'illiterate' or 'uneducated', not belonging to the elite. It is precisely this social ambivalence that fuels so much of the linguistic paranoia of second-century writers like Galen and Lucian.[73]

The same argument must apply to Luke (and indeed to other early Christian writers). He does not display the characteristic markers of Atticism, or even the more moderate classicism of his contemporaries. His default language – like that of writers of *Fachprosa* – is educated standard *Koine* (SHP). Theoretically, it is conceivable that this was only one of a number of linguistic competencies open to him – that Luke, like Galen, was capable of atticizing but chose not to

71.   Halliday, *Language as Social Semiotic*, p. 186. Cf. M.A.K. Halliday and R. Hasan, *Language, Context, and Text: Aspects of Language in a Social-Semiotic Perspective* (Oxford: Oxford University Press, 1989), p. 42: 'There is a close interconnection in practice between registers and dialects. There is division of labour in society: different social groups, speaking different dialects, engage in different kinds of activity. As a result of this, certain registers come to be associated with certain dialects.'

72.   Cf. Swain, *Hellenism and Empire*, p. 39: 'The linguistic competence of the elite was far broader than it was for the rest'.

73.   Swain, *Hellenism and Empire*, ch. 2, pp. 43–64. On the medical writers, see Rydbeck, *Fachprosa*; Alexander, *The Preface*, ch. 8, pp. 168–86.

because he did not consider Atticism appropriate for the genre and occasion of his writing. In this sense Luke's linguistic choice is a matter of register rather than of social dialect. But it must be acknowledged that the choice leaves him open to the charge (which is also in other respects more likely) that he writes standard educated *Koine* because it is the only language he knows, the highest register to which his education has given him access – in other words, that he belongs socially (and not just by choice) within the social location with which non-atticizing SHP was now associated, that is within the bureaucratic circles educated to use Greek for administrative, business and professional purposes.[74] And it must also be acknowledged that the linguistic choice itself very clearly identifies Luke's writings as not belonging to the prestige literary registers for which atticizing (or at least classicizing) Greek was fast becoming the norm.

But the other side of the argument must also be followed through. Luke, as we have argued, does in fact show himself highly adept and proficient in another form of classicism, in his *imitatio* (amounting at times to pastiche) of the Greek Bible. This linguistic facility should be analysed primarily in terms of register: it must tell us something about the literary matrix in which Luke wants to locate his account of Christian origins. It lends, in Wifstrand's words, 'a certain solemn and hieratic tone to Luke's diction, dignifying it and raising it above everyday life even more than a classicist style according to the Greek fashion of his day would have done'.[75] Not that this would cut any ice with the Greek elite. Functional parallels should not be taken to imply mutual recognition of linguistic standards: to classically-minded Greek readers, Luke's biblicizing Greek would be recognised simply as a distinctive form of standard educated Koine, and, like *Fachprosa*, subject to the same social stigma.

But Luke's dextrous manipulation of this register also has social implications. He could not deploy this biblicizing Greek in such a creative and wide-ranging fashion unless he had access to it – that is, unless he belonged to a social context in which this linguistic competence could be learned. That is not to say that Luke's biblical Greek was necessarily a spoken language, any more than the Herodotean Ionic dialect of Lucian's *De Dea Syria* was ever anything more than a *tour-de-force* of literary pastiche. But it does mean that Luke, like Lucian, must at the very least have had access to an educational context which socialized him at a profound level in the relevant literature – and, in Luke's case, that means a literary grounding in Jewish Greek literature far wider than the Pentateuch and operating at a level far deeper and more creative than conscious inter-textual allusion. In this sense, Luke's biblical Greek is clearly a matter of social dialect as well as register. Exactly how we should construct the social matrix for this sectarian idiolect is a matter for further investigation: but it seems to me reasonable to suggest that we are dealing with a prestige code of heightened, formal, religiously-charged language deployed at the very least in the preaching

74.   Horrocks, *Greek*, p. 83 speaks of 'the rigorous training of clerical officials (and indeed all who learned to read and write at a basic level) in the conventions of traditional "business Greek" '.

75.   Wifstrand, 'Septuaginta', p. 30.

and the liturgy of Greek-speaking Diaspora communities. As the H-code for these communities, it will be only one of a number of linguistic codes deployed by members whose everyday spoken language might display much more regional variation. All these codes are forms of Koine Greek: we are not talking about the distinct language-varieties found in some later Jewish communities, like Yiddish or Judeo-Arabic (though the parallels might repay some serious study). But, whatever we call it, 'Biblicism', like Atticism, is a real sociolinguistic phenomenon, a distinctive linguistic register deployed (in certain community-specific contexts) by particular communities or social networks in the Mediterranean world. To see this purely as a literary phenomenon is to misunderstand how such linguistic codes work: linguistic choices always have social implications. Like Atticism, Biblicism must have functioned *inter alia* as a cohesive factor in reinforcing cultural and religious identity for Jewish and Christian groups in the Roman world. It may also have played a part ultimately in their ability to construct a viable alternative to the classicism of the dominant elite, offering 'a very different set of priorities and paradigms to those who had no secure or direct interest in the Greek past and who were excluded from its benefits'.[76] But that – as they say – is another story.

76.   Swain, *Hellenism and Empire*, p. 422.

BIBLIOGRAPHY

Aberle, F., 'Exegetische Studien, Pt. 2: Über den Prolog des Lucas-evangeliums', *Theologische Quartalschrift* 45 (1863), pp. 98–120.

Albl, Martin C., *'And Scripture Cannot Be Broken': The Form and Function of the Early Christian Testimonia Collections* (NovTSup, 96; Leiden: Brill, 1999).

Alexander, Loveday C.A., 'Luke's Preface in the Pattern of Greek Preface-Writing', in *NovT* 28.1 (1986), pp. 48–74.

—— 'The Living Voice: Scepticism towards the Written Word in Early Christian and in Greco-Roman Texts', in Clines, Fowl and Porter (eds.), *The Bible in Three Dimensions*, pp. 221–47.

—— 'Schools, Hellenistic', in *ABD* V, pp. 1005–11.

—— *The Preface to Luke's Gospel: Literary Convention and Social Context in Luke 1.1–4 and Acts 1.1* (SNTSMS, 78; Cambridge: Cambridge University Press, 1993).

—— 'Acts and Ancient Intellectual Biography', in Winter and Clarke (eds.), *The Book of Acts in its First Century Setting*, I, pp. 31–63.

—— 'Paul and the Hellenistic Schools: The Evidence of Galen', in Troels Engberg-Pedersen (ed.), *Paul in his Hellenistic Context*, pp. 60–83.

—— '"In Journeyings Often": Voyaging in the Acts of the Apostles and in Greek Romance', in Tuckett (ed.), *Luke's Literary Achievement*, pp. 17–49.

—— 'Narrative Maps: Reflections on the Toponymy of Acts', in, Carroll, Clines, Davies (eds.), *The Bible in Human Society*, pp. 17–57.

—— 'The Preface to Acts and the Historians', in Witherington III (ed.), *History, Literature and Society in the Book of Acts*, pp. 73–103.

—— 'Ancient Book-Production and the Circulation of the Gospels', Bauckham, *The Gospels for All Christians*, pp. 71–111.

—— 'Marathon or Jericho? Reading Acts in Dialogue with Biblical and Greek Historiography', in David J.A. Clines and Stephen D. Mooore (eds.), *Auguries: The Jubilee Volume of the Sheffield Department of Biblical Studies* (JSOTSup, 269; Sheffield; Sheffield Academic Press, 1998), pp. 92–125.

—— 'Fact, Fiction and the Genre of Acts', *New Testament Studies* 44.3 (1998), pp. 380–99.

—— 'St. Paul and the Greek Novel', in Hock (ed.), *Ancient Fiction and Early Christian Narrative*, pp. 235–56.

—— 'Formal Elements and Genre: Which Greco-Roman Prologues Most Closely Parallel the Lukan Prologues?' in Moessner (ed.), *Jesus and the Heritage of Israel*, pp. 9–26.

—— 'Reading Luke-Acts from Back to Front', in Verheyden (ed.), *The Unity of Luke-Acts*, pp. 419–46.

—— 'The Acts of the Apostles as an Apologetic Text', in Edwards, Goodman and Rowland (eds.), *Apologetic among Pagans, Jews, and Christians*, pp. 15–44.

—— 'Intertextualité et la question des lecteurs', in Marguerat and Curtis (eds.), *Intertextualités: La Bible en échos*, pp. 201–14.

—— 'IPSE DIXIT: Citation of Authority in Paul and in the Jewish and Hellenistic Schools', in Troels Engberg-Pedersen (ed.), Paul beyond the Judaism-Hellenism Divide (Louisville: Westminster John Knox, 2001), pp. 103–27.

—— 'New Testament Narrative and Ancient Epic', in Emmanuelle Steffek and Yvan Bourquin (eds.), *Raconter, interpréter, announcer: Parcours de Nouveau Testament. Mélanges offerts à Daniel Marguera pour son 60e anniversaire* (Le Monde de la Bible, 47; Geneva: Labor et Fides, 2003), pp. 239–49.

—— 'Septuaginta, Fachprosa, Imatio: Albert Wifstrand and the Language of Luke-Acts', in Cilliers Breytenbach and Jens Schroter (eds.), *Die Apostelgeschichte und die hellenistische Geschichtsschreibung: Festschrift fur Eckhard Plumacher zu seinem 65. Geburtstag* (AGAJU, 57; Leiden: Brill, 2004), pp. 1–26.

—— 'The Four among Pagans', in M. Bockmuehl and D. Hagner (eds.), *The Written Gospel* (Cambridge: Cambridge University Press, 2005), pp. 235–36.

—— "The Passions in the Novels of Chariton and Xenophon,' in John T. Fitzgerald (ed.), *The Passions in Hellenistic Moral Philosophy Passions and Progress in Greco-Roman Thought* (London: Routledge, forthcoming).

—— *The Acts of the Apostles* (Black's NT Commentaries; London: Continuum, forthcoming).

Alexander, Loveday C.A., (ed.), *Images of Empire* (JSOTSup, 122; Sheffield: JSOT Press, 1991).

Alexander, P.S., 'Notes on the *Imago Mundi* in the Book of Jubilees', *JJS* 33 (1982), pp. 197–213.

—— 'Rabbinic Biography and the Biography of Jesus: A Survey of the Evidence', in Tuckett (ed.), *Synoptic Studies*, pp. 19–50.

—— 'Geography and the Bible, Early Jewish', *ABD* II, pp. 977–88.

—— '"The Parting of the Ways" from the Perspective of Rabbinic Judaism', in Dunn (ed.), *Jews and Christians*, pp. 1–25.

Allain, M.L., *The Periplous of Skylax of Karyanda* (PhD, Ohio State University, 1977).

Attridge, H., 'Josephus and his Works', in Stone (ed.), *Jewish Writings of the Second Temple Period*, pp. 185–232.

—— 'Historiography', in Stone (ed.), *Jewish Writings of the Second Temple Period*, ch. 4.

Auerbach, Erich, *Mimesis: The Representation of Reality in Western Literature* (trans. Willard R. Trask; Princeton: Princeton University Press, 1953).

Aune, David E., *The New Testament in its Literary Environment* (Cambridge: James Clarke, 1988).

—— 'Luke 1:1–4: Historical or Scientific Prooimion?', in Christopherson, *et al.* (eds.), *Paul, Luke, and the Graeco-Roman World*, pp. 138–48.

Avenarius, Gert, *Lukians Schrift zur Geschichtsschreibung* (Meisenheim/Glan: Hain, 1956).

Baird, W., *History of New Testament Research*. I. *From Deism to Tübingen* (Minneapolis: Fortress Press, 1992).

Barclay, John, *Jews in the Mediterranean Diaspora* (Edinburgh: T&T Clark, 1996).

Barrett, C.K., *Luke the Historian in Recent Study* (London: Epworth Press, 1961).

Bauckham, Richard, 'James and the Jerusalem Church,' in *idem* (ed.), *The Book of Acts in its First Century Setting*. IV. *Palestinian Setting* (Carlisle: Paternoster; and Grand Rapids: Eerdmans, 1995), pp. 415–80.

—— *The Gospels for All Christians* (Grand Rapids: Eerdmans, 1997).

Beissinger, M., J. Tylus, S. Wofford, (eds.), *Epic Traditions in the Contemporary World: The Poetics of Community* (Berkeley: University of California Press, 1999).

Berger, R.A. Klaus, 'Hellenistische Gattungen im Neuen Testament', *ANRW* 2.25.2, pp. 1034–1380.

Betz, Hans Dieter, *Der Apostel Paulus und die sokratische Tradition* (BHT, 45; Tübingen: Siebeck-Mohr, 1972).

Biber, D., and E. Finegan (eds.), *Sociolinguistic Perspectives on Register* (Oxford: Oxford University Press, 1994).

Black, M., (ed.), *Studies in the Gospels and Epistles* (Manchester: Manchester University Press, 1962).

Blomqvist, J., *The Date and Origin of the Greek Version of Hanno's Periplus* (Lund: Gleerup, 1979).

Bonz, Marianne Palmer, *The Past as Legacy: Luke-Acts and Ancient Epic* (Minneapolis: Augsburg Fortress, 2000).

Bowersock, G.W., *Fiction as History, Nero to Julian* (Sather Classical Lectures, 58; Berkeley: University of California Press, 1994).

Bowie, E., 'Apollonius of Tyana: Tradition and Reality', in *ANRW* 2.16.2 (1978), pp. 1652–99.

—— 'Lies, Fiction and Slander in Early Greek Poetry', in Gill and Wiseman (eds.), *Lies and Fiction*, pp. 1–37.

—— 'Philostratus, Writer of Fiction', in Morgan and Stoneman, (eds.), *Greek Fiction*, ch. 11, pp. 181–99.

Bowra, C.M., *From Vergil to Milton* (London: Macmillan, 1965 [1945]).

Braun, Martin, *History and Romance in Graeco-Oriental Literature* (Oxford: Basil Blackwell, 1938).

Brenk, Frederick E., 'A Gleaming Ray: Blessed Afterlife in the Mysteries', *Illinois Classical Studies* 18 (1993), pp. 147–64.

Brinkman, J.A., 'The Literary Background of the "Catalogue of the Nations"', *CBQ* 25 (1963), pp. 418–27.

Bruce, F.F., *The Acts of the Apostles: Greek Text with Introduction and Commentary* (Grand Rapids: Eerdmans, 3rd edn, 1990).

Burridge, R.A., *What are the Gospels?* (Grand Rapids: Eerdmans, 2nd edn, 2004; [SNTSMS, 70; Cambridge: Cambridge University Press, 1992]).

Byrskog, S., *Story as History – History as Story: The Gospel; Tradition in the Context of Ancient Israel* (WUNT, 123; Tübingen: Mohr-Siebeck, 2000).

Cadbury, H.J., *The Style and Literary Method of Luke* (Harvard Theological Studies, 6; Cambridge, MA: Harvard University Press, 1920).

—— 'The Purpose Expressed in Luke's Preface', *The Expositor* (June 1921), pp. 431–41.

—— 'Commentary on the Preface of Luke', in Jackson and Lake (eds.), *The Beginnings of Christianity*, II, Appendix C, pp. 489–510.

—— 'The Knowledge Claimed in Luke's Preface', *The Expositor* (Dec 1922), pp. 401–20.

—— *The Making of Luke-Acts* (New York: Macmillan, 1927).

—— *The Book of Acts in History* (London: Adam & Charles Black, 1955).

—— '"We" and "I" passages in Luke-Acts', *NTS* 3 (1956–57), pp. 128ff.

Cameron, Averil (ed.), *History as Text: The Writing of Ancient History* (London: Duckworth, 1989).

—— *Christianity and the Rhetoric of Empire: The Development of Christian Discourse* (Sather Classical Lectures, 55; Berkeley and Oxford: University of California Press, 1991).

Campbell, Robin, *Seneca: Letters from a Stoic* (Harmondsworth: Penguin Books, 1969).

Cancik, Hubert, 'The History of Culture, Religion, and Institutions in Ancient Historiography: Philological Observations Concerning Luke's History', *JBL* 116.4 (1997), pp. 681–703.

Caroll R., M. Daniel, *Rethinking Contexts, Rereading Texts* (JSOTSup, 299; Sheffield: Sheffield Academic Press, 2000).

Carroll R., M. Daniel, D.J.A. Clines, P.R. Davies (eds.), *The Bible in Human Society: Essays in Honour of John Rogerson* (JSOTSup, 200; Sheffield: Sheffield Academic Press, 1995).

Cassidy, Richard, *Jesus, Politics and Society: A Study of Luke's Gospel* (Maryknoll: Orbis, 1978).

—— 'Luke's Audience, the Chief Priests, and the Motive for Jesus' Death', in R.J. Cassidy and P.J. Scharper (eds.), *Political Issues in Luke-Acts* (Maryknoll: Orbis, 1983), pp. 146–67.

—— *Society and Politics in the Acts of the Apostles* (Maryknoll: Orbis, 1988).

Cassidy, R.J., and P.J. Scharper (eds.), *Political Issues in Luke-Acts* (Maryknoll: Orbis, 1983).

Casson, Lionel, *Travel in the Ancient World* (London: Allen & Unwin, 1974).

—— *The Periplus Maris Erythraei* (Princeton: Princeton University Press, 1989).

Chariton, *Callirhoe* (ed. and trans. G.P. Goold; LCL 481; Cambridge, MA: Harvard University Press, 1995).

Cheol-Won Yoon, 'Paul's Citizenship and its Function in the Narratives of Acts' (unpublished PhD thesis, Sheffield, 1996).

Christopherson, A., *et al.* (eds.), *Paul, Luke, and the Graeco-Roman World: Essays in Honour of Alexander J.M. Wedderburn* (JSNTSup, 217; Sheffield: Sheffield Academic Press, 2003).

Clarke, Katherine, *Between Geography and History: Hellenistic Constructions of the Roman World* (Oxford: Clarendon Press, 1999).

Clines, D.J.A., S.E. Fowl and S.E. Porter (eds.), *The Bible in Three Dimensions* (Sheffield: Sheffield Academic Press, 1990).

Conzelmann, H., *Die Mitte der Zeit* (Tübingen: Mohr, 1960).

—— 'Paulus und die Weisheit', *NTS* 12 (1965), pp. 231–44.

—— 'Luke's Place in the Development of Early Christianity', in L. Keck and J.L. Martyn (eds.), *Studies in Luke-Acts* (London: SPCK, 1968), pp. 298–316.

—— *Acts of the Apostles* (Hermeneia; Philadelphia: Fortress, 1987, trans. from 2nd German edn. of 1972).

Cook, S.A., F.E. Adcock, M.P. Charlesworth (eds.), *The Cambridge Ancient History* (Cambridge: University Press, 1st edn, 1934).

Corssen, P., Review of F. Blass, *The Philology of the Gospels* (1898), *GGA* 1899, pp. 305ff.

Cox, Patricia, *Biography in Late Antiquity* (Berkeley: University of California Press, 1983).

Croke, B., and A.M. Emmett (eds.), *History and Historians in Late Antiquity* (Sydney; New York: Pergamon Press, 1983).

Cross, Amanda, *No Word from Winifred* (London: Virago, 1987).

Cross, F.L., and E.A. Livingstone (eds.), *Oxford Dictionary of the Christian Church* (Oxford: Oxford University Press, 3rd edn, 1997).

Cross, Frank Moore, *From Epic to Canon: History and Literature in Ancient Israel* (Baltimore: Johns Hopkins, 1998).

—— 'Traditional Narrative and the Reconstruction of Early Israelite Institutions', pp. 22–52.

Crystal, D., *Linguistics* (Harmondsworth: Penguin, 1971).

Crystal, D., and D. Davy, *Investigating English Style* (London: Longmans, 1969).

Culpepper, Alan, *The Johannine School* (SBLDS, 26; Missoula: Scholars Press, 1975).

Cuntz, O., *Itineraria Romana* (Leipzig: Teubner, 1929).

Dalmeyda, Georges, *Xénophon d'Éphese: Les Éphésiaques* (Paris: Les Belles Lettres, 1962).

Darr, John A., *On Character Building: The Reader and the Rhetoric of Characterization in Luke-Acts* (Westminster: John Knox Press, 1992).

Desbordes, B.A., 'Introduction à Diogène Laërce. Exposition de l'Altertumswissenschaft servant de préliminaires critiques à une lecture de l'oeuvre', I and II (Doctoral Thesis, Utrecht, Onderwijs Media Institut, 1990).

Dibelius, Martin, *Studies in the Acts of the Apostles* (ed. H. Greeven; trans. M. Ling and P. Schubert; London: SCM Press, 1956); ET of *Aufsätze zur Apostelgeschichte* (Göttingen: Vandenhoeck & Ruprecht, 1951).

—— *The Book of Acts: Form, Style, Theology* (ed. K.C. Hanson; Minneapolis: Fortress Press, 2004).

—— 'The Acts of the Apostles as an Historical Source,' in *idem, Studies in the Acts of the Apostles,* pp. 102–108; now reprinted in *idem,* 'The Book of Acts as an Historical Source', in *idem, The Book of Acts: Form, Style, Theology,* pp. 27–31.

—— 'The Speeches in Acts and Ancient Historiography', in *idem, Studies in the Acts of the Apostles, pp. 138–85;* now reprinted in *idem, The Book of Acts:*

Form, Style, Theology, pp. 49–86.

—— 'The Acts of the Apostles in the Setting of the History of Early Christian Literature', in *idem, Studies in the Acts of the Apostles,* pp. 192–206; now reprinted in *idem, The Book of Acts: Form, Style, Theology,* pp. 3–13.

Dihle, Albrecht, *Studien zur griechischen Biographie* (Gottingen: Vandenhoeck & Ruprecht, 1956).

—— *Die Entstehung der historischen Biographie* (Sitzungsberichte der Heidelberger Akademie der Wissenschaften, phil.-hist. Klasse 1986/3; Heidelberg: Carl Winter, 1987).

Dilke, O.A.W., *Greek and Roman Maps* (London: Thames & Hudson, 1985).

Diller, A., *The Tradition of the Minor Greek Geographers* (American Philological Association Monographs, 14; New York: Lancaster Press, 1952).

Döring, Klaus, *Exemplum Socratis: Studien zur Sokratesnachwirkung in der kynisch-stoischen Popularphilosophie der frühen Christentum* (Hermes Einzelschriften, 42; Wiesbaden: Franz Steiner, 1979).

Droge, Arthur J., *Homer or Moses? Early Christian Interpretations of the History of Culture* (Hermeneutische Untersuchungen zur Theologie, 26; Tübingen: Siebeck-Mohr, 1989).

—— 'Apologetics, NT', in *ABD* I, pp. 302–307.

Dubrow, H., *Genre* (The Critical Idiom Series, 42; London: Methuen, 1982).

Dunn, J.D.G., 'The Question of Anti-Semitism in the New Testament', in *idem* (ed.), *Jews and Christians,* pp. 177–211.

Dunn, J.D.G., (ed.), *Jews and Christians: The Parting of the Ways A.D. 70 to 135* (Tübingen: Siebeck-Mohr, 1992).

Dupont, J., 'Le Salut des Gentils et la signification théologique du Livre des Actes', *NTS* 6 (1960), pp. 132–55.

—— 'La conclusion des Actes et son rapport à l'ensemble de l'ouvrage de Luc', in J. Kremer (ed.), *Les Actes des Apôtres: Traditions, rédaction, théologie* (BETL, 48; Leuven: Leuven University Press – Gembloux, 1978), pp. 359–404.

Düring, I., *Aristotle in the Ancient Biographical Tradition* (Studia Graeca et Latina Gothoburgensia, 5: Göteborg: Elanders, 1957), pp. 77–78.

Earl, D., 'Prologue-form in Ancient Historiography', *ANRW* 1.2, pp. 842–56.

Edwards, Douglas R., *Religion and Power: Pagans, Jews, and Christians in the Greek East* (New York: Oxford University Press, 1996).

Edwards, M., M. Goodman, S. Price and C. Rowland (eds.), *Apologetics in the Roman Empire: Pagans, Jews, and Christians* (Oxford: Clarendon Press, 1999).

Engberg-Pedersen, Troels, (ed.), *Paul in his Hellenistic Context* (Philadelphia: Fortress Press, 1994).

—— *Paul beyond the Judaism-Hellenism Divide* (Louisville: Westminster John Knox, 2001).

Esler, Philip F., *Community and Gospel in Luke-Acts* (SNTSMS, 57; Cambridge: Cambridge University Press, 1987).

Eucken, C., *Isokrates* (Berlin and New York: W. de Gruyter, 1983).

Fairweather, Janet, 'Fiction in the Biographies of Ancient Writers', *Ancient Society* 4 (1974), pp. 231–75.

Ferguson, Charles A., 'Diglossia', *Word: Journal of the Linguistic Circle of New York* 15 (1959), pp. 325–40.

Fiorenza, E. Schüssler, 'Miracles, Mission and Apologetics: An Introduction', in *eadem* (ed.), *Aspects of Religious Propaganda in Judaism and Early Christianity* (Notre Dame: Notre Dame University Press, 1976), pp. 1–25.

Fischel, H.A., 'Martyr and Prophet', *Jewish Quarterly Review* 37 (1946–47), pp. 265–80, 363–86.

Fitzmyer, J.A., *The Gospel According to Luke I–XI* (AB: New York: Doubleday, 1981).

Flashar, H., (ed.), *Le Classicisme à Rome aux I^{ers} Siècles avant et après J.-C.* (Entretiens sur l'Antiquité Classique, 25; Vandoeuvres-Genève: Fondation Hardt, 1978).

Flender, H., *St. Luke: Theologian of Redemptive History*, (trans. R. H. Fuller; London: SPCK, 1967).

Flueckiger, J.B., *Gender and Genre in the Folklore of Middle India* (Ithaca: Cornell University Press, 1996).

Fornara, C.W., *The Nature of History in Ancient Greece and Rome* (Berkeley: University of California Press, 1983).

Fraser, P.M., *Ptolemaic Alexandria* (Oxford: Clarendon Press, 1970).

Friedländer, P., *Plato: An Introduction*, (trans. and rev. Bollingen Foundation LIX; New York: Pantheon Books, 1958).

Frye, Northrop, *The Secular Scripture* (Cambridge, MA; London: Harvard University Press, 1976).

Fuhrmann, M., *Das systematische Lehrbuch: ein Beitrag zur Geschichte der Wissenschaften in der Antike* (Göttingen: Vandenhoeck & Ruprecht, 1960).

Gabba, Emilio, 'True History and False History in Classical Antiquity', *JRS* 71 (1981), pp. 50–62.

—— *Dionysius and the History of Archaic Rome* (Sather Classical Lectures, 56; Berkeley: University of California Press, 1991)

Gallo, Italo, *Frammenti Biografici da Papiri*, II (Rome: Ateno & Bizarri, 1980).

Gärtner, Bertil, *The Areopagus Speech and Natural Revelation* (Acta Seminarii Neotestamentici Upsaliensis, 21; Uppsala: Almqvist & Wiksell, 1955).

Gasque, Ward, 'A Fruitful Field: Recent Study of the Acts of the Apostles', *Int* 42 (1988), pp. 117–31.

—— *Dionysius and the History of Archaic Rome* (Sather Classical Lectures, 56; Berkeley: University of California Press, 1991).

Geiger, J., *Cornelius Nepos and Ancient Political Biography* (Historia Einzelschriften, 47; Wiesbaden/Stuttgart: Franz Steiner, 1985).

Gelzer, Th., 'Klassizismus, Attizismus, und Asianismus', in Flashar (ed.), *Le Classicisme à Rome aux Iers Siècles avant et après J.-C.*, pp. 1–55.

Gempf, Conrad, 'Public Speaking and Published Accounts ', in Winter and Clarke (eds.), *The Book of Acts in its First Century Setting*, pp. 259–303.

Genette, G., Palimpsestes: la littérature au second degré (Paris: Du Seuil, 1982).

—— *Seuils* (Paris: Du Seuil, 1987).

Gerhardsson, Birger, *Memory and Manuscript: Oral Transmission and Written Transmission in Rabbinic Judaism and Early Christianity* (Acta Seminarii

Neotestamentici Uppsaliensis, 22; Lund: Gleerup, 1961).

Gigon, O., 'Antike Erzählungen über die Berufung zur Philosophie', *Museum Helveticum* 3 (1946), pp. 1–21.

—— 'Biographie. A. Griechische Biographie', *Lexikon der Alten Welt*, pp. 469–71.

Gill, C., 'Plato on Falsehood—Not Fiction', in Gill and Wiseman (eds.), *Lies and Fiction*, pp. 38–87.

Gill, C., and T.P. Wiseman (eds.), *Lies and Fiction in the Ancient World* (Exeter: University of Exeter Press, 1993).

Gill, David W.J., and Conrad Gempf (eds.), *The Book of Acts in its First Century Setting.* II. *Graeco-Roman Setting* (Grand Rapids, MI: Eerdmans; Carlisle: Paternoster, 1994).

Glockmann, G., *Homer in der frühchristlichen Literatur bis Justinus* (Texte und Untersuchungen, 105; Akademie-Verlag, 1968).

Goodenough, E.R., 'Philo's Exposition of the Law and his De Vita Mosis', *HTR* 26 (1933), pp. 109–125.

—— *An Introduction to Philo Judaeus* (Oxford: Basil Blackwell, 2nd edn, 1962).

Gould, Peter, and Rodney White, *Mental Maps* (Boston and London: Allen & Unwin, 2nd edn, 1986 [Harmondsworth: Penguin, 1974]).

Grant, F.C., *The Gospels: Their Origin and their Growth* (New York: Harper, 1957).

Green, Joel, *The Gospel of Luke* (NICNT; Grand Rapids: Eerdmans, 1997).

Griffin, Miriam, *Seneca: A Philosopher in Politics* (Oxford: Clarendon Press, 1976).

Griffin, M.T., 'Urbs, Plebs and Princeps', in Alexander (ed.), *Images of Empire*, pp. 19–46.

Haenchen, E., *Der Weg Jesu* (Berlin: Topelmann, 1966).

—— *The Acts of the Apostles* (Oxford: Blackwell, 1971); ET (rev.) of *Die Apostelgeschichte* (Mayer Kommentar, Göttingen, 1961).

—— The Acts of the Apostles (Oxford: Blackwell, 1971); ET (rev.) of *Die Apostelgeschichte* (Mayer Kommentar, Göttingen, 1961).

Hägg, Tomas, 'Die *Ephesiaka* des Xenophon Ephesius: Original oder Epitome?', *Classica et Mediaevalia* 27 (1966), pp. 118–61.

—— *Narrative Technique in Ancient Greek Romances: Studies of Chariton, Xenophon Ephesius, and Achilles Tatius* (Skrifter Utgivna av Svenska Institutet i Athen, ser. 8, VIII; Uppsala: Almqvist & Wiksell, 1971).

—— *The Novel in Antiquity* (rev. English edn; Oxford: Blackwell, 1983).

Halliday, M.A.K., *Language as Social Semiotic* (London: Edward Arnold, 1978).

Halliday, M.A.K., and R. Hasan, *Language, Context, and Text: Aspects of Language in a Social-Semiotic Perspective* (Oxford: Oxford University Press, 1989).

Hamman, A.-G., *La Vie Quotidienne des premiers Chrétiens* (Paris: Hachette, 1971).

Hansen, William (ed.), *Phlegon of Tralles' Book of Marvels* (Exeter: University of Exeter Press, 1996).

Hays, R.B., *Echoes of Scripture in the Letters of Paul* (New Haven: Yale University Press, 1989).

Heidel, W.A., *The Frame of the Ancient Greek Maps* (New York: Arno Press, 1976; [repr. of original edn, New York: American Geographical Society, Research Series no. 20, 1937]).

Hemer, Colin J., *The Book of Acts in the Setting of Hellenistic History* (WUNT, 49; Winona Lake: Eisenbrauns, 1990; [Tübingen: Siebeck-Mohr; 1989]).

Hengel, M., *Acts and the History of Earliest Christianity* (London: SCM Press, 1979).

Herkommer, E., 'Die Topoi in der Proömien der Römischen Geschichtswerk' (Dissertation, Tübingen, 1968).

Hirsch, E.D., Jr, *Validity in Interpretation* (New Haven, CT: Yale University Press, 1967).

Hock, Ronald, 'Paul's Tentmaking and the Problem of his Social Class', *JBL* 97 (1980), pp. 555–64.

—— *The Social Context of Paul's Ministry: Tentmaking and Apostleship* (Philadelphia: Fortress Press, 1980).

Hock, Ronald (ed.), *Ancient Fiction and Early Christian Narrative* (SBL Symposium Series; Atlanta: Scholars Press, 1998).

Homeyer, Helene, *Lukian: Wie man Geschichte schreiben soll* (München: W. Fink, 1965).

Hornblower, Simon, *Thucydides* (London: Duckworth, 1987).

Horrocks, Geoffrey, *Greek: A History of the Language and its Speakers* (Longman Linguistics Library; London and New York: Longman, 1997).

Horsley, G.H.R., 'The Fiction of Jewish Greek', in G.H.R. Horsley (ed.), *New Documents Illustrating Early Christianity* (Ancient History Documentary research Centre; Macquarie University, 1989), pp. 5–40.

—— 'The Politarchs', in Gill and Gempf (eds.), *The Book of Acts in its First Century Setting*, pp. 419–31.

Howland, R.L., 'The Attack on Isocrates in the Phaedrus', *ClQ* 31 (1937), pp. 151–59.

Hudson, A., 'Diglossia as a Special Case of Register Variation', in D. Biber and E. Finegan (eds.), *Sociolinguistic Perspectives on Register* (Oxford: Oxford University Press, 1994).

—— *Sociolinguistics* (Cambridge: Cambridge University Press, 2nd edn, 1996).

Huntingford, G.W.B., (ed.), *The Periplus of the Erythraean Sea* (London: Hakluyt Society, 1980).

Jacoby, F., *Apollodors Chronik: eine Sammlung der Fragmente* (Philogische Untersuchungen, 16; Berlin: Weidmann, 1902).

—— *Die Fragment der groiechische Historiker* (Leiden: Brill, 1958).

Jackson, Foakes, and Kirsopp Lake (eds.), *The Beginnings of Christianity*. I.2. *The Acts of the Apostles* (London: Macmillan, 1922).

Jaeger, Werner, *Diokles von Karystos* (Berlin: de Gruyter, 1938).

—— *Aristotle: Fundamentals of the History of his Development* (trans. R. Robinson; Oxford: Clarendon Press, 2nd edn, 1948).

James, M.R., 'The Apocalypse in Art' (The Schweich Lectures of the British Academy 1927; London: Oxford University Press for the British Academy, 1931).

Janson, T., *Latin Prose Prefaces* (Studia Latina Stockholmiensia, 13; Stockholm: Almquist &Wiksell, 1964).

Jervell, J., *Luke and the People of God: A New Look at Luke-Acts* (Minneapolis: Augsburg, 1962).

—— 'The Problem of Traditions in Acts', ST 16 (1962), pp. 25–41; reprinted in *idem, Luke and the People of God*, pp. 19–39.

—— 'Paul: The Teacher of Israel: The Apologetic Speeches of Paul in Acts', in *idem, Luke and the People of God*, pp. 153–83.

Jewett, R., *Dating Paul's Life* (London: SCM Press, 1979).

—— *A Chronology of Paul's Life* (Philadelphia: Fortress Press, 1979).

Johnson, L.T., *The Acts of the Apostles* (Sacra Pagina, 5; Collegeville, MN: Liturgical Press, 1992).

Judge, E.A., 'Christian Innovation and its Contemporary Observers', in Croke and Emmett (eds.), *History and Historians in Late Antiquity*, pp. 13–29.

—— 'The Early Christians as a Scholastic Community', *JRH* 1 (1960), pp. 4–15, 125–37.

—— 'The Decrees of Caesar at Thessalonica', *Reformed Theological Review* 30 (1971), pp. 1–7.

Keck, L., and J.L. Martyn (eds.), *Studies in Luke-Acts* (London: SPCK, 1968).

Kenyon, F.G., *Books and Readers in Greece and Rome* (Oxford: Clarendon Press, 2nd edn, 1951).

Kiley, Mark, *Colossians as Pseudepigraphy* (Sheffield: JSOT, 1986).

Klein, G., 'Lukas 1:1–4 als theologisches Programm', in E.Dinkler (ed.), *Zeit und Geschichte*, (R.Bultmann Dankesgabe zum 80. Geburtstag; Tübingen: Mohr, 1964), pp. 193–216.

Klostermann, Erich, *Das Lukasevangelium* (HNT, 5; Tübingen: Mohr, 2nd edn, 1929).

Knox, W.L., *The Acts of the Apostles* (Cambridge: Cambridge University Press, 1948).

Koester, H., 'One Jesus and Four Primitive Gospels', *HTR* 2 (1968), pp. 206ff.

Kremer, J., (ed.), *Les Actes des Apôtres: Traditions, rédaction, théologie* (BETL, 48; Leuven: Leuven University Press – Gembloux, 1978).

Kunz, Margrit, 'Zur Beurteilung der Prooemien in Diodors historischer Bibliothek', (Dissertation, Zurich, 1935).

de Lagarde, P., *Psalterium Hieronymi* (Leipzig: Teubner, 1874).

Laqueur, R., 'Ephoros I: Die Proomien', *Hermes* 46 (1911), pp. 161–206.

Lefkowitz, Mary, *The Lives of the Greek Poets* (London: Duckworth, 1981).

Leo, F., *Die griechisch-romische Biographie nach ihrer Literarischen Form* (Leipzig: Teubner, 1901).

Lesky, Albin, *Thalatta der Weg der Griechen zum Meer* (New York: Arno Press, 1973 [1896]).

Liddle, Aidan, (ed.), *Arrian, Periplus Ponti Euxini*, (Bristol Classical Press; London: Duckworth, 2003).

Lindars, B., *New Testament Apologetic: The Doctrinal Significance of the Old Testament Quotations* (London: SCM Press, 1961).

Lown, John S., 'The Miraculous in the Greco-Roman Historians', *Foundations and Facets Forum* 2 (1986), pp. 36–42.

Lüdemann, G., *Paul, Apostle to the Gentiles: Studies in Chronology* (London: SCM Press, 1984).

—— *Early Christianity According to the Traditions in Acts* (London: SCM Press, 1989).

MacDonald, Denis R., 'The Shipwrecks of Odysseus and Paul', *NTS* 45 (1999), pp. 88–107.

—— *The Homeric Epics and the Gospel of Mark* (New Haven: Yale University Press, 2000).

—— 'Paul's Farewell to the Ephesian Elders and Hector's Farewell to Andromache: A Strategic Imitation of Homer's Iliad', in Penner and Vander Stichele (eds.), *Contextualizing Acts*, pp. 189–203.

MacDonald, Dennis R. (ed.), *Mimesis and Intertextuality in Antiquity and Christianity* (Claremont Studies in Antiquity and Christianity; Harrisburg: Trinity Press International, 2001).

MacMullen, Ramsay, *Christianizing the Roman Empire, A.D. 100–400* (New Haven: Yale University Press, 1984).

Maddox, Robert, *The Purpose of Luke-Acts* (Gottingen: Vandenhoeck & Ruprecht, 1982).

Magness, J.L., *Sense and Absence: Structure and Suspension in the Ending of Mark's Gospel* (Semeia Studies; Atlanta, GA: Scholar's Press, 1986).

Malbon, E.S., 'Ending at the Beginning: A Response', in D.E. Smith (ed.), *How Gospels Begin.*

Malherbe, A.J., *Social Aspects of Early Christianity* (Louisiana State University Press, 1st edn chs 1–3 only; Philadelphia: Fortress Press, 2nd edn enlarged; 1977).

Malherbe, A.J., (ed.), *The Cynic Epistles* (SBLSBS, 12; Missoula, MT; Scholars Press, 1977).

Maloney, E.C., *Semitic Interference in Marcan Syntax* (SBLDSS, 51; Chico, CA: Scholars Press, 1981).

Mansfeld, Jaap, 'Diogenes Laertius on Stoic Philosophy', *Elenchos* 7 (1986), pp. 295–382; reprinted in Jaap Mansfeld, *Studies in the Historiography of Greeek Philosophy* (Assen: Van Gorcum, 1990), pp. 343–428.

Marguerat, Daniel, ' "Et quand nous sommes entrés dans Rome": L'énigme de la fin du livre des Actes (28,16–31)', in *RHPR* 73 (1993), pp. 1–21.

—— 'Saul's Conversion (Acts 9, 22, 26) and the Multiplication of Narrative in Acts', in Tuckett (ed.), *Luke's Literary Achievement*, pp. 127–55.

—— 'Le Dieu du Livre des Actes', in Alain Marchadour (ed.), *L'Évangile Exploré: Mélanges offerts à Simon Légasse* (Lectio Divina, 166; Paris: Cerf, 1996), pp. 301–31.

—— *La première histoire du christianisme* (Lectio Divina, 180; Paris/Geneva: Cerf/Labor et Fides, 2nd edn, 2002 [1999]).

—— *The First Christian Historian: Writing the 'Acts of the Apostles'* (trans. Ken McKinney, Gregory J. Laughery and Richard Bauckham; SNTSMS, 121; Cambridge: Cambridge University Press, 2002).

—— 'The God of Acts', in *idem*, *The First Christian Historian*, pp. 85–108.

Marguerat, D., and A. Curtis (eds.), *Bible et Intertextualité* (Geneva: Labor et Fides, 1999).

—— *Intertextualités: La Bible en échos* (Geneva: Labor et Fides, 2000).

Marrou, H.-I., *History of Education in Antiquity* (ET; New York: Sheed & Ward, 1956; from the 3rd French edition, *Histoire de l'Education dans l'Antiquité*, Paris: Ed. du Seuil).

Marshall, I.H., 'Acts and the "Former Treatise"', in Winter and Clarke (eds.), *The Book of Acts in its First Century Setting*, I, pp. 163–82.

Matera, F.J., 'The Prologue as the Interpretative Key to Mark's Gospel', *JSNT* 34 (1988), pp. 3–20.

Mealand, David, 'Hellenistic Historians and the Style of Acts', *ZNW* 82 (1991), pp. 42–66.

—— 'Luke and the Verbs of Dionysius of Halicarnassus', *JSNT* 63 (1996), pp. 63–86.

—— 'Style, Genre, and Authorship in Acts, the Septuagint, and Hellenistic Historians', *LLC* 14.4 (1999), pp. 479–505.

Meeks, Wayne, 'The Social Context of Pauline Theology', *Int* 36 (1982), pp. 267ff.

—— *The First Urban Christians* (London and New Haven: Yale University Press, 1983).

Mejer, J., *Diogenes Laertius and his Hellenistic Sources* (Hermes Einzelschriften, 40; Wiesbaden: Franz Steiner, 1978).

Metzger, Bruce M., 'Ancient Astrological Geography and Acts 2.9–11', in W. Ward Gasque and Ralph P. Martin (eds.), *Apostolic History and the Gospel: Biblical and Historical Essays presented to F.F. Bruce on his 60th Birthday* (London: Paternoster Press, 1970), pp. 123–33.

Milroy, Lesley, 'Social Network and Linguistic Focusing', in Romaine (ed.), *Sociolinguistic Variation*, pp. 141–152.

Minyard, John Douglas, *Mode and Value in the De Rerum Natura* (Hermes Einzelschriften, 39; Wiesbaden: Franz Steiner, 1978).

Moessner, David P. (ed.), *Jesus and the Heritage of Israel* (Harrisburg: Trinity Press International, 1999).

Moles, J.L., 'Truth and Untruth in Herodotus and Thucydides', in Gill and Wiseman (eds.), *Lies and Fiction*, pp. 88–121.

Molinié, G., *Chariton: le Roman de Chairéas et Callirhoé* (Paris: Les Belles Lettres, 1979).

Momigliano, A.D., *Studies in Historiography* (London: Weidenfeld & Nicolson, 1969).

—— 'The Place of Herodotus in the History of Historiography', in *idem*, *Studies in Historiography*, pp. 127–42.

—— 'Historiography on Written and on Oral Tradition', in *idem*, *Studies in Historiography*, pp. 211–220.

—— *The Development of Greek Biography* (expanded edn. of 1971 *bis*; Cambridge, MA: Harvard University Press, 1993).

Morgan, J.R., 'Make-Believe and Make Believe: The Fictionality of the Greek Novels', in Gill and Wiseman (eds.), *Lies and Fiction*, pp. 175–229.

Morgan, J.R., and Richard Stoneman (eds.), *Greek Fiction: The Greek Novel in Context* (London and New York: Routledge, 1994).

Müller, C., (ed.), *Geographi Graeci Minores*, I and II (Paris: Didot, 1855, 1861).

Murray, Gilbert, *The Rise of the Greek Epic* (Oxford: Oxford University Press, 4th edn, 1934).

Murray, Oswyn, 'The "Quinquennium Neronis" and the Stoics', *Historia* 14 (1965), pp. 41–61.

Musurillo, H. (ed.), *Acts of the Pagan Martyrs: Acta Alexandrinorum* (Oxford: Clarendon Press, 1954).

Nagy, G., *Homeric Questions* (Austin: University of Texas Press, 1996).

—— 'Epic as Genre', in Beissinger, Tylus, and Wofford, (eds.), *Epic Traditions in the Contemporary World*, pp. 21–32.

Nettleship, H., and J.E. Sandys (eds.), *A Dictionary of Classical Antiquities* (London: Wm. Glaisher, 3rd edn, 1894).

Neyrey, J., 'The Forensic Defense Speech and Paul's Trial Speeches in Acts 22–26: Form and Function', in C.H. Talbert (ed.), *Luke-Acts: New Perspectives from the Society of Biblical Literature* (New York: Crossroads, 1984), pp. 210–24.

Nicolet, Claude, *Space, Geography and Politics in the Early Roman Empire* (Jerome Lectures, 19; Ann Arbor: University of Michigan Press, 1991); ET of *L'Inventaire du Monde: Géographie et Politique aux Origines de l'Empire Romain* (Librairie Arthème Fayard, 1988), chapter 5.

Nock, A.D., *Conversion* (Oxford: Clarendon Press, 1933).

—— 'Review of Dibelius, *Aufsätze*': *Gnomon* 25 (1953), pp. 497–506, repr. in *idem, Essays on Religion and the Ancient World*, (ed. Zeph Stewart; Oxford: Clarendon Press, 1972), pp. 821–32.

Norden, Eduard, *Agnostos Theos: Untersuchungen zur Formengeschichte religiöser Rede* (Stuttgart: Teubner 1956; [Leipzig and Berlin, 1913]).

—— *Antike Kunstprosa vom VI. Jahrhundert v. Chr. bis in die Zeit der Renaissance* (Stuttgart: Teubner, 1983; [based on the text of the 2nd and 3rd edns, Leipzig 1909, 1915]).

Oden, R.A., Jr, 'Philo of Byblos and Hellenistic Historiography', *PEQ* 110 (1978), pp. 115–26.

O'Neill, J.C., *The Theology of Acts in its Historical Setting* (London: SPCK, 1961).

Otis, Brooks, *Vergil: A Study in Civilized Poetry* (Oxford: Clarendon Press, 1963).

van Paassen, C., *The Classical Tradition of Geography* (Groningen: J.B. Wolters, 1957).

Pack, R.A., (ed.), *Artemidorus Daldiarnus. Oniro-crilion Libri V* (Leipzig: Teubner, 1963).

Palm, Jonas, 'Über Sprache und Stil des Diodoros von Sizilien: ein Beitrag zur Beleuchtung der hellenistischen Prosa' (Dissertation, Lund, 1955).

Palmer, D.W., 'The Literary Background of Acts 1.1–14', *NTS* 33 (1987), pp. 427–38.

—— 'Acts and the Ancient Historical Monograph', in Winter and Clarke (eds.), *The Book of Acts in its Ancient Literary Setting*, I, pp. 1–29.

Parsons, M.C., *The Departure of Jesus in Luke-Acts* (JSNTSup, 21; Sheffield: JSOT Press, 1987).

Parsons, M.C., and R.I. Pervo, *Rethinking the Unity of Luke and Acts* (Minneapolis: Fortress Press, 1993).

Pattison, Stephen E., 'A Study of the Apologetic Function of the Summaries of Acts', (Unpublished PhD thesis, Emory University, 1990; Ann Arbor: University Microfilms: order no. 9027934).

Paulston, C.B., 'Diglossia in First-Century Palestine', in Porter (ed.), *Diglossia and Other Topics,* pp. 79–89.

Pédech, P., *La méthode historique de Polybe* (Paris: Les Belles Lettres, 1964).

Pelletier, A., *Flavius Josèphe, adaptateur de la Lettre d'Aristée: une réaction atticisante cointre la koinè* (Études et Commentaires, 45; Paris: Libraire C. Klincksieck, 1962).

Pelling, C.B.R., *Literary Texts and the Greek Historian* (London: Routledge, 1999).

Penner, Todd, *In Praise of Christian Origins: Stephen and the Hellenists in Lukan Apologetic Historiography* (Emory Studies in Early Christianity, 10; New York and London: T&T Clark International, 2004).

—— 'Madness in the Method? The Acts of the Apostles in Current Study', in *Currents in Biblical Research* 2.2 (2004), pp. 223–93.

Penner, Todd, and Caroline Vander Stichele (eds.), *Contextualizing Acts: Lukan Narrative and Greco-Roman Discourse* (SBL Symposium Series, 20; Atlanta; Society for Biblical Literature, 2003).

Perret, J., *Les Origines de la légende troyenne de Rome* (Paris: Les Belles Lettres, 1942).

Perry, B.E., *The Ancient Romances* (Sather Classical Lectures, 37; Berkeley: University of California Press, 1967).

Pervo, Richard I., *Profit with Delight: The Literary Genre of the Acts of the Apostles* (Philadelphia: Fortress Press, 1987).

Pinault, Jody Rubin, *Hippocratic Lives and Legends* (Studies in Ancient Medicine, 4; Leiden: Brill, 1992).

Platt, John T., 'A Model for Polyglossia and Multilingualisim (with Special Reference to Singapore and Malaya)', *Language in Society* 6 (1977), pp. 361–78.

Plepelits, Karl, *Chariton von Aphrodisias, Kallirhoe* (Stuttgart: Anton Hiersemann, 1976).

Plümacher, E., *Lukas als hellenistischer Schriftsteller: Studien zur Apostelgeschichte* (Göttingen: Vandenhoeck & Ruprecht, 1972).

—— *Geschichte und Geschichten: Aufsätze zur Apostelgeschichte und zu den Johannesakten* (ed. J. Schröter, R. Brucker; Tübingen: Mohr Siebeck, 2004).

—— 'Die Apostelgeschichte als historische Monographie', in Kremer (ed.), *Les Actes des Apôtres*; repr. in Plümacher, *Geschichte und Geschichten*, pp. 1–14.

—— 'Cicero und Lukas: Bemerkungen zu Stil und Zweck der historischen Monographie', in *idem, Geschichte und Geschichten*, pp. 15–32.

Porter, Stanley E., 'Excursus: The "We" Passages', in Gill and Gempf (eds.), *The Book of Acts in its First Century Setting*, II, pp. 545–74.

—— 'The Functional Distribution of Koine Greek in First-Century Palestine', in *idem* (ed.), *Diglossia and Other Topics*, pp. 53–78.

—— 'Dialect and Register in the Greek of the New Testament: Theory', in M. Daniel Caroll R., *Rethinking Contexts, Rereading Texts*, pp. 190–208.

Porter, S.E., (ed.), *Diglossia and Other Topics in New Testament Linguistics* (JSNTSup, 193; Studies in NT Greek, 6; Sheffield; Sheffield Academic Press, 2000).

Powell, Mark A., *What Is Narrative Criticism?* (Minneapolis: Fortess Press, 1990).

Praeder, Susan M., 'Acts 27:1–28:16: Sea Voyages in Ancient Literature and the Theology of Luke-Acts', *CBQ* 46 (1984), pp. 683–706.

—— 'The Problem of First Person Narration in Acts', *NovT* 29.3 (1987), pp. 193–218.

Pride, J.B., and J. Holmes, *Sociolinguistics: Selected Readings* (Harmondsworth: Penguin, 1972).

Pritchett, W. Kendrick, *Dionysius of Halicarnassus: On Thucydides* (Berkeley: University of California Press, 1975).

—— *The Liar School of Herodotos* (Amsterdam: Gieben, 1993).

Rajak, Tessa, *Josephus: The Historian and his society* (London: Duckworth, 1983).

—— 'Was There a Roman Charter for the Jews?', *JRS* 74 (1984), pp. 107–23.

—— 'Friends, Romans, Subjects: Agrippa II's Speech in Josephus's Jewish War', in Alexander (ed.), *Images of Empire*, pp. 122–34.

Ramsay, W.M., *St. Paul the Traveller and the Roman Citizen* (London: Hodder & Stoughton, 1895).

Reardon, B.P., 'The Greek Novel', *Phoenix* 23, 1966, pp. 291–309.

—— *The Form of Greek Romance* (Princeton: University Press, 1991).

Reardon, B.P., (ed.), *Collected Ancient Greek Novels* (Berkeley: University of California Press, 1989).

Robbins, Vernon, 'Prefaces in Greco-Roman Biography and Luke-Acts', in P.J. Achtemeier (ed.), Society of Biblical Literature 1978 Seminar Papers (2 vols.; SBLSP, 13–14; Missoula, MT: Scholars Press, 1978), II, pp. 193–207.

—— 'By Land and by Sea: The We-passages and Ancient Sea-Voyages', in Talbert (ed.), *Perspectives on Luke-Acts*, pp. 215–42.

—— 'Luke-Acts: A Mixed Population Seeks a Home in the Roman Empire', in L.C.A. Alexander (ed.), *Images of Empire*, pp. 202–21.

Rogerson, J.W., *The New Atlas of the Bible* (Oxford: MacDonald, 1985).

Romaine, S., *Language in Society: An Introduction to Sociolinguistics* (New York: Oxford University Press, 1994).

Romaine, S. (ed.), *Sociolinguistic Variation in Speech Communities* (London: Edward Arnold, 1982).

Romm, James S., *The Edges of the Earth in Ancient Thought* (Princeton: Princeton University Press, 1992).

Ronconi, A., 'Exitus illustrium virorum', in T. Klauser (ed.), *Reallexikon für Antike und Christentum* (Stuttgart: Hiersemann, 1966), VI, cols. 1258–68.

Rosner, B.S., 'Acts and Biblical History', in Winter and Clarke (eds.), *The Book of Acts in its First Century Setting*, I, pp. 65–82.

Rothschild, Clare, *Luke-Acts and the Rhetoric of History* (WUNT, 2.175; Tübingen: Mohr Siebeck, 2004).

Rousseau, P., *Ascetics, Authority and the Church in the Age of Jerome and Cassian* (Oxford: Oxford University Press, 1978).

Ruch, M., *Le Prooemium Philosophique chez Cicéron* (Strasbourg: Publication de la faculté des lettre de Strasbourg, 1958).

Ruppert, J., 'Quaestiones ad historiam dedicationis librorum pertinentes', (Dissertation, Leipzig, 1911).

Russell, Joan, 'Networks and Sociolinguistic Variation in an African Urban Setting', in Romaine (ed.), *Sociolinguistic Variation,* pp. 125–40.

Rydbeck, Lars, *Fachprosa, vermeintliche Volkssprache und Neues Testament* (Acta Universitatis Upsaliensis: Studia Graeca Upsaliensia, 5; Uppsala: Berlingska Boktryckeriet, Lund, 1967).

—— '3. Sprache des Neuen Testaments', *RGG*[4] 1.1424–26 s.v. 'Bibel III: Neues Testament' (Tübingen: Mohr Siebeck, 1998).

—— 'Luke and Greek Classicism', forthcoming.

—— 'Luke and the Sepuagint', forthcoming.

Sacks, K.S., *Diodorus Siculus and the First Century* (Princeton: Princeton University Press, 1990).

Said, Edward, *Orientalism* (London: Routledge & Kegan Paul, 1978).

Sanders, E.P., *Paul* (Past Masters; Oxford: Oxford University Press, 1991).

Sanders, J.T., *The Jews in Luke-Acts* (London: SCM Press, 1987).

Sandmel, S., 'Parallelomania', JBL 81 (1962), pp. 1–13.

—— *Philo of Alexandria: An Introduction* (Oxford and New York: Oxford University Press, 1979).

Sandnes, Karl Olav, 'Paul and Socrates: The Aim of Paul's Areopagus Speech', *JSNT* 50 (1993), pp. 13–26.

Sayers, Dorothy L., *Unpopular Opinions* (London: Gollancz, 1946).

Schnabel, P., *Berossos und die Babylonisch-Hellenistische Literatur* (Leipzig and Berlin: Teubner, 1923).

Schubart, W., *Ein Jahrtausend am Nil* (Berlin: Weidmann, 1912).

Schürer, E., *The History of the Jewish People in the Age of Jesus Christ* (rev. G. Vermes and F. Millar; Edinburgh: T&T Clark, 1973).

Scott, James M., 'Luke's Geographical Horizon', in Gill and Gempf (eds.), *The Book of Acts in its First Century Setting,* II, pp. 483–544.

—— *Geography in Early Judaism and Christianity: The Book of Jubilees* (SNTSMS, 113; Cambridge: Cambridge University Press, 2002), esp. pp. 44–96.

Shuler, P.L., *A Genre for the Gospels* (Philadelphia: Fortress Press, 1982).

Smith, D.E., (ed.), *How Gospels Begin* (Semeia, 52; Atlanta, GA: Scholars Press, 1991).

Smith, Wesley D., *Hippocrates: Pseudepigraphic Writings* (Studies in Ancient Medicine, 2; Leiden: Brill, 1990).

Sparks, H.F.D., 'The Semitisms of St. Luke's Gospel', *JTS* 44 (1943), pp. 129–38.

—— 'The Semitisms of Acts', *JTS* n.s. 1 (1950), pp. 16–28.

Squires, J.T., *The Plan of God in Luke-Acts* (SNTSMS, 76; Cambridge:

Cambridge University Press, 1993).

Städter, P., *Arrian of Nicomedia* (Chapel Hill: University of North Carolina Press, 1980).

Städter, Philip A., (ed.), *The Speeches in Thucydides* (Chapel Hill: University of North Carolina Press, 1973).

Stark, Rodney, *The Rise of Christianity* (Princeton: Princeton University Press, 1996).

Steiner, Claire-Antoinette, 'Le lien entre le prologue et le corps de l'evangile de Marc', in Marguerat and Curtis (eds.), *Intertextualités: La Bible en échos*, pp. 161–84.

Steinmetz, P., 'Die Physik des Theophrastus', *Palingenesia* I (1964), pp. 14ff.

Stendahl, K., *The School of St. Matthew and its Use of the Old Testament* (Philadelphia: Fortress Press, 2nd edn, 1968; repr. Ramsey, NJ: Sigler, 1991).

Stepp, Perry
—— *Leadership Succession in the World of the Pauline Circle* (Sheffield: Sheffield Phoenix Press, May 2005).

Sterling, G.E., *Historiography and Self-Definition: Josephos, Luke-Acts and Apologetic Historiography* (NovTSup, 64; Leiden: Brill, 1992).

Stern, Jacob (ed.), *Palaephatus: On Unbelievable Tales* (Wauconda, IL: Bolchazy-Carducci, 1996).

Still, J.I., *St. Paul on Trial: A New Reading of the History in the Book of Acts and the Pauline Epistles* (London: SCM Press, 1923).

Stone, Michael E. (ed.), *Jewish Writings of the Second Temple Period* (CRINT, II; Assen: Van Gorcum; and Philadelphia: Fortress Press, 1984).

Stuart, D.R., *Epochs of Greek and Roman Biography* (Berkeley: University of California Press, 1928).

Swain, Simon, *Hellenism and Empire: Language, Classicism, and Power in the Greek World, AD 50–250* (Oxford: Clarendon Press, 1996).

Talbert, C.H., *Luke and the Gnostics* (Nashville: Abingdon Press, 1966).
—— *Literary Patterns, Theological Themes and the Genre of Luke-Acts* (SBLMS, 20; Missoula, MT: Scholars Press, 1974).
—— *What is a Gospel?* (Philadelphia: Fortress Press, 1977).
—— *Perspectives on Luke-Acts* (Edinburgh: T&T Clark, 1978).
—— 'Biographies of Philosophers and Rulers as Instruments of Religious Propaganda in Mediterranean Antiquity', *ANRW* 2.16.2, pp. 1619–1651.
—— 'Biography, Ancient', *ABD* I, pp. 745–49.

Talbert, C.H., and Perry Stepp, 'Succession in Luke-Acts and in the Lukan Milieu,' in Charles Talbert (ed.), *Reading Luke-Acts in its Mediterranean Milieu* (NovTSup, 107; Leiden: Brill, 2003), pp. 19–55.

Tannehill, R., 'Israel in Luke-Acts: A Tragic Story', in *JBL* 104 (1985), pp. 69–85.

Theissen, G., *The Social Setting of Pauline Christianity* (Edinburgh: T&T Clark, 1982).

Tolkien, J.R.R., *Tree and Leaf* (London: Unwin Books, 1964).

Toynbee, A.J., *Greek Historical Thought from Homer to the Age of Heraclius* (London: Dent, 1924).

Trebilco, Paul, 'Asia', in Gill and Gempf (eds.), *The Book of Acts in its First Century Setting*, II, pp. 291–362.

Trites, A.A., 'The Importance of Legal Scenes and Language in the Book of Acts', *NovT* 16 (1974), pp. 278–84.

Tuckett, C.M. (ed.), *Synoptic Studies* (JSNTSup, 7; Sheffield: JSOT Press, 1984).

—— *Luke's Literary Achievement: Collected Essays* (JSNTSup, 116; Sheffield: Sheffield Academic Press, 1995).

Turner, E.G., *Greek Papyri* (Oxford: Clarendon Press, 1968).

Tyson, J.B., 'The Birth Narratives and the Beginning of Luke's Gospel', in D.E. Smith (ed.), *How Gospels Begin*, pp. 103–20.

van Unnik, W.C., 'Opmerkingen over het doel van Lucas' geschiedwerk (Luc. 1:4)', *NedTTs* 9 (1954–55), pp. 323–33.

—— 'Luke's Second Book and the Rules of Hellenistic Historiography', in Kremer (ed.), *Les Actes des Apôtres*, pp. 37–60.

—— 'Once More St. Luke's Prologue', *Neotestamentica* 7 (1963), pp. 7–26.

Uspensky, Boris, *A Poetics of Composition* (Berkeley: University of California Press, 1973).

Verheyden, J. (ed.), *The Unity of Luke-Acts* (BETL; Leuven: Peeters, 1999).

Veyne, Paul, *Did the Greeks Believe in their Myths?* (trans. Paula Wissing; Chicago: University of Chicago Press, 1988; originally *Les Grecs ont-ils cru à leurs mythes?* [Paris: Editions du Seuil, 1983]).

Votaw, Clyde Weber, 'The Gospels and Contemporary Biographies in the Greco-Roman World', *AJT* 19 (1915), pp. 45–73 and 217–49; (repr. Facet Books, Biblical Series 27; Philadelphia: Fortress Press, 1970).

Walaskay, P.W., *'And So We Came to Rome': The Political Perspective of St Luke* (SNTMS, 49; Cambridge: Cambridge University Press, 1983).

Walbank, F.W., 'The Geography of Polybius', *Classica et Mediaevalia* 9 (1948), pp. 155–82.

—— *A Historical Commentary on Polybius* (Oxford: Clarendon Press, 1967).

Walzer, Richard, *Galen on Jews and Christians* (London: Oxford University Press, 1949).

Wasserberg, G., *Aus Israels Mitte – Heil für die Welt. Eine narrative-exegetische Studie zur Theologie des Lukas* (BZNW, 92; Berlin: de Gruyter, 1998).

Watt, J., 'The Current Landscape of Diglossia Studies: The Diglossic Continuum in First-Century Palestine', in S.E. Porter (ed.), *Diglossia and Other Topics in New Testament Linguistics* (JSNTSup, 193; Studies in NT Greek, 6; Sheffield: Sheffield Academic Press, 2000), pp. 18–36 .

Wehnert, J., *Die Wir-Passagen der Apostelgeschichte: Ein lukanisches Stilmittel aus jüdischer Tradition* (Göttingen Theologischer Arbeiten, 40; Göttingen: Vandenhoeck & Ruprecht, 1989).

Weinstock, Stefan, 'The Geographical Catalogue in Acts II, 9–11', *JRS* 38 (1948), pp. 43–46.

Wellmann, M. (ed.), *Dioscoridis Anazarbei De Materia Medica Libri V* (Berlin: Wiedmann, 1907–1914).

Westermann, A. (ed.), *Biographi Graeci Minores* (Amsterdam: Hakkert, 1964; [Braunschweig: 1845]).

Westlake, H.D., *Essays on the Greek Historians and Greek History* (Manchester: Manchester University Press, 1969).

Wheeldon, M.J., 'True Stories: The Reception of Historiography in Antiquity', in Cameron: *History as Text*, pp. 33–63.

Wifstrand, Albert, 'Lukas och den grekiska klassicismen', *Svensk Exegetisk Årsbok* 5 (1940), pp. 139–51.

—— 'Lukas och Septuaginta', *STK* 6 (1940), pp. 243–62.

—— *L'Eglise ancienne et la culture grecque* (Paris: Editions du Cerf, 1962).

—— *Epochs and Styles* (eds. L. Rydbeck, S.E. Porter; WUNT 179; Tübingen: Mohr Siebeck, 2005).

—— 'Classicism', in *Epochs and Styles*, pp. 17–27.

—— 'Septuagint', in *Epochs and Styles*, pp. 28–45.

von Wilamowitz-Moellendorff, Ulrich, *Geschichte der griechischen Sprache* (Vortrag gehalten auf der Philologenversammlung in Göttingen am 27. Sept. 1927; Berlin, 1928).

Wilkinson, John, *Egeria's Travels* (London: SPCK, 1971).

Wills, Lawrence M., 'The Jewish Novellas', in Morgan and Stoneman (eds.), Greek Fiction: *The Greek Novel in Context*, pp. 223–38.

—— *The Jewish Novel in the Ancient World* (Ithaca; London: Cornell University Press, 1995).

Wimmer, F. (ed.), *De Signis Tempestatum*, 1.1. Texts in *Theophrasti Opera Omnia* (Frankfurt on Main: Minerva, 1964; [Paris: Didot, 1866]).

Winter, Bruce W., and Andrew D. Clarke (eds.), *The Book of Acts in its First Century Setting*. I. *Ancient Literary Setting* (Grand Rapids, MI: Eerdmans, 1993).

Wiseman, T.P., *Clio's Cosmetics* (Leicester: Leicester University Press, 1979).

—— 'Lying Historians: Seven Types of Mendacity', in Gill and Wiseman, *Lies and Fiction*, pp. 122–46

Witherington, Ben, III (ed.), *History, Literature and Society in the Book of Acts* (Cambridge: Cambridge University Press, 1996).

Witherup, Ronald D., 'Cornelius over and over and over again: "Functional Redundancy" in the Acts of the Apostles', *JSNT* 49 (1993), pp. 45–66.

Wodehouse, P.G., *Bill the Conqueror* (London: Methuen, 1924).

Woodman, A.J., *Rhetoric in Classical Historiography* (New South Wales: Croom Helm, 1988).

Zeegers-Vanderhorst, N., *Les citations des Poètes Grecs chez les apologistes Chrétiens du IIᵉ siècle* (Louvain: Bibliothèque de l'Université, Bureau du Recueil, 1972).

INDEX OF ANCIENT AUTHORS AND TEXTS

PASSAGES

INDEX OF BIBLICAL REFERENCES

INDEX OF MODERN AUTHORS